BAPTISTS, GOSPEL, AND CULTURE

The James N. Griffith Series in Baptist Studies

This series on Baptist life and thought explores and investigates Baptist history, offers analyses of Baptist theologies, provides studies in hymnody, and examines the role of Baptists in societies and cultures around the world. The series also includes classics of Baptist literature, letters, diaries, and other writings. For a complete list of titles in the series, visit www.mupress.org and visit the series page.

—C. Douglas Weaver, Series Editor

Baptists, Gospel, and Culture

Papers from the Eighth International Conference
on Baptist Studies

Edited by William L. Pitts Jr.

Foreword by *David Bebbington*

MERCER UNIVERSITY PRESS
Macon, Georgia

MUP/ P625

Published by Mercer University Press
1501 Mercer University Drive
Macon, Georgia 31207

25 24 23 22 21 5 4 3 2 1

Books published by Mercer University Press are printed on acid-free paper that meets the requirements of the American National Standard for Information Sciences—Permanence of Paper for Printed Library Materials.

Printed and bound in the United States.

This book is set in Adobe Caslon Pro.

Cover/jacket design by Burt&Burt.

ISBN 978-0-88146-789-5
Cataloging-in-Publication Data is available from the Library of Congress

Contents

MERCER UNIVERSITY

MERCER UNIVERSITY PRESS

Endowed by

TOM WATSON BROWN

and

THE WATSON-BROWN FOUNDATION, INC.

Contributors

David Bebbington, Professor of History, University of Stirling, Stirling, Scotland, UK

Terry Carter, Professor of History of Christianity, Pruet School of Christian Studies, Ouachita Baptist University, Arkadelphia, Arkansas, USA

Ivan Dias da Silva, President of the Sul Fluminense Baptist Theological Seminary, Volta Redonda, Rio de Janeiro, Brazil

Nathan Finn, Provost and Dean of the University Faculty, North Greenville University, Tigerville and Greer, South Carolina, USA

Curtis Freeman, Professor of Theology and Baptist Studies and Director of the Baptist House of Studies, Duke University Divinity School, Durham, North Carolina, USA

Rosalind Gooden, Retired missionary and Research Professor of History of Religion, Faculty of Theology, Tabor, Adelaide, Australia

George Hancock-Stefan, Associate Professor of Church History, Palmer Theological Seminary, Philadelphia, Pennsylvania, USA

Narola Imchen, Principal, Eastern Theological College, Rajabari, Jorhat, Assam, India

Wado Kawthoolei, ThD, Kawthoolei Karen Baptist Churches, Thai-Burma Border

Adina Kelley, PhD candidate in History, Baylor University, Waco, Texas, USA

Samuel J. Kelley, PhD candidate in Religion, Baylor University, Waco, Texas, USA

Melody Maxwell, Associate Professor of Church History, Acadia Divinity College, Wolfville, Nova Scotia, Canada

William L. Pitts Jr., Professor of History of Christianity, Department of Religion, Baylor University, Waco, Texas, USA

Robert Pope, Reader in Theology and Joint Head of School of Theology, Religious Studies and Islamic Studies, University of Wales, Cardiff, Wales, UK

Constantine Prokhorov, historian and writer, Omsk, Russia

Jake Raabe, graduate student at George W. Truett Theological Seminary, Baylor University, Waco, Texas, USA

David Rathel, Associate Professor of Christian Theology, Gateway Seminary, Ontario, California, USA

Laine Scales, Professor and Associate Dean of Graduate Studies, Baylor University, Waco, Texas, USA

Stuart Sheehan, President and CEO of World Hope Ministries International, Director of World Hope Bible Institute, Houston, Texas, USA

Malkhaz Songulashvilli, Metropolitan Bishop of Tbilisi, Georgia

Brian Talbot, Minister of Broughty Ferry Baptist Church, Dundee, Scotland, UK, and Extraordinary Professor, North West University Faculty of Theology, South Africa

Valdis Teraudkalns, Professor of Religion, University of Latvia, Riga, Latvia

John Tucker, Lecturer in History and Homiletics, Carey Baptist College, Auckland, New Zealand

Marina Xiaojing Wang, Associate Director, Christian Study Center on Chinese Religion and Culture, Divinity School of Chung Chi College, Chinese University of Hong Kong

Foreword

David Bebbington

The theme of gospel and culture has come to the fore in recent years as a subject for scholarly analysis. Missiologists led the way. In particular, Lesslie Newbigin, an English Presbyterian missionary who in 1947 had become a founding bishop of the Church of South India, explored the issue in a wealth of writings following his retirement in 1974 from a second term of episcopal service in India. In *Foolishness to the Greeks: The Gospel and Western Culture* (1986) and several other books he expounded the view that the West was showing resistance to the Christian message because it had become captive to the assumptions of the Enlightenment.[1] His work inspired a Gospel and Our Culture Network, which endured after Newbigin's death in 1998, encouraging continuing research on the issue. The questions Newbigin raised call for examination over the long term and relate to all Christian denominations. They can therefore be fruitfully explored by historians concerned with the Baptists.

On the one hand, the gospel has been a molder of culture over the centuries. The edifice of Western Christendom, however flawed in its structure, was erected on the foundation of faith in Christ. After the Reformation, whole nations were fashioned by their confessional allegiance, whether Catholic or Protestant. The Baptists, as part of the greater Protestant Dissenting movement, played their part in shaping the English-speaking world. Martin E. Marty once suggested in an influential article that postwar America had witnessed a "baptistification" that extended beyond religion to the culture.[2] The process spread far outside the bounds of the United States, though usually in lesser degree, to encompass lands to which Baptists had conveyed the gospel. Instances of this development, clarifying the nature and extent of Baptist influence, are included in this volume.

On the other hand, culture in all its varied dimensions has made a major impact on the form the gospel has assumed. The faith and practice of the Baptists have been drastically affected over the years by their setting. Their

---

[1] Lesslie Newbigin, *Foolishness to the Greeks: The Gospel and Western Culture* (Geneva: World Council of Churches, 1986).

[2] Martin E. Marty, "Baptistification Takes Over," *Christianity Today*, September 2, 1983: 32–36.

original aim, the reproduction of the New Testament pattern of the church, was largely superseded during the Enlightenment of the eighteenth and early nineteenth centuries by the priority of bringing people to Christ. The pragmatic temper of the age of reason, for example, was illustrated by the creation of the Baptist Missionary Society, an organization modeled on contemporary joint stock companies and entirely lacking in biblical warrant. In particular places, elements in the existing culture have served as models for Baptist practice. Thus, among the Seminole people of the Indian Territory in the modern state of Oklahoma, the protracted annual camp meetings that the Baptists enjoyed showed affinities with the Green Corn Festivals that the tribe customarily celebrated. A particularly striking instance, the adoption of traditional Orthodox ways by the Baptists of Georgia in the Caucasus, is examined in this book.

Culture, then, has molded the gospel at least as much as the gospel has molded culture. The two-way interaction in its various expressions among Baptists is the subject of this book. The papers were presented at the Eighth International Conference on Baptist Studies held at Baylor University, Texas, in July 2018. They cover America, Europe, and the majority world and address issues between the seventeenth and the twenty-first centuries. Their common ground is how the eternal message of Christ has been embodied in the ever-changing phenomena of human affairs.

Introduction

William L. Pitts, Jr.

This book is devoted to Baptist engagement with culture. Broadly defined, "culture" comprises a range of practices that may include virtually all aspects of life in which people are involved, including shared knowledge, beliefs, moral practices, gender relations, customs, habits, rituals, music, arts, and leisure activities. Evaluation of cultural history examines both diversity and commonalities of cultures as well as ways that cultures change. During the twentieth century, historians revolutionized the understanding of their tasks. Whereas nineteenth-century historians focused first on political developments, twentieth-century historians recognized the great impact of economic and social practices on human experience. Sociologists and anthropologists also pointed to the importance of the transmission of people's cultural values and practices including their religion, and during the 1980s cultural history emerged as a self-aware and distinct approach to human experience. Cultural history offered academic legitimacy to the study of religion and its significant place in societies. Whereas denominational histories tend to focus on internal developments, cultural history recognizes the limitations and opportunities afforded by its larger social context.

By the mid-twentieth century, scholars interested in the mutual impact of religion and culture had already offered notable insights into this question. Three examples suffice. Influenced by reading sociologists of religion Max Weber and Ernst Troeltsch, theologian H. Richard Niebuhr, in his *Social Sources of Denominationalism* convincingly demonstrated that Christianity was powerfully shaped by social sources. Different social contexts in America—race, region, class—shaped American expressions of Christianity just as fully as did theological belief.[1] Informed by historical awareness, in *Christ and Culture* Niebuhr identified in church history five competing patterns of Christian engagement with its surrounding culture.[2] Together these

---

[1] H. Richard Niebuhr, *Social Sources of Denominationalism* (New York: Henry Holt and Co., 1929).

[2] H. Richard Niebuhr, *Christ and Culture* (New York: Harper and Brothers, 1951).

two books have convinced many readers of the reality of mutual interaction between Christianity and its culture.

Named as Gifford Lecturer in Edinburgh (1947–1949), English Roman Catholic scholar Christopher Dawson made the case for the influence of religion in shaping societies. In the first set of lectures he examined the pervasive impact of world religions on their respective cultures.[3] He devoted his second series of lectures to the European Middle Ages. In this study he argued for the centrality of Christianity as a shaper of Western culture.[4] Dawson specifically used the terms "religion" and "culture" in the titles of these influential books. A third example of recognizing the power of culture appears in the work of missiologist Kenneth Scott Latourette, who chronicled the spread of Christianity throughout the world. Latourette identified seven criteria for exploring the establishment of Christianity, including the influence of the environment on Christianity and, conversely, the influence of Christianity on the environment.[5] Planting Christianity in non-Western societies sharply accented the role of cultural context in shaping varieties of Christian churches in the majority world. Missiologists clearly recognized and stressed the importance of contextualization and accommodation of Christianity to non-Western cultures in their assessment of missionary tasks and practices.

The chapters in this volume address Baptist engagement with a wide variety of cultural influences, including local limitations imposed by state authority; engagement with races and ethnicities as a result of immigration; alternative gender beliefs and practices, including polygamy; and establishment of new educational institutions and appropriation of new technologies. Cultural changes have influenced the shape of theologies from Enlightenment stress on free will and the human role in the salvation experience to current divisive theological battles reflecting "culture wars" in the United States. These articles demonstrate that some Baptists have sought to advance their cause by blending with the dominant culture while others thought their best strategy was to resist conformity with the majority and emphasize their distinctiveness. In short, culture is now readily recognized

[3] Christopher Dawson, *Religion and Culture: The Gifford Lectures 1947* (New York: Meridian, 1958).

[4] Christopher Dawson, *Religion and the Rise of Western Culture* (New York: Image Books, 1958).

[5] Kenneth Scott Latourette, "Introduction," in *A History of the Expansion of Christianity*, vol. 1: *The First Five Centuries* (New York: Harper and Brothers, 1937), xii–xvi.

as an important influence in shaping the Christian and Baptist experience worldwide.

Chapter arrangement in the book is chronological and geographical. One paper treats early Baptist experience in the seventeenth-century American colonies and another in eighteenth-century England. Since the nineteenth century, Baptists have planted their churches in many new cultures in the majority world as well as exercising increasing influence where they were already established in Europe and the United States. Baptist numbers and geographical reach continued to accelerate during the twentieth and twenty-first centuries. In each setting, Baptist engagement with culture is a significant issue: no church exists without a specific social context. Because cultures experience change, the question of the relationship between religion and culture is dynamic, challenging, and relevant. In an era of globalization, it is helpful to hear from Baptist voices worldwide: the studies provided here offer a wide array of analyses of how Baptists have coped with challenges posed by their cultural contexts.

Curtis Freeman's article explores Roger Williams's concept of freedom of conscience and its role in forming American identity. Freeman argues for the value of practicing dissent while maintaining civility in discourse, noting that while Williams strongly opposed the theology of the Puritan establishment and the Quakers, he held tenaciously to liberty of conscience for all citizens. The author celebrates tolerance as a Baptist legacy to the American democratic process and also a constructive model for political discourse in the current era of deep polarization.

David Mark Rathel assesses the influence of Enlightenment thought on eighteenth-century Baptists by contrasting the views of John Gill with those of Andrew Fuller. Whereas Gill emphasized salvation by God's election from eternity, Fuller stressed the role of evangelical preaching and human response to God through a personal conversion experience, thus laying a strong theological basis for revivalism and missions. Rathel concludes that although these two Baptists represent different traditions, both drew heavily on divergent strands of their Enlightenment cultural context.

Robert Pope examines the role of Baptists and other Nonconformists in shaping Welsh identity during the first half of the nineteenth century. Noting the pervasive poverty of the masses of the population, Pope declares that for the people of Wales, "identity and self-worth were to be found not in work, in accumulation of wealth, or in seeking political influence, but in religion. For the Welsh during the nineteenth century, that religion was Nonconformist." Pope makes the case that Nonconformity (Methodists, Independents, Baptists) and the Welsh language together exercised decisive influence in shaping Welsh culture and identity.

Because the consequences of drunkenness were seen as pressing problems, the question of alcohol consumption became a major social issue among Protestants during the nineteenth and twentieth centuries. Brian Talbot describes the role Scottish Baptists played in the long-lived temperance movement in Scotland from 1829 to 1929. While focusing on Baptists, his narrative also includes other denominations in this national social enterprise. The Scottish people and churches divided over the issue. Some advocated temperance, others moderate consumption, others abstinence, and still others preferred that alcohol consumption be left to individual choice. Talbot assesses the social and health impacts of the campaign on his nation as well as the successes and failures of the movement.

Terry Carter examines Baptists and nativism. Nativism is ultimately the question of who owns the nation and who deserves to live in it. Most of the immigrants to the United States were European, comprised of a Protesteant majority and a Roman Catholic minority. Baptists expressed strong anti-Catholic sentiment. Carter's study focuses on the era from 1830 to 1860 and documents a variety of Baptist expressions of nativism. Some Baptist rhetoric included the fear that Catholics would do as directed by the pope, thereby undermining democracy. Baptists involved in missions sought to convert non-Protestant immigrants. Some Baptists refused to vote for Catholics; other Baptists opposed use of the pulpit for political engagement. Carter realistically observes that there is no way to know what percentage of Baptists North and South shared nativist views, but the movement is strongly represented in the Baptist newspapers.

Baptists planted churches around the world during the nineteenth century. John Tucker's chapter addresses the question of Baptists and race during their mission experience with the Maori of New Zealand. For this study he solicited a response from a practicing Maori Baptist minister and historian. In Tucker's telling of the story, Baptists initially displayed cultural insensitivity in their relationships with the Maori from the 1880s to the 1920s. Only in the 1930s did Baptists recognize that they had been patronizing in delivering the gospel to the Maoris. As awareness of racism in other parts of the world continued to increase (notably in South Africa and the United States), churches working in New Zealand responded with a higher level of biculturalism. Nevertheless, even then only a minority of Baptist leaders adopted the progressive approach first practiced by the Methodists. The Maori Baptist response offers insight into ways European Baptists viewed whiteness as normative and thereby failed to recognize their own racist presuppositions.

Melody Maxwell notes that the relationship between the gospel and culture is a key source of ongoing debate in Christian missions. She illustrates her claim by exploring the work of Southern Baptists among the Yoruba people of Nigeria from 1875 to 1905. The literature of the era already shows that Americans assumed the superiority of their culture and religion, refusing to accommodate the Yoruba practice of polygamy. For the Yoruba, this was the normal social arrangement, with benefits for both men and women. For the missionaries, however, polygamy was sinful, and they would not permit converts to continue the practice. Yoruban Christians resisted and responded by forming the Independent Native Baptist Church. These churches embraced African customs—not only polygamy but also deference to tribal chiefs, traditional clothing, and worship in indigenous languages. Maxwell concludes that Western missionary racism clearly hindered the spread of the gospel.

Rosalind Gooden explores the work of the Australian Baptist Zenana Mission in Bengal, India. Zenanas were secluded women's quarters: the only viable missionary access to them was by single women. The women in the mission sought to distance themselves apart from British imperialism. They learned the Bengali language and respected native gender roles assigned to women. They adopted national dress, learned to eat local food, and lived with the Zenana women despite the risk of malaria. This chapter documents missionary sensitivity to cultural practices: the strategy of the mission was to conform as far as possible with Bengali practice in order to open doors to evangelization.

Narola Imchen demonstrates how nineteenth-century American feminist thought influenced the work of some American female missionaries in their missionary activities. Her test case is the work of Mary Mead Clark, an American missionary who served with her husband in North East India (later Nagaland) in the 1870s. Imchen identifies two characteristics of first-wave feminism salient for missions, namely their focus on education for women and on creating societies formed of women, by women, and for women only—where women had the opportunity to learn organizational and leadership skills. Imchen shows how Clark instuituted both programs among Naga women. Although the Naga culture remained patriarchal, Imchen concludes that Clark's ministry elevated Naga women by opening new opportunities for them.

Wado Kawthoolei describes Baptist work in Myanmar (formerly Burma), beginning with work in planting Baptist churches, especially the establishment of the Karen Baptist Church which is often viewed as one of the more successful efforts of the modern missionary enterprise. Cultural dimensions loom large in this story. From the outset, the Baptists faced serious opposition from the dominant Buddhist culture. In the current climate, Myanmar culture stresses the importance of one race, one language, and one religion for the nation, thereby marginalizing and persecuting such minority groups as the Baptists, who nevertheless have sustained a long-lived presence in the nation.

In the twentieth century, Baptists continued to engage their cultures, sometimes in surprising ways. Stuart Sheehan's study of Baptist hymnody in the twentieth century provides a perspective on changing theological understanding reflected in hymnology among Southern Baptists. By analyzing Baptist hymnals he notes a shift in the subject content of hymns from a predominant focus on God to a more frequent focus on human religious experience. The change reflects growing individualism in the culture, which Sheehan also sees in influential theologians working in Southern Baptist seminaries and the most influential compilers of hymnals used by Southern Baptists.

Deeply influenced by late-nineteenth-century New Testament and theological studies, Walter Rauschenbusch accepted the idea that the kingdom of God was Jesus's central message. Rauschenbusch dramatically enlarged his view of the gospel, coming to the conviction that the gospel is twofold: Jesus came to redeem society as well as individuals. As a pastor, Rauschenbusch witnessed the economic suffering of parishioners. Although capitalism was highly productive for owners, it left most workers insecure and impoverished. The church should lead in transforming American culture by insisting on justice. His social gospel has been widely adopted and also widely challenged by virtually every major denomination during the past century.

How have Baptists engaged their message of the gospel in the most intensely urbanized cultures of the world? George Hancock-Stefan explores the differing roles in four leading Baptist churches located in New York City: Abyssinian, Concord, Calvary, and Judson Memorial. Each of the churches proclaimed the gospel under the leadership of outstanding preachers. Moreover, they engaged in attempts to alleviate human suffering or to transform society. The most obvious division among twentieth-century Protestants has been between the liberal Protestant mainstream and conservative evangelicalism. This chapter shows that three of the Baptist churches were deeply committed to social ministry whereas one focused on evangelical conversionism. All four managed to flourish in the metropolitan culture. The author offers reasons for their sustained success.

Restricted by cultural norms, Baptist women of the southern United States were barred from preaching but were encouraged to pursue mission and educational work. Laine Scales surveys theological education for women throughout the twentieth century at one location, the Southern Baptist Theological Seminary (Louisville, Kentucky). Copying Northern models, in 1907 Southern Baptists established the Carver School of Missions and Social Work, a training school for women. In 1948, the courses for the Bachelor of Divinity (BD) and the Doctor of Theology (ThD) degrees were opened to women. During the next generation, many women pursued ministerial roles in church music, religious education, and social work. However, following the fundamentalist takeover of the Southern Baptist Convention in the 1980s, new restrictions were imposed on theological education for women. Nevertheless, Scales notes that the Me Too cultural movement countering sexual abuse of women has recently found expression among conservative Baptist women, thus placing the gender issue in question.

Sam Kelley's chapter examines the role of Kenneth Scott Latourette as a Christian historian working in a modern secular university. Latourette wrote on the history of Christian missions and also on the history of East Asia. Mission history was marginalized by leading universities during the interwar era, where missions was interpreted as a form of Western imperialism and therefore unworthy of academic pursuit. Latourette's Asian histories were soon eclipsed by scholars who knew the languages of these cultures. Latourette also took a highly confessional view of history in general, whereas the American Historical Association generally did not accept confessional accounts of the historical past. Thus, in all of his endeavors Latourette was eventually seen as a throwback to an outdated nineteenth-century perspective. However, there was another American cultural audience that celebrated a triumphalist-hopeful perspective on Christian history and its missions expansion, and his books sold over a million copies.

Adina Kelley addresses Baptist views of gender roles in Southern Baptist literature during the postwar period of 1945–1960. Kelley examines Southern Baptist publications of the era and finds that housekeeping and rearing children were the dominant ideals projected for women. Although authors occasionally addressed the problem of boredom from the mind-numbing repetition of relentless household tasks, most of the stories published ended up with the woman finding her deepest calling in life and fullest satisfaction in her role as wife, mother, and housekeeper. The stories conveyed the notion that if a woman could look back on success in these areas, she would have lived the most fulfilled life possible.

Nathan Finn addresses a cultural shift on the question of Baptists and the culture of higher education by assessing the career of David Dockery, who served as president of Union University, a Tennessee Baptist institution located in Jackson, Tennessee. Finn shows how evangelical concerns shaped Dockery's views, noting that evangelicals emphasized promoting a Christian worldview and integrating faith and learning in higher education. Baptists and evangelicals share commitment to personal salvation, but then their identities diverge. Key traditional Baptist identity markers of democratic congregationalism and separation of church and state receive little emphasis in this study of Dockery. Finn's study illustrates how the Southern Baptist Convention identity has clearly shifted due to its growing acceptance of the cultural influence of an evangelical/fundamentalist worldview.

Baptists in the twentieth century have devoted much effort to growth through evangelism and mission. That they would adopt new technologies influential in popular culture to mass-market their message is not surprising. Jacob Raabe demonstrates this development in the American context. He shows how various individual Baptist ministers and also conventions appropriated radio programming locally and nationally. Producing high-quality movies is enormously expensive, but for a limited time the Billy Graham Evangelistic Association produced effective religious films. The third major media—television—surpassed both earlier technologies and carried throughout the nation messages of influential Baptist voices as diverse as Jerry Falwell's Moral Majority and Martin Luther King Jr.'s civil rights movement.

Despite opposition, Baptists have enjoyed a favorable response in Russia. Constantine Prokhorov's chapter documents religious sensibilities common to Russian Baptists and Russian Orthodox monasticism. He suggests that both groups employ similar language and imagery, such as the spiritual ladder one climbs on the path to heaven. Both Baptists and Russian Orthodox monks have been influenced by *The Lives of the Saints*, which stresses holiness, ascetic self-denial, voluntary poverty, and accepting roles as "God's fools." Prokhorov contends that these commonalities derive from a shared Russian spirituality. The Russian denominations may be distinctive in thought and organization, but in his view the "Russian soul" produced a common cultural spirituality that transcends doctrine.

Noting the pervasive influence of the Orthodox Church in his country from its centuries-long presence, Malkhaz Songulashvili explores the story of Baptist appropriation of many features of the dominant Orthodox culture, including their use of Georgian music, literature, liturgy, icons and practices of piety common in the Orthodox Church. Structurally, the Baptists also created bishops, granting them power and vestments symbolic of their authority. Georgian Baptists have thereby displayed a unique level of accommodation to their surrounding society while also being prepared to reject aspects of the dominant culture—especially its nationalism and exclusivism.

Valdis Tēraudkalns's study of Latvian Baptists from 1900 to 1915 demonstrates how broadly the category of culture can be applied to historical interpretation. Examining Baptist publications, it is clear that Baptist readers, like other Latvians, showed general interest in travel, geography, science, and technological advances. On the other hand, the prevailing sense of Baptist opposition to the dominant German Lutheran and Russian Orthodox cultures is evident in their Baptist publications. Baptists in Latvia opposed consumption of alcohol; modern developments in church music and liturgy, education, and theology; and the thought and practice of emerging Pentecostalism. In short, Latvian Baptists adopted some of the prevailing cultural norms and rejected others. This chapter firmly asserts that no form of Christianity is free of cultural influence.

The book concludes with two examples from Baptists in the majority world. Marina Wang's chapter examines the Baptist experience of creating higher-level education amid Chinese culture from 1906 to 1952. Her focus is on the Shanghai college and seminary established by collaborative efforts of American Baptists North and South in 1906. She focuses especially on the presidency of Chinese-born, American-trained educator C. E. Liu, who served as president of the institution from 1928 to 1938. Despite close governmental scrutiny he was able to sustain the school under the motto "More Christian, More Chinese, and More Efficient," and by interpreting Christian instruction in terms of character formation and practical vocational education, values that would benefit the state interest in promoting Chinese nationalism and patriotism. Wang's study thus engages the issue of how Baptists might seek to sustain their identity while having to operate in a political culture that articulated secular goals and carried enough coercive power to enforce them.

Southern Baptist missionaries established churches in Brazil in the 1880s. Brazilian Baptists grew rapidly and organized their own convention so that they could begin operating on a self-governing basis. Nevertheless, the cultural influence of Baptists in the United States have remained powerful. Ivan Dias da Silva's study documents how Brazilian Baptists have divided over national versus missionary control and over Pentecostalism. Moreover, he argues that the Moral Majority influenced Southern Baptists in America, and in turn, that influence permeated Brazilian Baptists. Not content with traditional focus on personal salvation, Southern Baptists and likewise Brazilian Baptists identified as "warriors" by endorsing political involvement in the culture wars. Moreover, they copied Reagan's anticommunism campaign. The author contends that Brazilian Baptists were copying what they saw in the American culture, the source of their foundation.

Baptists, like all Christians, inevitably engage their surrounding cultures. Different contexts present different situations. There is no single Baptist context but rather a plurality of contexts. These chapters share with readers a great variety of challenges and opportunities faced by Baptists around the world and the ways in which they have managed to survive or flourish in many different contexts. This book addresses only two dozen examples of thousands of local regional and national situations. Baptists and culture constitutes a vast field for fruitful reflection.

PART I

EARLY BAPTISTS AND THEIR CULTURES (17TH—18TH CENTURIES)

1

Roger Williams and the American Conscience

Curtis W. Freeman

There is an old saying that Baptists become Methodists when they learn to read; Methodists become Presbyterians when they make money; and Presbyterians become Episcopalians when they inherit the family business. There are, to be sure, exceptions to the rule, such as Thomas Hollis, the wealthy Baptist merchant and benefactor of the Hollis Chair of Divinity at Harvard College; or Samuel Colgate, the wealthy manufacturer whose philanthropic contributions include the establishment of Colgate University and numerous other Baptist causes for education and civic life; and of course, John D. Rockefeller, whose legacy includes the University of Chicago and Riverside Church in New York City. Such notable examples notwithstanding, "culture," at least in the sense of high culture, is not usually the first thing that comes to mind when one is asked to name contributions of the Baptists. Though their impact on *culture as civilization* may be small by comparison to other religious groups, the Baptist influence on *culture as civility* is considerable, especially as it pertains to American culture.

The word "civility" is often used as a kind of shorthand for polite and respectful speech and behavior, as a set of social and cultural norms, as the basic equivalent of good manners. But this narrow and more restrictive understanding misses a richer and deeper meaning. The English word "civility" derives from the Latin term *civilitas*, which connotes the art of good citizenship. In this broader sense, civility denotes not just polite speech and behavior but a whole range of habits and practices that constitute the successful engagement of citizens in civic life. It is something that Alexis de Tocqueville tried to capture in his lovely phrase, "habits of the heart," which he used to describe "the whole moral and intellectual condition of [the American] people."[1] When Robert Bellah offered his account of these habits, he looked

[1] Alexis de Tocqueville, *Democracy in America*, trans. Phillips Bradley (1835; New York: Vintage, 1945), 310.

first to John Winthrop as their progenitor, but he eventually came to see Roger Williams, who founded the first Baptist church in America in 1638, as the fountainhead of American culture.[2] Bellah argued that Williams's emphasis on liberty of conscience was quintessentially American, noting that the freedom to "do almost anything within reason and still not raise an eyebrow…is all ultimately thanks to [Roger Williams and] the Baptists, even though some Baptists today find it rather upsetting!"[3]

However, Bellah's…focus on individualism as the key to understanding American culture distorted Williams in ways that ignored or confused his contributions to the social dimensions of civic life. Williams's zeal for religious and governmental protections of the *liberty of conscience* was matched by his recognition of the political realities of the *limits of conscience* that made civility possible. It is a profound mistake to portray Williams as elevating the convictions of individual conscience over the claims of civic good. To the contrary, Williams's account of conscience relates to his understanding of civility, and thus contributes to the lively experiment called democracy. This chapter examines Williams within the tradition of religious dissent with an eye to the way that American civic culture has continuity with his political legacy.

The Liberty of Conscience

Any attempt to understand Roger Williams's account of liberty of conscience cannot begin in colonial America, for his views were shaped by the

---

[2] Robert N. Bellah, "Religion and the Shape of National Culture," *America*, July 31, 1999, 10; and Bellah, "Is There a Common American Culture?" *Journal of the American Academy of Religion* 66 (Fall 1998): 620. See also Bellah et al., *Habits of the Heart*, updated ed. (Berkeley: University of California Press, 1996); Bellah et al., *The Good Society* (New York: Vintage Books, 1992); and J. Stanley Lemons, *First: The First Baptist Church in America* (Providence, RI: Charitable Baptist Society, 2001), 1–11. Though Williams soon left the Baptists and held membership with no church or religious society, he nevertheless remained a Baptist in conviction. A decade after his own baptism, Williams stated that the Baptist practice of believer baptism by immersion "comes nearer the first practice of our great Founder Christ Jesus than other practices of religion do" (Letter to John Winthrop Jr., December 10, 1649, in *The Complete Writings of Roger Williams*, 7 vols. [New York: Russell and Russell, 1963; reprinted Paris, AR: Baptist Standard Bearer, 2005], 6:188). Near the end of his life, Williams defended the Baptist practice of believer baptism in an essay written in encrypted code. See Linford D. Fisher, J. Stanley Lemons, and Lucas Mason-Brown, *Decoding Roger Williams: The Lost Essay of Rhode Island's Founding Father* (Waco, TX: Baylor University Press, 2014).

[3] Bellah, "Religion and the Shape of National Culture," 10.

long tradition of religious dissent issuing from English Free Church Protestantism.[4] Williams grew up in Smithfield on the northwest side of London, near the infamous execution site of the Marian martyrs, for which Queen Mary earned the epithet "Bloody Mary." Williams may have witnessed the execution of Bartholomew Legate, the next to last "heretic" to be burned at the stake in London, on March 18, 1612. But there is no doubt that his convictions about "the bloody tenet of persecution" were shaped by the public display of state-sponsored tyranny so close to home.[5] The first generation of English Baptists were strong defenders of religious liberty. Leonard Busher addressed his tract *Religion's Peace* (1614) to King James I, making a full-throated plea for liberty of conscience for all, beginning with the declaration that "Christ hath not commanded any king, bishop, or minister to persecute the people for difference of judgment in matters of religion."[6] Thomas Helwys and John Murton defended freedom of conscience in matters of religion in *Persecution for Religion Judg'd and Condemn'd* (1615) and *A Humble Supplication to the King's Majesty against Persecution of Any of the King's Subjects for Differences in Religion* (1620).[7] In his most famous book, *The Bloudy Tenent of Persecution for Cause of Conscience* (1644), Williams drew on this Baptist tradition of dissent, especially a letter written by Murton from which he quoted extensively.

Roger Williams arrived in Boston on February 5, 1631, and was banished four years later by the general court of Massachusetts for teaching

[4] Curtis W. Freeman, *Undomesticated Dissent: Democracy and the Public Virtue of Religious Nonconformity* (Waco, TX: Baylor University Press, 2017), 1–37. I am describing "dissent" as a tradition in the sense that Alasdair MacIntyre defined it as a lively argument extended over time about how the goods and values of the tradition are best understood and defended (Alasdair MacIntyre, *After Virtue* [Notre Dame, IN: University of Notre Dame Press, 1981], 175).

[5] Ola Elizabeth Winslow, *Master Roger Williams: A Biography* (New York: Macmillan, 1957), 28–29.

[6] Leonard Busher, *Religion's Peace: Or a Plea for Liberty of Conscience* (London: John Sweating, 1646), in Edward Bean Underhill, *Tracts on Liberty of Conscience and Persecution, 1614–1661* (New York: Burt Franklin, 1966), 27. Busher's *Plea* was first published in 1614, but no copy of the original survives.

[7] Thomas Helwys, *Persecution for Religion Judg'd and Condemn'd* (1615), and John Murton, *A Humble Supplication to the King's Majesty against Persecution of Any of the King's Subjects for Differences in Religion* (1620), in Underhill, *Tracts on Liberty of Conscience and Persecution*, 86–231.

"new and dangerous opinions."[8] Boston minister John Cotton defended the banishment of Williams, on the basis that society must be protected from the contamination of undomesticated dissenters, whose errors were "fundamental, or seditiously and turbulently promoted."[9] After being exiled, Williams set out to establish a colony at Providence as "a shelter for persons distressed of conscience."[10] He acquired land by customary law, agreeing to a fair purchase price with the local tribal leaders. Rhode Island soon became a haven for Baptists, Quakers, Jews, and other religious dissenters. Williams returned to England, where he secured a Parliamentary charter for his colony in July 1644, and after the restoration of the monarchy in England, he obtained a royal charter in 1663, which ensured religious liberty for all its residents, proclaiming that no person would be punished for their religious opinions and that all were free to follow the convictions of conscience in religious matters.[11]

Williams never formally defined what he meant by "conscience," though he clearly understood it as a moral faculty distinct from reason or will. He described it as "a *perswasion* fixed in the minde and heart of a [hu]man, which inforceth him [or her] to judge…and to doe so and so with respect to *God*."[12] His understanding of conscience was roughly the same as the standard Protestant accounts of his day.[13] This view was deeply shaped by

---

[8] Nathaniel E. Shurtleff, ed., *Records of the Governor and Company of Massachusetts Bay in New England* 1628-1686, 5 vols. in 6 (Boston: William White, 1853), 1:160–61.

[9] Cotton, *The Bloudy Tenent, Washed, and Made White in the Bloud of the Lambe* (London: Matthew Symmons, 1647), chap. 56: 118f.

[10] "Confirmatory Deed of Roger Williams and his wife, of the lands transferred by him to his associates in the year 1638," in *Records of Rhode Island*, also known as *Records of the Colony of Rhode Island and Providence Plantations*, 10 vols. (Providence, RI: A. Crawford Greene & Brother, 1856–1865), 1:22–25.

[11] The Charter of Rhode Island and Providence Plantation, in Benjamin Perley Poore, *Federal and State Constitutions, Colonial Charters*, 2 vols. (Washington: Government Printing Office, 1878) vol. 2: 1596–97; full charter:1594–1603.

[12] Williams to Governor John Endicott, August–September 1651, in *The Correspondence of Roger Williams*, 2 vols., ed. Glenn W. LaFantasie (Hanover, NH: University Press of New England, 1988), 1:340.

[13] E.g., William Perkins, *A Discourse of Conscience*, in *The Workes of That Famous and Worthy Minister of Christ in the Universitie of Cambridge, Mr. William Perkins*, 3 vols. (London: John Legatt, 1626), 1:515–54. See Edmund Morgan, *Roger Williams: The Church and State* (New York: Harcourt, Brace and World, 1967), 130–35, for a treatment of Williams's view of conscience in relation to the accounts of William Perkins and William Ames. Roger Williams's understanding of conscience moves in a decidedly Calvinist direction, by allowing for dissent based on convictions of conscience, as opposed to a Hobbesian one, which tends

the Apostle Paul, who described the conscience as a testimony of the moral law imprinted on the heart of every person, which stood between God and humanity (Rom. 2:15).[14] Following Calvin, Williams thought of conscience as having to do with the internal government of the soul over which God alone is sovereign. Williams conceived of conscience as a kind of innate sense of natural law. Yet as important as conscience was for Williams and other Protestants, it did not stand alone as the solitary moral authority to discern God's will. The consensus Protestant anthropology reflected the doctrine of original sin, which taught that no human faculties escaped free from corruption. Conscience was no exception. It could, and indeed, was inclined to err. As William Ames put it, "A Conscience hath never so sure a ground, as that there needeth not further examination and inquiry into things."[15] To put it simply: though not infallible, conscience is inviolable.[16] And because conscience is prone to error, it is subject to correction by the Spirit and the Word of God.

But Williams took the inviolability of conscience to a radical conclusion, arguing that compelling the conscience of those who differ in judgment amounted to "soul-rape,"[17] and he added that any religion "which needs such instruments of violence to uphold it" cannot be true.[18] He argued that because conscience is subject to God alone, those who differ in judgment must be respected and tolerated, persuaded but never compelled. The

---

toward a totalitarian account of political power, where the sovereign exercises complete control to enforce uniformity over personal conscience and freedom of speech (Thomas Hobbes, *Leviathan or The Matter, Forme and Power of a Common Wealth Ecclesiasticall and Civil* 2.29 [London: Andrew Crooke, 1651; reprinted Chicago: University of Chicago, 1952], 148–49); and Richard Tuck, "Hobbes, Conscience, and Christianity," in *The Oxford Handbook of Hobbes*, ed. Al P. Martinich and Kinch Hoekstra (New York: Oxford University Press, 2016), 481–99. For a more detailed account of how this dissenter tradition is grounded in a Reformed theological outlook, see Freeman, *Undomesticated Dissent*, 4–15.

[14] John Calvin, *Institutes of the Christian Religion*, III.19.15 and IV.10.3, ed. John T. McNeill and trans. Ford Lewis Battles (Philadelphia: Westminster, 1960), 848 and 1181.

[15] William Ames, *Conscience, with the Power and Cases Thereof, Devided into V Bookes*, in *Works*, (London: W. Christiaens, E. Griffin, J. Dawson, 1639), 1:14.

[16] Calvin distinguished between the *forum internum* and the *forum externum*, in which he argued that human laws do not necessarily establish a religious obligation. Calvin suggested that because conscience has to do with the internal government of the soul over which God alone is sovereign, human laws cannot be used to bind the conscience (*Institutes* IV.10.3–5 [McNeill and Battles, 1181–84]).

[17] Williams, *The Bloudy Tenent of Persecution*, in *Complete Writings of Roger Williams*, 3:182, 219.

[18] Williams, *The Bloudy Tenent of Persecution*, in *Roger Williams*, 3:139.

weak conscience, and even the faulty conscience, must never be bound or coerced by civil or ecclesial authorities. To violate the conscience by force was "the bloody tenet," which Catholics and Protestants alike (even Calvin himself) had at times endorsed.[19] Williams proposed a different tenet of universal protection of conscience. Its roots were watered by the blood of martyrs like Thomas Helwys, who gathered the first Baptist congregation in England in 1612 and addressed his claim to King James I, declaring that "the king has no more power over their consciences than over ours, and that is none at all." Helwys continued, asserting that the judgments of conscience must be respected regardless of whether they are "heretics, Turks, Jews, or whatsoever, it appertains not to the earthly power to punish them in the least measure."[20] Williams shared and defended this tenet that provided universal protection of liberty of conscience.

Williams differed sharply from other Protestants on how to deal with the erring conscience after persuasion fails. For example, when an English translation of *The Racovian Catechism*, a compendium of Socinian theology, appeared in print in the spring of 1652, there was a public outcry led by John Owen, Oliver Cromwell's chaplain. Owen, who had considerable influence in political matters, argued that liberty had become license. Parliament responded by ordering all copies of the catechism to be "seized" and "burnt."[21] Owen and his Protestant allies published a set of proposals that urged Parliament to prevent "persons of corrupt judgements, from publishing dangerous Errours, and Blasphemies."[22] One of the Baptists who rose to the defense of John Biddle, the translator of the catechism, was (not surprisingly) Roger Williams, who was in England at the time, seeking a repeal of

[19] In his answer to the question posed by Williams, "whether persecution for the cause of conscience, be not against the doctrine of Jesus Christ," John Cotton rejected Williams's argument that Christians are never justified in using secular power against the erring conscience, but are only warranted to use spiritual weapons, exhorting not compelling. Cotton argued that the church may use the civil sword to stop heretics from sinning against their own conscience and from corrupting others. He cited in support of his argument Calvin's approval of the execution of Michael Servetus for the heresies of antitrinitarian and antipedobaptism, in *The Answer of Mr. John Cotton of Boston in New England to the aforesaid Arguments against Persecution for Cause of Conscience*, in *Complete Writings of Roger Williams*, 3:51–52. Servetus was burned at the stake in Geneva on October 27, 1553.

[20] Helwys, *A Short Declaration of the Mystery of Iniquity* (1611/1612), ed. Richard Groves (Macon, GA: Mercer University Press, 1998), 53.

[21] *Votes of Parliament Touching the Book Commonly Called The Racovian Catechism* (London: John Field, 1652).

[22] John Owen et al., *The Humble Proposals* (London: Robert Ibbitson, 1652), title page.

William Coddington's commission as governor of Rhode Island. Though he disagreed with Biddle's heterodoxy, Williams criticized any use of civil power to punish in religious matters. Williams did not advocate for Biddle's Arianism, but he defended liberty of conscience, even one he considered to be in error, when it was under threat by Owen and Parliament. Williams exclaimed, "Oh that it would please the Father of Spirits to affect the heart of the Parliament—to proclaim a true and absolute Soul-freedom to all the people of the land impartially."[23] He suggested "that the Judgement and Condemnation of such false Teachers and Hereticks be left to" God and added that "for the Civil powers to assume a Judgement in Spirituals, [was] against the Liberties given by Christ Jesus to his people."[24] Williams and other dissenters made a convincing case, and in the end Owens and the heresy-hunting faction failed to achieve a politically established trinitarian settlement.

This difference between Williams and his Protestant contemporaries in Massachusetts Bay was grounded in his conviction that "the magistrate ought not to punish the breach of the First Table," a reference to the first four of the Ten Commandments.[25] Williams argued forcefully in *The Bloudy Tenent* that civil magistrates were restricted to affairs of "law" named in the second table,[26] that is, Commandments Six to Ten, and that they had no "power over the Soules or Conscience of their Subjects, in the matters of

---

[23] Williams, *A Testimony to the 4th Paper Presented by Major Butler to the Honorable Committee for Propagating the Gospel*, in *The Writings of Roger Williams*, 7:135.

[24] Williams, *Certain Proposals from the Scriptures, Humbly Presented to the Honourable Committee for the Propagating of the Gospel*, in *Complete Writings of Roger Williams*, 7:124–25. Williams makes it clear that Biddle was not a heretic in the strict sense of "one *obstinate* in *Fundamentalls*," namely, the six principles of "Repentance from dead workes, Faith towards God, the doctrine of Baptismes, and of laying on of hands, the Resurrection, and eternall Judgement, *Heb. 6.2.&c.*," in *Bloudy Tenent of Persecution*, in *Complete Writings of Roger Williams*, 3:88–89.

[25] Winthrop, July 8, 1635, *Journal of John Winthrop, 1630–39*, abridged ed., ed. Richard S. Dunn and Laetitia Yeandle (Cambridge, MA: Belknap Press, 1996), 82. When the general court considered Williams's case, Winthrop, who was on friendly terms with Williams and considered him to be a "godly minister," was no longer governor and could not guide the process to a peaceful resolution (Francis J. Bremer, *John Winthrop: America's Forgotten Founding Father*, [New York: Oxford University Press, 2003] 249–52).

[26] Williams, *Bloudy Tenent of Persecution*, 46–47, in *Complete Writings of Roger Williams*, 3:150–55.

God," stipulated in the first table.[27] Protestants like John Winthrop and John Cotton based the applicability of both tables on their interpretation that civil magistrates typologically fulfilled the Old Testament kingly office, which justified their duty to preserve true religion as a responsibility of civil government.[28] They believed that magistrates acting in this enforcing royal role were therefore God's agents. Williams rejected this theocratic understanding of government, arguing that Israel was a type of Christ's church, not the Puritan commonwealth or any other civil government, thus obliterating the basis for any union of church and state based on the Old Testament.[29] For Williams, soul liberty was forever established by the divine kingship of Jesus Christ, making government interference in matters of faith disobedience to Christ.[30] He argued that the soul is free, not because the human will is supreme, but because Jesus Christ is king.[31]

---

[27] Williams, *Bloudy Tenent of Persecution*, 7, in *Complete Writings of Roger Williams*, 3:76.

[28] Williams, *Bloudy Tenent of Persecution*, 109, in *Complete Writings of Roger Williams*, 3:312; and Cotton, *Bloudy Tenent*, 35.76.

[29] Perry Miller, *Roger Williams: His Contribution to the American Tradition* (Indianapolis: Bobbs-Merrill, 1953), 33–38. Sacvan Bercovitch suggests that the conflicting interpretations of Williams and Cotton and the Massachusetts Bay Puritans reflected two rival versions of the use of typology among Protestants. Williams followed the *developmental typology* of the Geneva Bible, which understood the Old Testament figures as shadows of Christ's incarnation or eschatological revelation, whereas Puritans like Cotton were closer to the *correlative typology* grounded in the covenant theology that made connections between Israel and (in the case of English Puritans) England and New England (Bercovitch, ed. *Typology and Early American Literature* [Boston: University of Massachusetts Press, 1972], 251). E. Brooks Holifield, however, suggests that the difference lies in the fine but often confusing distinction in Puritan exegesis between biblical *examples*, which were patterns of imitation, and biblical *types*, which were figures of Christ. Some types (*typus destinatus*) were shadows of Christ and had no exemplary force. Other types (*typus fictus*) were also examples, having some reference to Christ as well as possessing ongoing exemplary power. Holifield indicates that the disagreement between Cotton and Williams may reflect this blurry distinction: Williams conceiving all typology as the *typus destinatus*, thus ending the royal office in Christ, and Cotton imagining an ongoing exemplary appeal to the kings for the New England magistrates (Holifield, *Era of Persuasion: American Thought and Culture, 1521–1680* [Boston: Twayne, 1989], 43–48). Bercovitch's etic analysis and Holifield's emic both offer a helpful explanation of the difference of interpretation.

[30] Williams, *Bloudy Tenent of Persecution*, 119, in *Complete Writings of Roger Williams*, 3:346–47. On Williams's use of typology see James P. Byrd Jr., *The Challenges of Roger Williams: Religious Liberty, Violent Persecution, and the Bible* (Macon, GA: Mercer University Press, 2002), 31–52.

[31] Williams, *Bloudy Tenent of Persecution*, in *Complete Writings of Roger Williams*, 3:76.

Soul freedom for Roger Williams applied to all impartially, so that, in his words, "no person [should] be forced to *pray* nor *pay*, otherwise then as his Soul believeth and consenteth."[32] Williams was not a champion of religious liberty in the same way as Thomas Jefferson, James Madison, or Hugo Black. Nevertheless, Williams indicates how the theological interests of Baptists and the political interests of civil libertarians have converged to shape what can rightly be called the American conscience.[33] Full freedom of conscience for those who joined in the lively experiment with Roger Williams did not rest on religious uniformity. Instead it presupposed a rich and robust diversity. On issues theological, Williams disagreed strongly with Quakers. He considered George Fox and his Society of Friends to be "lying spirits" propagating a religion of "horrible wickedness."[34] But in matters political, Williams defended their religious freedom and their civil liberties. It is no surprise, then, that Quakers were free to live and worship in Providence at a time when they were still being hanged for heresy in Boston. Civility in the tradition of Roger Williams and the Baptists demands full protection of religious liberty—and not one's own religious liberty, but the liberty of others, even those with whom we disagree. This is the American conscience. Yet liberty of conscience is under threat and in need of defense today as much as ever. Where are the sons and daughters of Roger Williams when modern magistrates and purveyors of purity deploy their political and legal powers to ban entire religious and people groups from entry into America and block their participation from civic life? All too many Baptists these days seem to be supporting the theocratic fantasies of politicians rather than challenging their flawed sense of religious authority. And no doubt Roger Williams, were he still buried under that apple tree on his property in Providence, would be rolling over in his grave.

---

[32] Williams, *The Fourth Paper, Presented by Major Butler to the Honourable Committee of Parliament*, in *Complete Writings of Roger Williams*, 7:135.

[33] William Lee Miller, *The First Liberty: Religion and the American Republic* (New York: Alfred A. Knopf, 1986), 170. The relation between religious and civil freedom from Williams to Jefferson and beyond was complicated by the existence of slavery, which recognized the liberty of conscience of African slaves but did not extend that to civil and political liberty.

[34] Williams, *George Fox Digg'd Out of His Burrowes*, in *Complete Writings of Roger Williams*, 5:148 and 155.

The Limits of Liberty

To protect liberty of conscience in matters of religion, Roger Williams favored establishing a "wall of Separation between the Garden of the Church and the Wilderness of the world."[35] Williams invoked the metaphor of "the wall of separation" long before Thomas Jefferson,[36] and they employ the image differently. For Williams, the "wall of separation" protected the church from the world, while for Jefferson, the "wall" protected the state from the church.[37] But Williams did not propose or imagine a wall of separation between individual interests and the common good. Indeed, for Williams the proper exercise of conscience created a web of connections that supported the practices of civility, though he and his contemporaries worried about the corruption of conscience and civility through selfish and carnal interests, especially the pursuit of economic gain.[38] Though the primary interest of Williams was in the freedom of the church, he was not disinclined altogether from thinking about the freedom of the state, and though his main con-

---

[35] Williams, *Mr. Cottons Letter Lately Printed*, in *Complete Writings of Roger Williams*, 1:392. Thus Perry Miller aptly described Williams as "a churchless man seeking the pure fellowship," in *Williams: His Contribution*, 52. Clark Gilpin argues that millennialism was not only the basis of Williams's separating ecclesiology but was "the axis of his religious thought," in *The Millenarian Piety of Roger Williams* (Chicago: University of Chicago Press, 1979), 51, 174.

[36] Jefferson, "Draft Reply to the Danbury Baptist Association," https://jeffersonpapers.princeton.edu/selected-documents/draft-reply-danbury-baptist-association (accessed November 19, 2017), in *The Papers of Thomas Jefferson*, 36:254–56; "Jefferson's Letter to the Danbury Baptists," January 1, 1802, *Library of Congress Information Bulletin* 57, no. 6 (June 1998), Library of Congress, https://www.loc.gov/loc/lcib/9806/danpost.html.

[37] Leroy Moore, "Religious Liberty: Roger Williams and the Revolutionary Era," *Church History* vol. 34, no. 1 (March 1965): 61. Williams's reasons for separating were grounded in his religious separatism, by which he sought to purify the church by weeding the garden, first according to the Congregationalists and later the Baptists. Eventually his hopes of a pure church faded. He lamented that God had caused the wall to be broken down and the worldly vines had choked out the garden. Though he retained a thoroughly baptistic theology, Williams left the Baptists while he awaited the coming of Christ, who would send out his messengers to reestablish his church. As Perry Miller observed, unlike Jefferson, Williams was interested in building a wall of separation, "not to prevent the state from becoming an instrument of 'priestcraft,' but in order to keep the holy and pure religion of Jesus Christ from contamination by the slightest taint of earthly support" (Perry Miller, "Roger Williams: An Essay in Interpretation," in *Complete Writings of Roger Williams*, 7:6).

[38] John Winthrop, "A Model of Christian Charity," in *The Puritans*, 2 vols., ed. Perry Miller and Thomas H. Johnson (New York: Harper, 1963), 1:198.

cern in politics was to ensure liberty of conscience for all, he did not conceive of liberty without limits.

In his "Ship of State" letter, written to the town of Providence in January 1655, at a time when some citizens of the colony were resisting the attempt to establish a militia, Williams declared that liberty of conscience was not infinite. Individual conscience had limits that were subject to the judgment of civil authorities.[39] He compared the commonwealth to a ship at sea, in which "Papists, Protestants, Jews, and Turks" were all on board.[40] Every passenger was to be regarded liberty of conscience, which, he explained, has only two requirements: that none be forced to attend the worship not of their choice and that none be compelled from participating in the worship of their choosing. Here Williams declared his core conviction to be that all persons must be permitted to believe and practice their faith both as they choose and that all must be protected from compulsion against their basic beliefs and practices. This provision is what Jefferson called the "free exercise" of religion. But, Williams added, the ship's commander also is at liberty "to command the Ship's Course," and any who resist or refuse or disobey the common law of the ship should be punished as "Transgressors, according to their Deserts and Merits." In other words, there are limits to liberty of conscience, and the state may determine those limits. The expression of liberty must be congruent with civil peace and must not threaten the "Common Peace and Preservation."[41] Williams thus made the important recognition that the claims of individual conscience are subject at points to the judgments of the common good.

Williams in his relations with the Narragansett serves as a model of radical democracy based on receptive generosity of the other.[42] While this

---

[39] Williams, "Ship of State Letter," January 1655, in *Correspondence of Roger Williams*, 2:423–24.

[40] Williams's reference to a "commonwealth" in 1655 is understandable given that his native England had thrown off the yoke of monarchy and established a commonwealth (or republic) under the leadership of Oliver Cromwell as Lord Protector, with whom Williams was closely associated.

[41] Bellah, "Religion and the Shape of National Culture," 10.

[42] Freeman, *Contesting Catholicity: Theology for Other Baptists* (Waco, TX: Baylor University Press, 2014), 45–53. For this account of "radical democracy" I drew on political theorist Romand Coles, who describes radical democracy (over against liberal democracy) as the politics exemplified by local communities that maximizes the practices of listening, receptivity, tabling, and generosity, in *Beyond Gated Politics: Reflections for the Possibility of Democracy* (Minneapolis: University of Minnesota Press, 2005), 216.

aspect of Williams's politics offers a model of how to practice civil life in ways that do not underwrite notions of totalizing power motivated by colonial assumptions, it fails to take account of how respect for individual liberty and pursuit of common good in the lively experiment of Rhode Island might suggest a way through the current crisis of civility in America. In her book *Mere Civility*, political theorist Teresa Bejan looks to Williams as the unlikely hero to show how it is possible to express political difference and disagreement without suffering the corrosive effects of incivility on the social bonds that make civic life possible.[43] Bejan finds in Williams a model of (in her terms) "mere civility," which demands "a minimal conformity to norms of respectful behavior and decorum expected of all members of tolerant society as such."[44] She sees in Williams an alternative to modern liberal political theories, which work to make what is *polemic* become *irenic*. Whereas this full sense of *more civility* expects differences to become harmonized, the basic sense of *mere civility* allows for the expression of difference and dissent without resolution or suppression.

Williams framed his basic text on civility, *The Bloudy Tenent*, as a conference between Truth and Peace, suggesting that mere civility must be both truthful and peaceable, though it may not necessarily be either polite or courteous.[45] Indeed, as Bejan points out, "mere civility made toleration possible by allowing individuals to *permit*, while nevertheless *protesting against*

---

[43] Teresa M. Bejan, *Mere Civility: Disagreement and the Limits of Toleration* (Cambridge, MA: Harvard University Press, 2017).

[44] Bejan, *Mere Civility*, 9. Bejan stands within a wider discussion in political theorists described by Susan Herbst, *Rude Democracy: Civility and Incivility in American Politics* (Philadelphia: Temple University Press, 2010).

[45] This pattern of dialogue is an ancient Christian tradition reflecting on Psalm 85:10: "Mercy and truth meet" and "righteousness and peace have kissed." Often described as "the Four Daughters of God," Christian preachers and teachers have used it as a rhetorical and dramatic device to show how the tensions within the basic attributes of the divine nature are resolved in the incarnation. See Hope Traver, "The Four Daughters of God: A Mirror of Changing Doctrine," *Modern Language Association* 40, no. 1 (March 1925): 44–92; and Mary Immaculate, "The Four Daughters of God in the Gesta Romanorum and the Court of Sapience," *Modern Language Association* 57, no. 4 (December 1942): 951–65. It is a common device found in Catholic writers from Bernard of Clairvaux to Anselm of Canterbury. John Milton uses it in the opening scene of *Paradise Lost.* In *The Bloudy Tenent*, Roger Williams, addressing English Parliament, employs it in an abbreviated form, with two of the virtues, Truth and Peace, in dialogue about "Whether Persecution for the cause of Conscience be not against the Doctrine of Jesus Christ the King of Kings."

that which they could not approve."[46] Williams favored what he called an "ingenious Civility," whose citizens like the noble Christians of Berea searched the Scriptures daily to determine whether things were so (Acts 17:11), over the so-called civility of the English colonists, who perpetuated their version of Christendom, not by truth or peace, but by coercion and violence.[47] The mere civility practiced by Williams, because it was true to his convictions, could be, and often was, obnoxious and rude.[48] Williams, like Daniel Patrick Moynihan, believed that "everyone is entitled to [their] own opinion but not to [their] own facts."[49] And when Williams caught his political opponents making pants-on-fire claims, he was neither meek nor lowly in heart, though he was always truthful and peaceable.

When Williams returned from London to Providence in 1654, he was welcomed by residents and elected to serve as president of the colony. Quakers began flocking to Rhode Island. Even Williams's old nemesis William Coddington joined the Friends. With their numbers and political power growing, Williams tried to discredit their teachings by publishing a long treatise titled *George Fox Digg'd Out of His Burrowes*, which, as some have noted, succeeded only in raising questions about the sincerity of his commitment to liberty of conscience.[50] Notwithstanding his objections to Quaker theology, which he abhorred, Williams never attempted to restrict their religious beliefs or worship. His chief concern was that Quakers epitomized the politics of extremist enthusiasm that refused to regard non-Quakers as equals, and consequently they refused to engage in basic social relations with those outside their sect, upon which civil order depended. In his public debate against several Quakers in Newport in 1673, Williams wrote that he

[46] Bejan, *Mere Civility*, 65.

[47] Bejan, *Mere Civility*, 67. See Williams, *The Hireling Ministry None of Christs*, in *Complete Writings of Roger Williams*, 7:151. Williams expressed astonishment at the "strange truth that a man shall generally finde more free entertainment and refreshing amongst these Barbarians, then amongst thousands that call themselves Christians" (Williams, *Key into the Language of America*, in *Complete Writings of Roger Williams*, 1:106).

[48] Here Bejan's appeal to Williams anticipates some of the moves of Herbst, *Rude Democracy.*

[49] Steven R. Weisman, ed., *Daniel Patrick Moynihan: A Portrait in Letters of an American Visionary* (New York: Public Affairs, 2010), 2.

[50] Williams, *George Fox Digg'd Out of His Burrowes*, in *Complete Writings of Roger Williams*, vol. 5, 1-582. The strong theological and political rhetoric of Williams is consistent with earlier conflicts between Baptist and Quakers; see, e.g., T. L. Underwood, *Primitivism, Radicalism, and the Lamb's War: The Baptist-Quaker Conflict in Seventeenth-Century England* (New York: Oxford University Press, 1997).

endured "insulting" and "grievous language," despite his protests that "such practices were against the sober rules of *Civility* and *Humanity*."[51] Though they were committed in principle to religious liberty, what made Quakers *incivil* was not just their bad behavior, but their attempts to "cut off" their opponents in religious matters from civil life altogether.[52]

The ability of religious groups to disagree agreeably, even if sharply, is no small matter. As Harvard historian Jill Lepore has noted, the recognition of and capacity to live with fundamental religious differences is foundational to the basic political tolerance on which American democracy depends.[53] This robust pluralism of mere civility left a legacy of liberty of conscience that operated not merely as the "loser's creed" but rather became a crucial factor in the formation of American democracy and remains essential for its flourishing today. Reinhold Niebuhr famously wrote that "[hu]man[ity]'s capacity for justice makes democracy possible, but [hu]man[ity]'s inclination to injustice makes democracy necessary."[54] It is a great theological sentence that Niebuhr spent the rest of his life unpacking. Roger Williams provides a maxim worth considering that *democracy depends on dissent and dissent defends democracy*. To understand this practice of forbearing those with whom we differ deeply demands the telling of a story older than the memory of American democracy. This conviction of mere civility was transmitted through the tradition of English Protestant dissent that was shared by a wide range of groups, but none better than Roger Williams and the Baptists. Yet the question that remains is whether the spiritual sons and daughters of Roger Williams will own their family tradition and stand by the convictions of civility that were so hard won.

Liberty beyond Limits

The contribution of Roger Williams to the American conscience described thus far does not easily fit into the liberal account of civility and democracy

---

[51] Williams, *George Fox Digg'd Out of His Burrowes*, in *Complete Writings of Roger Williams*, 5:38–39.

[52] Bejan, *Mere Civility*, 72. Cf. Williams, *Bloudy Tenent of Persecution*, in *Complete Writings of Roger Williams*, 3:94; and Williams, *George Fox Digg'd Out of His Burrowes*, in *Complete Writings of Roger Williams*, 5:5.

[53] Jill Lepore, "Prior Convictions: Did the Founders Want Us to Be Faithful to Their Faith?" *New Yorker*, April 14, 2008: 71-75.

[54] Reinhold Niebuhr, *The Children of Light and the Children of Darkness: A Vindication of Democracy and a Critique of Its Traditional Defense* (New York, C. Scribner's Sons, 1944), xi.

as harmonious disagreement. Modern political theorists often have been inclined to see history as a story of inevitable progress from cruelty to civility, which is sometimes known as "whig history."[55] Though revisionists have critiqued this progressive narrative, it has not put an end to placing Roger Williams within the liberal democratic narrative.[56] Two recent treatments of Williams illustrate the problem: the biography by John Barry and the political philosophy by Martha Nussbaum. Both come up short in different ways: Barry by wrongly reading Williams as a proto-Jeffersonian democrat, and Nussbaum by transforming him into the forebear of a neo-Kantian secular liberalism.[57] These valuations of Williams as the forerunner of liberal democracy are profoundly mistaken.[58] Williams was a Calvinist, not a progressivist. His primary interest was "theological not political."[59] But to the extent

---

[55] In his history of England, Thomas Babington Macaulay showed how from the settlement of 1689, England rose "from a state of ignominious vassalage...to the place of umpire among European powers" (Macaulay, *The History of England from the Accession of James II*, ed. Charles Harding Firth [1848; London: Macmillan, 1913), 1. It is summarized by Herbert Butterfield, *The Whig Interpretation of History* (New York: Scribner, 1951), and "Toleration in Early Modern Times," *Journal of the History of Ideas* 38 no. 4 (1977): 573–84.

[56] Alexandra Walsham, *Charitable Hatred: Tolerance and Intolerance in England, 1500–1700* (Manchester: Palgrave, 2006). The modern story is neither as easy as the liberals assume nor as inconclusive as the revisionists assert. The history of the liberty of conscience is a muddled and complex story, as shown by John Coffey, *Persecution and Toleration in Protestant England, 1558–1689* (New York: Longman, 2000), 1–20. See Bejan, *Mere Civility*, 21 and 187n8.

[57] John M. Barry, *Roger Williams and the Creation of the American Soul: Church, State, and the Birth of Liberty* (New York: Viking, 2012); and Martha Nussbaum, *Liberty of Conscience: In Defense of America's Tradition of Religious Equality* (New York: Basic Books, 2008), 34–71.

[58] The progressivist reading of Williams is not new. It was expressed by Vernon Louis Parrington, *Main Currents in American Thought*, 3 vols. (New York: Harcourt, Brace, and Company, 1927), 1:62–75. Parrington presented Williams as a seminal thinker, describing him as an individualistic mystic and forebear of Transcendentalism, as a speculative seeker and precursor of Unitarianism, but most of all as a political philosopher and forerunner of democratic liberalism. Baptist historian Winthrop S. Hudson argued that "such a valuation casts a false light on a deeply religious spirit and misinterprets the place of the Christian faith in our American heritage," in "Roger Williams No Secularist," *Christian Century*, August 22, 1951, 963. James Emanuel Ernst and Samuel Hugh Brockunier continued the progressivist interpretation, celebrating Williams as a heroic figure in American history and a defender of inalienable rights (James Emanuel Ernst, *The Political Thought of Roger Williams* [Seattle: University of Washington Press, 1929]; Ernst, *Roger Williams: New England Firebrand* [New York: Macmillan, 1932]; and Samuel Hugh Brockunier, *The Irrepressible Democrat: Roger Williams* [New York: Ronald Press, 1940]).

[59] Miller, "Roger Williams: An Essay," in *Complete Writings of Roger Williams*, 7:10.

that his theology had political implications, Williams had more in common with the earlier tradition of English Protestant dissenters like John Lilburne and the Levellers than with the American liberal democratic tradition that followed him.[60]

Indeed, the dynamic account of Williams's "mere civility" presented thus far stands in stark contrast to the progressive narrative of history, which so much modern liberal social and political theory presumes. Yet Williams may still be instructive for those engaged in the constructive task of politics. By anticipating the problems that irresolvable conflicts of conscience pose to democratic stability, Williams actually moves along similar lines as an important new stream of thought, which imagines the construction of a common life in terms of "agonistic democracy" rather than the "deliberative democracy" that earlier liberal theorists proposed. Agonistic democracy does not seek to resolve political differences in a grand consensus, as deliberative democracy does, but rather attempts to improve democracy's functioning by reducing the antagonism between friends and enemies.[61] The danger is that the fragile social order, which arises from agonistic politics, is never more than an unresolved truce between political adversaries. There is an ever-present risk that agonism may devolve into antagonism, that political adversaries will become enemies, and that enemies will be demonized and rendered evil or subhuman, resulting in intractable polarization. This kind of cascading Manichaeism makes civil politics impossible. The prospect of civil order in an agonistic democracy demands the capacity to imagine an eschatological end to antagonism, which makes politics possible.[62]

The adversarial exchanges between Williams and the Boston Puritans on the one hand and the Quakers on the other seem to fit the description of

---

[60] Freeman, *Undomesticated*, 21.

[61] Chantel Moufee, "Religion, Liberal Democracy, and Citizenship," in *Political Theologies: Public Religions in a Post-Secular World*, ed. Hent de Vries and Lawrence Sullivan (New York: Fordham University Press, 2006), 318-326; Moufee, *Agonistics: Thinking the World Politically* (London: Verso, 2013); Moufee, "Deliberative Democracy or Agonistic Democracy," Reihe Politikwissenschaft / Political Science Series 72 (Vienna: Department of Political Science, Institute for Advanced Studies, 2000), https://www.ihs.ac.at/publications/pol/pw_72.pdf; and Mouffe, "Agonistic Democracy and Radical Politics," *Pavilion*, http://pavilionmagazine.org/chantal-mouffe-agonistic-democracy-and-radical-politics/. See also Mark Wenman, *Agonistic Democracy: Constituent Power in the Era of Globalisation* (Cambridge: Cambridge University Press, 2013).

[62] Luke Bretherton, *Resurrecting Democracy: Faith, Citizenship, and the Politics of a Common Life* (New York: Cambridge University Press, 2015), 211–16.

the sort of antagonism that makes the construction of a peaceable social and political order difficult, if not impossible. The Quaker conscience moved toward a kind of sectarian withdrawal from civility where the Inner Light was an infallible moral voice like the pope, and the Puritan conscience seemed inclined toward the pursuit of selfish interests and economic gain that pushed against the common good. Williams, however, imagined an eschatological reconciliation between these conflictual forces. He believed that the guarantee to exercise conscience freely not only removed the threat of violent disorder but was also the means of political agency for the pursuit and preservation of civil order. He described this vision in a never-published manuscript that he titled "Esau and Jacob's Mystical Harmony."[63] Williams presents the brothers as types, which is common in the history of interpretation. Yet his account is unique. Other interpreters portray Jacob and Esau as types of Israel and the church, belief and unbelief, or election and unelection.[64] But Williams's typology is different. He sees the struggling brothers as figures for "All darkness; All Bondage; All discord, All Enmity; All Hate, All wrath, All vengeance, All Corruption; All Judgments; All Condemnation, all Hell; And all Misery."[65] In short, the struggles of Esau and Jacob

---

[63] "Esau and Jacob's Mystical Harmony" (Ms. N-313, Old shelf marks: 16.7, 101.87) in the Massachusetts Historical Society Library, Boston, Massachusetts. The flyleaf contains a handwritten note that mentions the suggested manuscript was from the hand of Roger Williams. The catalogue note states, "Manuscript (96 pp.) dated 1666 attributed to Roger Williams by Caleb Gannett in 1813. A preface page was signed 'R Ws.' The volume also contains the manuscript of a title page for 'The Second Harmonious on the Second Mystical Order of the Letter,' 1667." Although it was apparently not known to Perry Miller, who included new material from Williams in volume 7 of *The Complete Writings of Roger Williams*, it was known by others. It is attributed to Williams and listed in *A History of American Literature*, vol. 1, W. P. Trent, ed., *Supplement to the Cambridge History of English Literature* (New York: Putnam, 1918), 394; and James D. Knowles, *Memoir of Roger Williams* (Boston: Lincoln, Edmands, 1834), 386. The authenticity of the manuscript has been thoroughly examined on physical, contextual, stylistic, and thematic grounds, confirming Roger Williams as the author. See Jennifer H. Smith, "Unbinding Order in History: Conscience and Civil Good in the Thought of Roger Williams, 1603–1683" (PhD diss., University of Leicester, October 2001), see appendix 2, 278–90. The text is transcribed and included at the end of Smith's study. References to it will be from that transcription.

[64] *Encyclopedia of the Bible and Its Reception*, vol. 13, ed. Dale C. Allison Jr., Christine Helmer, et al., (Berlin: De Gruyter, 2016), s.v. "Jacob," by Candace Kohli; and David Lyle Jeffrey, ed., *A Dictionary of Biblical Tradition in English Literature* (Grand Rapids: Eerdmans, 1992), s.v. "Jacob," 385–87.

[65] Williams, "Esau and Jacob's Mystical Harmony," 64. Page numbers indicate the pages in the handwritten manuscript.

signify all human conflict, spiritual and civil. The discord between the brothers is only resolved when God's mystical unity is finally unveiled, offering the possibility of reconciliation for the political and religious disagreements throughout human history, and especially important for Williams, in the civil life of Rhode Island.

The literary structure of the text is a dialogue, a rhetorical form Williams used effectively in *The Bloudy Tenent.* The conversation between Esau and Jacob occurs, not in the heavenly realm removed from time, but within the arena of natural history after their reconciliation (Gen 33). Williams describes the struggle of the brothers in their mother's womb as prefiguring the struggle between nations and people.[66] Yet the mystery of God's providence lies hidden in the figures. Following the Apostle Paul's distinction between the letter and the spirit (2 Cor. 3:6), Williams suggests that on the literal level Esau and Jacob are types of two groups of people—Jews and Gentiles, showing the visible division of humanity. But in the spiritual sense the two brothers represent an invisible unity, the mystery of one universal humanity.[67] Williams thus gestures to the possibility of resolving spiritual and civil conflict by virtue of participation in this shared peoplehood. Letter and the spirit meet and embrace as Esau and Jacob reconcile, finding their common life in the mystical unity of God. Williams's typology takes a surprising turn as he traces the mystery further back to the sons of Noah, with Shem signifying the Jews, Japheth the Gentiles, and Ham the heathen.[68] Toward the end of the dialogue, Jacob confesses his deceit and tells Esau that he is not destined for reprobation as the letter seems to indicate, but rather that both alike have been ordained eternally unto the same spiritual blessing.[69] The upshot is that the typology provided Williams with a way of understanding social conflict in matters civil and religious, as well as how human struggle is ultimately reconciled in God's mystical unity.

Looping back to Robert Bellah's claim that Roger Williams is representative (or perhaps even constitutive) of something distinctively American, it should now be clear that Williams indeed embodied and contributed

---

[66] Williams, "Esau and Jacob's Mystical Harmony," 11–12.

[67] Williams, "Esau and Jacob's Mystical Harmony," 32.

[68] Williams, "Esau and Jacob's Mystical Harmony," 40–48. This rendering of "heathen" as the unbelieving people of the world differs from his identification of "heathen" with Gentiles in his earlier tract, *Christening Makes Not Christians*, in *Complete Writings of Roger Williams*, 7:31.

[69] Williams, "Esau and Jacob's Mystical Harmony," 52–53.

something important to American culture, but his gift was not the notion of individual liberty that simply prepared the way for John Locke and Thomas Jefferson. Rather, Roger Williams's contribution is something that might be called the American conscience, which is deeply rooted in his Baptist experience and in his inherited tradition of religious dissent. Moreover, Williams understood conscience, not as a private privilege, but as a public practice, one that is essential to civility. Indeed, far from a kind of Manichean vision that divides humanity between good and evil, saved and damned, elect and non-elect, friends and enemies, Williams's political theology imagined the possibility of overcoming and reconciling civil and spiritual disagreements, not by tyranny of violence or through the force of law, but by a vision of a common humanity engaged in common good, in which "mercy and truth meet, and righteousness and peace kiss one another" (Ps. 85:10).[70] Thanks to Roger Williams, the Baptist tradition is four hundred years ahead in recognizing the religious and political importance of protecting and preserving liberty of conscience for all: "Papists, Protestants, Jews, and Turks," for those who believe in one God, twenty gods, or no god.[71] If ever there was a time when democratic societies needed such a vision, it is now.

---

[70] "Esau and Jacob's Mystical Harmony," 2. Psalm 85:10 from the Geneva Bible, which was Williams's translation of choice. The image of the four virtues coming together in harmony is a trope that is revealed in the reconciliation of Esau and Jacob, in "Esau and Jacob's Mystical Harmony," 12 and 95. The universal humanity serves for Williams as a model of social and spiritual reconciliation, which makes civility and the common good possible. John D. Inazu argues along these lines in his essay, "Between Liberalism and Theocracy," *Campbell Law Review* 33 no. 59 (March 23, 2011): 591–607.

[71] Williams, "Ship of State Letter." As Jefferson put it pointedly, "It does me no injury for my neighbor to say there are twenty gods, or no god. It neither picks my pocket nor breaks my leg" (Jefferson, *Notes on the State of Virginia* [New York: Harper, 1964], Q 17, 152).

2

Baptist Theology in the Age of Enlightenment: Contextualizing the Soteriological Proposals of John Gill and Andrew Fuller

David Mark Rathel

Reflecting on Particular Baptist life during the early eighteenth century, Andrew Fuller, Kettering pastor, remarked that his denomination had at one point almost become a "dunghill in society."[1] With this graphic descriptor, Fuller referred to the apparent numerical and spiritual decline that Particular Baptists experienced prior to the evangelical revival.

Fuller charged a rigid form of Calvinism with creating much of this decline. Often branded high or hyper-Calvinism, this offshoot from the broader Reformed tradition denied the legitimacy of gospel offers and duty-faith. According to the tenets of hyper-Calvinism, a minister may preach the indicatives of the gospel but must not instruct hearers that the benefits of the gospel might apply to them. A minister should also not imply that hearers possess any obligation to respond positively to the gospel's message.

Historians of the Baptist tradition rightly portray Fuller (1754–1815) as a modernizer, a theologian who employed the resources of the evangelical revival to rescue Particular Baptists from this extreme form of Calvinism. They often present John Gill (1697–1771), an influential London-based minister, as the chief proponent of hyper-Calvinism. Although Fuller infrequently interacted with Gill's published works, the differing soteriologies that these two men possessed and the influence that they enjoyed do allow them to stand as the representative heads of two divergent traditions in eighteenth-century Particular Baptist life. The gulf between what became

---

[1] Andrew Gunton Fuller, *The Complete Works of Andrew Fuller*, 3 vols., ed. Joseph Belcher, vol. 3: *Expositions—Miscellaneous* (Harrisonburg, PA: Sprinkle Publications, 1988), 478.

known as Fullerism and Gillism appears so regularly in the secondary literature that it has become something of a trope in Baptist research.[2]

Interestingly, contemporary interpretations of Gill and Fuller have not sufficiently explored how cultural context influenced the way that these two ministers developed their convictions. Researchers have focused mainly on biographical details or on delineating soteriological and ecclesial commitments. They have not sought to contextualize the theological claims that both men offered. I briefly do so in this chapter by addressing aspects of Gill's and Fuller's thought relevant to debates over hyper-Calvinism. I contend that Gill sought to preserve an older theological tradition often known as "contra-Puritanism," partly in an attempt to counter cultural changes ushered in by Enlightenment epistemology. His position resulted in a hyper-Calvinism that emphasized human passivity. Fuller took a different direction. He appropriated some of the intellectual resources provided by the Enlightenment to promote an evangelical form of Calvinism. This evangelical Calvinism proved conducive to open gospel preaching and a more active understanding of human agency. This study of contrasting positions reveals that cultural context shaped the theological development of these important Baptist theologians.

John Gill

Gill did not arrive at his hyper-Calvinist conclusions in a vacuum, and one can adequately assess his thought only by first considering its source: contra-Puritanism. This theological movement, codified in the writings of early seventeenth-century figures such as John Saltmarsh, John Eaton, and Tobias Crisp, represented a reaction to the perceived legalism found in much of Puritan theology.[3] Contra-Puritans expressed particular concern with the manner in which many Puritan theologians framed covenant theology. In popular presentations of the divine covenants, the elect must fulfill the con-

---

[2] E.g., Joseph Ivimey, *Memoir of the Life and Writings of Rev. Joseph Ivimey,* ed. George Pritchard (London: George Wightman, 1835), 126; David Benedict, *Fifty Years among the Baptists* (New York: Sheldon & Company, 1860), 135–36; William H. Brackney, *The A to Z of the Baptists* (Lanham: Scarecrow Press, 2009), 23.

[3] The term "contra-Puritan" originates from T. D. Bozeman, "The Glory of the 'Third Time': John Eaton as a Contra-Puritan," *Journal of Ecclesiastical History* 46, no. 4 (1996): 638–54. Contra-Puritan theologians sometimes receive the descriptor "doctrinal antinomians" in the secondary literature, e.g., Randall J. Pederson, *Unity and Diversity: English Puritans and the Puritan Reformation, 1603–1689* (Leiden: Brill, 2014), 213.

ditions of a covenant of grace—faith and repentance—before they receive salvation. Contra-Puritan authors feared that the use of such language as "conditions" and "fulfill" framed salvation as a human work and not an act of divine grace.

Anglican minister Tobias Crisp (1600–1644) served as the most able of the contra-Puritan theologians, and he devised a new account of Christian conversion to combat the alleged excesses found in the Puritan approach. He presented Christ—not the believer—as the one who fulfilled the covenant of grace. By dying a substitutionary death, Christ could accomplish all the necessary conditions for salvation's actualization. This move made Christ the sole agent in the economy of salvation. The elect could now receive justification before God and adoption into God's family apart from any action on their part.[4]

Crisp used his covenant theology to posit that justification precedes faith in the order of salvation. In his scheme, God justifies the elect at conception—while they are in the womb.[5] Human faith serves not as the instrumental means by which the elect procure justification; human faith only brings about an awareness that one has already been justified by God.

Crisp rejoiced that by minimizing human agency he could ensure assurance of salvation. Only complete human passivity could magnify divine grace and remove a sense of duty from a sinner's conscience. Crisp wrote, "Ye may easily perceive, beloved, what I drive at in all this discourse, namely, to strip the creature stark naked, leave it shiftless, and unable any way to help itself, that all the help that it receives may appear to be of the free grace of God, merely, without its concurrence in it."[6]

---

[4] For introductions to Crisp's theology, consider David Parnham, "The Humbling of 'High Presumption': Tobias Crisp Dismantles the Puritan *Ordo Salutis*," *Journal of Ecclesiastical History* 56, no. 1 (2005): 50–74; Parnham, "The Covenantal Quietism of Tobias Crisp," *Church History* 75, no. 3 (2006): 511–43. For Crisp's works, consider the definitive version of his published sermons edited by John Gill: Tobias Crisp, *Christ Alone Exalted: The Complete Works of Tobias Crisp*, 2 vols., ed. John Gill (London: John Bennett, 1832).

[5] Cf. Kendall who inaccurately concluded that Crisp taught eternal justification (R. T. Kendall, *Calvin and English Calvinism to 1649* [Oxford: Oxford University Press, 1981], 186–88). Contrary to Kendall's reading, Crisp was emphatic that justification could not occur in eternity and "must needs be in time" because "before a man is in being, there cannot be a personal application of the grace of God unto him; God cannot apply his grace to nothing" (Crisp *Christ Alone Exalted*, 1:355).

[6] Crisp, *Christ Alone Exalted*, 1:320–21.

Joseph Hussey, a Congregationalist minister in Cambridge, imbibed Crisp's concepts as he wrestled with his search for assurance of salvation. Hussey espoused Crisp's covenant theology and belief in justification before faith, but he offered additional innovation to the Crispian approach. He desired to separate salvation not just from any human action but any temporal referent whatsoever. Only then, Hussey concluded, might salvation appear as solely a work of God.

Hussey's approach moved the entire economy of salvation into eternity, locating God's saving work in a pre-temporal arrangement between the Father and Son. He argued that in a covenantal agreement made between Father and Son before the world's creation, the Son agreed that he would at some future point die for the sins of the elect. The Son's promise to do so was so secure that the Father could consider the Son's death as having already occurred. The Father was then able to apply the benefits of the Son's death to the elect—even though they were not yet born. The elect, therefore, receive justification, union with Christ, and adoption not just before their faith in Christ but before their actual creation. Human faith only serves as a means by which the elect receive an existential awareness of their status as eternally justified people.[7]

Importantly, Hussey allowed his belief in salvation from eternity to influence his understanding of evangelism. Since salvation occurs not in time but eternity, he argued that ministers should not offer the possibility of salvation to sinners who hear the gospel; salvation remains only for those who have been eternally justified. Also, ministers should not call sinners to respond to the gospel with faith and repentance because such actions might imply that an action remains necessary for salvation to occur. Calls to respond only betray the fact that salvation has already occurred in eternity. Ministers must only preach the indicatives of the gospel and wait for the Spirit to make application to the hearts of the elect—revealing to them their eternal status before God.[8]

---

[7] For introductions to Hussey's theology, consider Peter Toon, "The Growth of a Supralapsarian Christology," *Evangelical Quarterly* 39, no. 1 (1967): 23–29; Toon, *The Emergence of Hyper-Calvinism in English Nonconformity, 1689–1765* (London: Olive Tree, 1967; repr., Eugene, OR: Wipf & Stock, 2011), 75–83. For Hussey's most explicit remarks about salvation in eternity see Joseph Hussey, *The Glory of Christ Unveiled: The Excellency of Christ Vindicated* (London: J. and D. Bridge, 1706).

[8] See the argument in Joseph Hussey, *God's Operations of Grace: But Not His Offers of Grace* (London: D. Bridge, 1707).

Gill spent his formative years in Northamptonshire, a region in which many Nonconformists accepted the teachings of Crisp and Hussey. Richard Baxter, for example, served with several Nonconformists from Northamptonshire during his time with Cromwell's New Model Army. This experience led him to cast Crisp and his followers as antinomians—people who were promoting lifestyles contrary to divine law. As a young man, Gill studied under many of these reputed antinomians. He received personal tutoring from Richard Davis, a man condemned in Kettering for promoting the theology of Tobias Crisp. Gill's first pastoral service occurred under the tutelage of John Davis, a minister who sympathized with Hussey's teachings.[9]

Later in his life, Gill did not depart from the instruction he received as a youth. His systematic theology, *A Complete Body of Doctrinal and Practical Divinity,* exhibits the convictions of Crisp and Hussey in their most potent forms.[10] For Gill, salvation must occur in eternity—not in time—in the covenantal arrangements of God. He explicitly condemned the Protestant doctrine of justification by faith alone by arguing that it presented salvation as a work.[11] He contended that faith serves as the means by which the elect receive knowledge of their eternal union with Christ—not as the way they procure salvation's benefits. Gill also steadfastly promoted Hussey's approach to evangelism—or, more specifically, lack of approach to evange-

---

[9] For a brief biography of Gill, see Robert W. Oliver, "John Gill (1697–1771): His Life and Ministry," in *The Life and Thought of John Gill (1697–1771): A Tercentennial Appreciation*, ed. Michael A. G. Haykin (Leiden: Brill, 1997), 7–50. For a survey of Gill's indebtedness to the contra-Puritan tradition, see Curt Daniel, "John Gill and Calvinistic Antinomianism," in *Life and Thought of John Gill*, 171–90; Barry H. Howson, *Erroneous and Schismatical Opinions: The Question of Orthodoxy Regarding the Theology of Hanserd Knollys (c. 1599–1691)* (Leiden: Brill, 2001), 158–71.

[10] Gill expressed these convictions most clearly in John Gill, *A Complete Body of Doctrinal and Practical Divinity,* 2 vols. (London: Tegg & Company, 1839), 246–356. For an introduction to Gill's willingness to locate the economy of salvation in eternity, see David Mark Rathel, "John Gill and the History of Redemption as Mere Shadow: Exploring Gill's Doctrine of the Covenant of Redemption," *Journal of Reformed Theology* 11, no. 4 (2017): 377–400; Richard A. Muller, "The Spirit and the Covenant: John Gill's Critique of the *Pactum Salutis*," *Foundations* 24, no. 1 (1981): 4–14. For a critique of recent works that seek to argue that Gill did not promote hyper-Calvinism, see David Mark Rathel, "Was John Gill a Hyper-Calvinist?: Determining Gill's Theological Identity," *Baptist Quarterly* 48, no. 1 (2017): 47–59.

[11] For Gill's attacks on justification by faith alone, see his remarks in the tract *The Doctrines of God's Everlasting Love to His Elect* in John Gill, *A Collection of Sermons and Tracts,* 3 vols. (London: George Keith, 1778), 3:198. Gill repeated these attacks in Gill, *Complete Body,* 1:292–94.

lism—by rejecting universal gospel offers and universal calls to respond to the gospel.[12]

When interpreted in this manner, little innovation is apparent in Gill's soteriology; Gill followed almost exactly the pattern set by Crisp and developed later by Hussey. What Gill did offer was a systematization and maturation of Crisp's and Hussey's ideas. He bemoaned the fact that, during his day, new epistemological trends associated with the Enlightenment sought to minimize the careful systematization of Christian truth. He opened his systematic theology with an attack on this development and a call to return the primacy of an ordered account of religious knowledge.[13] Partly for this reason, Richard Muller has deemed Gill the eighteenth century's most significant preserver of seventeenth-century Reformed Scholasticism.[14]

Interestingly, Gill's theology represents the codification and systematization of what were originally radical and countercultural proposals. His *Complete Body of Doctrinal and Practical Divinity* presents the thought of the contra-Puritans and Joseph Hussey in an orderly manner. It makes no admission of the controversial nature of these theologians and instead presents their proposals not only as a defense against the alleged excesses of Puritan theology but also as an antidote to the experimental religion favored by the growing evangelical movement.[15] For Gill, calls for personal conversion and a conversion experience matter little; indeed, such calls may unhelpfully

[12] For analysis of Gill's position on Gospel offers, see David Mark Rathel, "Was John Gill a Hyper Calvinist?: Determining Gill's Theological Identity," *Baptist Quarterly* 48, no. 1 (2017): 47-59; Peter Naylor, *Picking Up a Pin for the Lord: English Particular Baptists from 1688 to the Early Nineteenth Century* (London: Grace Publications, 1992), 145-191.

[13] Gill, *Complete Body,* 1:vii–xxx. Robison demonstrates that Gill concerned himself with rebutting developments associated with Enlightenment epistemology as he composed his systematic theology. See O. C. Robison, "The Particular Baptists of England, 1760–1820" (DPhil thesis, University of Oxford, 1963), 34–36. Sell connects Gill's systematic theology with pre-Enlightenment trends in Alan P. F. Sell, *Philosophy, Dissent, and Nonconformity, 1689–1920* (Cambridge: James Clarke & Co., 2004), 55–58, 96.

[14] Richard A. Muller, *The Divine Essence and Attributes*, vol. 3 of *Post-Reformation Reformed Dogmatics: The Rise and Development of Reformed Orthodoxy* (Grand Rapids: Baker Academic, 2003), 150. See also Muller, "John Gill and the Reformed Tradition: A Study in the Reception of Protestant Orthodoxy in the Eighteenth Century," in *Life and Thought of John Gill*, 51–68.

[15] Consider the exchanges Gill had with Abraham Taylor, an advocate of a more warm-hearted and evangelistic form of Calvinism. Gill steadfastly defended his belief in eternal salvation in the face of Taylor's concerns. For an overview of the Gill-Taylor exchange, see Anthony R. Cross, *Useful Learning: Neglected Means of Grace in the Reception of the Evangelical Revival among English Particular Baptists* (Eugene, OR: Pickwick, 2017), 116–18.

highlight human agency and frame salvation as a work. Only a careful and organized description of salvation occurring in eternity will preserve divine grace.

Andrew Fuller

Fuller's mature theology represents a departure from Gill's. Fuller at first accepted key tenets of the hyper-Calvinist position—partly because he grew up in Kettering, Gill's hometown. He soon changed his commitments, however, and began to oppose hyper-Calvinist theology, most famously through the publication of his tract *The Gospel Worthy of All Acceptation.*[16]

Though known for his direct attacks on hyper-Calvinism, Fuller went beyond offering a mere rebuttal of hyper-Calvinism. He provided a constructive account of human faith as a way to offer a competing narrative. He developed his understanding of faith throughout his writings, but his considerations of a movement known as Sandemanianism feature some of his most detailed and developed remarks on the matter.

Sandemanianism, a set of beliefs originating in Scotland with John Glas and formed later by Robert Sandeman, envisioned human faith as mental agreement with the truths of the gospel. Fearing that calls for repentance or a strong emphasis on human action might present faith as a meritorious work, Sandemanians favored a minimalist understanding of faith that encouraged human passivity.[17]

Fuller associated Sandemanianism with the hyper-Calvinism favored by such theologians as Gill. Both hyper-Calvinism and Sandemanianism advocated a nonparticipative view of human action that framed faith as mental assent to certain truths. Hyper-Calvinism presented faith as assent to the knowledge that one is eternally justified; Sandemanianism presented faith as assent to the truth of the gospel message itself. Apparently noting this similarity, Fuller attached an appendix to his *Gospel Worthy* that addressed Archibald McLean, a Scotch Baptist minister who imbibed some Sandemanian

[16] For Fuller's biography and theological contributions, see Peter J. Morden, *Offering Christ to the World: Andrew Fuller (1754–1815) and the Revival of Eighteenth-Century Particular Baptist Life* (Milton Keynes: Paternoster, 2003). For an introduction into the current state of Fuller research, see Nathan A. Finn, "The Renaissance in Andrew Fuller Studies: A Bibliographic Essay," *Southern Baptist Journal of Theology* 17, no. 2 (2013): 44–61.

[17] For material on Sandemanianism that gives special attention to concerns relevant to Fuller, see Nathan A. Finn, introduction to Fuller, *Strictures on Sandemanianism* (Berlin: De Gruyter, 2016), 1–35.

tenets.[18] Fuller also highlighted that many Sandemanians denied duty-faith—although he admitted that McLean had not explicitly done so. Fuller was not the first to draw this connection between hyper-Calvinism and Sandemanianism. Church of Scotland minister John Erskine once assessed that the positions of Joseph Hussey and Robert Sandeman were surprisingly similar in how they defined faith.[19]

To counter Sandemanianism, Fuller appropriated aspects of Jonathan Edwards's work, particularly Edwards's understanding of the sense of the heart and the role the affections play in motivating the human will. As Nathan Finn has explained, "Fuller made a multi-pronged Edwardsean case." Fuller argued that "spiritual blindness is ultimately an aversion of the heart to true religion." The Holy Spirit counters this aversion by allowing sinners to appreciate God's glory; the Spirit provides them a "spiritual perception of religious truth." This perception enlivens the will toward spiritual reality.[20]

By employing Edwards, Fuller displayed an indebtedness to categories of thought that emerged during the Enlightenment. To be sure, considerable debate exists over the precise way the Enlightenment might have formed Edwards's theology. To cite but two examples, David Bebbington has pointed to Edwards's remarks on faith and the will to demonstrate that evangelicalism emerged from a context shaped deeply by Enlightenment thought.[21] Garry Williams has countered that scholars should interpret Edwards as primarily standing in continuity with earlier Reformed thinkers and not as a theologian influenced by Enlightenment philosophers.[22]

Regardless of one's position on this matter, even Bebbington's critics admit that Edwards shaped his rhetoric about the religious affections in a Lockean key. For his work on the affections, Edwards used concepts like a simple idea and a sense of the heart, concepts that appeared prominently in

---

[18] See the appendix provided to Fuller's second edition of *Gospel Worthy* in Fuller, *Complete Works*, 393–416. See also Fuller's address to McLean in *Strictures on Sandemanianism.*

[19] See the description provided in Jonathan M. Yeager, *Enlightened Evangelicalism: The Life and Thought of John Erskine* (Oxford: Oxford University Press, 2011), 181.

[20] Finn, introduction to *Strictures*, 24–25.

[21] David W. Bebbington, *Evangelicalism in Modern Britain: A History from the 1730s to the 1980s* (London: Routledge, 1993), 1–17, 20–74. For a thorough examination of Edwards in his historical context, see the helpful Norman Fiering, *Jonathan Edwards's Moral Thought and Its British Context* (Chapel Hill: University of North Carolina Press, 1981).

[22] E.g., Garry J. Williams, "Was Evangelicalism Created by the Enlightenment?," *Tyndale Bulletin* 53, no. 2 (2002): 283–312.

Locke's work.[23] Even if Edwards only appropriated Locke's thought to describe positions that appeared earlier in the Reformed tradition, he still drew heavily from his cultural context, a context shaped by Locke's epistemology.

Most significant for this chapter, the Edwards passages from which Fuller quoted in his account of faith are the ones that appear most often in contemporary debates about Edwards's relationship to the Enlightenment. They feature some of Edwards's most significant allusions to Locke. Using Edwards in this way made Fuller's theology at a minimum also dependent on the conceptual categories provided by Locke.[24] Fuller was undoubtedly aware of this fact. His personal library featured a copy of Locke's *Essay concerning Human Understanding*—a work that proved important to Edwards—and he cited Locke by name on four separate occasions in his published sermons and tracts.[25] Two such citations featured lengthy quotations from Locke's *Essay*.

In likely the most revealing quotation, Fuller referenced Locke in a tract titled *Dialogues and Letters between Crispus and Gaius* to explain human agency. There he used the same reading of Locke advanced by Edwards in *Freedom of the Will*, but he made no direct mention of Edwards.[26] Fuller interpreted Locke in an Edwardsean fashion and then placed this interpretation directly into his writing without referencing Edwards explicitly. This fact reveals that Fuller was not an unsophisticated reader of Edwards. He was aware of the contours of Edwards's thought and also knew of its origins. He knew that Edwards drew from Locke, and he apparently approved of

---

[23] Chris Chun provides a survey of the various ways scholars have interpreted Edwards's use of Locke. See Chris Chun, *The Legacy of Jonathan Edwards in the Theology of Andrew Fuller* (Leiden: Brill, 2012), 84–109. See also Paul Helm, "Jonathan Edwards, John Locke, and the Religious Affections," *Jonathan Edwards Studies* 6, no. 1 (2016): 3–15; Terrence Erdt, "Sense of the Heart," in *The Jonathan Edwards Encyclopedia*, ed. Harry Stout (Grand Rapids: Eerdmans, 2017), 525–28. For primary source material, consider Jonathan Edwards, *The Works of Jonathan Edwards*, vol. 18: *The Miscellanies*, ed. Ava Chamberlain (New Haven, CT: Yale University Press, 2000), 452–66; Edwards, *The Works of Jonathan Edwards*, vol. 2: *Religious Affections*, ed. Paul Ramsey (New Haven, CT: Yale University Press, 1959).

[24] See the lengthy quotation from *Religious Affections* in Fuller, *Strictures on Sandemanianism*, 97–100.

[25] For details on Fuller's personal library, see the appendix provided in Andrew Fuller, *Diary of Andrew Fuller*, ed. Michael D. McMullen and Timothy D. Whelan (Berlin: De Gruyter, 2016), 215–36. For references to Locke in Fuller's corpus, see Fuller, *Complete Works*, 1:465; 2:6, 658; 3:680.

[26] Fuller, *Complete Works*, 2:658.

this move. In this instance, Fuller followed Edwards when he employed Locke.

Conclusion

Gill bemoaned the epistemological shifts that were occurring during his day and sought refuge in the contra-Puritan and hyper-Calvinist theologies he received during his youth. He repackaged those theologies in the fashion of seventeenth-century Scholastic theologians in an attempt to promote a passive understanding of human faith. Fuller rejected this method. Throughout his attacks on hyper-Calvinism and Sandemanianism, he framed faith in a manner conducive to personal conversion and uninhibited gospel preaching. He did so by utilizing the writings of Jonathan Edwards, particularly the sections of Edwards's works reliant on Lockean epistemology. In this way, Gill's writings and Fuller's writings represent different approaches to the Enlightenment—one reactionary and the other more accommodating. The cultural context in which these men ministered therefore has great significance, and it merits more attention than it often receives.

PART II

BAPTIST EXPANSION THROUGHOUT THE WORLD (19TH CENTURY)

Baptists in the United Kingdom

3

Baptists and the Invention of Culture in Early-Nineteenth-Century Wales

Robert Pope

In 1803 John Evans, "late of Jesus College, Oxford," but at that time a schoolmaster in Bristol, made a tour of south Wales.[1] He recorded visiting a cottage in Cardiganshire, in the southwest of the country. The house, he wrote, was "partly formed by an excavation in the slate rock, and partly by walls of mud mixed with chopped rushes....A wall of turfs for fuel served as a partition for the bed-room, furnished with a bed of heath and dried rushes in one corner." The woman of the house, he reported, was "as happy as any of the *great folk*, for that [her husband] loved her and his children, and worked very hard, and they wanted for nothing he could get for them." She explained that she could endure such abject poverty because "all we have is the gift of God, and that if we possess health and strength, we possess more than we deserve." Nevertheless, she had come to accept "that state of life in which it has pleased God to call us," living in hope that "we shall, after death, change this poor uncertain life for a better, where we shall be for ever happy." She added an ominous note: "the frequent interment of our friends and neighbours informs us daily this event can be at no great distance."[2]

Some forty years later, the *Times* sent its correspondent Thomas Campbell Foster to southwest Wales in order to investigate the frequent episodes of civil unrest that had broken out. At Newcastle Emlyn, Cardiganshire, he recorded,

---

[1] For John Evans (1767/8–c. 1812), see entry at *Welsh Biography Online*, http://wbo.llgc.org.uk/en/s-EVAN-JOH-1768.html (accessed June 22, 2018).

[2] J. Evans, *Letters Written during a Tour through South Wales in the Year 1803 and at Other Times, etc.* (London: C. & R. Baldwin, 1804), 348–51; J. E. Thomas, *Social Disorder in Britain, 1750–1850: The Power of the Gentry, Radicalism, and Religion in Wales* (London: I. B. Taurus, 2011), 53–54.

> On my way I entered several farm labourers' cottages by the roadside, out of curiosity to see the actual condition of the people, and found them mud hovels, the floors of mud and full of holes, without chairs or tables, generally half-filled with peat packed up in every corner, the only articles of furniture being a wretched sort of bedstead and a kettle.[3]

If living conditions, at least in rural Wales, had changed very little, then the attitude of the poor had been transformed. Foster was generally sympathetic to their plight and asserted, "Content to live like swine they should be fitly treated as such. But the people, to their honour be it said, are not content with this."[4]

The first description aptly summarizes Welsh life at the beginning of the nineteenth century. The vast majority of the population was located in rural settings where living conditions were primitive, life was hard and short, but this "mortal coil" was somehow made bearable by the claims of a benevolent and all-pervading providence that had promised to the faithful their reward in the afterlife. The second description demonstrates that, four decades later, Welsh rural life was still characterized by poverty, toil, and squalor (and it has to be said that life for the urban poor was not much different).[5] Many retained a subservient acceptance of their lot through the adoption of a religious hope inspired and sustained by what was a generally accepted modified but nonetheless fatalistic Calvinism, but others no longer felt content to do so. The first description upholds the image of the Welsh as loyal, peaceful, hardworking, but passive people, an image that is not far from the truth but that achieved mythlike status among Welsh political and religious leaders over the course of the nineteenth century.[6] The second de-

---

[3] *The Times*, October 6, 1843, quoted in David J. V. Jones, *Rebecca's Children: A Study of Rural Society, Crime, and Protest* (Oxford: Clarendon, 1989), 104.

[4] *The Times*, October 6, 1843, quoted in Jones, *Rebecca's Children*, 104.

[5] Though slightly later than the period under scrutiny here, a description of working-class housing in Dowlais—an industrial area of south Wales—by Jack Jones bears testimony to this. See his *Unfinished Journey* (London: H. Hamilton, 1937), 18–19. By the early twentieth century, health inspectors claimed that conditions in Wales were worse than in any comparable district in the United Kingdom. See D. L. Thomas and Herbert Morgan, *Housing Conditions in Wales* (London: Welsh Housing Association, 1912).

[6] For example, Henry Richard (1812–1888), Independent minister and Liberal MP, claimed that "sedition, tumult, or riot is very rare in the principality" (*Letters on the Social and Political Condition of the Principality of Wales* [London: Jackson, Walford & Hodder,

scription at least suggests that there exists an alternative narrative, and the social transformation brought about by the Industrial Revolution had at least raised the possibility that life this side of eternity could be more bearable, if not more comfortable, than it seemed to be, even if this could be achieved only through struggle, protest, and agitation.

Both descriptions reveal historical actuality and some imaginative interpretation that characterize Welsh life and its development in the early nineteenth century. They point to a context where life was perceived as something to give meaning to rather than something to be endured. As a result, "culture" could be developed and also constructed. Gwyn Alf Williams, one of the twentieth century's more colorful Welsh historians, claimed in his intriguing and vivid *When Was Wales?* that "A country called Wales exists only because the Welsh invented it. The Welsh exist only because they invented themselves."[7] In this chapter I trace the promotion—even the creation—of a particular Welsh culture in which Nonconformists came to be the spokespeople for the peasantry against the landed and privileged establishment, both political and ecclesiastical. During the period here under scrutiny (roughly 1800 to 1850) they labored in a context that was being transformed socially, economically, politically, and theologically. Their enduring legacy was to lay the foundations on which a sense of national identity, based thoroughly on a Nonconformist, Welsh-speaking culture, could be constructed, and they supported it by providing a mythology rooted in both an ancient and a quite recent past.

Transformation

The first half of the nineteenth century witnessed major development in Wales. Between 1801 and 1851 the population virtually doubled—from 587,245 to 1,163,139—though numerical growth itself disguises the more crucial transformation where the rural areas were depleted by migration of men to the burgeoning coalfields of Glamorgan and Monmouthshire in the southeast of the country, areas that also experienced considerable emigration from outside Wales. The change was drastic as the rural masses converged on the new industrial districts. While in 1801 the population was relatively

1866])—quoted by modern historian Chris Williams, who dismissed it as "Nonconformist whitewashing," in his foreword to David J. V. Jones, *The Last Rising: The Newport Chartist Insurrection of 1839* (1985; Cardiff: University of Wales Press, 1999), xvi.

[7] Gwyn A. Williams, *When Was Wales? The History, People, and Culture of an Ancient Country* (Harmondsworth: Penguin Books, 1991), 2.

evenly shared with each of the Welsh counties containing between 3 and 12 percent of the inhabitants, by 1851 a quarter of Welsh residents lived in Glamorgan and Monmouthshire.[8]

For most of this period, the ordinary folk did little more than toil, whether in agriculture or in industry. They were excluded from the benefits that accrued to capital by those who controlled it, and there was no role for them to play in politics. Identity and self-worth were to be found not in work, in the accumulation of wealth, or in seeking political influence, but in religion. For the Welsh, during the nineteenth century, that religion was Nonconformist.

It has been calculated that, during the first half of the century, a chapel was opened in Wales on average once every eight days.[9] Some were primitive: one record has a Baptist chapel in southwest Wales finally adding a roof in 1816, not so much because of the climate and for protection from the elements but in order to assist preachers with weak voices.[10] Nevertheless, growth, if difficult to measure accurately, was remarkable. As the historian David Jones somewhat wryly remarked of rural west Wales, "From Aberaeron [on the west coast] to Felinfoel [on the edges of the industrial heartlands], new Independent chapels appeared every year and the brooks were full of bobbing Baptists."[11] The Baptists and Independents of Old Dissent were joined by the majority of Methodists outside the Established Church of England from 1811 and the much-vaunted ordinations at the Bala and Llandeilo Association meetings. While Old Dissent never quite embraced the enthusiasm of their Methodist counterparts, they certainly shared common characteristics, namely "sound doctrine, perspicuous style, richness of thought, an animated delivery, an earnestness, a solemnity, and a directness of appeal."[12] By 1851, and the first religious census to be conducted in England and Wales, Nonconformists apparently outnumbered Anglicans in Wales by four to one.[13]

---

[8] D. Gareth Evans, *A History of Wales, 1815-1906* (Cardiff: University of Wales Press, 1989), 81.

[9] John Davies, *A History of Wales* (Harmondsworth: Penguin, 1994), 359; John I. Morgans and Peter C. Noble, *Our Holy Ground: The Welsh Christian Experience* (Talybont: Y Lolfa, 2016), 111.

[10] T. M. Bassett, *The Welsh Baptists* (Swansea: Tŷ Ilston, 1977), 59.

[11] Jones, *Rebecca's Children*, 83.

[12] Evans, *History of Wales, 1815–1906*, 78.

[13] Morgans and Noble, *Our Holy Ground*, 110. I. G. Jones and D. Williams, eds., *The Religious Census of 1851: A Calendar of Returns relating to Wales*, vol. 1: *South Wales* (Cardiff:

While they remained third on the list, behind Methodists and Independents, Baptists had also experienced considerable growth. In 1800 there were around 9,200 of them; by 1851 this had increased to 76,865.

The proliferation of Nonconformity was due in part to population growth and in part to the fact that the State Church was hindered by its association with the Establishment. Parish boundaries had been unchanged for centuries and could not easily be adapted to the demographic emerging as a result of the Industrial Revolution. New parishes required acts of Parliament; a dissenting chapel required committed and generous members or benefactors. The same was true of industrial England, but in Wales it was more prominent due to the concentration of population and to the primary defining factor of the Welsh people. At this point, around 80 percent of people in Wales spoke Welsh, the vast majority of them being monoglot. They became increasingly alienated from the landed gentry, often descended from ancient Welsh families whose progeny had been educated at Oxford or Cambridge and had adopted English language and culture, meaning they were Anglican in practice if not in conviction and often spent extensive time outside Wales. While it is true that the Established Church tried to make arrangements for their spiritual needs, it never quite succeeded. For the common folk, it remained an alien church, a foreign imposition, a symbol of social stratification. And this claim was only too readily exploited by Nonconformist preachers.

Conditions in Wales in the early nineteenth century were not conducive to the development of "high" culture. Nevertheless, definite attempts were made to create a Welsh culture characterized by a distinctive language and adherence to the Christian faith. Early in the nineteenth century, the famous Baptist preacher Christmas Evans claimed,

> Perhaps there has never been such a nation as the Welsh who have been won over so widely to the hearing of the gospel. Meeting houses have been erected in each corner of the land and the majority of the common people, nearly all of them, crowd in to listen.... There is virtually no other nation, whose members have, in such numbers, professed the gospel so widely, in both south Wales and the north.[14]

University of Wales Press, 1976); *Volume II: North Wales* (Cardiff: University of Wales Press, 1981).

[14] Owen Davies, ed., *Gweithiau y Parch Christmas Evans*, 3 vols. (Caernarfon: W. Gwenlyn Evans, 1899), vol. 2: 13; D. Densil Morgan, *Wales and the Word: Historical Perspec-*

Alongside its Nonconformist religion, this culture would be literate. Building on the success of the circulating schools of the eighteenth century,[15] it would champion education as a means of self-improvement and character building, it would encourage temperance and abstinence[16] as part of holy living, and it would support itself and try to instill a confidence in the population by promoting a particular mythology regarding the ancient inhabitants of the British lands as well as the significance and value of the language itself. And Baptists came to the fore in the creation and promotion of this culture.

Seren Gomer

In 1801 Joseph Harris (1773–1825) was the minister of Back Street Baptist Church, Swansea, at that time one of Wales's larger towns, with a population of 6,831. Born the son of a farm bailiff from Pembrokeshire in 1773, he was baptized around 1792 and soon came to prominence as a hymn writer. Although a number of Baptist hymnbooks were published between 1796 and 1821,[17] not all welcomed the development. Christmas Evans continued

tives on Religion and Identity in Wales (Cardiff: University of Wales Press, 2009), 29. For Christmas Evans (1766–1838), see David Meyrick Evans, *Christmas Evans: A Memoir...with Selections from His Sermons* (London: J. Heaton & Sons, 1863); D. Densil Morgan, *Christmas Evans a'r Ymneilltuaeth Newydd* (Llandysul: Gwasg Gomer, 1991); Tim Shenton, *Christmas Evans: The Life and Times of the One-Eyed Preacher of Wales* (Darlington: Evangelical Press, 2001).

[15] The system of "circulating schools" had been initiated in the eighteenth century by the clergyman Griffith Jones (1683–1761). Peripatetic teachers would travel around the country, settling in an area for a number of months in order to train others who would continue, on a more permanent basis, to teach the locals to read once the peripatetics had moved on to another area. The aim was to enable people to read their Bibles. The result, in Geraint H. Jenkins's words, was "a literate peasantry." For more information see Glanmor Williams, *Religion, Language, and Nationality in Wales: Historical Essays* (Cardiff: University of Wales Press, 1979); W. T. R. Pryce, "The Diffusion of the 'Welch' Circulating Schools in Eighteenth-Century Wales," *Welsh Historical Review* 25, no. 4 (2011): 486–519.

[16] See W. R. Lambert, *Drink and Sobriety in Victorian Wales, 1820–1895* (Cardiff: University of Wales Press, 1983). It was not entirely certain that teetotalism would win the day in the period under scrutiny here. While some advocated it (see, e.g., *Seren Gomer*, March 1838, 73-77; May 1838, 141–42; July 1838, 202–5; April 1840, 102–3) the vast majority felt it legalistic and unscriptural and therefore advocated moderation (see, e.g., *Seren Gomer*, October 1836, 291–93; June 1837, 176–77; August 1837, 236; January 1838, 12–13; February 1838, 42–44; June 165–71; July 1838, 304–5; August 1838, 234–35; February 1844, 40–42; June 1849, 167–69).

[17] Bassett, *Welsh Baptists*, 183.

to support the former practice of "canu o'r galon" (singing from the heart) where hymns had been committed to memory. When he saw someone in his congregation open a hymnbook he responded, "You won't have those in heaven. Put it back in your pocket."[18]

Harris was a studious youth, it being recorded that he read voraciously, much to his father's annoyance. His formal education amounted to no more than four months at the Bristol Academy, at that time under the guidance of John Ryland (1753–1825), one of the Baptist movement's most significant moderate Calvinists. Ryland exercised sufficient influence for Harris to name his son after him and, indeed, it was said of Harris that his Calvinism was like "sugar in his tea, to sweeten the whole, but nowhere in the lump."[19] However, he was not entirely convinced by the Fullerite revision, most fully promoted in Wales by John Philip Davies (1786–1832), Baptist minister at Tredegar, Monmouthshire. As in the ancient creeds, Davies linked atonement with Christ's person, or with incarnation, rather than with his death. While Davies still limited salvation to the elect in whom redemption worked effectively, his tendency to downplay Christ's suffering and cross caused disagreement between him and Harris in the 1820s. Moderate in his Calvinism Harris might have been, but he proved his orthodoxy by combatting encroaching Arminianism and Socinianism in his *Bwyall Grist yng Nghoed Anghrist* (Christ's axe in Antichrist's forest, 1804) and his more positive *Tracthawd ar Briodol Dduwdod ein Harglwydd Iesu Grist* (Essay on the proper divinity of our Lord Jesus Christ, 1816–1817).

Though largely self-taught, Harris was a learned man and he believed that the Welsh needed to be educated. To that end, he operated a day school, a printing office, and a bookshop. His greatest desire was to provide a regular newspaper or journal in Welsh that discussed current events as well as classical history, poetry and theology. With Titus Lewis (1773–1811), Harris published *Y Drysorfa Efengylaidd* (The evangelical treasury) in 1806, but it folded after two issues. An initial attempt to publish a weekly broadsheet in 1814 failed after eighty-six issues. Harris persisted and finally saw success with *Seren Gomer*, published from January 1818 initially as a weekly journal, becoming a monthly publication from 1820. While Harris was neither the "father" nor the "founder" of the Welsh periodical (the first such publication appeared a century and a half earlier), the advent of *Seren Gomer*

[18] Bassett, *Welsh Baptists*, 185.

[19] Quoted in Glanmor Williams, *Grym Tafodau Tân: Ysgrifau Hanesyddol ar Grefydd a Diwylliant* (Llandysul: Gomer, 1984), 243.

"was a great event in Wales's history" because it was the first truly *national* newspaper.[20] *Seren Gomer* was intended to be nonsectarian in order to appeal to all Welsh people. It was regularly recorded that the intention was to "publish the stories sent to us from all parties without distinction," the tracks being covered sufficiently by the assertion also that "if it appears that there is less of a list of one party than another, the cause will be the fault of that party" for not sending material for publication.[21] In fact the journal largely supported Nonconformist religion and reported far more on Baptist activity than that of any other denomination. Its editors and owners were Baptists, though it did not formally become a denominational journal until 1850. Nevertheless, the aim was to educate and to inform. Harris, in the words of D. R. Stephen (his son-in-law), "saw himself as teacher to his nation,"[22] and *Seren Gomer* became the means by which he shared his vision with his fellow Welsh people and sought to create what we might now call a "culture."

Harris's bardic name was "Gomer," and in choosing *Seren Gomer* (Gomer's star) as the title of his journal he was also promoting the Welsh as the heirs of the original inhabitants of Britain, inheritors of an ancient and noble tongue that it was their duty to preserve, and the direct descendants of a biblical tribe, this final point justifying the belief that the Welsh were inherently religious. The link arose from a dubious, and subsequently discredited, etymological claim about the word that the Welsh used to describe themselves, namely "*y Cymry*." Tudor antiquarian William Camden (1551–1623) had claimed in 1586 that the word was derived from the Cimbri, a tribe hailing from Jutland (modern Denmark) around the year 200 BC. The Cimbri, in turn, were said to be descended from Gomer, son of Japheth, son of Noah. The notion was adopted by the clergyman Theophilus Evans (1693–1767) in his *Drych y Prif Oesoedd* (Mirror of the early centuries) published in 1716, a book described by one Welsh scholar as "a prejudiced and uncritical but very entertaining version of the early history of Wales."[23] An alternative, and by today majority, view was suggested, in 1853, by Johann

---

[20] Thomas Shankland, "Joseph Harris a Chychwyniad Llenyddiaeth Gyfnodol yng Nghymru," *Trafodion Cymdeithas Hanes y Bedyddwyr* (1912–1913), 9–58, 43–44.

[21] *Seren Gomer*, January 28, 1818, 2.

[22] D. ap Rhys Stephen, ed., *Gweithiau Awdurol y Diweddar Barchedig Joseph Harris (Gomer)* (Llanelli: Swyddfa'r Diwygiwr, 1839), xxiv; Glanmor Williams, "Gomer a'i Gydfedyddwyr," *Trafodion Cymdeithas Hanes y Bedyddwyr* (1983), 7.

[23] Enid Pierce Roberts in the entry for Theophilus Evans in *Welsh Biography Online*, http://wbo.llgc.org.uk/en/s-EVAN-THE-1693.html (accessed October 2, 2018). See e.g., *Seren Gomer*, June 1836, 162.

Kaspar Zeuss (1806-1856), the German historian usually credited with founding Celtic philology, namely that the word derived from the Brythonic *Combrogos*, or "fellow countrymen."

Zeuss's revision came after Harris's death. For him, the Welsh were the descendants of the first inhabitants of the island of Britain, and their claim to it is consequently greater than that of subsequent people who came to possess it by force, especially given that the ancient Britons had inhabited the land "through peaceful infiltration, with no one trying to prevent them." These early inhabitants of Britain, and the Welsh who descended from them, held principles of equality where "each one lived independently on a piece of land which belonged to him, without any obligation on them to pay tax or tithe to each other, but all living together charitably and peaceably, humanely and beneficently." They were a free people, "without an alien nation oppressing them, and inflicting on them oppressive laws and violence," and being self-sufficient they "did not have to exert themselves to the point of wretchedness to support the wealthy, but rather the wealthy sponsored and supported the poor."[24]

Alongside this, Welsh (the word used was "Yr Omeraeg," i.e., "Gomerish") was the only language spoken on the whole island. Again, Harris addressed his fellow Welsh with a mixture of legend and, it should be said, wishful thinking:

> Our fathers who were famous in their day, not only in military campaigns, the extent of their territory, and the abundance of their nation but also in their dedication to foster learning, through which they were able to educate barbarous and oppressive nations in various beneficial matters, relating to the two worlds; and especially their steadfast loyalty to the language of their ancestor (as a particular nation) Gomer, in the face of great difficulties, the bloody laws and every kind of cruel hardship of oppressive foreigners.[25]

The Welsh language was superior in every way to English. The Welsh might have lost most of their land "because of violence and deceit" but they had retained their "comprehensive, expressive language," which "descends from Gomer's age, or," he added rather fancifully, "as nothing is known to the contrary, it is the language of the sweetness of the old paradise, that in which Adam and Eve conversed about the ineffable might and infinite wis-

---

[24] *Seren Gomer*, January 1, 1818, 1.

[25] *Seren Gomer*, January 1, 1818, 1.

dom of their blessed creator." It is difficult to be sure that this was not simply hyperbole, but Harris seems to have been of a sufficiently sober and serious disposition to have believed the essential truth of what he was saying. Either way, the Welsh belonged to an ancient, biblical tribe, and the most enduring sign of that pedigree was their language, which, Harris believed, they had to master and also keep pure from the corrupting influences of the English.[26]

Alongside the myth of their ancient origins and noble language, the Welsh had also been an adventurous people, and Harris both promoted the claim that the Welsh were the first to immigrate to the Americas and supported the widespread appeal to prove this by locating Welsh-speaking tribes among the first peoples in the land.[27] The former claim was grounded in the legendary story of Madog ab Owain Gwynedd, a prince of the northern part of Wales who, it was said, left the land in 1169–1170, discovered America, returned, and then left again, taking ten ships and 323 men with him. While there is no firm evidence to support the claim, in what appears to be a logical conclusion but might also be historically naïve, John Solomon Jones asked rhetorically, "In what way did it become a tradition if it is not true in the first place?"[28] The same author went on to claim that, three hundred years later, Columbus had found some tribes among the inhabitants who knew of Christianity, who respected the sign of the cross and who formed "a much more moral nation, who had a better government between them than others." Despite the fact that Madog's Christianity was corrupted by its commitment to Rome, it was Christianity nevertheless and therefore it "much surpassed the pagan traditions of the Indians."[29] The Reverend Morgan Jones had discovered "Welsh Indians" in 1660, he claimed;[30] lists were produced of those who had met such groups[31] and Solomon Jones concluded, "It appears to me, beyond all doubt, that such Indians, those who are sometimes called the White Indians, the Welsh Indians or the *Madogion*"

---

[26] *Seren Gomer*, January 28, 1818, 1. Cf. also June 1836, 161–63; July 1836, 193–96; November 1836, 324–25; December 1836, 361–64; May 1837, 129–32; June 1837, 174–75; August 1837, 232–34; April 1838, 107–8; October 1838, 305–6.

[27] G. M. Ashton, "*Seren Gomer* I and II, 1818–1819," *Trafodion Cymdeithas Hanes y Bedyddwyr* (1980), 20.

[28] *Seren Gomer*, November 7, 1818, 296; also 341, 342, 374.

[29] *Seren Gomer*, November 7, 1818, 297.

[30] *Seren Gomer*, November 7, 1818, 298.

[31] *Seren Gomer*, October 21, 1818, 316; cf. July 15, 1818, 198.

certainly exist.[32] The story has little basis in fact, and some, even at the time, concluded that "the whole story from the beginning is nothing more than *a deceit*,"[33] but it received significant airing in *Seren Gomer* as the editor sought to encourage the idea that the Welsh were adventurous, courageous, and resourceful people and were not restricted to the land they at that time called Wales but could be found throughout the world—or at least in the Americas.

Alongside promotion of the mythology, articles and sermons were published on points of theology or on biblical texts. One such article, on the names of God, demonstrated the depth of Harris's learning as he explained the meaning of various Hebrew words.[34] Clearly the promotion of Christian faith was one part of educating the Welsh. The assumption, of course, was that its readers were Christian. Nevertheless, Harris was keen to remind his readers that judgment awaits, despite the fact that "many spend their time in this world so unperturbed and impertinently."[35] The death of Dafydd Dafis the Smith at Newport was recorded as a solemn omen: "he was called to judgment without a moment's notice; rather his sudden departure gave a grave warning to us to be ready for the important change which may be before us."[36] But the doctrines of unconditional election and predestination continued to lose favor. Such teaching was "rather harmful" to people who either then wait for a miraculous intervention that bestows their salvation or else they make no effort at living the holy life. "I say," he wrote, "let such men beware lest they go to judgment with the blood of men on their hands through proclaiming such a narrow system to the world."[37]

While the aim was evidently a pious culture, it was acknowledged that this also had to be an informed, even learned culture. Alongside theology and the Bible, *Seren Gomer* intended to publish articles on ancient and modern history, linguistics, as well as poetry, and so on, "in order that the progeny and descendants of Gomer may grow in knowledge and wisdom equal with any from neighbouring nations."[38] News was given considerable space, with a regular column reporting the business of Parliament. Local events

[32] *Seren Gomer*, November 7, 1818, 301; cf. May 26, 1818, 135.

[33] *Seren Gomer*, July 15, 1818, 196.

[34] *Seren Gomer*, August 12, 1818, 225–29.

[35] *Seren Gomer*, March 6 1818, 113–16, 113.

[36] *Seren Gomer*, July 1, 1818, 188.

[37] *Seren Gomer*, February 1843, 42.

[38] *Seren Gomer*, May 26, 1818, 186.

were recorded, including cases heard at the Quarter Sessions. Something of the brutality of the early-nineteenth-century penal system, often referred to as the "Bloody Code," becomes clear, though it was recorded without comment, for example, that John Evans from Carmarthen was transported for seven years for stealing clothes from a hedge[39] while Ioan Lewis from Aberystwyth was to be imprisoned for a year and flogged publicly, twice, for a similar offense.[40] Debora Puw was sentenced to three months prison for stealing a Welsh Bible while Joseph and John Dafis were condemned to death for theft, the former for stealing a horse and the latter for stealing a watch.[41] The arrest, trial, and subsequent execution of the Cato Street conspirators was reported with almost indecent detail in 1820, their fate serving to remind the readers that their duty was to honor and obey their rulers.[42] On a lighter note, Joseph Jones was acquitted of the charge of falsifying the will of one Rees Price on account of the rather conclusive fact that he could not write.[43] Perhaps more sobering was the record that Ann Richards was sentenced to a week's imprisonment for being married twice. It is likely that this was the result of the mercy of the court, it being known that she had been sold publicly in Merthyr Tydfil by her first husband, though there was no suggestion that he should be the subject of any legal redress.[44]

Births, marriages, and deaths were recorded, but interest was not merely parochial. Articles were published on what were considered to be interesting subjects, including "The Science of Acoustics" and "Persian,"[45] while news was recorded from France, Russia, the Middle East, India, and the United States, though the record would have been made some time after the events had taken place. Clearly successive editors believed that education was something broader than the nurturing of piety:

---

[39] *Seren Gomer*, January 1, 1818, 15. The term means removed to a penal colony.

[40] *Seren Gomer*, February 11, 1818, 29.

[41] *Seren Gomer*, September 9, 1818, 269.

[42] *Seren Gomer*, April 1820, 122; May 1820, 155; June 1820, 188–89. The Cato Street conspiracy involved a group of malcontents who, allegedly, had plotted to assassinate members of the UK government's cabinet as they dined at the home of Lord Harrowby. One of their number proved to be a police spy, and thirteen were arrested on February 23, 1820, in a brawl that saw one policemen killed by a sword. Five conspirators were later executed and five others transported to Australia.

[43] *Seren Gomer*, May 1839, 153.

[44] *Seren Gomer*, April 1843, 123–24.

[45] *Seren Gomer*, April 1843, 104–7; May 1843, 140–41; October 1843, 298–99.

> The phrase which is often heard "that the holy Bible is sufficient for a Welshman and that he needs no other book" is very repugnant; it is true, this is the book of books, this is God's book, this contains the words of eternal life, yet it was never intended to hinder the increase in knowledge of natural things; those who oppose extending knowledge generally to useful things are rushing towards the superstitious church of Rome, and it would not be a great surprise if it were said before long "the mother of godliness is ignorance."[46]

One of the more entertaining parts of the journal was the section where readers sent in questions, some of which would elicit responses in future issues. Some were serious and helpful, others a little on the lighter side. The question "As there was a reference in the first issue of Seren Gomer to the good people of the moon, what are the strongest reasons to prove the unscriptural claim that there are men on the moon?"[47] received no response. "Ab Siencyn" of Pontneddfechan asked how to weigh a bull without the necessary scale and received the appropriate arithmetical directions about two months later.[48] The question "Who is the oldest Dissenter in Wales?"[49] received a somewhat convoluted response from someone calling himself "Philotheorus" (the use of pseudonyms being common in the press at the time):

> Because the word Dissenter signals "think the opposite, disagree, separate," &c., from a person or a body, it is appropriate to say that the whole race of Adam are dissenters, namely, have separated from God, and in this sense [the oldest dissenter is] the oldest man in the Principality; but the devil separated from God before Adam did so and without means of him reconciling with that which he separated from, and as he is still alive in Wales, he is the oldest Dissenter and the most hopeless in our land.[50]

Correspondents appear to have enjoyed highlighting apparent contradictions in Scripture, such as that found in Proverbs 26:4: "Do not answer fools according to their folly, or you will be a fool yourself," but the very next verse reads: "Answer fools according to their folly, or they will be wise in

---

[46] *Seren Gomer*, January 28, 1818, 4.
[47] *Seren Gomer*, March 23, 1818, 67.
[48] *Seren Gomer*, March 1839, 83; May 1839, 142.
[49] *Seren Gomer*, May 26, 1818, 134.
[50] *Seren Gomer*, August 28, 1818, 247–48.

their own eyes."[51] Someone calling himself "Tom of the Mountain Top" saw a contradiction in the book of Genesis between "So God created humankind in his image, in the image of God he created them; male and female he created them" (1:27) and "but for the man there was not found a helper as his partner" (2:20).[52] The response reassured Tom that there was no contradiction, though this was done without reference to the emerging field of biblical criticism.[53] A reader who inquired as to the difference between the words "redemption" and "atonement" perhaps could have chosen a more appropriate pseudonym than "Calfin."[54] A correspondent calling himself "Antipope" from Newport asked a number of questions. One concerned the scriptural mandate (or otherwise) for publishing illustrated Bibles and asked, if it is permissible, why were Nonconformist chapels not so adorned? Another of his questions drew a rather disturbing picture of congregational comportment:

> Is it appropriate to take tobacco and snuff during worship? And to spit the tobacco juice until there is a pool of it about the place? And the old women (yes, indeed, the young women in this country) to send the [snuff] box around as you might see boys passing the beer cup in the taverns?[55]

An anonymous answer claimed to have asked two men, Dafydd Howel of Banc y Ffrydiau and Rees Williams of Llan-newydd, who replied that "they preferred not to go to worship than to go without a morsel of tobacco in their mouths, given that they could not understand a word the speaker said without it." He claimed also to have asked Johana Blwchclawmynydd, Wiliam y Wadd (i.e., "the Mole") and others who had replied that "they preferred to have snuff than to have their Sabbath day dinner and they could not go to worship without it." They did, however, draw a line at passing the snuff box around the congregation and, it is a relief to know, also at spitting.[56]

Another correspondent asked whether it was appropriate for booksellers who profess Christian faith to stock and to sell "all kinds of

---

51 *Seren Gomer*, May 26, 1818, 134.

52 *Seren Gomer*, January 1839, 19.

53 *Seren Gomer*, March 1839, 82.

54 *Seren Gomer*, July 1843, 206.

55 *Seren Gomer*, August 12, 1818, 235.

56 *Seren Gomer*, October 21, 1818, 311.

books which contain fictional news, novels and romances," all of which he considered to be potentially harmful to those who read them.[57] Indeed, the general consensus was that to publish fiction would cause harm, presumably because it did not take life and truth seriously enough. During the period under scrutiny, *Seren Gomer* published no fiction, apart perhaps from the support given to the Gomer and Madog legends, and fiction writing in Welsh would gain real popularity only with the works of Daniel Owen (1836–1895) in the 1880s. Nevertheless a poem was regularly published under the title "Dychymyg" (Imagination), such as,

Wyf destun siarad gwych a gwael,
Er nad all neb fy nghwm'ni gael;
Ni'm delir byth, er ymlid maith,
Ni'm gwelwyd ac ni'm gwelir chwaith.

Given the sense of elusiveness, it is perhaps significant that this particular example was signed "Madog" from Swansea.[58]

Despite the fact that Nonconformists at this point still suffered particular legal restraints, Harris appears to have possessed little desire for reform. Instead, he emphasized the protection of Nonconformists under the law. It was reported with gratitude that William Easton, the parish incumbent at Anstey in Wiltshire, appeared with eight others, including James Gerrard, the constable, before the King's bench for "disrupting a dissenting service" taking place in a licensed chapel. They were all fined and bound over to keep the peace for three years. The comment was, "Great indebtedness lies on the religious believers of our land to be grateful for the tender laws of our kingdom."[59]

---

[57] *Seren Gomer*, January 1839, 20.

[58] *Seren Gomer*, November 4, 1818, 330. A loose translation might be "I am the subject of good and bad talk / Although no one can have my company / I will never be caught, despite strenuous effort / I have not been seen, and nor will I be seen." The poem was later republished under the title "Dychymmyg" in *Seren Gomer* (April 1843, 114), with the poet recorded as "James Jones, Blaensulgen."

[59] *Seren Gomer*, May 26, 1818, 142. The terms of the so-called Act of Toleration (1689) protected properly licensed preachers and dissenting chapels from having their meetings disrupted. Nevertheless, in the early nineteenth century, "much of the violence [suffered by Nonconformists] was connived at, if not positively encouraged, by Anglican clergymen and justices" (Kenneth D. Brown, *A Social History of the Nonconformist Ministry in England and Wales, 1800–1930* [Oxford: Clarendon, 1988], 9).

Following the repeal of the Test and Corporation Acts in 1828, Nonconformists could play a fuller part in civic life without having to celebrate Communion at the parish church. Attention subsequently turned more toward the injustices suffered by Nonconformists at the hands of the Church Establishment. The church tithe was a particular bone of contention, especially the extreme ways in which nonpayment was treated.[60] This was perceived as ecclesiastical oppression, made possible by the privileged relationship with the state enjoyed by the Established Church.[61] The Nonconformists were promoted as noble in the best sense of the word,[62] while the leading English Congregationalist, Thomas Binney (1798–1874), was quoted approvingly as saying, "The Established Church damns more souls than it saves."[63] Perhaps the most remarkable piece written against ecclesiastical oppression came in an article titled "Victoria's Captivity." It began with a gushing, though loaded, statement of loyalty:

> Every sincere heart beats for her Majesty, and she swims in the fullest floods of the warmest affections of her subjects; and we know of no one who makes an indignant look but some old selfish and callous Tory. Our hearts are warm towards her; our feet would quickly work for her service and our tongues easily say, "Long live Victoria!"[64]

However, the queen was imprisoned in a system where she was unable to choose her religion. Willingly or otherwise, she had to be a member of the Church of England and adhere to the Thirty-Nine Articles and the Book of Common Prayer, rather than search the Scriptures,[65] the article complained, before ending with a rallying cry: "Listen Churchmen! Listen Nonconformists! Victoria is fettered! Do you intend this? Freedom for Victoria! Energise yourselves until it is achieved, and extinguish for ever the scandalous bondage!"[66] The whole matter was exacerbated by the rise of Puseyite practices. This was little more than papist religion in disguise, accord-

---

[60] Such as the occasion in June 1843 when John Jones, a Quaker shopkeeper in Rhuthun, north Wales, had 30s worth of goods removed from his shop in order to pay the 7s 6d he owed for the tithe (*Seren Gomer*, September 1843, 278).

[61] See a further example at *Seren Gomer*, January 1839, 29–30; February 1839, 58.

[62] *Seren Gomer*, December 1843, 363–66.

[63] *Seren Gomer*, February 1839, 57.

[64] *Seren Gomer*, June 1839, 193.

[65] *Seren Gomer*, June 1839, 193.

[66] *Seren Gomer*, June 1839, 195.

ing to correspondents.[67] Such priests, "unchristian brutes,"[68] "would prefer to have England back in the bosom of the Papist Church than to win the whole world to be Papists; *and so long as there is an Established Church in Britain* THERE WILL BE DANGER."[69] This was the problem with a "State Church," and the answer was disestablishment. The antiestablishmentism aimed toward the State Church and the injustices that arose from its support in law signaled a degree of change in Nonconformist attitudes toward society.

Church and Society

While modified or moderate Calvinism had increased in popularity among Welsh Baptists following the revivals of the eighteenth century, it had not been completely established by the beginning of the nineteenth century—and for some there remained something of a fatalism in their outlook. In this life, human beings had been born in a particular station and to seek to alter it was considered an attack not just on social order but on the providence that had established it in the first place. During an industrial dispute at the Paris Mountain copper mine on Anglesey in 1817, the redoubtable Christmas Evans, along with eight other Baptist ministers, drew up a declaration and sent it to a justice of the peace. Part of it read,

> It is not the province of Christians to debate and discuss politics—but to behave humbly towards our superiors....Sir, we do not feel the least interest in the great noise about Universal Suffrage, Annual Parliaments, Reform in Parliament, abolishing of the Tythes and many other things....From Agrarian laws, and Spencean principles, good Lord deliver us....We do cordially hate the political leaven of Cobbett, Tom Payne and other anarchists.[70]

---

[67] *Seren Gomer*, February 1836, 82–83; March 1836, 89; July 1836, 197–202; August 1836, 254; May 1837, 135–36; May 1839, 137–38; June 1840, 186–89; June 1842, 161–64; July 1842), 193–95; May 1844), 134–37, 152; June 1844, 184; August 1844, 245; November 1844, 341–343; December 1844, 375–80; January 1845, 28–29; February 1845, 56; November 1845, 332–33; June 1846, 184–85; September 1846, 269–70; August 1847, 227; August 1848, 230–31; January 1849, 1–4; February 1849, 44–47; April 1849, 97–100; June 1849, 161–65; 173–75; November 1848, 349–50.

[68] *Seren Gomer*, July 1843, 203.

[69] *Seren Gomer*, January 1843, 4.

[70] Bassett, *Welsh Baptists*, 131–32. See Morgan, *Christmas Evans a'r Ymneilltuaeth Newydd*, 78. Meeting held at Llangefni, Anglesey, March 4, 1817 (*North Wales Gazette*,

As with other religious leaders of the time, Christmas Evans and company were fearful that agitation from the grass roots would lead to godless chaos and bloody horror similar to that of the French Revolution. However, there seems something obsequious, almost sycophantic, in these words. Those who spoke of the king or the government in a critical or disparaging way were to be excommunicated. Perhaps worse than that, the declaration denied even the possibility that distress and hardship among the people might have something to do with those who governed, or who lived privileged lives, whether monarch, government, or gentry. Instead this, too, was the result of providence. It was the case, they claimed, that "the supreme disposer of all sublunary events did tenderly smite us with his rod, wherefore our duty is to consider who hath ordained it, and to hear his voice unto us by his rod." They concluded, "How unbecoming, how vain and infuriating it is for the common people to engage in political debates! It is as fruitless as it is foolish."[71] T. M. Bassett, one of the Welsh Baptists's most comprehensive chroniclers of the twentieth century, commented that "servility could hardly grovel lower." But knowing one's station in life was considered to be part of obedience to the providence which, it was believed, had dictated it in the first place. The South-Western Association of Baptists, in 1826, told parents that their children should be dressed appropriately, displaying no ambition either to change or to deny their social status,[72] while as late as 1857 another Baptist minister, J. A. Jones, asserted that the poor are to be content in all circumstances and to submit themselves to what was clearly God's will. While entitled to their own opinion, they were to listen to those whose station in life dictated that they possessed the greater wisdom.[73]

Under Harris's editorship, *Seren Gomer* had contained no political radicalism, hardly a surprising fact, given that Harris died before the first Parliamentary Reform Act was passed in 1832. But from the late 1820s and into the 1830s, Welsh society was more turbulent and journalism had become "more aggressive and argumentative."[74] Readers of *Seren Gomer* were

---

March 27, 1817). T. M. Bassett, "Cymreictod a Phrydeindod: Dau Lythyr (ii) Llythyr Christmas Evans ac eraill (1817)," *Trafodion Cymdeithas Hanes y Bedyddwyr* (1981), 16–20. Bassett was not convinced that Evans et al. had drafted the declaration, but they clearly endorsed it.

[71] Bassett, *Welsh Baptists*, 131-32.

[72] Bassett, *Welsh Baptists*, 132.

[73] *Y Bedyddiwr*, September 1857, 263–64.

[74] Prys Morgan, "Daucanmlwyddiant Seren Gomer," *Y Casglwr* 112 (2014): 22–23.

aware of radical and even revolutionary events occurring in Welsh society, and the editor's comments reveal a willingness to acknowledge that, rather than oppressive reprisal by the forces of the law, some social reform was necessary. From 1827, the sub-editor (editor from 1830) was Samuel Evans (1793–1856). Known as "Gomerydd," Evans was a Baptist layman, considered to be one of the greatest Liberal journalists of his day. The owner (from 1837) was the radical Baptist minister Huw William Jones (1802–1873)[75] who also assisted with the editing. His radicalism was beyond doubt; it was daring, blatant, overt. He published articles on Robespierre as well as a translation of the Declaration of the Rights of Man.[76] The radical sympathies of both men were seen in the journal especially in the recording of, and reaction to, social disorder. The ideal was that of a peaceful, pious, literate, and sober populace. But this was never quite realized and appeared increasingly further from reality as remarkable outbreaks of organized intimidation, violence, and destruction of property occurred in the second quarter of the century.

During the 1820s and 1830s, there were countless episodes in the eastern coalfields involving "herds" of "Scotch Cattle."[77] Even today, little is known about the organization that appears to have been a secret society made up of Welsh colliers. Threatening letters were sent before a nocturnal visit by a group of men disguised and with blackened faces (itself a capital offense) who would conduct a mock trial before destroying property and assaulting those identified as a threat to the community. These included Irish or English immigrants, bailiffs, or employers who had exploited their workers. Despite the trial and execution of Edward Morgan in 1834 for killing a miner's wife on such an occasion, the authorities failed to break the organization. *Seren Gomer* consistently denounced acts of violence and encouraged readers to use the legal processes available for change (whatever

---

[75] *Y Bedyddiwr*, October 1856, 316; *Yr Haul*, October 1856, 324; *Seren Gomer*, October 1856, 476; T. M. Jones, *Llenyddiaeth fy Ngwlad: Sef Hanes y Newyddiadur a'r Cylchgrawn Cymreig yn Nghymru, America ac Awstralia, yn nghyd a'u dylanwad ar fywyd Cenedl y Cymry* (Holywell: P. M. Evans and Son, 1893), 84–86.

[76] Bassett, *Welsh Baptists*, 140; *Seren Gomer*, May 1837, 138–41; June 1837, 171–73. Not all were convinced; see July 1837, 202.

[77] See David J. V. Jones, "The Scotch Cattle and Their Black Domain," *Welsh History Review* 5, no. 3 (1971): 220–49; Marie-Elaine Bidder, "The Scotch Cattle in Monmouthshire, c. 1820–1825," *Gwent Local History* 63 (1981): 3–16; Rhian Eleri Jones, "Symbol, Ritual, and Popular Protest in Early Nineteenth-Century Wales: The Scotch Cattle Rebranded," *Welsh History Review* 26, no. 1 (2012): 34–57.

they were). Nevertheless, it was possible to denounce violence and lawlessness while also acknowledging it to be a response to wider injustices. The cause of this activity was clear. On the one hand there was the indifference of the Tory government: "all their measures are so narrow, as if they do not wish to serve anyone but the gentry." On the other there was the genuine concern of the peasantry: "our trade has declined, our manufacturing destroyed, the people starve, the poor's prisons are overcrowded" and yet the Tories claim "there is nothing wrong."[78]

Doubtless as a result of recognizing social and economic changes brought by industrialization, the sense that station in life was solely the responsibility of providence was being replaced by a culture whose piety and education sought social improvement and began to acknowledge that divine justice and righteousness should be mirrored in human relationships, even if they remained fundamentally those between governors and governed, owners and employees. Thus it could be written, "If something is not done soon to improve the state of the workers we would not be surprised to hear that the whole land has turned into Scotch cattle, or something worse."[79]

Chartism emerged in the 1830s as a popular movement agitating, among other things, for universal male suffrage. The failure of the first petition to Parliament in 1839 was followed by riots in Llanidloes and, famously, in Newport. Around five thousand workers marched on Newport on a miserable, wet November 4, 1839. Soldiers lying in ambush at the Westgate Hotel shot twenty-two protesters dead. The Newport Rising received extensive coverage in *Seren Gomer*, in what was a descriptive rather than evaluative article. While "the futility of winning their claims through unlawful means" was emphasized, it was widely known that Samuel Evans and Hugh Jones supported the People's Charter. Virtually no comment was made until the end of the article when the editor noted his support for vote by ballot, and that "there are burdens on the country which should be removed" but that violence would not help and that the Newport rising was little more than "leading men to the slaughter."[80]

The attack on Newport was roundly condemned, and the trial of the Chartists was given extensive coverage in *Seren Gomer*.[81] The three leaders of the rising—John Frost, Zephaniah Williams, and William Jones—were

---

[78] *Seren Gomer*, April 1843, 122.

[79] *Seren Gomer*, April 1843, 122.

[80] *Seren Gomer*, December 1839, 374.

[81] *Seren Gomer*, January 1840, 28; February 1840, 51–59. See also Jones, *Last Rising*.

charged with high treason, found guilty, and on January 16, 1840, became the last men in British history to be sentenced to death by being hanged, drawn, and quartered. Micah Thomas (1778–1853), president of the Baptist Academy at Abergavenny, despite having no personal acquaintance or connection with the Chartists or Chartism, and abhorring their violent activities, wrote to Lord Normanby, the home secretary, advocating clemency for the Newport three. Normanby replied on February 1, 1840, informing Thomas that the sentence had been commuted to transportation for life.[82]

While the Chartists' actions were condemned as "foolish," it was stated "at the same time, we regret that our governors make no efforts to lighten the people's burdens. And their hard-heartedness is now beginning to bear its moral fruit."[83] This had been a consistent theme and, at times, bordered on the audacious:

> If our politicians read Seren Gomer, we would give them a word of counsel—namely, that they strive to remove the people's burdens, and arrange bills for the benefit of the country; because as long as cause exists, effect will surely follow.[84]

A final example of popular unrest was the series of so-called Rebecca Riots.[85] Initially in 1839 and then again in 1843–1844, smallholders rose up against what they saw as symbols of their oppression by disguising themselves and attacking the tollgates on the turnpikes of southwest Wales. Legend has it that one early leader had borrowed clothes from a large woman named Rebecca, while another suggested a biblical source: "And they blessed Rebekah and said unto her, let thy seed possess the gates of those which hate thee" (Gen. 24:60). Again, some kind of secret organization developed and each attack had its own leader, dressed as Rebecca, while their targets included tollgates, weirs where landowners had restricted fishing rights, workhouses, landlords and their agents, magistrates, bailiffs, Anglican clergymen, and absent fathers of children born outside wedlock.

Seren Gomer provided a relatively sympathetic response to the events, though once again made it clear that it did not support lawbreaking. When

---

[82] David Williams, "Micah Thomas and the Chartists," *Trafodion Cymdeithas Hanes y Bedyddwyr* (1950): 28–31.

[83] *Seren Gomer*, March 1940, 93.

[84] *Seren Gomer*, December 1839, 374.

[85] See Jones, *Rebecca's Children*; David Williams, *The Rebecca Riots* (1955; Cardiff: University of Wales Press, 2015); Rhian E. Jones, *Petticoat Heroes: Gender, Culture, and Popular Protest in the Rebecca Riots* (Cardiff: University of Wales Press, 2015).

Rebecca was at its height, in 1843, there were monthly accounts of its activity, all of which contained little, if any, condemnation. So while the editor could say, at the end of the year, "We do not support the use of *physical force*, at all, to remove the people's burdens, but with all earnestness we plead them to reject this dangerous path, and adopt measures which are compatible with the content of the constitution," he could also say, "The country is being severely crushed, and the burdens must be urgently removed."[86]

While never encouraging the rioters, the blame was squarely placed on the authorities for not dealing with root causes. While at times the root cause appeared to be the greed and mismanagement of the turnpike trusts, in fact correspondents understood that the destruction of the tollgates and tollhouses constituted a tangible symbol of frustration at social and economic hardship: "Business on stop; workers in their thousands unemployed; farmers almost shattered; education bill; raising taxes of the poor; no hope to repeal the Corn Law; Ireland in tumult; exceptional hardship in the land."[87] Nevertheless, the government succeeded in making it a matter about the turnpikes, and a commission of inquiry placed the roads in the hands of a number of boards that then simplified and reduced the tolls.

The Welsh were, perhaps, forging or adopting an identity encouraged by publications such as *Seren Gomer* to acknowledge they belonged to an ancient and noble people. Events, however, revealed also the frustration arising from economic depression and social transformation that opened them simultaneously to the radical currents in contemporary politics and led to at least some of them taking matters into their own hands. At times the Establishment certainly felt under siege; something had to be done. The response came from an unexpected source when the commissioners appointed to investigate the state of education in Wales reported in 1847. The report, and the evidence gathered by the commissioners, were published with blue covers and thus became known as "the Blue Books."

The report rightly recorded that the provision of education in Wales was poor, but the findings were nullified by the commissioners' indictment of the culture, social conditions, (Nonconformist) religion, and morals of the people of Wales. "The Welsh were portrayed as ill-educated, poor, dirty, unchaste and potentially rebellious."[88] The commissioners assumed that ignorance of English language and literature was synonymous with illiteracy

[86] *Seren Gomer*, Introduction 1843.
[87] *Seren Gomer*, June 1843, 185.
[88] Evans, *History of Wales, 1815–1906*, 126.

and that the Welsh language was associated with immorality due, in no small part they thought, to the overwhelming influence of Nonconformity.[89]

The response was swift, and churchmen as well as Nonconformists rushed to condemn the reports. In 1853 a satirical play was published by Baptist preacher R. J. Derfel (1824–1905), who later became a pioneering socialist, under the title *Brad y Llyfrau Gleision* (The treachery of the Blue Books).[90] The play is remarkably imaginative, though as it was written in rhyming couplets it belongs more to the ancient tradition of poetry and storytelling rather than a new tradition of fiction writing. In the play, Satan and his minions are portrayed as planning an attack on Wales because of the nation's godliness, a fact attributed to the strength of Nonconformity. Three spies (representative of the three commissioners) are sent to Wales to analyze the state of the country, and the play closes with the spies having their conclusions endorsed by the bishops while the representatives of the Nonconformists gather in the People's Village in order to condemn them.[91]

The publication of the Blue Books demonstrates that, despite the efforts of Welsh Nonconformist leaders to create a culture in which their language and religion were at the fore, and despite their commitment to education, the London government, boosted by the lawlessness witnessed in the preceding two or three decades, could still be persuaded that it was precisely this culture that lay behind the violence, destruction, and intimidation witnessed in Wales. The conclusion could still appear reasonable that what the Welsh needed more than anything else was to learn English and be civilized through the State Church. It is a classic response of a dominant culture to a minority one, where the former considers the latter to be alien and other.

That being said, in effect the Blue Books galvanized the Welsh. In Kenneth O. Morgan's words, instead of acting "to remedy the under-provision and under-endowment of education, [they] became the most effective starting point for a renewal of national self-consciousness." Though this "national feeling" was characterized by "struggle against contempt rather

[89] It is worth noting, perhaps, that Walter Jones, a doctor who had been attacked, claimed that the Rebecca Riots were organized by the Baptist and Independent chapels (Jones, *Rebecca's Children*, 333).

[90] The title echoed an episode from Welsh legend, namely "Brad y Cyllyll Hirion" [The treachery of the long knives], when Celtic leaders were duped into feasting with Saxon neighbors only for the latter to draw out hidden "long knives" during the meal and slaughter the former.

[91] Prys Morgan, "R. J. Derfel a'r Ddrama *Brad y Llyfrau Gleision*," in *Brad y Llyfrau Gleision: Ysgrifau ar Hanes Cymru*, ed. Prys Morhhan (Llandysul: Gomer, 1991), 14–16.

than physical oppression," it constituted "a campaign for national recognition."[92] The attempts to create a Welsh culture through religion and education alone had not entirely succeeded. A feeling of helplessness among the ordinary folk, as well as frustration at their lot in life, had spilled over into violence and intimidation. The Establishment, both political and religious, was intent on blaming the violence on the Nonconformity that had sought to create a cultured populace. Ironically, then, it was not the heavy-handed response of the British government that drew the Welsh into line, but the Nonconformity that the Establishment viewed with considerable suspicion. The Blue Books enabled Nonconformists to claim more forcibly than ever that they were spokespeople for the ordinary folk against a privileged Anglican establishment. In turn, this boosted Nonconformity's appeal and ensured that the ideal of the law-abiding, chapel-going, Welsh-speaking, teetotaling, literate, and educated Welshman—however aspirational it was in reality—would endure for around a hundred years.

[92] Kenneth O. Morgan, *Wales in British Politics, 1868–1922* (1963; Cardiff: University of Wales Press, 1991), 16.

4

Scottish Baptists and Temperance, 1829–1929

Brian R. Talbot

The Context for Temperance Reforms

The catalyst that led to the launch of temperance activities in the British Isles was the widespread drunkenness caused by excessive consumption of spirits in the early decades of the nineteenth century across the United Kingdom and Ireland.[1] The Beer Act of 1830 intended to address this problem had the unintended consequence of significantly increasing the number of licensed premises selling alcohol—44,134 new beer houses operating by 1836—and this free trade in beer resulted in far greater drunkenness than previously experienced prior to the legislation being passed.[2] The phenomenon of hard drinking previously associated primarily with the upper classes had now spread down to the middle and working classes as a result of strong liquors becoming both cheaper and easier to obtain. At that time, water in many urban areas was unfit to drink, and nonintoxicating drinks were both less accessible than alcohol and often more expensive to purchase. When these factors are added to the social expectations of alcohol consumption in that era, it reveals the scale of the obstacles that these reformers had to address.[3]

Although the formation of temperance societies had some impact, widespread consumption of alcohol did continue to rise in Scotland until the middle of the nineteenth century.[4] The number of licensed traders at this

---

[1] Norman Longmate, *The Waterdrinkers: A History of Temperance* (London: Hamish Hamilton, 1968), 15–20.

[2] Henry Carter, *The English Temperance Movement* (London: Epworth Press, 1933), 24–26; Lilian Lewis Shiman, *Crusade against Drink in Victorian England* (New York: St. Martin's Press, 1988), 15.

[3] Brian Harrison, *Drink and the Victorians* (Keele, UK: Keele University Press, 1994), 38–45.

[4] Stewart Mechie, *The Church and Scottish Social Development, 1780–1870* (London: Oxford University Press, 1960), 81–83.

time was extraordinary. In Edinburgh in 1833, for example, there was a license to every fifteenth family, and in Glasgow in 1832 it was one to each fourteenth family.[5] The problem continued to grow in Glasgow so that by 1840 as many as one in ten inhabited houses was licensed to sell alcohol, meaning that there were more drink-sellers than butchers, bakers, fishmongers, greengrocers, cheesemakers, and other grocers combined.[6] Smaller towns were not much better. Renfrew had one spirits dealer to every eighteen families; Greenock one to nineteen; Port Glasgow one to fifteen; and Dumbarton one to eleven and a half families.[7] In the working-class parish of St. David's Dundee in 1841, for example, there were 9,264 inhabitants served by eleven bakers's shops and 108 public houses.[8]

The seriousness of the problem in Scotland by the early 1840s was that the annual consumption of spirits had risen to twenty-three pints per head of the population, as compared to thirteen pints in Ireland and seven in England. The excessive amounts of money spent on alcohol at that time in Scotland had a serious impact on the quality of food many poorer families could afford.[9] The impact on crime since the significant drop in the price of liquor in 1822 had seen the number of convictions for related serious offenses rise from 1,479 in 1823 to 3,126 in 1837. In Glasgow and Edinburgh alone the number of crimes had doubled in the years since the reduction of the duties on spirits.[10] Targeted temperance campaigns to reduce the num-

---

[5] James Silk Buckingham, ed., *Report of the Select Committee Appointed to Inquire into the Extent, Causes, and Consequences of the Prevailing Vice of Intoxication among the Labouring Classes of the United Kingdom* (London: House of Commons, 1834), 136, 410.

[6] "Temperance," in *Oxford Companion to Scottish History*, ed. Michael Lynch (Oxford: Oxford University Press, 2007), 595–96.

[7] Buckingham, *Report of the Select Committee*, 136. It was no different in England with the rapid rise in beer shops, following the passing of the Sale of Beer Act in Parliament in October 1830. See Longmate, *Waterdrinkers*, 23–26.

[8] George Lewis, *State of St David's Parish, Dundee*, 1841, 14–15. The section "Parochial Expenditure on Ardent Spirits" is found on pages 14–20.

[9] Thomas Ferguson, *Dawn of Scottish Social Welfare* (London: Thomas Nelson, 1948), 27. Figures for England and Wales from 1831 to 1931 showing the two-thirds decline in licenses held and the remarkable reduction in alcohol consumption, especially of spirits, over this century, is given in Harrison, *Drink and the Victorians*, 38.

[10] Archibald Alison, *Principles of Population*, 2 vols. (Edinburgh: W. Blackwood and Sons, 1840), 2:113–14. A fuller discussion of this subject is given at 112–23. George Bell, *Blackfriar's Wynd Analysed* (Edinburgh: Johnstone and Hunter, 1850), 17, gives the financial data on this subject to explain the rise in crime. See also T. Christopher Smout, *A Century of the Scottish People, 1830–1950* (London: Fontana, 1986), 138–39.

ber of licenses permitted did have a significant effect. In Aberdeen, for example, there was one public house for every 66 homes in 1837; this was reduced to 1 to 117 in 1851 and by 1901 it was now 1 to 406. In this time period (1837 to 1851) there was a decrease of 511 licenses at a time when the population had increased to ninety-five thousand.

In the second half of the century, when the population more than doubled, there was a further reduction of 256 licenses. One of the most significant causes of the decrease in alcohol consumption in the second half of the nineteenth century was the adoption of the Forbes Mackenzie Act of 1853 that forced the closure of public houses on Sundays and fixed a closing time of 10 p.m. on weekdays.[11] However, other factors also played a part. It was noticeable that in years of prosperity—between 1870 and 1877, for example—there was a marked increase in the consumption of alcohol that can be contrasted with an even greater fall in the 1880s and 1890s when for many people their finances were more limited in economically challenging times.[12] There was no doubt that a heavy drinking culture was engrained in Scottish society in the nineteenth century. Temperance campaigners would face a major challenge as they sought to change this culture.

The Early Years of Temperance Reform

In the early nineteenth century, campaigners in this field appeared first in North America and then in Northern Ireland and Scotland.[13] John Dunlop, a Presbyterian church elder who began giving lectures promoting temperance in 1828, is credited with founding the first temperance society in Scot land at Greenock in October 1829.[14] He was soon joined by publisher Wil-

[11] A. C. Cook, *The Evolution of the Temperance Movement 1837 to 1901* (Aberdeen: n.p., 1901), 3–4.

[12] Cook, *Evolution of the Temperance Movement,* 4. See also Harrison, *Drink and the Victorians*, 22.

[13] Edward Morris, *The History of the Temperance and Teetotal Societies in Glasgow from their Origin to the Present Time* (Glasgow: City of Glasgow United Total Abstinence Association, 1855), 12; Orfhlaith Campbell, "A Platform upon Which All Could Unite?: Temperance in Ulster and the Irish Temperance League, 1858–1914" (PhD diss., the Open University, 2017), 33; Harrison, *Drink and the Victorians*, 98–99.

[14] Morris, *History of the Temperance and Teetotal Societies*, 12–14; Robert Reid, "The Early History of the Temperance Movement in Scotland, and of the Scottish Temperance League," in *Scottish Temperance League Register and Abstainers' Almanac* (1897), 62–66; The first Irish temperance societies in Belfast and Dublin also appeared in late 1829 (Elizabeth

liam Collins, a Presbyterian colleague, as they promoted this cause in Glasgow. However, the first seven years of the movement were extremely difficult and demoralizing as even the majority of clergymen and doctors had serious doubts about the campaign's credibility.[15] Although activists were beginning temperance work in the 1820s, it was during the following decade that the movement gained a firm footing in different parts of the United Kingdom and embraced people from different Protestant denominations as well as in the Roman Catholic Church.[16] Such ecumenical character is important to stress because people who otherwise would never have stood together on the same platforms did so to combat this social evil.[17]

There were also significant temperance advocates who also were involved in the newly formed Evangelical Alliance, such as Scottish Baptists Robert Kettle and James Patterson of Hope Street Baptist Church, Glasgow.[18] William Reid, a leading eastern Scotland advocate of total abstinence, suggested to members of the newly formed Edinburgh Association for the Promotion of the Temperance Cause through means of the Church (EAPTCC), on March 14, 1847, that they ought to view their body as a local equivalent of "an evangelical alliance," given that member churches included Baptist, Secession, Relief, Cameronian, Free, Established and Methodist connexions."[19] In the 1840s, temperance principles were still held only by a small minority of Christians. The church leaders who espoused

---

Malcolm *'Ireland Sober, Ireland Free': Drink and Temperance in Nineteenth-Century Ireland* [Dublin: Gill and Macmillan, 1986], 56).

[15] Olive Checkland, *Philanthropy in Victorian Scotland* (Edinburgh: John Donald, 1980), 92–93.

[16] Studies that give a wider overview of this subject include Brian Harrison, *Drink and the Victorians*, 167–81, and Brian Harrison, "The British Prohibitionists, 1853–1872: A Biographical Analysis," *International Review of Social History*, XV, no. 3 (1970): 375–467. For a contemporary analysis from a participant in temperance work, see D. Burns, "Baptists and the Temperance Reform," in *The English Baptists*, ed. John Clifford (London: E. Marlborough, 1881), 163–80. One of the best overviews specifically of this movement in Scotland is D. C. Paton, "Drink and the Temperance Movement in Nineteenth-Century Scotland" (PhD diss., University of Edinburgh, 1976).

[17] Brian R. Talbot, *Search for a Common Identity: The Origins of the Baptist Union of Scotland, 1800–1870* (Carlisle, UK: Paternoster, 2003), 240–42, gives examples of this ecumenical cooperation in temperance work. However, there were still examples of communities where sectarian pressures prevented such cooperation. See P. T. Winskill, *The Temperance Movement and Its Worker,* 4 vols. (Glasgow: Blackie & Son Ltd., 1893), 2:76.

[18] See William Reid, *Temperance Memorials of the Late Robert Kettle, Esq* (Glasgow: Scottish Temperance League, 1853), lxxix.

[19] *Scottish Temperance Review* 2 (April 1847): 154–57.

total abstinence were vital recruiters for this movement. It was natural that they would seek to maximize their efforts by working together across denominational boundaries, where that was possible, to promote this cause.

The key decision that enabled this moment to progress in the United Kingdom was that of Baptist minister Joseph Livesey and six working-class Preston colleagues and friends from Manchester and Liverpool, who sharpened the focus to promoting total abstinence from all alcoholic beverages.[20] The Scottish branch of this cause was relaunched as the Glasgow Radical Temperance Society with thirty-seven members on September 16, 1836. The consistency of the abstinence message appealed more to the skilled working classes, but at least initially diminished support among the "ladies and gentlemen" and clergymen.[21] Doctors who relied quite heavily on recommending alcoholic drinks as a remedy for many medical ailments at that time were even less enthusiastic toward the abstinence message. In 1846 the *Scottish Temperance Review* reported that "of the ministers of religion only one in eight are members! Of medical men, only one in forty!!"[22] However, the majority of the societies converted to the stricter abstinence cause, although the effectiveness of some of them was diminished as a result of conflict with those who wished to retain the more moderate pledge.[23] What is beyond question, though, is that the sharper focus of the abstinence message did ensure greater clarity in future campaigns.

Some encouraging developments emerged from strong interchurch co-operation. An example comes from Paisley in 1845 to 1846 where the Protestant clergymen had met together in the autumn of 1845 to discuss the drinking customs practiced as part of social gatherings in their community. They came to an agreement that a united challenge should be given beginning with funeral customs. A thousand copies of a proclamation were printed for distribution following the reading of the document from the pulpits of each of the churches on the first Sabbath of January 1846. The document included the following statement:

---

[20] John William Kirton, *The World's Workers: Dr. Guthrie, Father Matthew, Elihu Burritt, Joseph Livesey* (London: Cassell & Company, 1887), 118; Morris, *History of the Temperance and Teetotal Societies in Glasgow*, 18; Carter, *English Temperance Movement*, 21; Shiman, *Crusade against Drink in Victorian England*, 18.

[21] Morris, *History of the Temperance and Teetotal Societies in Glasgow*, 15, 54–55. See also Checkland, *Philanthropy in Victorian Scotland*, 92–93.

[22] *Scottish Temperance Review* 1 (October 1845–December 1846), (Edinburgh: McDowall, Greig and Wahler) (May 1846): 328.

[23] Shiman, *Crusade against Drink in Victorian England*, 21.

> We the ministers of various denominations, having a common interest in the social and religious well-being of the community, give it as our decided and deliberate opinion, that the present custom of giving wines or spirits at funerals might be relinquished with great advantage; and we are persuaded that the substitution of a simple devotional service would be attended with less trouble to the friends, would not encroach on the time of the company, and would be in harmony with the saddening and melancholy duties to be discharged in the chamber of death.[24]

The signatories included John Taylor, "pastor of the Baptist Church."[25] John Taylor and Walter Shanks had been set apart as elders at the formation of the George Street Baptist Church, Paisley, in 1842. This congregation had formed as a result of a doctrinal difference within the Storie Street Scotch Baptist Church in Paisley.[26] This step by the churches was warmly welcomed in the wider community and was followed by a similar public statement by Provost David Murray, together with the other civic officials, on January 12, 1846. As a result, almost every funeral in Paisley in the months that followed adopted the simple pattern proposed by the ministers and was conducted without drinking.[27] A similar decision was taken in March 1846 by nearly all the Protestant clergymen and civic leaders in Dundee.[28] This cultural change was also agreed by the ministers and magistrates in Edinburgh and Kirkcaldy in early 1847.[29] It was a significant early step forward in changing the drinking culture of Scotland.

It was inevitable that there would be differences of opinion as to how far it was reasonable to go in adopting abstinence principles. James Inglis, one of the pastors of the Scotch Baptist Church in Dunfermline, issued a challenge in February 1946 to the Established Church in his town. He asked them to revoke the membership privileges of those who were "spirits venders selling their wares on the Sabbath."[30] It was clear that this Baptist pastor was equally convinced about Sabbatarian principles as well as total

---

[24] *Scottish Temperance Review* 1 (March 1846): 243.

[25] *Scottish Temperance Review* 1 (March 1846): 243.

[26] George Yuille, *History of the Baptists in Scotland* (Glasgow: Baptist Union Publications Committee, 1926), 201–2.

[27] *Scottish Temperance Review* 1 (March 1846): 243–44.

[28] *Scottish Temperance Review* 1 (April 1846): 267.

[29] *Scottish Temperance Review* 2 (March 1847): 106; 2 (April 1947): 162.

[30] *Scottish Temperance Review* 2 (February 1847): 59.

abstinence. The absence of evidence of a response to his plea is probably due to the rejection of his appeal. This is confirmed in a later comment about the progress of temperance in Dunfermline the following year: "Comparatively few, however, of the middle or higher classes have adopted the principle, and several of the ministers were once teetotallers, but not since they came to town."[31] It is likely that it was viewed as too extreme a measure to take against church members of good standing.

Scottish Baptists in Dunfermline, however, were strongly supportive of the Dunfermline Total Abstinence Society. The president was David Dewar from James Street Scotch Baptist Church, and at the January 17, 1848, meeting in the Free Abbey Church schoolroom, the main speaker was Robert Thomson, minister of Viewfield Baptist Church, Dunfermline.[32] It was not only in Fife where the majority of adherents were of working-class backgrounds: "The temperance movement in Aberdeen has never been much indebted to what is termed the middle class or the aristocracy. With a few honourable lay and clerical exceptions, this great reformation has been left entirely in the hands of the working classes."[33] It was clear that those of higher social rank were slower to support this cause once it was reconstituted on total abstinence grounds. It would take into the second half of the nineteenth century for their numbers to increase significantly. However, the younger Scottish Baptist ministers, together with some Scotch Baptist elders, had been quick to associate themselves with the temperance movement in the 1830s and early 1840s. There were also twenty-three out of seventy-three Scottish Baptist churches associated with this cause prior to 1842.[34]

What is particularly significant is that a majority of the key influential Scottish Baptist leaders in this period were strong advocates of this cause. In an era of significant tensions between proponents of Reformed and Arminian convictions, temperance was one of the key causes that united them. It is also likely that support within their congregations was higher than the surviving records of temperance agencies might imply, as many ordinary people

---

[31] *Scottish Temperance Review* 2 (December 1847): 537.

[32] *Scottish Temperance Review* 3 (March 1848): 141.

[33] *Scottish Temperance Review* 3 (June 1848): 216.

[34] Talbot, *Search for a Common Identity*, 240–46, and Appendix 5.2, "Scottish Baptist Churches, Ministers and Lay Leaders Involved in the Total Abstinence Cause before 1842," 362–63, give details of the individuals supporting this cause. This information was obtained from the *Scottish Temperance Herald*, 1840–1842; the *Scottish Temperance Journal*, January 1839–August 1841 issues; together with Winskill, *Temperance Movement*, vols 1-4.

of limited means did not subscribe as members. However, the changes in the practices of individuals and congregations in this Scottish denomination in the nineteenth century could not have taken place without the support of the majority of church members.[35] Baptists in Scotland were among the more enthusiastic bodies for this particular cause. However, pride of place belongs to the Evangelical Union of Scotland, formed in 1843, that was founded as a denomination committed to abstinence. All the members of its churches were required to be committed to teetotal principles, and by implication, not work in the licensed trade. From the start, unfermented wine was used in its Communion services.[36] In summary, commitment to the temperance cause clearly was firmly established within Scottish Baptist churches prior to the formation of the Baptist Union of Scotland in 1869.

Consolidation of the Movement in the Later Nineteenth and Early Twentieth Centuries

There were many social issues on which Scottish Baptists had concerns in these years, but there would have been little doubt that for the majority of them, the problem of drunkenness and its consequences would have been among the most pressing.[37] The tide was now beginning to turn in favor of temperance reform, with societies being established in communities throughout Scotland. What is more, there was now significant progress being made among both the medical profession and the clergy, with the former now largely supportive by 1908.[38]

The picture among the clergy was more complex than first assumed. The Nonconformist Conscience in the United Kingdom that was influential in the later nineteenth century was not uniformly committed to the temperance cause prior to the First World War. The United Kingdom Alliance formed in 1853 to encourage the passage of legislation to restrict the liquor trade was significantly influential in the second half of the nineteenth century with its targeted campaigns to influence causes as diverse as the army and

---

[35] Talbot, *Search for a Common Identity*, 240–46, gives more information on this point.

[36] George Gladstone, Glasgow, "Scottish Denominational Temperance Societies," in *Temperance in All Nations: History of the Cause in All Countries of the Globe*, ed. J. N. Stearns (New York: National Temperance Society and Publication House, 1893), 276–77.

[37] An excellent overview of this movement in Scottish churches in this era is provided by N. D. Denny, "Temperance and the Scottish Churches, 1870–1914," *Records of the Scottish Church History Society* 23, no. 2 (1988): 217–39.

[38] Denny, "Temperance and the Scottish Churches," 221.

navy, the medical profession, and the churches.[39] Unlike America, where denominational temperance bodies were established early in support of this cause, only the Primitive Methodists and the Bible Christians formally organized in England.[40] Individual campaigners had to take the initiative in the first few decades of this work. In the Church of England, for example, the catalyst for a change of perspective was the publication of Mrs. Wightman's *Haste to the Rescue* (1859), which described the devastating impact of alcohol on the lives of the poor. Twenty-six thousand copies of this work were issued in its first fourteen months alone. Wightman, wife of the vicar of St. Alkmond's, Shrewsbury, was a persuasive advocate of this cause. She modeled her approach on the style of English-born American temperance campaigner J. B. Gough, whose temperance tours in 1853 and then in 1857–1860 had convinced her of the need to address this social issue. A copy of her book was sent to every clergyman and theological college in the country, led to the formation of temperance work in many parishes, and nationally helped the launch of the Church of England Total Abstinence Society in 1862. The society was renamed the Church of England Temperance Society in 1872 because a decision was taken to admit moderate drinkers as well as abstainers.[41] The book doubtless spurred progress in this particular denomination.

In the 1870s in England there were few teetotal Wesleyan Methodist ministers, although Primitive Methodists with working-class roots were largely dedicated to this cause. The Wesleyans did set up a temperance committee in 1875, but its influence was limited and assurances were given that the new agency must be open to moderate drinkers as well as total abstainers.[42] Likewise the Congregational Total Abstinence Society was established in 1874 but took until 1885 to have a significant influence over its national meetings.[43] Voices opposing abstinence advocates in its ranks were not silent. For example, in 1886 Edward White, chair of the Congregational Union, chose to attack the "wild excesses of teetotalism" at the fifty-fourth

---

[39] K. Heasman, *Evangelicals in Action* (London: Geoffrey Bles, 1962), 128–29.

[40] Heasman, *Evangelicals in Action,* 132.

[41] Heasman, *Evangelicals in Action,* 131–32.

[42] *Minutes of Wesleyan National Conference,* (1875): 210–11, cited by D. W. Bebbington, *The Nonconformist Conscience: Chapel and Politics, 1870–1914* (London: George Allen & Unwin, 1982), 46.

[43] Bebbington, *Nonconformist Conscience,* 46.

Annual Meeting of the Congregational Union.[44] However, in the previous year at the 1885 Annual Meetings, representatives of the Congregational Total Abstinence Society were informed at their own gathering that a majority of their ministers were now abstainers, with 84 of the 94 newly settled young ministers also declared abstainers, together with 303 out of the 353 ministerial students in the theological colleges.[45] As late as 1879 there had been only 760 out of 2,000 Congregational ministers committed to total abstinence, though it had been transformed by 1904 when 2,500 out of 3,000 had declared their commitment to this cause.[46]

In English Baptist ranks only one in six were teetotallers in 1860, though it had risen to 1,100 out of 1,900 by 1886, and of the remaining 800 it was reported that many of them were "practically abstainers";[47] and in 1907, 211 out of 214 Baptist theological students were identified with this position.[48] The Baptist Union of Great Britain and Ireland was more supportive than the equivalent Congregational body, but its Annual Assembly in 1897 still rejected the requirement of total abstinence as a qualification for an officeholder in its member churches.[49] However, at least 6 million people were members of one of the temperance bodies by 1900,[50] but the lack of unanimity in the aspirations and campaigns of the different temperance agencies undoubtedly hampered the advocacy of this cause both in the later nineteenth and early twentieth centuries.[51] In England it was in the early years of the twentieth century, rather than in the nineteenth, before this movement consolidated its position in the churches.

Other Scottish denominations were quicker than Baptists to form temperance committees, including the Free Church of Scotland and the United

---

[44] *Christian World*, May 13, 1886, 385.

[45] *Christian World*, October 8, 1885, 745–46.

[46] *Christian World*, October 8, 1885, 745; and September 29, 1904, 21.

[47] *Christian World*, May 20, 1886, 411.

[48] *Christian World*, October 3, 1907, 21.

[49] Bebbington, *Nonconformist Conscience*, 46.

[50] Annemaire McAllister, "The Alternative World of the Proud Non-Drinker," *Social History of Alcohol and Drugs* 28, no. 2 (Summer 2014): 161.

[51] Geoffrey R. Treloar, *The Disruption of Evangelicalism* (London: InterVarsity Press, 2016), 110; D. W. Bebbington, *Evangelicalism in Modern Britain* (London: Unwin Hyman, 1989), 136. An example from the early twentieth century is given in Stuart Mews, "Urban Problems and Rural Solutions: Drink and Disestablishment in the First World War," in *The Church in Town and Countryside*, ed. Derek Baker, Studies in Church History 16 (Oxford: Basil Blackwell, 1979), 465–76.

Presbyterian Church in 1847 and the Church of Scotland in 1848.[52] It is probable that the greater autonomy of Baptist congregations had contributed to the delay in forming a collective Baptist agency to promote this cause.[53] A prominent Baptist supporter of this cause, John Bone, acknowledged this in 1901: "The democratic element which enters so largely into their communion, leaving each individual church complete autonomy in its internal affairs, free of control of Presbytery, Synod, or Assembly, had in turn, however, until recent years, stood in the way of any manifested agreement on the subject of Total Abstinence."[54] The number of abstaining ministers in Scottish churches had risen steadily from around 1,573 in 1891 to 1,861 in 1899. By 1903, 30 percent of Church of Scotland ministers, 68 percent of the Free Church's, 65 percent of United Presbyterians, 97 percent of Congregational Union ministers, together with all Baptist and Evangelical Union ministers, and with the great majority of Original Secession, Reformed Presbyterians, Wesleyan, and Primitive Methodist clergymen in Scotland were abstainers.[55] Alexander Wylie, then a Glasgow Baptist minister, proposed that Scottish Baptists form a society to address this issue at the 1876 Annual Assembly.

This issue was raised each year until in 1879 the Assembly unanimously agreed to the formation of the Scottish Baptist Total Abstinence Society (SBTAS), an agency formally inaugurated on October 25, 1881. The wording of the pledge was clear: "I agree to abstain from all intoxicating drinks as a beverage and to promote the practice of Abstinence in the Community." The earliest roll of members contained 135 names, of which approximately 40 were ministers,[56] and a high proportion of those training for pastoral ministry were also advocates of this cause. A correspondent to the SBTAS in 1907 wrote that the "cursed traffic [of alcohol] ruins more souls in a week

---

[52] Denny, "Temperance and the Scottish Churches," 223–24. Fuller details are given in N. D. Logan, "Drink and Society: Scotland, 1870–1914" (Ph.D. diss., University of Glasgow, 1983), 438–66.

[53] This explanation was also suggested by Denny, "Temperance and the Scottish Churches," 229.

[54] Bone, "Scottish Baptist Total Abstinence Society," 64.

[55] Logan, "Drink and Society," 451.

[56] Some confusion exists as to the exact number of subscribing Baptist ministers in 1881. For example, *Baptist Union of Scotland Temperance Committee Special Jubilee Number 1881–1931* lists "thirty-five out of seventy" on p. 10, though "forty" on p. 5. See John S. Bone, "The Scottish Baptist Total Abstinence Society," *Scottish Temperance Annual* (1901): 67. The number of ministers listed was forty-three.

than the preaching of the gospel rescues in a year."[57] These sentiments would have been commonly held in Scottish Baptist ranks at the start of the twentieth century. However, temperance advocates were not downcast but very confident in the future success of their cause. Institutional organization of temperance activities in Scottish Baptist ranks had taken place much later than the personal adoption of its principles by many individuals within this denomination.

As early as 1901 Bone took great satisfaction in recording: "It is believed that there are not more than six non-abstaining Baptist Ministers in Scotland....The Society [SBTAS] is also entitled to much credit for the fact that almost every church in the Union now celebrates the Communion with unfermented wine."[58] It had been a long battle to persuade a majority of members in some churches to change their Communion practice. Irvine Baptist Church, for example, at a church meeting on March 19, 1882, had for the third time discussed "the propriety of using non-alcoholic wine at the Lord's Supper in place of that which has hitherto been in use."[59] It would take longer for institutional church practices to change than to change many members. Protracted debate in the pages of the *Scottish Baptist Magazine* from advocates of the opposing positions ensured a full airing of this topic with Oliver Flett of Paisley insisting that "wine should be wine" and Robert Lockhart of Dublin Street Baptist Church, Edinburgh, that it should be the natural unfermented juice of the grape.[60] Lists of ministers advocating temperance principles and churches using unfermented wine at Communion were published in the *Scottish Baptist Yearbook* up to World War I, by which time the vast majority of Baptist ministers and congregations were supportive of this cause.[61] In fact, by the end of the nineteenth century almost every

---

[57] "The Scottish Baptist Total Abstinence Society Twenty-Seventh Annual Report, 1907–1908," *Scottish Baptist Yearbook 1909*, 270–71.

[58] Bone, "Scottish Baptist Total Abstinence Society," 67.

[59] Irvine Baptist Church, Church Meeting Minutes, March 19, 1882, cited in David and Ron Polland, eds., *Great Is Thy Faithfulness: A History of Irvine Baptist Church* (Edinburgh: private publication for the church, 2006), 164.

[60] For example, R. Lockhart, "A Few Thoughts about the Cup at the Lord's Table," *Scottish Baptist Magazine* 9, no. 12 (December 1883): 281–82; Oliver Flett, "The Communion Wine," *Scottish Baptist Magazine* 10, no. 1 (January 1884): 20–21; see also 10, no. 2 (February 1884): 48–51; 10, no. 3 (March 1884): 75–78; 10, no. 4 (April 1884): 100–103 for this continuing correspondence.

[61] *Baptist Union of Scotland Temperance Committee Special Jubilee Number 1881–1931*, 10–11.

Baptist congregation was using unfermented wine at Communion.[62] Out of a printed list of 112 churches, only Dublin Street Baptist Church, Edinburgh, was offering both fermented and unfermented wine by 1898.[63] The Presbyterian Church most committed to advocating this cause, the Free Church of Scotland, had 70 churches using nonalcoholic Communion wine in 1887, but by 1914 this had risen to 734 congregations.[64]

The Church of Scotland, like the Church of England, by contrast, sought to unite both total abstainers and moderate drinkers in its temperance agency.[65] It took longer in Scottish Baptist churches for the change to individual Communion cups to be used in place of a single shared cup. The Scottish Baptist Individual Cup Communion Association launched a campaign on October 6, 1907, distributing five thousand in Glasgow churches advocating use of "the hygenic individual cup."[66] This proposal was resisted at first; the change likely took place in most Scottish Baptist congregations in the 1920s. In Maxwelltown Baptist Church, Dundee, for example, they were introduced as a special feature of the Church Semi-Jubilee Celebrations on December 16, 1923.[67] In Helensburgh Baptist Church the change was introduced in the early 1920s with the option of the common cup retained for those who preferred it, but by 1925 the church minutes record that everyone preferred the individual cups.[68] In Broughty Ferry Baptist Church the change occurred in 1928 against the wishes of the deacons who had hoped to retain both the individual and the common cup.[69] However, it was not a universal change, as Keiss Baptist Church in Caithness, for example, was committed in 1925 to retaining the common cup.[70] However, although the battle for the temperance cause within the denomination was

---

[62] Murray, *First Hundred Years,* 68. One English Independent congregation launched a campaign in its ranks to go even further and replace the wine with water at Communion; see *Scottish Temperance Review* (November 1845): 68–69.

[63] "The Scottish Baptist Total Abstinence Society Seventeenth Annual Report 1897–1898," *Scottish Baptist Yearbook 1899*, c14–c15.

[64] Logan, "Drink and Society," 451.

[65] Denny, "Temperance and the Scottish Churches," 234.

[66] *Christian World*, October 10, 1907, 12.

[67] *Scottish Baptist Magazine* 50, no. 1 (January 1924): 9.

[68] Kenneth McNeish, *A History of Helensburgh Baptist Church, 1881–1998* (Helensburgh: For the church, 1998), 14.

[69] Ramsay G. Small, *Broughty Ferry Baptist Church: The First Hundred Years* (Dundee: private publication, c. 1995), 12.

[70] *Scottish Baptist Magazine* 51, no. 3 (March 1925): 39.

won, much was still to be accomplished within the wider society and in promoting this cause among young people.[71]

Scottish Baptists, in line with other mainstream churches in Scotland, were also active in political representations supporting the tightening of licenses in, for example, the Forbes Mackenzie Act of 1853. Seventy Baptist congregations sent petitions supporting the unsuccessful Local Options Bill,[72] an attempt by the Liberal government in 1894 to provide opportunities for local communities to restrict the sale of alcohol in their communities. However, by 1914 morale was high among reformers as the new Temperance (Scotland) Act came into force, restricting opening hours of public houses and granting an opportunity for local ratepayers to vote on this subject in 1920.[73] The SBTAS took satisfaction that one of its vice presidents, Sir John Mills McCallum a soap manufacturer, the Liberal M.P. for Paisley, and a deacon of Thomas Coats Memorial Church, Paisley—"had a prominent share in promoting in parliament the Temperance (Scotland) Act, 1913."[74] This was one of the high points of this cause on the threshold of World War I.

From the 1870s a significant shift to prioritize advocacy of this cause among young people took place because education was seen as crucial in changing attitudes in the country.[75] When the SBTAS was formed in 1881 there were only seven Bands of Hope promoting temperance principles among young people in Scottish Baptist churches. Over the course of the next fifty years, adult temperance societies and Bands of Hope were formed in all Scottish Baptist churches.[76] This movement had grown dramatically over the following years in the United Kingdom, with a rise in Scotland alone to 570 branches in 1887 and 700 by 1897.[77] The Baptist Union of

---

[71] *Baptist Union of Scotland Temperance Committee Special Jubilee Number 1881–1931*, 5.

[72] Yuille, *History of the Baptists in Scotland*, 247.

[73] "The Scottish Baptist Total Abstinence Society Thirty-Third Annual Report 1914," *Scottish Baptist Yearbook 1915*, 6.

[74] *Baptist Union of Scotland Temperance Committee Special Jubilee Number 1881–1931*, 6. See also D. W. Bebbington, "Baptist Members of Parliament in the Twentieth Century," *Baptist Quarterly* 31, no. 6 (April 1986): 270.

[75] D. W. Bebbington, *The Dominance of Evangelicalism* (Leicester: InterVarsity Press, 2005), 228.

[76] *Baptist Union of Scotland Temperance Committee Special Jubilee Number 1881–1931*, 6–7.

[77] Frederick Smith, ed., *The Jubilee of the Band of Hope Movement* (London: United Kingdom Band of Hope Union, 1897), 292.

Great Britain and Ireland (BUGBI) Annual Assembly in Liverpool in 1907 was informed that there were now 2,275 Band of Hope Temperance Societies associated with Baptist churches affiliated to that body.[78] The first Juvenile Temperance Associations were formed in Scotland in 1830 in Saltcoats and Paisley.[79] The first specifically Band of Hope cause had been formed in Leeds in 1847.[80] The Scottish Band of Hope was formed in 1871 with seven societies affiliated, but this movement grew dramatically to have 130,000 juvenile members and four thousand workers by 1897.[81]

Scottish Baptists reported seventy-five Baptist congregations having a Band of Hope by April 1898.[82] In addition, the first chairman of the Band of Hope Union in Glasgow was William Quarrier, the Baptist figurehead of the Orphan Homes at Bridge of Weir, who had witnessed firsthand the devastating consequences of drunkenness in the families of many children he had rescued. Educating the young on this subject was a priority for Quarrier. Band of Hope provided activities for children up to age sixteen. Out of this organization came the idea for a Christian youth organization, Crusaders, to take care of young people too old for the Band of Hope but too young for adult temperance societies. It would prove a great success.[83] Temperance committees had also developed as part of another Christian youth movement, Christian Endeavour (C.E.) at this time.[84] More than a century later, it is difficult to appreciate the passion for and the success of this cause in Scotland in the decades prior to World War I.[85] However, in partnership with other measures to alleviate poverty and improve the lives of people in many of the poorer communities in Scotland, the temperance movement clearly made a significant contribution to the progress undoubtedly made at that time.

---

[78] *Christian World*, October 3, 1907, 21.

[79] Smith, *Jubilee of the Band of Hope Movement*, 15.

[80] Smith, *Jubilee of the Band of Hope Movement*, 44.

[81] Smith, *Jubilee of the Band of Hope Movement*, 292.

[82] "Scottish Baptist Total Abstinence Society Seventeenth Annual Report 1897–1898," c8–c13.

[83] David Strachan, *Scottish Band of Hope Union Diamond Jubilee Brochure* (Glasgow, 1931), cited by King, *Sober and Free*, 13. The organization's current name is Urban Saints; see www.urbansaints.org for more information.

[84] *Baptist Union of Scotland Temperance Committee Special Jubilee Number 1881–1931*, 6–7.

[85] "Scotland Back in the Day: Spirited Souls Led the Fight to Defeat the Demon Drink," *The National*, April 11, 2016.

Progress and Decline in the Postwar Years

The temperance battle was one in which Scottish Baptists were keen to engage. On October 23, 1918, Alexander Bremner proposed at the Annual Assembly, "That this Assembly of the Baptist Union of Scotland most respectfully approaches His Majesty's Government asking for the Prohibition of the Traffic in Intoxicants; being convinced that Public Opinion in Scotland is in favour of such a measure."[86] The Assembly adopted this motion, which was followed by a second from the same minister: "That the Assembly earnestly urges all Baptist congregations to at once begin to organize and educate, so as to be able to take full advantage of the provisions of the Temperance (Scotland) Act, 1920, for clearing communities of the Traffic in Drink." It was adopted.[87] Already high morale was boosted by the votes in Norway and the United States of America to adopt Prohibition by 1920.[88] There had also been a remarkable drop in alcohol consumption in England during the war years, which continued into the 1920s. In 1914, 89 million gallons of alcohol had been consumed, a figure reduced to 37 million by 1918, and the number of cases of drunkenness in England and Wales fell from 184,000 to 29,000 while deaths from alcoholism had been cut by five-sixths.

By 1929, convictions for drunkenness in England and Wales had fallen to 27.5 percent of the 1913 level, and public houses were less prominent in many people's lives. What factors had led to this social transformation? The absorption of many men in particular into the armed forces during the war, together with shorter opening hours and restricted supply of alcohol, had certainly been major factors in this remarkable change. Higher taxation had also been significant in raising the price of beer to 7d a pint in 1922, double the prewar price, which, combined with lower disposable incomes, had significantly reduced the total consumption of beer. In addition, new leisure activities were extremely popular. The appearance of the cinema offering tickets at prices even the poorest could afford attracted approximately a third of the population by 1931. New sports clubs promoting, for example, foot-

---

[86] *Scottish Baptist Yearbook 1919*, 23.

[87] *Scottish Baptist Yearbook 1919*, 23.

[88] "The Scottish Baptist Total Abstinence Society Thirty-Eighth Annual Report (1919)," 3, in the *Scottish Baptist Yearbook 1920*.

ball, swimming, and cycling also improved the health and social habits of many citizens.[89]

However, the success of social control in this area weakened the case of the temperance movement for Prohibition to effect the necessary change. The majority of abstinence campaigners were seeking abolition, not government control or regulation of the trade. In addition, the influence of the abstinence campaigners was diluted as the different temperance agencies had no coherent aims and objectives. They were also politically weak in the postwar years, and the political system in the Westminster Parliament favored the anti-Prohibitionists as Liberal and Labour Party support had weakened and the Tory Party upheld freedom for the trade.[90] Ironically, many of the aims of the temperance campaigners in the United Kingdom had been achieved in reducing social harm, but the means most effective in bringing about the change had come from outside their ranks.

Expectations in Scotland for a result similar to America had seemed quite reasonable in the light of votes for Prohibition, but advocates of this cause would soon be disappointed. The odds were stacked against them after a strong campaign by the licensed trade and the restrictive nature of the Temperance Act. A poll could only be held if a tenth of the electorate requested one; then a minimum of 35 percent of the electorate had to vote and a majority of 55 percent was required for a "No License" campaign to succeed. In total, there were 584 polls sought and held in the 1,215 voting areas in 1920, of which 508 voted for no change, 35 for license limitations, and 41 for "No License"; 308 of the voting areas had no licenses, and no polls were held there.[91] Licenses were lost in burghs such as Kirkintilloch, Kilsyth, Stromness, and Wick. In the city of Glasgow, the middle-class residential

[89] James Dunn, "A Force to Be Reckoned With? The Temperance Movement and the 'Drink Question,' 1895–1933," (PhD diss., University of Central Lancashire, 1999), 96; Callum G. Brown, "Charting Everyday Experience," in Lynn Abrahams and Callum G. Brown, *A History of Everyday Life in Twentieth-Century Scotland* (Edinburgh: Edinburgh University Press, 2010), 38–39.

[90] Dunn, "A Force to Be Reckoned With?," 104–6.

[91] Tom Honeyman, *No License! The New Campaign* (Glasgow: National Citizens' Temperance Council, 1921), 18–19. See also John Douglas Kemp, "Drink and the Labour Movement in Early Twentieth-Century Scotland with Particular Reference to Edwin Scrymgeour and the Scottish Prohibition Party" (PhD diss., University of Dundee, 2000), 286–87.

areas of Cathcart, Pollokshields, Kelvinside, and North Kelvin voted for "No License" and limitations, rather than the most deprived inner-city areas.[92]

Overall in the areas where votes were cast, 40 percent of the total, 450,000 votes, were in favor of local Prohibition, which is a large proportion of the electorate by any standard, with a respectable turnout of 69.6 percent of eligible voters.[93] "No License" supporters were not restricted to one social class or particular geographical locations, as they included, for example, miners in Kirkintilloch and Kilsyth, shipbuilders in Clydebank, the middle classes in Glasgow, and remote northern fishermen and agricultural workers.[94] Two examples illustrate the significance of the votes. In the city of Dundee there were three polls at three-year intervals in the 1920s. The first poll campaign in November 1920 saw the Christian community split on the issue. Despite the General Assembly of the Church of Scotland promoting the "No License" campaign, some local parish ministers were demonstrating in favor of "an Honest Christian Dram and the citizens right to have one," claiming that only 10 percent of the attendees of the General Assembly who voted for Prohibition were teetotallers.[95]

Edwin Scrymgeour,[96] a prominent temperance campaigner who would famously oust Winston Churchill from the Dundee seat at the 1923 election on a temperance manifesto, was suitably outraged by the non-teetotallers' actions. Scrymgeour and his Prohibition Party were blamed by the mainstream temperance campaigners as a major factor in their losing the vote in Dundee in 1920 because they were denouncing the proposal before the electorate as too modest a change.[97] The result was 36,452 for "No Change" and 15,491 for "No License," a majority of 20,961. The later votes had a similar result, with the majority reduced to 16,037 in 1923 and 17,556 in 1926. The Town Council had voted itself dry in January 1920, but not enough citizens shared those convictions. However, the unconfirmed reports that the "No Change" campaign in the city had spent approximately £50,000 on their

---

[92] Honeyman, *No License!*, 36–39, gives full details of the results. See also Elspeth King, *Scotland Sober and Free: The Temperance Movement, 1829–1979* (Glasgow: Glasgow Museums and Art Galleries, 1979), 24, and Smout, *Century of the Scottish People*, 133–48.

[93] Kemp, "Drink and the Labour Movement," 286–87, 292.

[94] Honeyman, *No License!*, 19.

[95] Kemp, "Drink and the Labour Movement," 299.

[96] D. G. Southgate, "Edwin Scrymgeour," in *Three Dundonians* (Dundee: Abertay Historical Society, 1968), 16–23.

[97] Honeyman, *No License!*, 127–28.

campaign compared to the "No License" team's £1,100 indicated they had held genuine fears of a different result at the polls, at least in 1920.[98]

Some initial successes gave encouragement to the reformers—for example, at Cambuslang in 1920,[99] but it turned wet in the 1926 vote. What led to this change? Cambuslang Baptist Church minister J. O. Hagger, in his analysis of the result, highlighted a number of factors. First of all, the drink trade had predicted a victory of their cause in 1920 based on the high number of licenses held and subsequently ran a weak campaign.[100] In subsequent polls they "saw Cambuslang invaded by such a fleet of motor cars as she had never seen before," and trade supporters were brought to canvass from "all over the west of Scotland." As a result, their support in the ballot box increased, with the winning margin being a comfortable twelve hundred votes in 1926.

Other factors included a division in the local Labour Party, with a minority siding with the trade over a local political issue, whereas in previous votes it was wholeheartedly for the temperance cause, together with the formal neutrality of the Roman Catholic Church in 1926 compared to its active support on previous occasions, although individual members of that church were prominent in the dry campaign. Hagger concluded, "I confess that with the defeat which has come to us here I am pessimistic of success in any part of Scotland."[101] The editor of the *Scottish Baptist Magazine* in his reflection on the loss of Cambuslang noted that some significant grounds for optimism remained. City councils in Glasgow, Aberdeen, and Dundee, for example, had voted against the provision of alcoholic refreshments at civic functions.

The battleground for the future had to be won through work among the young people, convincing them of the rightness of this cause.[102] Moves in this direction had already begun in 1923 when the work of the SBTAS was scaled back after the loss of its evangelist who had combined temper-

---

[98] "Wet or Dry," in David Phillips, *The Hungry Thirties: Dundee between the Wars* (Dundee: David Winter & Son, 1981), 37–39. For fuller details and analysis, see Kemp, "Drink and the Labour Movement in Early Twentieth-Century Scotland," 285–318.

[99] *Baptist Union of Scotland Temperance Committee Special Jubilee Number 1881–1931*, 11.

[100] Hagger's claim is supported by James Jamieson, "Cambuslang 'Dry' a Sweeping Change," in Honeyman, *No License!*, 123.

[101] J. O. Hagger, "The Temperance Defeat in Cambuslang," *Scottish Baptist Magazine* 52, no. 2 (February 1926): 15–16.

[102] "Temperance," *Scottish Baptist Magazine* 52, no. 2 (February 1926): 13.

ance advocacy with evangelistic ministry. In October 1923, delegates at the Baptist Union Assembly voted for the SBTAS to cease its work as a separate campaigning group to become the temperance committee of the Baptist Union of Scotland, with the wider denomination agreeing to fund T. A. McQuiston, minister of Rutherglen Baptist Church, as a "Gospel Evangelist." The future focus would be on work among young people and the production of suitable literature for supporters to promote this cause.[103] It was a recognition that although the vast majority of Scottish Baptists and a significant minority of the wider society had accomplished much for commitment to this cause, the majority of Scottish people now saw other social issues as more pressing concerns.

Conclusions

Christian temperance advocates in the mid-nineteenth century had identified a very serious social problem in Scotland and resolved against the odds to attempt to change their culture for good. They had to battle against the power interests of the drinks trade and initially against the medical profession and many Scottish clergy. However, by the end of the nineteenth century, doctors and increasingly the clergy, together with a growing minority of the population, were committed to this cause. The passing of the Temperance (Scotland) Act in 1913 was a high point in their campaign as it allowed for votes in local communities to address this issue. Initial confidence was high about the outcome of votes in the 1920s, and in the most hotly contested poll in 1920, 40 percent of the electorate voted for "No License"—but it was insufficient to bring change in the majority of constituencies. Scottish Baptists had been totally committed to this cause in the early twentieth century.

The momentum in the political campaigns for temperance reforms had dissipated by the end of the 1920s. It was not necessarily a decline in the convictions of supporters of this cause, but a growing recognition that they would not gain a majority in a national vote on the issue. However, many of the social changes they had campaigned for, such as a significant reduction in alcohol consumption and the resultant healthier lifestyles they had sought, had come about not by Prohibition but by other factors. First, at a time of reduced incomes in the postwar period, a government law to reduce

[103] *Scottish Baptist Yearbook 1924*, 99. *Baptist Union of Scotland Temperance Committee Special Jubilee Number 1881–1931*, 12–13.

the opening hours of licensed premises limited the supply of alcohol; combined with higher taxes on its purchase, effectively doubling the price of a pint of beer by 1922 from its prewar price, demand fell. Second, very cheap tickets at cinemas provided alternative entertainment to an evening in the public house, and for others, healthier lifestyles through participation in football, cycling, and swimming clubs also contributed to lower demands for alcohol.

Baptists in American Culture

5

Baptists and American Nativism, 1830–1860

Terry G. Carter

Current events often prompt historians to look to the past for clarity or at least for comparisons to provide clarity. Recent political, social, and even religious movements have fueled the quest to look back. The catalyst for this study is the rising wave of American nativism, which not only touches political and social structures but has also invaded many of the more conservative American religious groups. Baptists have not escaped. An outspoken Baptist pastor echoed a growing attitude by stating that "America is not a church where everyone should be welcomed regardless of race and background." The pastor went on to say that the country has the right to restrict immigration on any grounds, including race or various other qualifications.[1] While I do not intend in this chapter to engage the current political debate over immigration, I do explore contemporary attitudes that seem particularly nativist and seek to survey the past to understand how these same attitudes surfaced among Baptists in the 1800s.

According to Cas Mudde, a political science professor at the University of Georgia, nativism may loom as one of the largest movements in the West at this time. In an article titled "Why Nativism, Not Populism, Should Be Declared Word of the Year," Mudde argued that in 2017 the nativist impulse dominated social life. Although what has happened in America and Europe has often been termed "populism," Mudde argues that is a false designation:

> If anything, 2017 was the year of nativism, or more correctly, yet another year of nativism, as we have had many of these years since the turn of the century. Nativism is an ideology that holds states should be inhabited exclusively by members of the native group ("the na-

[1] Bob Allen, "Evangelical Supporter Sees Nothing Racist about Trump Immigration Stance," *Baptist News Global*, January 17, 2018, https://baptistnews.com/article/evangelical-supporter-sees-nothing-racists-trump-immigration-stance/#.Wz5_eNVKipo.

tion"), and that non-native people and ideas are fundamentally threatening to the homogenous nation-state.[2]

Irma Leonard and Robert Parmet, who explored the beginnings of American nativism in the 1830–1860 era, stated that almost from the beginning the new nation was seen as a "sacred nation with a divine purpose." Americans saw themselves as "chosen people," and underlying that belief was also the strong sense that America was a Protestant land. For them, Americanism and Protestantism were synonymous. Democracy, institutions, the way of life, and even the founding American documents—the Declaration of Independence and the Constitution—were believed to derive from the Protestant faith. Therefore, any immigrant who entered with another religious perspective or was loyal to another authority represented a threat. American nativism erupted when the numbers of arriving strangers grew noticeably. Nativists in America believed the newcomers to be either unfit for citizenship, unable to assimilate, or unacceptable because they resisted Americanization. Anxiety gave rise to fear, and fear prompted nativism. "Nativism, then, is defined by historians and sociologists as a deep-seated American antipathy towards internal 'foreign' groups of various kinds—cultural, national, religious, racial—which has erupted periodically into intensive efforts to safeguard America from such perceived threats."[3]

Historically in America, waves of nativist attitude occurred between 1830 and 1860 and again between 1870 and 1930 due to massive immigration. During that time, many native-born Americans felt a "purported inability of specific immigrant groups to assimilate, described them as 'dangerous to the native-born population,' and perceived them as a threat to 'American workers.'"[4] This may sound like familiar rhetoric in our time. The late-nineteenth-century wave of nativism merely continued an earlier movement that rose between 1830 and 1860. During that time immigration increased dramatically with most of the newcomers being Roman Catholic,

---

[2] Cas Mudde, "Why Nativism, not Populism, Should Be Declared Word of the Year?," *The Guardian*, December 7, 2017. Mudde describes populism as a "political ploy by cynical leaders who mobilize the 'ordinary people' by promising them whatever they want."

[3] Irma M. Leonard and Robert D. Parmet, *American Nativism, 1830–1860* (New York: Robert E. Krieger, 1971), 3–6. See also Ray Allen Billington, *The Origins of Nativism in the United States, 1800–1844* (1938; New York: Arno Press, 1974), for further discussion on the anti-Catholic factor in the development of American nativism.

[4] Julia G. Young, "Making America 1920 Again? Nativism and US Immigration Past and Present," *Journal on Migration and Human Security* 5, no. 1 (2017): 217.

which complicated the nativist impulse by adding an antireligious fervor—which is not unusual for extreme nativism; religion often plays a role. But simply being against a particular religion does not qualify as pure nativism.

In previous work I focused on Baptists and anti-Catholicism between 1830 and 1860. However, one must distinguish between an anti-Catholic sentiment and American nativism, which is understood as against immigrants or foreign influences. Some who were anti-Catholic rejected Roman Catholic Church theology and practice. They did not recognize the pope's authority and believed that many Catholic practices were anti-Christian or immoral. One could be anti-Catholic and not be nativist. However, most nativists between 1830 and 1860 were also anti-Catholic and tended to express their negative response to Catholicism by admitting a fear that these new immigrants were a threat to the American way of life and its freedoms.

Most American Protestant groups showed at least some signs of American nativism during eras of heavy immigration. The pulpit, periodicals, mission organizations, and denominational gatherings were often peppered with nativist sentiment. Baptists in America were no exception. Many Baptists, in rhetoric and attitude, exhibited negative responses to immigrants. Neither of the major Baptist denominations as denominational entities embraced American nativism in its pure form, but both Northern and Southern branches had members and periodicals that either mildly or radically supported nativist notions. My task in this chapter is to reveal how some Baptists in America between 1830 and 1860 reflected a clearly nativist attitude and openly feared that foreigners might destroy liberty, institutions, and the nation. Examples of Baptist nativist rhetoric, nativism and Baptist missions, Baptists and nativist political movements, and Baptist support of nativist organizations are investigated.

Nativist Rhetoric

W. Darrell Overdyke in his study of the Know-Nothing Party in the South made a comment that we hope was true of most Baptists in the United States between 1830 and 1860: "Southern Baptists, while anti-Catholic, were not universal supporters of Americanism." By "Americanism," Overdyke meant nativist political and social attitudes and actions. He used as his example J. L. M. Curry, a Virginia Baptist. In a letter written to Clement Claiborne Clay on July 5, 1855, Curry denounced nativism: "To choke up the spontaneous convictions of an immortal soul, is what I fear.—My Baptist principles revolt at anything that militates against individuality of character and the right of private judgment."[5] Understanding that Baptists have historically stood for religious liberty and freedom of conscience, it stands to reason that Curry's opinion should have constituted the then-common belief of most Baptists. However, gauging the attitudes of the many laypeople in the pews is difficult. We can, however, survey what they were hearing and reading and assume that at least some agreed with the proposed nativist opinions.

Baptists may have taken their nativist cue from well-known American Protestant spokespersons. Samuel F. B. Morse, a non-Baptist, enlarged the nativist conversation by publishing *A Foreign Conspiracy against the Liberties of the United States* in 1834. He claimed that Catholics, through an organization called Leopoldine Shiftung, sent missionaries to undermine American liberty; he saw this activity as a political strategy.[6] Lyman Beecher added to the anxiety with his *Plea for the West* in 1835.[7] Baptists along with other Protestants followed suit with statements of similar alarm.

Baptist papers often published articles from other newspapers that included nativist sentiments. In the *True Union*, an article titled "Catholics and Rum" blamed Catholics for the negative issues associated with alcohol in the United States. In addition, the editors laid responsibility for a large majority of crime in the country on Catholic immigrants. The *Western Recorder* in Kentucky charged Catholics with being anti-Republican and despotic in spirit. Unmistakably anti-Catholicism and nativism merged in the article. The paper also printed a speech by a Mr. Putnam of the New York legislature commenting on Roman Catholic antagonism toward liberty. Putnam argued that Catholic loyalty is to the pope not the country, and that Catholics would abolish the Constitution if asked to do so by the church. In this light, the writer feared Rome would use political interference that would put America into grave danger.[8]

Some Baptist pastors were particularly vocal in expressing native Americanism, fearing that Roman Catholic immigration threatened liberty and democracy. George B. Ide, a Baptist pastor who served in Vermont, New

---

[5] W. Darrell Overdyke, *The Know-Nothing Party in the South* (Baton Rouge: Louisiana State University Press, 1950), 238.

[6] Samuel F. B. Morse, *A Foreign Conspiracy against the Liberties of the United States* (1834; New York: Arno Press, 1977).

[7] Lyman Beecher, *A Plea for the West* (Cincinnati: Truman and Smith, 1835).

[8] "Political Power of the Pope," *Western Recorder*, March 14, 1855.

York, Pennsylvania, and Massachusetts, avidly shared the nativist fears. Ide wielded some influence among Baptists in the North. Cathcart describes Ide as "one of the most vigorous and effective preachers that the Baptist denomination has had in this century."[9] Ide served as a signer of the invitation for the establishment of the American Protestant Association, thereby indicating his anti-Catholic stance. Then in 1843 the *Quarterly Review of the American Protestant Association* printed one of his essays, in which Ide enumerated the enemies of Christianity and of America, claiming that the pope intended to transplant his power to America. In Ide's words, the pope's votaries

> scruple at no means, and shrink from no labour, to accomplish their end; founding colleges and seminaries in order to control education, and gain ascendency over youth; assailing the Bible in our public schools; tampering with the ballot-box; and striving, by every wily stratagem, to subvert our civil and religious liberties, and establish, in their place, the spiritual domination of Rome.[10]

Ide considered the Roman Catholics not so much as objects of contempt but rather a source of fear and abhorrence. He believed they would dazzle and enthrall with pomp and ritual and then, when in a position of power, become a monster of destruction, crushing all opposition.[11]

Without doubt one of the most outspoken Baptist nativists was the editor of the *Tennessee Baptist* and promoter of Landmarkism, J. R. Graves. He openly pushed nativist sentiment in editorials and published nativist articles with his personal comments attached. In September 1854 Graves included an article titled "To the Friends of Religious and Civil Liberty," signed simply "Liberty." The article discussed the supposed intentions of Catholics and then issued a warning: "These are not imagined dangers....They are real dangers, which as Protestants, as patriots, and Christians, we must avert." The author believed that of all the threats to the Union, Catholic immigrants were the greatest. He called all to action: "Countrymen! Americans! Be up and doing. The liberties of your country

---

[9] William Cathcart, ed., *The Baptist Encyclopedia. A Dictionary of the Doctrines, Ordinances, Usages, Confessions of Faith, Sufferings, Labors, and Successes, and of the General History of the Baptist Denominations in All Lands*, rev. ed., vol. 1 (Philadelphia: Louis H. Everts, 1883), 36.

[10] George B. Ide, "The Ministry Demanded by the Present Crisis," *Quarterly Review of the American Protestant Association* (April 1845): 190.

[11] Ide, "Ministry Demanded by the Present Crisis."

are in danger. Rally under the banner of the nation. Stand by your countrymen, and let your rallying point be, the grave of Washington."[12]

Graves also published an article from the *New York Day-Book* in October 1854 denouncing Roman Catholics as anti-republican and opposed to what the American government represents. The article questioned whether a man can be a good republican "whose religion is anti-republican." If a person's religion makes war with republican ideals, it would be impossible for that man to support a republican form of government. Logically that man would be an enemy to either his religion or the republic and most likely he would support his religion. Therefore, such a man could not be trusted. He would betray republicans and must do so as his religious duty demands. "So we say, in this country, no man who professes to believe in a religion which is anti-republican in principle should be allowed to either hold office or vote."

J. R. Graves added his own opinion: "We agree with the writer. No man can be a good republican whose religion is anti-republican." He accused Catholics of violently opposing "the spirit of our government" and seeking to subvert it. Graves reasoned that the political sentiment and character of a person "is always informed, if not always determined, by the religious system under which he is trained." Graves was referring to increasing Catholic immigration when he wrote, "The Catholic element in this country is dangerous to our republican government and the tendency of it is to subvert our free institutions."[13] Graves urged his readers to recognize the threat.

Some Baptists, like other Protestants in the United States, clearly exhibited fear that Catholic immigrants would destroy American ideals. But how much of this attitude was shared by the Baptist in the pews? That is not easily determined. Perhaps, as for their Conventions and mission boards, immigration provided a catalyst for missions.

Baptist Missions and Nativism

Some Baptists in the United States used nativist ideas to promote missions to convert the dangerous immigrant. The *Western Recorder* noted the increase in immigration as a reason to act, reminding the reader that the Roman Catholic Church had rapidly gained strength in the 1800s. Citing the

---

[12] "To the Friends of Religious and Civil Liberty," *Tennessee Baptist*, September 30, 18 54.

[13] "Anti-Republican Religion," *Tennessee Baptist*, October 28, 1854.

existence of sixteen hundred priests and seventeen hundred Catholic churches in 1855, the article suggested that readers who regarded this as an insignificant issue were either mistaken or had their eyes clouded.[14]

Some prominent Baptists between 1830 and 1860 shared this opinion. R. B. C. Howell's *The Baptist* featured a sermon titled "Dangers to Our Nation" preached by the most notable Baptist home missionary, J. M. Peck. Preaching at the First Baptist Church of Nashville, Tennessee, on November 3, 1844, Peck declared the dangers to the United States resulting from Catholic immigration. He cautioned his audience that they were living in an age of Romanism with its superstitions, despotic character, and priests who formerly served as "ultra despots in Europe." Peck believed that Catholics were "destroying the very foundations of truth, morality and justice." His concern increased with the rising numbers of immigrants: "Our country is receiving annually vast accessions of population from Europe and about one third of this class are Roman Catholics and all are defective of those principles which are indispensable to the conservation of our country." He conceded that we could not drive them back and "ought not to stay this influx of immigration" but rather win them to Protestant Christianity.[15]

The Tennessee Board of Domestic Missions in 1853 included in its proceedings a circular letter sent out by J. M. Peck suggesting that missions begin in "our Jerusalem" because half a million foreigners were pouring into the Mississippi Valley annually. Peck warned that these immigrants exerted pressure to subvert the American Constitution and threatened the nation's government and free institutions: "For the sake of Europe and of the world we must seek to save America." Peck came just short of equating Christian mission endeavors with the acts of being a good American citizen.[16]

After the formation of the Southern Baptist Convention, similar calls were issued year after year from the South. The "Report of New Orleans" in 1853 clarified the danger and need, describing a mighty conflict between the friends of pure Christianity and Romanists. The Board of Domestic Missions report reflected the same urgency. Catholics were considered absent "of all moral principles" and seldom people of character. The call to missions

---

[14] "The Intolerant Spirit of Romanism," *Western Recorder*, August 1, 1855.

[15] J. M. Peck, "Dangers to Our Nation," sermon to First Baptist Church of Nashville, TN, *The Baptist*, November 3, 1844.

[16] "The Board of Domestic Missions of the General Association of Tennessee and North Alabama to the Churches Composing That Body," *Tennessee Baptist*, November 12, 1853.

remained the solution.[17] The American Baptist Home Mission Society early on recognized the danger of increased immigration to interests cherished by American Christians. The society believed immigration was an organized Roman effort to send thousands annually and have them "located at places selected with systematic regard" to gain influence in the United States. The immigrants were disciplined to the will of the Roman Catholic Church and came from places that practiced habits and possessed prejudices incongruent with those of America. The society predicted that these immigrants would issue forth corrupting influence because "aspiring political demagogues" (a favorite phrase) had control over them.[18] The same year Peck preached in Nashville, the American Baptist Home Mission Society echoed the missions call, asserting that Baptists could not overlook the corrupting influence of "aspiring political demagogues" or the dangers to civil and religious liberties. The only safeguard was the free dissemination of the gospel, and they urged Baptists to employ all their energies more directly to promote the gospel or else the Catholics would win.[19]

D. C. Eddy, a politically active Baptist minister, addressed the Executive Committee of the American Baptist Home Mission Society in 1855, recommending missions action for responding to the threat. Eddy's concern was that papists on all sides were trying to bring the United States prostrate to Rome. He suggested that Baptists "not talk of political organizations"; even though these might do some good, they could not drive back the wave of skepticism and superstition rolling in like a flood. Eddy acknowledged the worth of statute law but cautioned that it also would not arrest the tide of immigration. "Party politics, however pure, carries nothing but the popular will; the law carries nothing but the statute book." Eddy advised Baptists instead to turn to the home mission enterprise, which goes forth with the

---

[17] "Report of New Orleans"; "Seventh Annual Report of the Board of Domestic Missions," *Southern Baptist Convention Proceedings*, 1853, 22, 62.

[18] "Reasons for Vigilance and Activity," *Fifteenth Report of the Executive Committee of the American Baptist Home Mission Society* (New York: American Baptist Home Mission Society, 1847), 17; "Popish Efforts—Protestant Supineness," *Twelfth Annual Report of the Executive Committee of the American Baptist Home Mission Society* (New York: American Baptist Home Mission Society, 1844), 61–62.

[19] "Work before Us," *Twelfth Annual Report of the Executive Committee of the American Baptist Home Mission Society*, 14.

Bible—older than Romanism, stronger than the church, and more infallible than the pope.[20]

In the 1840s and 1850s another immigration wave occurred on the West Coast of the United States. Chinese immigrants began arriving in California in great numbers. Initially Baptists exhibited little evidence of nativist concerns directed toward this group but rather saw them as the mission field coming to the United States. At the Southern Baptist Convention meeting in 1849 J. L. Dagg addressed the Chinese immigration into California, urging Baptists to act. "Within the last few months many thousands of our fellow men, of our own and other countries have emigrated to that distant territory...destitute of ordinary means of grace. They will likely die without the gospel if we do not send missionaries." Dagg saw the possibility of the mission reaching all the way to China. It will be the only means "to eradicate the spiritual darkness from the Isles of the ocean, the empires of the East."[21] Similar statements were made in SBC meetings to follow. In 1853 the "Report on California" explained that "it is supposed that the Chinese population in California is about 40,000 and their number is increasing rapidly. It is probable that millions instead of thousands will ultimately settle in California from China....God in his providence, is bringing these multiplied thousands of pagans to our land, that we may give them the gospel."[22]

Initially, California Baptists held the same opinion concerning the Chinese immigrants. In the 1854 state Convention's "Committee on the Chinese Report," a resolution was proposed that the Convention sympathize with the "trying circumstances which surround them as residents in California and that we pledge our sympathy and co-operation with Brother Shuck in his missionary efforts."[23] For some in California, this attitude changed to a nativist, anti-immigration stance as the Chinese population grew to what was interpreted as fearful proportions.[24] However, this view did not prevail

---

[20] "Address of D. C. Eddy," *Twenty-Third Report of the Executive Committee of the American Baptist Home Mission Society* (New York: American Baptist Home Mission Society, 1855), 79–80.

[21] "J. L. Dagg—Immigrants from China—Need Churches on the Pacific Coast to Teach Gospel," *Proceedings of the Southern Baptist Convention Second Triennial Meeting*, 1849, 36–38.

[22] "Report on California," *Proceedings of the Southern Baptist Convention*, 1853, 14–15.

[23] "Proceedings of the California Baptist State Convention: Committee on the Chinese People," *Religious Herald*, November 9, 1854.

[24] Laurence Davis, *Immigrants, Baptists, and the Protestant Mind in America* (Urbana: University of Illinois Press, 1973), 22. Davis agrees that initially the Baptist approach to the

among Baptists generally. The mission societies and most other pastors continued to recognize the Chinese immigrants as a target for missions.

Baptists and Political Nativism

Nativism in the United States took on a political flavor in the 1840s. As early as 1839, local native American associations formed in several cities across the nation. In June 1843 many of these were politically unified with the establishment of the American Republican Party in New York City. It spread quickly to other cities with some success.[25] Then during the 1850s, as the Catholic immigration problem appeared more acute in the eyes of Protestants, a new party emerged. The American or Know Nothing Party developed in the 1850s and provided a venue for the nativist "propagandists demands" to be put into a party platform.[26] The party, secretive by nature, was shrouded in mystery and claimed George Washington as its first adherent. The movement began when Charles Allen formed a secret society called the Order of the Star-Spangled Banner in 1849. Beginning small, it surged in April 1852 under the leadership of James W. Barker, growing to more than a thousand in four months. The order consisted of two degrees. The first degree required proper age, birth in the United States, Protestant parents, and proof the candidate was not married to a Catholic. The member promised to use influence to vote only for native-born American citizens and to keep the secrets of the society. The second degree allowed members to hold offices in the society and become political candidates. Two princi-

---

Chinese immigration issue was simply to convert them to Christianity and to oppose restrictions on immigration. But by the 1880s some California Baptist pastors expressed new concerns. A. A. Denison of Oakland shared his resentment of the immigrants: "If the Baptist admirers of the Mongols could come face to face with them in Chinatown, it would no doubt dispel some Eastern illusions as to their desirability as a permanent population.'" Speaking at the Home Mission Society in 1882, Denison shared a very negative view of the Chinese while just two years earlier he argued the ports should not be closed to "Asiatics." In his address to the society he strongly stated that the nation could not "endure a slave or helot group such as the Chinese." He did support what he called "desirable immigration" but did "not believe in any force or vigor coming to us, as a Republic, from the scum of the world." They were a different and of an unacceptable "race stock." Denison claimed Caucasian or Indo-Germanic blood as different and more acceptable or a more "desirable immigration." (Laurence Davis, 22, 28-29.)

[25] Ray Allen Billington, *The Protestant Crusade: 1800–1860* (New York: Macmillan, 1938), 200–202.

[26] Billington, *Protestant Crusade*, 327.

ples guided the order: "opposition to the foreigner and opposition to the Catholic."

The political expression of American nativism proved distasteful for many Baptist leaders. The *Western Recorder* of Kentucky published several articles challenging Baptist engagement in political movements. The paper denied any interest in political parties that championed nativist ideas and attacked ministers who used their pulpits to urge partisan voting. One article even suggested ministers who did so should resign: "The Lord does not wish his ministers to use any carnal weapons in his behalf for the purpose of maintaining his honor on earth."[27] Some of these statements referred to the slavery issue rather than Catholic immigration. Another *Recorder* article accused ministers who used their pulpit influence for political purposes of being "religio-political demagogues." Since the editor believed Archbishop Hughes fit that description, he disparaged similar efforts by Protestants. "Religion, pure and undefiled, seeks no such measures in its support." The article further attacked the use of political votes to gain objectives for religion which it believed constituted threats to political and religious groups.[28] This did not mean that Protestants should be unconcerned with politics, but they should never approach it in a violently partisan way. The article discouraged overzealous involvement since the church should not serve as an electioneering headquarters.[29] The *South Western Baptist* (Marion, AL) agreed, admitting that they fought "Roman Catholicism as a system of iniquity and religious oppression" but did not feel obliged to give up their "weapons into the hands of politicians."[30] Charles F. Williams, who wrote the circular letter for the New Jersey Baptist Association in 1853, admitted the presence of threats to civil and religious liberty. However, he urged Baptists not to rely too heavily on statesmen but rather on the cultivation of correct religious sentiment in order to maintain the republic. Williams believed the perpetuity of the republic depended on the faithfulness of the American citizens, and he suggested nonpolitical options.[31]

---

[27] "Politicians," *Western Recorder*, February 8, 1857; "Clerical Politicians in the North," *Western Recorder*, March 29, 1854. (By 1859 the *Recorder* had around fifteen thousand subscribers.)

[28] "Methodism and Politics," *Western Recorder*, December 31, 1851, 2.

[29] "Religious Politicians," *Western Recorder*, August 26, 1856; "Political Excitement," *Western Recorder*, November 5, 1856; September 7, 1856.

[30] "Efforts to Keep Out of Politics," *Christian Index*, August 23, 1855. This article is a reprint of an earlier appearance in the *South Western Baptist*.

[31] *Minutes of the New Jersey Baptist Association of New Jersey*, 1853, 19–22.

Some Baptists appeared to reject political activity while nodding agreement to the nativist platform. The *Baptist Banner and Pioneer* as early as 1844 dealt with the nativist political question when responding to a letter to the editor. In a previous edition the paper had reported that the "highhanded" activity of Catholics prompted the establishment of several native American associations, and the editor, William Buck, projected that after the election there may also be new political associations. The editor of the *Catholic Advocate* accused the *Banner* of persecution. Buck responded with a clarification: "We have never meddled in party politics, and in this capacity we never intend to do so." In fact, the paper suggested that its political views were not even known by many, Democrats or Whigs, who followed the paper. An emphasis was added: "We are the opponent of Popery, and the friend of foreigners and as a religious journal we have nothing to do with Native Americanism as a political party matter." Finally, the editor added a caveat that could be interpreted as betraying a nativist leaning. He declared, "We are opposed to admitting foreigners to the elective franchise under 21 years in residence and it doesn't matter if they are Catholic or other 'religionists.'"[32]

Again in 1844 William C. Buck predicted that the American future would be one of nativism versus antinativism. He attributed his opinion to the "high-handed" (clearly a favorite term) and daring encroachments of the Catholics in the country. He believed the attacks targeted particularly republican institutions, the "elective franchise," and the use of the Bible in schools. Buck described these encroachments as an "insidious policy of the Pope and the papal sovereigns of Europe, against the peace and permanence of our government." The politicians have issued the alarm and "Native American Associations" have sprung up in every direction. "We opine, that as soon as the present Presidential election is over, new political combinations will be formed, and Whigism and Democracy will be merged into Nativism and Anti-Nativism."[33] In the same year Buck borrowed an article from the *Louisville Courier* that displayed the full creed of the native American party. It included a twenty-one-year naturalization law, natives only in office, every man's right to worship as he pleases, limitations on immigration, and the presentation of a pure and uncorrupted elective franchise. Although the party did not appear extremely anti-Catholic, it targeted Catholic

[32] "The Catholic Advocate," *Baptist Banner and Pioneer*, November 28, 1844.

[33] Quoted in Agnes Geraldine McGann, *Nativism in Kentucky to 1860* (Washington, DC: Catholic University of America, 1944), 15–16.

immigrants. While claiming to reject political involvement, Buck clearly wanted to make sure his readers knew the nativist platform proposals. At the same time he revealed some of his own feelings in addressing the party. He clearly believed Catholic immigration had encroached on the institutions of the country, the elective franchise, and the schools.[34]

Other Baptists endorsed the political form of nativism without apology. Baptist pastor Daniel C. Eddy preached a sermon in April 1854 openly calling for Baptist preachers and laypeople to engage politically to stop the Catholic threat. He described the times as a "death struggle with Romanism. They have sent an army of priests and legates who have no sympathy for American institutions. Their method is not to shoot you but rather to suppress schools, control ballots, overthrow the press and silence the pulpit." Eddy claimed Catholics had wormed their way into the cabinet and the Supreme Court. "The country is filling with foreigners who cannot read or write and are filling the prisons, almshouses and asylums." Eddy argued he "would not prevent the naturalization of them; but I would require every foreigner, to be in our country from fifteen to twenty one years, before he can cast his vote. I would make an ability to read and write a qualification for voting."[35] He did propose that he "would have every ship owner placed under bonds to keep all he brings here off the State for at least five years." Undoubtedly, Eddy believed shipowners would be more selective if financially responsible for how their passengers fared in the New World. His intention was to limit emigrants to the intelligent and industrious while excluding all paupers.[36]

Eddy called Baptists to action: "To be a good citizen is the next thing to being a good Christian; and love of country is the next thing to love of God. The peculiar Phases of our time do not involve merely the political question, for the gaunt form of Romanism menaces not merely the ballot box but free speech and public schools, but also the altars of the church, and the liberty to worship God." Eddy ended with an interesting metaphor to describe the acute danger the United States faced. "Pray for the Republic—the ship in a storm, with broken compass, an incorrect chart, a blind pilot, a

---

[34] "Native Americanism," *Baptist Banner*, November 14, 1844.

[35] Daniel C. Eddy, *Political Rights of Ministers: A Sermon Preached on Fast Day, April 6, 1854* (Boston: Dayton Wentworth, 1854), 40–44.

[36] Eddy, *Political Rights of Ministers.*

mutinous crew, and an insane commander."[37] Eddy patently held that Catholic immigrants constituted a threat to liberty and political rightness.

Some Baptist associations encouraged political involvement during the Know Nothing era. A circular letter written by J. R. Murphy, included in the 1852 minutes of the New Jersey Baptist Association, rejected any strong party allegiance. However, it encouraged ministers and deacons to "mingle with the noisy crowd around the ballot box." Murphy promoted the use of the ballot box to safeguard liberty, especially since the "man of sin" desired to use politicians to accomplish his purpose. Ministers should avoid an active role in political meetings but laypeople have more freedom as long as their motives are not sectional or partisan.[38] The East New Jersey Baptist Association in 1856 urged its members to deal with the present national affairs through prayer and "such use of their political franchises and influence as they believe are demanded of them as followers of truth and righteousness."[39]

By far the most outspoken advocate of Know Nothingism was J. R. Graves, editor of the *Tennessee Baptist* and a very popular spokesman for a significant segment of Baptist life. At least twice in 1854 Graves provided column space for the Know Nothing Party agenda. He recognized that the party was reaching great strength. The reasons for such growth related to the political climate of 1854. The political parties were deplorable, and politicians were like "wolves" fighting for spoils and pandering to foreigners. Graves characterized Congress as shameful and disgraceful with drunkenness and carousing common. And then there was the foreign immigration issue. "The foreign element is increasing in fearful ratio." According to Graves, warfare against the schools, Sabbath, laws and the Constitution provided the backdrop for the rise of the Know Nothing Party. He claimed that thousands and hundreds of thousands of American citizens who love their country better than any party were willing to shed their blood to save the legacy of the forefathers who were "martyrs of the Revolution."[40]

The article concluded that citizens had banded themselves together to know nothing "but the safety and best good of their country." Graves listed what were said to be the leading principles of the party: the repeal of the

---

[37] Eddy, *Political Rights of Ministers*, 46.

[38] J. R. Murphy, "Circular Letter," in *Minutes of the New Jersey Baptist Association of New Jersey*, 1852, 17–20.

[39] *Minutes of the East New Jersey Baptist Association of New Jersey*, 1856, 9.

[40] "Know Nothing," *Tennessee Baptist*, August 26, 1854.

naturalization laws, only native Americans for offices, a pure American school system, opposition to military companies composed of foreigners, "war on Romanism," hostility to papal influence, promotion of American institutions and sentiment, more stringent and effective immigration laws, protection of Protestant interests, the doctrines of the "revered Washington," sending foreign paupers and convicts home, the formation of societies to protect American interests, enmity against all who carry out the principles of a foreign country or church, and finally a pure American law designed to put foreign influences to death. In the midst of the list appeared a motto statement characterizing nativist sentiment. "Our Country, Our Whole Country, and Nothing but our Country." Graves unambiguously agreed with most of the platform and added that if "we could be allowed to add one or two more, we would Know Nothing in politics save these principles." He predicted the existence of two parties: Protestant and Foreign Catholic / Infidel. True Christians would be compelled to take sides. "Then it will be the duty of the minister as well as the member to become a politician—and the politics of the day will needs be preached from the pulpit and prayed around the family altars, and enter into and effect all the interests and relations of life." The article ended with a commendation of Know Nothing platform principles and the desire to add even "a few more to serious and favorable attention of Christians and Patriots."[41]

In December of the same year, a reader wrote to Graves asking if he approved of secret societies, a well-known characteristic of the Know Nothing Party. The writer approved of Graves's "American Principles" but wanted his opinion specifically on secret societies. Graves responded that he was not much for secret societies but that may be due to a lack of acquaintance with them. He did not favor them, but "with a certain provisio" (the desire to add to the party platform) he commended the principles of the Know Nothing Party. "We have nothing to do with a secret political party, 'of Know Nothingism,' we positively Know Nothing; but if the principles are indeed American, let it come forth into the light of day and originate a great American party upon Great American principles, and we shall be very apt to be found on that side."[42]

It is nearly impossible to gauge the feelings of the average Baptist in the pew—North or South—concerning nativist political parties. This brand of

---

[41] "Know Nothing," *Tennessee Baptist*, August 26, 1854.

[42] "Know Nothingism," *Tennessee Baptist*, December 2, 1854.

politics had a following in many sections of the United States. Books have chronicled the party in places like New Orleans, Maryland, Kentucky, and the whole South. The readership of some Baptist magazines that provided column space for nativist concerns often reached significant numbers, but how much those readers shared the views of people like Graves may never be known. Nativism and its propaganda existed, but the extent of the influence it exerted is difficult to determine.

Baptists and Nativist Societies

There remains one more query concerning Baptist involvement with nativism between 1830 and 1860. Admittedly this discussion may indicate more anti-Catholicism than pure American nativism, but many of the Protestant societies formed between 1830 and 1860 revealed nativist leanings. Baptist involvement in them warrants discussion. In 1842 the American Protestant Association formed in Philadelphia. The purposes outlined were openly anti-Catholic but also revealed nativist fears over the loss of American liberties. The purpose statement explained that the organization was formed by Protestant ministers "to give their several congregations instruction on the difference between Protestantism and Popery…to awaken the attention of the community to the dangers which threaten the liberties…of the United States from the assaults of Romanism." A. D. Gillette and George B. Ide, both Baptists, joined the association.[43] A few years later, the new American Protestant Society included in its constitution the nativist idea that "the Society will aim to enlighten Protestants concerning the nature, operation, and influence of Romanism, as well as to guard against its encroachments upon our civil and religious institutions."[44] Again several Baptists played prominent roles in this society, including M. J. Gonsalves (an ex–Roman Catholic turned Baptist), John Dowling, Duncan Dunbar, and D. W. Lathrop.[45]

Conclusion

American nativism experienced strong surges between 1830 and 1860. The cause of these surges can be traced directly to foreign immigrants arriving in the United States in such numbers that fear erupted for the loss of liberty

---

[43] John R. Bodo, *The Protestant Clergy and Public Issues, 1812–48* (Princeton, NJ: Princeton University Press, 1954), 7–8.

[44] Billington, *Protestant Crusade,* 244–45.

[45] "American Protestant Society," *Christian Watchman,* May 27, 1849, 83.

and the American way of life. This intensified due to the Roman Catholic background of the vast majority of those immigrants. Anti-Catholicism, combined with a tendency to equate Americanism with Protestantism, produced nativist feelings and rhetoric as well as political and organizational activity within most Protestant groups in the United States. An antiforeign, anti-immigrant, and, during the thirty years in question, anti-Catholic sentiment regularly appeared in religious venues. Ray Allen Billington in his work *The Origins of Nativism in the United States, 1800–1844*, refers regularly to Protestant nativism in documenting his study.[46] Protestant papers, leaders, and organizations fueled the nativist crusade that plagued America throughout the 1800s and 1900s.

Baptists in the North and the South showed signs of this nativist mindset. Some of the most vocal Baptist preachers and leaders openly professed nativist ideas, and a few openly supported political parties that embraced the movement. Some Baptist papers provided column space for the propaganda or even promoted it in editorial comments or articles. People like Graves represented the basest form of nativism as he openly espoused the nativist political platforms calling for restrictions in immigration and limitations on newcomers. While the Baptist story in the United States frequently contains evidence of unseemly actions and attitudes, support for American nativism should certainly be added to that list.

However, even with clear evidence that some Baptists were nativist, many took a higher road in the discussion. While aware of the great number of immigrants entering the country and expressing concern over their influence for the American future, Baptists generally rejected a hateful nativist option. Many overruled use of political solutions, feeling that those options belonged outside the church and denomination. In addition, their most common response involved a mission impulse directed at converting the immigrants to Christianity and no doubt to Americanism. While even this reaction might be considered narrow and restrictive in today's America, in the 1800s it was a much gentler option. As would be expected, Baptists appeared to resort to their historic principles of freedom of conscience and soul liberty. In addition, the general sense at the denominational and mission meetings normally leaned against the restriction of immigration. They chose not to stem the flood but to influence the newcomers toward true Christianity. Many today in the United States might also interpret this as biased, but

[46] Billington, *Origins of Nativism in the United States.*

again, for the nineteenth century it embodied a milder approach to the immigration issue than political nativism.

Absolute assurance of the feelings of the lay Baptists in the pew during this time is difficult to ascertain. These members were not as vocal as those who regularly wrote or preached their views. Yet undoubtedly Baptist laypeople heard the arguments for nativism, and many lived in areas where large immigration populations settled. The influence of both environment and propaganda surely moved some to the nativist camp. A very broad investigation into associational and church minutes in every state would likely reveal additional information concerning that ordinary Baptist in the pew—but such investigation remains a work for the future.

Baptists in the Majority World

6

Baptist Mission among Māori in New Zealand, 1840–1990

John Tucker
(followed by a response from Rāwiri Auty)

In February 1883 the editor of the *New Zealand Baptist* magazine declared with some pride that "[our] section of the Christian Church has always been to the front in fulfilling our Saviour's commission." "Our honoured fathers," he wrote, "led the van of the great missionary movement of the last century." They were "the pioneers of that large and noble army of the messengers of peace, which since then has continued to go forth from the English and American churches to proclaim the glad tidings of salvation to the regions beyond."[1] The editor was referring to William Carey, the so-called father of modern missions and author of the *Enquiry*.[2] In that essay Carey urged his fellow Baptists to take the gospel to all those parts of the world "where the Sons of Adam still lived in the most deplorable state of heathen darkness." In section 3 he makes particular mention of "the New Zealanders."[3] Carey was referring to Māori, the indigenous people of New Zealand.

In this chapter I attempt to trace the story of Baptist interaction with Māori. I examine Baptist attempts to proclaim the gospel among Māori and Baptist discourse about Māori. In the chapter I identify three phases or episodes in this story. Baptist engagement with Māori was characterized first by cultural insensitivity, then by a more patient contextualization on the part of some, and finally by a growing commitment on the part of some leaders to what might be called "covenantal biculturalism." Overall, my narrative highlights the extent to which racist attitudes in New Zealand culture impeded Baptist attempts to proclaim the Christian gospel. Given that the

---

[1] *New Zealand Baptist* (hereafter *NZB*), February 1883, 217.

[2] William Carey, *An Enquiry into the Obligations of Christians to Use Means for the Conversion of the Heathen* (London: Kingsgate Press, 1792).

[3] Carey, *Enquiry*, 63.

telling of history is never neutral but always reflects the narrator's priorities and perceptions, I conclude the chapter with a word of response from Rev. Rāwiri Auty, a Māori minister and historian.

Proclaiming the Gospel to Māori: Cultural Insensitivity

The story begins in 1840 with the signing of *te Tiriti o Waitangi*, the Treaty of Waitangi. This agreement between the British Crown and the Māori chiefs of New Zealand is remarkable, if not unique, in colonial history. It did not just guarantee Māori all the rights and protections of British subjects; it brought Māori and Pākehā (Europeans) together as one people. From the early missionaries, Māori understood the treaty to be a *kawenata tapu*, a sacred covenant in which power would be shared. It created "a bond with all the spiritual connotations of the biblical covenants; there would be many tribes, including the British, but all would be one under God."[4] With this covenantal relationship or partnership in place, British settlement began in earnest. The first Baptists from Britain arrived in the 1840s.[5]

These Baptists did not, it seems, carry with them the missionary enthusiasm of William Carey, at least insofar as the Māori were concerned.[6] It was not until 1882 that Baptists began mission work among Māori. A wealthy American tourist visiting the Lakes around Rotorua was deeply moved by the condition of local Māori. Being Baptist he approached the Auckland Baptist Tabernacle and offered to help fund a Baptist missionary in the area. The tabernacle's pastor, the Reverend Thomas Spurgeon, wrote to his famous father, Charles Haddon Spurgeon, asking him to send a graduate from his Pastor's College in London. Spurgeon Sr. sent the Reverend Alfred Fairbrother. On his arrival the *New Zealand Baptist* magazine announced, "By a singular coincidence the missionary's name is Fairbrother. A fair brother is going to proclaim the gospel to his dark brethren. In this we

[4] Claudia Orange, *The Treaty of Waitangi* (Wellington: Allen and Unwin, 1987), 57, 90–91. See also Susan Healy et al., *Ngāpuhi Speaks: Commissioned by Kuia and Kaumātua of Ngāpuhi. He Wakaputanga o te Rangitiratanga o Nu Tireni and Te Tiriti o Waitangi. Independent Report. Ngāpuhi Nui Tonu Claim* (Kaitaia: Te Kawariki and Whangarei: Network Waitangi Whangarei, 2012).

[5] The first Baptist church to be formally constituted in New Zealand was Nelson Baptist Church, established in 1851.

[6] The *New Zealand Baptist* magazine admitted, "There is no doubt the important claims of missionary effort, if not lost sight of, have been kept in the background by many of our colonial churches" (February 1883, 217).

do and will rejoice."[7] Thomas Spurgeon, appealing for support from the New Zealand churches, predicted that Fairbrother would "be the means of doing great good in the gross darkness."[8]

Spurgeon's predictive powers, it seems, were a little off. In just over two years, local Māori sent a letter to the Tabernacle with one request: "Can you please remove Mr. Fairbrother?" One commentator, reflecting on Fairbrother's ministry, says that he "lacked the tolerance and sympathy required of a missionary. One gains the impressions that 'he despised the sinner and the sin.'"[9] Once, when a local Māori came drunk into a meeting, Fairbrother declared he would never preach in that "polluted" place again. Sometimes he would snatch the pipes out of his parishioner's mouths, following this up with a sharp public rebuke. When Māori women caused disturbances in his meetings, he would throw his walking stick at them. If meetings went over time, he would simply turn out the lights and leave.[10] It turns out that in the eyes of Māori, at least, Fairbrother wasn't such a "fair brother" after all.

The reality is, he "found it hard to adjust to Māori ways and customs."[11] In his written reports Fairbrother poured undiluted contempt on Māori practices. The *haka*, or traditional Māori dance, was, according to Fairbrother, "lewd in...its postures, indecent in its language, and demoralising to all." The *moko*, or facial tattoo, another important feature of Māori culture, was a "hideous" mark of heathenism. Fairbrother writes of "one old man, whose contour was unmistakably cannibalistic," that he refused to "give up his heathen customs as to dressing."[12] Living with these "semi-civilized, semi-clad natives" was, he said, like living in a "modern Sodom," a "land of shadows."[13] Fairbrother clearly carried with him a sense of cultural superiority.[14] And it wasn't just him. Other Baptist ministers described Māori in equally derogatory terms: they were "noble savages," "poor dark

---

[7] *NZB*, October 1882, 187.

[8] *NZB*, January 1883, 193.

[9] Roy Bullen, "Failure of a Mission," New Zealand Baptist Research and Historical Society Archive, MA 127/4, M 20/1. (MA stands for "main archive.")

[10] Bullen, "Failure of a Mission," 1–2. See also A. D. Mead, "Baptist Mission to the Maoris: An Early Venture and a New Beginning," *Bulletin of the New Zealand Baptist Historical Society* 4 (December 1954): 1–2.

[11] Roy Bullen, "Return to Rotorua," *NZB*, December 1965, 321.

[12] A Fair Brother, "News from 'The Front,'" *NZB*, July 1883, 289.

[13] Letter from Alfred Fairbrother to Thomas Spurgeon, *NZB*, December 1883, 369.

[14] R. F. Keam, *Dissolving Dream: The Improbable Story of the First Baptist Maori Mission* (Auckland: R. F. Keam, 2004), 165.

Māori," the "cannibal children of the letterless stone age."[15] Reflecting on other English-speaking settler societies, David Bebbington says Baptists had the "assumption that the original inhabitants were at a lower level of civilization, and so needed to be brought out of savagery as well as out of paganism. There was an insensitivity to indigenous culture that few were able to transcend."[16] This description fits nineteenth-century New Zealand Baptists perfectly.

With the failure of the first mission, there were occasional appeals to the Baptist Union to launch another mission among the "poor Māori."[17] But the denomination did not seem interested in mission to Māori.[18] At the turn of the century one minister charged his denomination with criminal neglect for refusing to evangelize the Māori.[19] This provoked a fierce reply from H. H. Driver, secretary of the New Zealand Baptist Missionary Society, a society formed just two weeks after Fairbrother's resignation. It was supporting a fledging work in India, and according to Driver, the society did not have the resources to fund both mission to India and mission to Māori. India was the more strategic investment because, Driver said, "the Māoris are plainly a vanishing race....Education, civilisation and evangelisation may delay the passing away of this fine branch of the human family; but it is very unlikely that they can ensure its permanent continuance....In India, however, we have one of the largest, the most ancient and the most enduring and influential races. They will affect the world's destinies when the Māoris have ceased to be."[20] This notion that Māori were a noble but dying race was common currency in New Zealand—and among Baptists—until the 1930s. Alfred Simmons expressed the opinion of many when he observed of Māori in 1879 that "the race is fast degenerating, and even now is of little political

[15] "Book Reviews," *NZB*, July 1938, 205.

[16] David W. Bebbington, *Baptists through the Centuries: A History of a Global People* (Waco, TX: Baylor University Press, 2010), 143.

[17] S. B. Ingold, letter to the editor, *NZB*, October 1892, 159; Gordon Kelly, letter to the editor, *NZB*, March 1899, 39.

[18] G. T. Beilby, *Road to Tomorrow: A Popular Account of One Hundred Years of Baptist Work in New Zealand* (Wellington: Baptist Union, 1957), 34; C. D. B. Jones, "The Long Painful Birth of Baptist Maori Ministry," *New Zealand Journal of Baptist Research* 1 (October 1996): 47.

[19] T. A. Williams, "The Pagans of Our Own Land: A Plea for the Maori," *NZB*, May 1900, 66.

[20] H. H. Driver, "The Pagans of Our Own Land: A Rejoinder by the Missionary Secretary," *NZB*, June 1900, 83.

importance. They will ultimately become a drivelling herd of servile beings."[21]

Ani Mikaere argues that colonizing powers needed to create myths about the natural inferiority of indigenous people in order to justify the way they treated them.[22] The impending and inevitable passing of the noble but weaker Māori race was one such myth. As Darwin had indicated in his *Descent of Man*, the stronger civilized races were destined to supplant the weaker, primitive races, like Māori.[23] It was simply natural selection. So, in November 1881 when troops invaded Parihaka, a peaceful Māori settlement waging a campaign of nonviolent resistance against the government's unlawful confiscation of its land, one church newspaper commented,

As the Pākehā [or European] fly has driven out the Māori fly;
As the Pākehā rat has killed the Māori rat;
As the Pākehā clover has starved the Māori fern;
So will the Pākehā destroy the Māori.[24]

It was simply "survival of the fittest." Natural selection. When Baptist preachers described Māori as a dying race, a "child-nation cursed by the too great nearness of a civilisation" like Britain's, they were simply reinforcing that narrative.[25] Willie Jennings observes that in the modern colonial era, Christianity, "captured and contorted inside imperial procedures of conquest," was deeply complicit in the process of colonization.[26] The history of Baptists in nineteenth-century New Zealand supports that claim.

Literature on the comparative conditions of indigenous people in settler societies generally indicates that New Zealand's race relations were better than those of Australia, South Africa, Canada, or the United States.[27] But

---

[21] Quoted by David Hackett Fischer, *Fairness and Freedom: A History of Two Open Societies—New Zealand and the United States* (Oxford: Oxford University Press, 2012), 267.

[22] Ani Mikaere, "Kairangi: Expanding a Māori Conception of Excellence," in *He Takuhanga Whakaaro: Conference Proceedings for Tuia Te Ako 2013*, 69, https://akoaotearoa.ac.nz/download/ng/file/group-4188/tuia-te-ako-2013proceedings.pdf.

[23] Charles Darwin, *The Descent of Man and Selection in Relation to Sex*, 2nd ed. (London: John Murray, 1874), 197, 283, 286–89.

[24] *New Zealand Free Methodist*, November 1881, 182.

[25] J. J. North, "A Missionary Address," *Missionary Messenger*, November 1906, 3.

[26] Willie James Jennings, "Theology and Race," in Chad Meister and James Beilby, *The Routledge Companion to Modern Christian Thought* (London: Rouledge, 2013), 789.

[27] For a good summary, see Fischer, *Fairness and Freedom*, 293–95.

"better" does not mean "great."[28] For generations, the New Zealand government systematically stripped Māori of their land and their culture in violation of the Treaty of Waitangi.[29] Colonial Baptists, however, were largely silent in the face of these injustices. With no mission to Māori, with no real connection to the victims of colonization, Baptist rhetoric about Māori could be quite troubling. Take, for instance, Rev. Charles Williams's reflections on the land wars of the 1860s, when the government unjustly invaded and confiscated millions of acres of Māori land: "I allow that conflict with Māoris was inevitable. Where Britain plants her foot, she demands submission to her authority." However, he said, "I believe that…no nation but ours would have dealt with them so justly; that there is no right or privilege enjoyed by the white man that is denied to them." So, Williams concluded with the blessing, "May they speedily attain to Christian manliness…and forget the real or imagined wrongs of the past in the enjoyment of equality and friendship with their English Christian brothers!"[30] This call to forget the past and move on, a recurring refrain, clearly reinforced and enabled the process of colonialism.

Other Baptists acknowledged that wrongs were done, no doubt. But their account of history was equally troubling. New Zealand's destructive land wars were not, they said, about land. They were about liquor. Māori chiefs took up arms because the government did not honor its promises to protect their settlements from "the demon drink."[31] This, Baptists argued—liquor—was the primary cause of Māori decline.[32] Given their attitudes to alcohol at this time, Baptists were very willing to come to the defense of Māori against the liquor traffic, the "cannibal trade." So, in 1924, for example, the Baptist Conference vigorously protested against attempts to introduce the liquor traffic in the King Country: "Such a violation of the sanctity of a national covenant, solemnly made and frequently reaffirmed, would be

---

[28] James Belich, *Paradise Reforged: A History of the New Zealanders from the 1880s to the Year 2000* (Auckland: Penguin, 2001), 190.

[29] For a basic summary of these historical injustices, see Laurie Guy, *Shaping Godzone: Public Issues and Church Voices in New Zealand, 1840–2000* (Wellington: Victoria University Press, 2011), 33–82, 285–302, 338–55.

[30] Charles Williams, "An English Baptist's Impressions of New Zealand," *NZB*, January 1902, 16.

[31] "Baptist Union of New Zealand: Fortieth Annual Conference," *NZB*, November 1922, 218; J. J. North, "Passing Notes," October 1924, 218.

[32] F. W. Boreham, "Between Ourselves," *NZB*, July 1904, 289.

an unspeakable offence against the living and the dead of the Māori race."[33] However, when a royal commission into the invasion of the King Country reported its findings just two years later, Baptists were again silent. They seem to have been blind to the sanctity of the Treaty of Waitangi—so much so that, during this period, the pages of the *New Zealand Baptist* magazine often celebrated military veterans who had fought in government campaigns against Māori. These men—with their "gallant" regiments—were, according to the *Baptist*, "good soldiers of Christ."[34]

Proclaiming the Gospel among Māori: Patient Contextualization

The demise of the first Baptist mission to Māori did not mean the end of all evangelism among Māori. Throughout the late nineteenth and early twentieth centuries, several Baptist churches led open-air services, ran Sunday schools, and organized boys' camps for Māori.[35] The Auckland and Tauranga churches supported missionaries working among the Māori in their districts.[36] Until the 1930s, however, these efforts to carry the gospel to Māori were spasmodic and largely ineffective, marked as they were by a sense of cultural superiority and insensitivity.[37] The late 1930s, though, signaled a new chapter in the history of Baptist interactions with Māori, one that featured patient contextualization.

In 1939 Rev. E. P. Y. Simpson wrote a thoughtful piece on the failure of Baptist mission among Māori. Most Baptists, he said, who come into contact with Māori brand them as primitive savages simply because Māori culture is different from European culture. Consequently, they pile on their indigenous converts a Europeanized form of Christianity. But Māori, Simp-

---

[33] S. Morris, "Second Day: Friday," *NZB*, November 1924, 249.

[34] "Death of a War Veteran," *NZB*, June 1915, 113.

[35] "Auckland District Association of New Zealand Baptist Union," *NZB*, June 1896, 91; "Mt Eden," *NZB*, April 1925, 110; "South Auckland Baptist Association," *NZB*, June 1938, 172; H. A. Harris, "Auxiliary Activities," *NZB*, August 1939, 243.

[36] "Back Blocks' Mission, Whangarei District," *NZB*, January 1910, 15; "Whangarei District Baptist Mission," *NZB*, August 1914, 160; D. H. Stewart, "Mission Work in Maoriland," *NZB*, May 1933, 150.

[37] Caleb Haurua, "'Korero Tuku Iho'—Mission to Merger: Exploring the Stories of Maori-Baptist Engagement in the Lower Waikato" (MAppTheol, Carey Graduate School, 2017), 23. According to the 1945 New Zealand census, when the Maori population numbered some 100,000 people and Baptist adherents numbered 27,500, there were only 21 Maori Baptists in New Zealand (Elaine E. Bolitho, *Meet the Baptists: Postwar Personalities and Perspectives* [Wellington: Christian Research Association, 1993], 28).

son said, are justifiably indignant when they are "patronized" in this way. The best work is done when the missionaries have

> "gone native" in [their] speech, thinking, and living, so that [their] life as well as [their] speech is a witness that Christ is mighty to save.... If it is worth taking the gospel of salvation to people, it is also worth seeking to understand them—their thought life, their social problems, their history, their culture. The missionary who strives to know all about the life and problems of those to whom he carries God's message—the missionary showing sympathetic love—is the one who shall inspire confidence, rouse responsive love, and be a worthy ambassador of Christ Jesus.[38]

From the late 1930s a growing number of young Baptists started volunteering for interdenominational mission service among Māori, mainly with the newly formed United Māori Mission.[39] Many of them, like Norman Perry and Phyllis Conway, adopted Simpson's approach by living among Māori to build indigenous Māori churches.[40] Baptist churches across the country took an eager and growing interest in their work, with United Māori Mission missionaries speaking at Baptist Women's Missionary Union meetings, men's events, and youth meetings.[41] Demands for a denominational mission among Māori grew until, in 1954, the Baptist Union launched a new work among Māori in the lower Waikato area, picking up on work done by Baptists in Pukekohe. At Assembly that year the president of the Baptist Union, a direct descendant of William Carey, inducted the first worker, Joan Milner. The second worker, Des Jones, was commissioned by the principal of the Baptist College, who quoted Carey's Serampore Covenant and urged him to live by its principles. Des and his colleagues tried to do that. They tried to esteem and treat Māori as their equals. They tried to

---

[38] E. P. Y. Simpson, "NZ Baptists and the Maori: A Reconsideration of the Problem," *NZB*, August 1939, 245.

[39] Report on Whangarei Baptist Church, *NZB*, July 1937, 228; reports on the Ashburton and Cambridge churches, *NZB*, March 1939, 91; "Missionary Roll of Honour," *NZB*, April 1940, 122.

[40] Norman Perry, who became active in the Presbyterian Church, entered Maori mission as a Baptist. See the reports on Lower Hutt Baptist Church in *NZB*, February 1937, 61; February 1941, 61. He was awarded a knighthood in 1977 for his services to Maori.

[41] "New Zealand Baptist Women's Missionary Union," *NZB*, July 1938, 221; "New Zealand Baptist Women's Missionary Union," *NZB*, June 1945, 136; "North East Valley," *NZB*, August 1945, 194; "New Plymouth," *NZB*, November 1945, 288.

abstain from whatever deepens Māori prejudice against the gospel. For them, Des says, it meant trying to "distinguish what was essentially Christian and what was essentially Western." It meant "entering into Māori life as far as we were able."[42] It meant living among Māori, learning their language and culture. Jones and his colleagues embodied Simpson's call to enter the Māori world—and Māori responded. Such was his regard for Des Jones that the local *kaumatua* or Māori elder gave each of Des's children a Māori name at their birth.[43] At her farewell, local Māori said of Dora Whitehead, one of the mission workers, "She might have a Pākehā face, but she has a Māori heart."[44]

Following William Carey's example in Serampore, the missionaries committed themselves from the beginning to raise up indigenous leaders. Māori converts led cottage meetings.[45] They conducted evening services, much of it in the Māori's language.[46] They taught Sunday school and led youth clubs.[47] In 1960 the mission's prayer letter was calling Baptists to special prayer for Māori men to feel the call to full-time mission work. A Māori teacher for the Māori people was, they said, "one of the greatest needs for the spread of the gospel."[48] By the early 1960s, Māori Christians were organizing their own *hui* or traditional Māori camps to reach out to their own people.[49] Before the decade had closed, the Māori board had commissioned the first full-time Māori worker and opened Puna o te Ora, a Māori church in Pukekohe where Māori leadership and Māori culture were normative.[50] From the 1960s, a number of local Baptist churches appointed Māori leaders to minister among Māori within their catchment.

It is fascinating to see how Baptist discourse about Māori shifted during this time. Until the 1960s the dominant narrative in New Zealand and in the Baptist Union was that the country possessed an enviable reputation for its race relations. As such, R. P. Staples, the New Zealand delegate to the Baptist World Congress in 1947, could proudly assure his fellow dele-

---

42 C. D. Jones, "25th Jubilee of the Maori Department," *NZB*, April 1979, 1.

43 I am indebted to my colleague Andrew Picard for this information.

44 H. G. Massam, "Farewell to Sister Dora Whitehead," *NZB*, April 1968, 16.

45 "Maori Work," *NZB*, September 1955, 227.

46 "Maori Work," *NZB*, August 1956, 208; Joan Milner, "Among the Maoris," *NZB*, July 1957, 156.

47 Ian D. Brown, "Maori Work," *NZB*, March 1962, 70.

48 Des Jones, "Need of Maori Work," *NZB*, February 1960, 40.

49 "Maori News," *NZB*, February 1963, 44.

50 Caleb Haurua, "Korero Tuku Iho," 79.

gates that "there is no race problem in New Zealand."[51] "In this lovely land," declared the *Baptist*, "our two races live together in harmony."[52] The chief reason, however, for the harmonious relations between Māori and Pākehā was the striking lack of social interaction between them. Until World War II, Māori generally lived in rural districts, while the majority of Pākehā lived in the towns and cities. As one American observer noted, "When Māori lived in rural villages, out of sight and out of mind, white New Zealanders could take a benign view of them."[53] Once Māori began to migrate into urban areas, latent racial prejudice came to the surface.

This was particularly evident in Pukekohe, where the Baptist Māori Mission was based. In the 1950s Pukekohe became known as "the capital of New Zealand racism."[54] Māori were made to sit downstairs at the movie theatre, they were assigned a separate chair at the barber's shop, and they were refused service at public bars. Māori children were quarantined in separate classrooms, forced to use separate toilets, and permitted to use the swimming pool only on the last day of the week, before the water was renewed. Māori families were forced to live in ramshackle houses made of packing cases or cabbage boxes.[55] Des Jones's personal engagement with local Māori gave him a deep desire to address these injustices. He spoke with the local parliamentary representative about substandard housing for Māori.[56] He wrote to the local newspaper, protesting the editor's racial prejudice.[57] He published opinion pieces in the *Baptist* magazine.

From the 1950s discussion about racism and prejudice against Māori started to appear in the pages of the *New Zealand Baptist* magazine. Baptist leaders began calling for a vital rethinking of the relationship between Pākehā and Māori. Initial calls for Baptists to show "tolerance" or "friendly concern" toward Māori were soon overtaken by more challenging analyses.[58] In 1958 the editor discussed the resistance of Māori people toward Christianity, tracing it directly to the unjust seizure of Māori land and the devastating

---

[51] "Baptist World Congress—Copenhagen," *NZB*, October 1947, 294.

[52] N. R. Wood, "God's Own Country," *NZB*, October 1957, 299.

[53] David P. Ausubel, *Maori Youth* (Wellington: Price Milburn, 1961), 43–44 (quoted in Guy, *Shaping Godzone*, 287).

[54] Belich, *Paradise Reforged*, 190.

[55] Guy, *Shaping Godzone*, 289.

[56] *Franklin Times*, February 12, 1958, 4.

[57] *Franklin Times*, July 15, 1959, 6.

[58] "Assembly Public Questions," *NZB*, December 1953, 273.

wars that followed.[59] Two years later, Arthur Mead, secretary of the Māori Mission Board, expanded this analysis. In his opinion, gospel work among Māori was also hindered by the way government agencies and church organizations had displaced Māori culture with Pākehā processes and practices, which tended to bewilder and alienate Māori people. "It is easy," he said in relation to our work among the Māori, "to counsel patience, prayer, and giving; we want also understanding"—an understanding of history.[60]

In the early 1960s, Des Jones moved the discourse a stage further. When the government released a report encouraging the "integration" of urban Māori and Pākehā, Jones expressed his grave concern that integration would mean assimilation—the "compulsory Europeanization" of Māori. He noted, by way of example, that some Pākehā, though they are purists when it comes to Latin and Greek, have no qualms at all about murdering Māori place names, and yet Māori boys and girls were beaten for speaking Māori in the school playground. He was referring, very possibly, to the native school system, which provided special primary schools for Māori children, separate from the normal state schools. These native schools were required by statute to conduct all education in English. The system, which continued until 1969, was designed to eradicate the native language because, in the words of Parliament, "civilization cannot be attained through the medium of an uncivilized and imperfect language."[61] Jones asked, why, in the process of integration, should Māori have to make all the adjustments? It was not fair. He called on Baptists to subvert the system. Get to know your Māori neighbors, he said. Enter their world. Embrace their culture. Participate in their activities.[62]

The editor of the *New Zealand Baptist* magazine, Bert Whitten, was even more forthright in his assessment of New Zealand society: "We are far from living up to our boasted no-colour-bar towards the Māori people. It is only Pākehās who boast that no colour-bar exists and that here there is no discrimination against the Māori people. No Māori makes that claim. Every Māori knows how false it is. He sees quite clearly what most Pākehās do not want to see and so refuse to see. There may be equality in law. But there is

---

[59] N. R. Wood, "Sparks from the Anvil," *NZB*, August 1958, 479.

[60] A. D. Mead, "A History Needed," *NZB*, October 1960, 266.

[61] *Native Schools Report, Appendices to the Journals of the House of Representatives* (1962), E-04, 16. (E-04 is the number of this report given to the House of Representatives.)

[62] C. D. Jones, "Integration and the Maori," *NZB*, February 1964, 40–41.

little true social acceptance, and very little real equality of opportunity."[63] Growing relational engagement with Māori sensitized a number of Baptist leaders to the complex challenges that Māori in the mid-twentieth century experienced due to colonization. Most leaders, though, showed very little interest in drawing alongside Māori. Throughout the 1960s the Baptist Theological College hosted an annual School of Māori Studies. Attendance was not strong. In 1966 the college reported, with frustration, that "a disappointing number of our ministers attended the course designed to help them to minister to Māori people."[64]

Proclaiming the Gospel with Māori: Covenantal Biculturalism

This brings us to the 1970s, and the third episode in this story. If the first part of the narrative was characterized by cultural insensitivity, and the second by a more patient contextualization on the part of some, the third featured a growing commitment by some leaders to justice and biculturalism.

From the 1970s, Baptists in New Zealand became increasingly sensitized to the reality of racial injustice and the need to honor the covenantal commitments expressed in the Treaty of Waitangi. There were several factors. Internationally, the campaign against apartheid in South Africa and the civil rights movement in the United States had broadened New Zealand consciences on the issue of race. So, in 1971 the National Council of Churches urged its members to make eradication of racism in New Zealand a major objective during the 1970s. The same year, New Zealand's Parliament introduced a Race Relations Act, creating an office to investigate complaints of racial discrimination and to promote racial harmony. Even more significant was the emergence of a new wave of Māori protest movements. In 1975 Māori mounted a major campaign—a great land march—to highlight the loss of their lands and assert their rights under the Treaty of Waitangi. Shortly thereafter, the government established the Waitangi Tribunal, a quasijudicial body with a mandate to investigate breaches of the Treaty of Waitangi and recommend compensation. In 1977, Māori protestors staged a protracted and very visible occupation of their ancestral land in central Auckland, attracting considerable public attention to their claims.

In this climate, Baptist leaders began offering a more penetrating—and controversial—analysis of Māori-Pākehā relations. The Reverend John

[63] H. E. Whitten, "Race and the Christian," *NZB*, June 1968, 1.

[64] "Maori News in Brief," *NZB*, August 1966, 211.

North attributed the massive overrepresentation of Māori in prison statistics to a British justice system that many Māori did not understand. A significant number of them, he argued, were in prison simply because they'd never received legal representation. North called for the immediate introduction of a comprehensive, nationwide duty solicitor scheme. He also warned, however, that it "would be naive to assume that simply by providing lawyers for defendants in the courts discriminatory practices against Māori offenders will cease. The inequalities will persist until such time as this and all other Pākehā-dominated institutions in New Zealand are demolished and a new society, created jointly by and serving the needs of all ethnic groups in the community, is achieved."[65] North recognized that Māori, to use Willie Jennings's phrase, were living under "the pigmentocracy of white preference."[66] Pākehā or Western institutions privileged white people by positioning white values as normal. North would have agreed with those scholars who argue that colonization is not just a historical phenomenon. It is very much a contemporary one.[67]

In 1980 New Zealand's Human Rights Commission published a statement on racial harmony. Trevor Donnell, former *tumuaki* (or superintendent) of the Baptist Māori work, responded to it by saying that any harmony in New Zealand was only skin deep. "There is," he said, "growing frustration amongst minority groups concerning insensitivity, ignorance, [and] institutionalised discrimination through our Pākehā orientated systems of politics, justice, education and employment....Many people, particularly Māoris, are feeling the system is not giving them a fair go. The system must change." Donnell claimed that Baptist churches tended to disregard differences between cultures and to stress instead our unity as "New Zealanders." However, he said, if we take the gospel seriously we must "acknowledge there are differences and work towards a multi-cultural society where cultural needs and identity are valued and developed and where minority groups are not presented with the 'take it or leave it' option but instead can have real power in shaping society."[68]

Māori Baptist leaders went even further. At the annual national Assembly, Charles Joe, the *kaiwhakahaere* (or secretary) of the Māori Depart-

---

[65] J. L. North, "Spotlight on Maoris in Court," *NZB*, June 1973, 17.

[66] Jennings, "Theology and Race," 788.

[67] Alistair Reese, "Reconciliation and the Quest for Pakeha Identity in Aotearoa New Zealand" (PhD thesis, University of Auckland, 2013), 212.

[68] Trevor Donnell, "Race Relations: A Superficial Calm," *NZB*, October 1980, 5.

ment, preached a sermon charging the church with being an "ally" of colonialism. The early missionaries, he argued, wanted to create converts in their own image and suppressed Māori culture. It was unjust and destructive. The great challenge for the church today, he said, is to "carefully and sensitively unwrap the Christian Faith from its dominant Western forms."[69] In 1982 Rua Turner declared to the Baptist Women's League that racism in New Zealand "permeates our basic power structures," but white New Zealand Christians are determined to push the issue under the carpet. They point to all the "assimilated" Māori in their congregations and pretend that everything is fine.[70] White evangelical Christians, she suggested, were perpetuating the racial division and inequity they claimed to oppose, something Emerson and Smith have argued in relation to the United States.[71]

In 1983 the Methodist Church decided to structure its decision-making processes in light of the Treaty of Waitangi and its principles of power sharing and partnership. The Anglican and Presbyterian Churches would later follow suit. The Baptist Union was not prepared to take this step, but at its annual Assembly that year it issued an important statement on Māori. It urged the churches, first, to appreciate and honor Māori culture and language. Second, the statement acknowledged that many past injustices against Māori were still causing hurt in the present and encouraged Baptists to support all realistic attempts to redress those wrongs. Third, it accepted that a solemn responsibility lies on Baptist people—as well as on the government—to honor the provisions of the Treaty of Waitangi and declared that more needs to be done in this respect.[72]

These were not empty words. In the following years the Baptist Union invested considerable energy helping churches embark on a "bi-cultural journey." Since the early 1970s the Baptist Māori mission had transitioned into the Baptist Māori Department, focusing its efforts mainly on assisting and resourcing those churches that wanted to become more multiracial.[73] From the mid-1980s, however, under the leadership of Lionel Stewart, the Māori Department launched a more vigorous program to assist *all* Baptist churches in understanding and embracing Māori culture, to the extent that

---

[69] Charles Joe, "A New Obedience," *NZB*, December 1980, 10.

[70] Rua Turner, "Racism—If You Ignore It, It May Go Away," *NZB*, June 1982, 3.

[71] Michael O. Emerson and Christian Smith, *Divided by Faith: Evangelical Religion and the Problem of Race in America* (Oxford: Oxford University Press, 2000).

[72] "Baptists Go Bi-Cultural," *NZB*, December 1983, 9.

[73] "Union Council Meets," *NZB*, August 1972, 8.

it was consistent with Scripture. Through a series of *wananga*—residential learning courses—hundreds of Baptists came to experience, understand, and appreciate Māori culture. In many instances, misconceptions were dispelled, and racism exposed.[74]

A number of Baptist leaders and laypeople experienced a profound awakening toward Māori. They recognized that "guarantees given [to Māori] under the Treaty of Waitangi [had] not been honoured."[75] They realized that both state and church had pursued policies of cultural assimilation. These Baptists acknowledged that Pākehā settlement had severely disadvantaged Māori, and they confessed that it continued to do so. Colonization was not just a historical phenomenon but an ongoing reality.[76] This is how the *New Zealand Baptist* magazine put it: "Today's society reflects ongoing discrimination against Māori. This discrimination is not always obvious. It is frequently subtle, institutionalised, cultural and has its roots in a colonial era. It contributes to disproportionately high numbers of Māori amongst the unemployed, the homeless, and the low-income workers."[77]

What was the Christian response to this injustice? One minister adamantly insisted, "We need to acknowledge our Pākehā guilt. We did not commit the injustices. It was our forebears. But we have inherited the fruits. We have inherited a system that privileges Pākehā." He also spoke of the need to rebuild Māori culture: "If Māori have to compete in the Pākehā world, adopting Pākehā values, and Pākehā ways, most will fail."[78] For some Baptists, this at least meant putting their own house in order: embracing Māori traditions and practices in their church life, preferencing Māori forms of worship that were strange to Pākehā but normal to Māori, and making space for Māori voices to be heard in the Baptist Union's decision-making processes.[79] It meant intentionally laying down power and privilege, and

---

[74] Lionel Stewart, "Maoritanga and Kingdom Life," *NZB*, July 1988, 3; Susan Hayes, "Removing Cultural Blinkers on Somebody Else's Turf," *NZB*, August 1988, 8; "Te Wananga Hapai Ako," *NZB*, September 1989, 14.

[75] "Te Christian," *NZB*, March 1987, 4.

[76] Reese, "Reconciliation and the Quest for Pākehā Identity," 68.

[77] "Common Pakeha Questions on the Treaty of Waitangi," *NZB*, September 1988, 14.

[78] Laurie Guy, "Waitangi—Why Bother?" *NZB*, November 1990, 8.

[79] Alistair McKenzie, "Of Bishops, Deacons, Elders," *NZB*, March 1987, 12.

partnering with Māori in accordance with the Treaty of Waitangi.[80] By 1990, when New Zealand celebrated the 150th anniversary of the treaty, there were signs that these changes were beginning to occur. The worship in some churches had a distinctively Māori flavor.[81] The annual Baptist Assembly met that year for the first time on a *marae*, a traditional Māori meeting ground. The president of the Baptist Union was a Māori and urging the movement along the bicultural journey.

At a local level, however, most churches were far from bicultural in their practices, personnel, or power structures.[82] For most white Baptists—the overwhelming majority of Baptists—any talk of biculturalism or justice for Māori provoked a mild shrug at best, or fierce resistance at worst. Some struggled to see the structural nature of racism or the privileges associated with whiteness.[83] One frustrated correspondent informed the editor of the *New Zealand Baptist*, "You would help many ordinary people like myself if you would publish evidence of significant discrimination against the Māori people....One needs something better than the apparently irrational statement...that Māoris are oppressed because in proportion to their population there are more of them in prison."[84] Another correspondent raged that it was simply "evil to suggest to Māori people that their health problems are due to discrimination against them rather than to factors within their control." In "a free and just society" like New Zealand, people make their own choices between "diligence or idleness, self-discipline or self-indulgence." Some will progress, and some will go backward.[85]

For other Baptists, pandering to Māori culture was itself a form of racism. One exasperated correspondent asked, "Why is it that today everything Māori is good, and everything Pākehā is not good?...Why do [you] persist in making me feel guilty?"[86] Another responded with "disgust and anger" to

---

[80] Cf. Soong-Chan Rah, *The Next Evangelicalism: Freeing the Church from Western Cultural Captivity* (Downers Grove, IL: InterVarsity Press, 2009), 123–24, 161–62.

[81] "Christian Beliefs in a Maori Idiom," *NZB*, October 1980, 6; Phillip Donnell, "How We Made a Maori and Pakeha Church in Gisborne," *NZB*, September 1988, 1.

[82] "Maori Ministry," *NZB*, April 1985, 9; "Te Christian," *NZB*, March 1987, 4. See also Haurua, "Korero Tuku Iho," 60–63.

[83] Scholars have pointed out that those who enjoy privilege are often the ones most blind to it. See, for example, Claire Gray, Nabila Jaber, and Jim Anglem, "Pakeha Identity and Whiteness: What Does It Mean to Be White?" *Sites* 10, no. 2 (2013): 82–106.

[84] E. L. Sellens, "Racism Reaction," *NZB*, August 1982, 4.

[85] R. N. S. Sandbrook, "Brethren, Come Ye Out," *NZB*, May 1986, 2.

[86] L. Jenson, "Mourning Comment," *NZB*, May 1989, 2.

claims that "the Pākehā majority who control the institutions of our society receive more benefits from these institutions (education, justice, industry and the like) than Māori people." This statement was, he said, "a malicious indictment of our nationality." He took particular exception, however, to use of the term "Pākehā." It was "insulting" and bad taste "to separate those of Māori ancestry and the rest." It reeked of racism.[87] These Baptists wanted to forget the past and move on as one big happy amnesiac nation.[88]

In comparison with New Zealand's other mainline denominations, New Zealand Baptists in 1990 were far less committed to pursuing justice for or reconciliation with Māori. Several reasons exist for this relative apathy. It can be explained, partly, by the strongly evangelical orientation of most Baptists. In New Zealand, their preoccupation with individual conversion blinded many Baptists to the systemic realities of racism and the social implications of the gospel.[89] When in November 1959 the editor of the *Baptist* magazine devoted a whole column to the exclusion of Māori from the All Blacks' rugby tour of South Africa, one correspondent angrily responded, "The duty of every fundamental and evangelical church is to preach Christ and Him crucified and risen again, to succour and encourage those who have put their trust in Him, and to build up His Saints in their most Holy Faith." It was not the church's duty to address patterns of structural injustice.[90] Another correspondent went even further: "When Jesus left this world he left us one job, and one job only—evangelism—seeking and winning lost souls."[91] For this reason, the president of the Baptist Union could declare that the church "knows neither race nor nation, but only individuals and their need of God and a living Christ."[92] This emphasis on the individual rendered many Baptists colorblind.

This colorblindness was exacerbated by theological developments in the second half of the twentieth century. From the 1960s onward, the rise of

---

[87] Gordon Haycock, "Reeking of Racism," *NZB*, December 1983, 4.

[88] This call to forget past wrongs is common among those who enjoy the fruits of colonization. See Ani Mikaere, "Are We All New Zealanders Now? A Māori Response to the Pākehā Quest for Indigeneity," in *Colonising Myths—Māori Realities: He Rukuruku Whakaaro* (Wellington: Huia, 2011), 106.

[89] In *Divided by Faith* Emerson and Smith argue that white evangelicals in the United States, because of their preoccupation with evangelism and the individual, have also tended to perpetuate the racial divisions and inequities they ostensibly opposed.

[90] "Maoris and the All Blacks," *NZB*, November 1959, 312.

[91] "Christian Life Crusades," *NZB*, June 1963, 160.

[92] A. R. Jordan, "Heroic Christianity," *NZB*, November 1956, 266.

neo-liberalism within mainline Protestant churches had a profound effect on conservative evangelical Baptists, who came to associate social justice with liberal theology.[93] Polarization between evangelism and social justice caused many Baptist churches to became "more retreatist, more pietistic and more narrow in their understanding of the gospel."[94] It helps to explain why the members of Tauranga Baptist Church, for example, chose to formally disassociate themselves from the National Council of Churches' protests in relation to the Treaty of Waitangi.[95] During this period, the charismatic renewal also had a profound impact on the New Zealand Baptist movement.[96] In many churches, charismatic renewal tended to foster an introspective emphasis on personal experience rather than social concern. It also often generated a heightened awareness of spiritual warfare, demons, and the occult. Many charismatics classified all Māoritanga—Māori culture—as demonic.[97] Even some young Māori within the Baptist movement became afraid that efforts to integrate Māori culture in church life and worship would "only bring people back into the darkness of the occult again."[98]

Apathy among Baptists toward Māori and their welfare can also be traced, finally, to the limited relational engagement between the two groups. From its beginnings, the Baptist movement has been almost exclusively Pākehā in its composition. In 1990, it was still very much that way.[99] This lack of relational engagement with Māori deprived most Baptists of any real sensitivity to the challenges facing Māori, either in society or in the church.[100] Consequently, as the twentieth century drew to a close, it could not be said that the Baptist churches of New Zealand clearly embodied, in

---

[93] See John Tucker, *A Braided River: New Zealand Baptists and Public Issues, 1882–2000* (Bern: Peter Lang, 2013), 232–38.

[94] Laurie Guy, ed., *Baptists in Twentieth-Century New Zealand: Documents Illustrating Baptist Life and Development* (Auckland: NZ Baptist Research and Historical Society, 2005), xiv.

[95] Report on Tauranga Baptist Church, *NZB*, June 1983, 14.

[96] For a discussion of the influence of charismatic Christianity on New Zealand Baptists, see Tucker, *Braided River*, 230–32.

[97] Lionel Stewart, "Church Must Set Own House in Order in Aotearoa," *NZB*, June 1988, 8.

[98] "Cultural Signposts Point to Gospel," *NZB*, April 1987, 4.

[99] Of the seventy thousand people who identified as Baptist in the 1986 New Zealand census, fewer than three thousand claimed Maori ethnicity. See Bolitho, *Meet the Baptists*, 28.

[100] For a similar analysis in relation to the churches of Aotearoa more generally, see Guy, *Shaping Godzone*, 301.

their life together, Carey's gospel of reconciliation—at least not insofar as most Māori were concerned.

This narrative of Baptist interaction with Māori in New Zealand bears some similarities to the story of Baptists and indigenous people in other settler societies. Early attempts to preach the gospel were marred by a sense of superiority and insensitivity to Māori culture. These were followed in the mid-twentieth century by a period of patient and careful contextualization, at least on the part of a few Baptist missionaries and a small number of Baptist churches. This relational connection with Māori served to awaken some Baptists to the realities of racial discrimination in New Zealand. During the 1970s and 1980s a few Baptist leaders became increasingly vocal about the systemic nature of racism and called for radical changes in both church and society. They were motivated both by the gospel of the kingdom and by the covenantal commitments expressed in the Treaty of Waitangi. It must be said, though, that these leaders constituted a very small minority. The reality is that racist attitudes embedded in New Zealand culture generally impeded Baptist attempts to proclaim the Christian gospel.

A Māori Response by Rāwiri Auty (Ngāti Kahungunu ki te Wairoa)

I am grateful to Dr. John Tucker for inviting a Māori response to his story of Baptist mission among Māori. My perspective, shared briefly here, is drawn from experience as a Māori Baptist pastor and interviews with seventeen prominent Māori Baptists.[101] As a rhetorical device I have chosen to reframe the titles in Dr. Tucker's account into questions that suggest a Māori view of Baptist and Māori engagement for each of the three periods identified.

Cultural Insensitivity or Superiority?

The first section, "Proclaiming the Gospel to Māori: Cultural Insensitivity," traces the taking of the gospel to Māori, albeit in a culturally insensitive manner. In many ways, the Baptist situation epitomized "the historic missions community...seeing its purpose through a lens of ethnic superiority and con-

[101] What I present here is my personal view, informed by historical research and interviews on the topic of Māori and Baptist engagement. I do not speak for all Māori. There may be other equally valid Māori viewpoints not articulated here.

trol,"[102] and I would argue that this is far more than cultural insensitivity. Māori were marked as inferior to Europeans by skin color as much as by a culture that appeared uncivilized. An 1881 *New Zealand Baptist* provided an example of marking people by color when it proclaimed that "in Christ the dusky Māori now clasps hands with the swarthy Negro, or the Red Indian, or the pale European."[103] The reference to Fairbrother being "a fair brother...going to proclaim the gospel to his dark brethren" is another example. Depictions such as these, of multicolored brethren clasping hands in Christ, obfuscate the racist hierarchy that underpinned such sentiments—a construct whereby whiteness was pure and blackness considered evil or cursed.[104]

I acknowledge that the early efforts at mission to Māori were not deliberately racist but also that the mission's sense of cultural superiority was detrimental to the spread of the gospel among Māori. It is little wonder that Māori asked for the first Baptist missionary to be removed and that Baptist mission work among Māori faltered. Soon after, the mission focus shifted to saving souls elsewhere, leaving a seventy-year gap until the next concerted attempt to engage with Māori.

Patient Contextualization by Whom?

The section on "Proclaiming the Gospel among Māori: Patient Contextualization" describes a more contextual mission among Māori. It developed in a few selected areas and was not representative of the prevailing Baptist preoccupations of the time. As Dr. Tucker points out, Baptists were largely a settler movement serving a settler society. From a Māori perspective, however, the term "settler" is highly problematic. It masks an erasure of Māori from society that is painful for Māori to consider, even now. A "settler" society leaves no space for the indigenous people of the land.

During this period, however, Baptists were beginning to notice Māori again. The mission among Māori launched in 1954 signaled the beginning of a new concerted Baptist effort to evangelize Māori. The more contextualized

---

102 George E. Tinker, *Missionary Conquest: The Gospel and Native American Cultural Genocide* (Minneapolis: Fortress, 1993), 3, quoted in Richard Twiss, *Rescuing the Gospel from the Cowboys: A Native American Expression of the Jesus Way* (Downers Grove: InterVarsity Press, 2015), 72.

103 T. L. Davies, "Regeneration—An Exposition and an Appeal," *NZB*, October 1881, 132.

104 Willie James Jennings, *The Christian Imagination: Theology and the Origins of Race* (New Haven: Yale University Press, 2010), 47, 190.

Māori work opened up in the lower Waikato, and the handful of wonderful Pākehā missionaries of the time are rightly celebrated by Pākehā and Māori Baptists alike. But a wider view shows the Anglicans and Catholics had been operating contextualized missionary efforts among Māori for over one hundred years by the time the Baptists started in earnest. Baptists were very slow to come to the party.

Covenantal Biculturalism at Māori Expense?

The third period of "Proclaiming the Gospel with Māori: Covenantal Biculturalism" saw Baptists begin a bicultural journey with Māori—an ongoing journey that continues to this day. I would contend, though, that the significant shifts of this period, including the appointment of Charles Joe as the first Māori leader of the Māori Mission, and then Lionel Stewart as the first Māori *tumuaki* (superintendent), came at the expense of ongoing mission and discipleship to and by Māori. Māori leaders were quickly co-opted to the task of educating the largely Pākehā church on how to become bicultural. Lionel's catch-cry of "Kia Kotahi Tatou" (Let us all be one together) was embraced by the denomination, while work with and for Māori was put to one side. Although seeds of unity were sown, the fruits of this unity can be difficult for Māori to see. David Moko, the current *kaihautu* (leader) of Mānatu Iriiri Māori (Baptist Māori Ministries) shares his reflection on these times:

> There was...a cost for Māori...around that bicultural *kōrero* [conversation]....It was great that Lionel traveled around the country to all our Baptist churches and educated Pākehā...but...[Māori] lost more, they sacrificed more to what Pākehā gained....If you were to quantify the knowledge equity, that went Pākehā way, as opposed to what wasn't developed [for Māori], that equity never came the other way.[105]

Dr. Tucker's accurate and compelling history of Baptist mission among Māori is a welcome addition to the historical record. I am honored to have been invited to provide a Māori perspective on that story. Mine is noticeably less positive, and less optimistic, but it is not without gratitude to Pākehā Baptists who have labored among us and with us. We are certainly not without hope. We pray and look forward to a time when we will worship and minister together in true bicultural covenantal relationship, for the sake of the gospel of Jesus Christ.

---

[105] David Moko and Denise Moko interview by Rāwiri Auty, Auckland, September 10, 2016.

7

Saving "Primitive" Peoples: Southern Baptists' Mission to the Yoruba, 1875–1905

Melody Maxwell

The relationship of gospel and culture is an ongoing debate in Christian mission. Does becoming a Christian mean accepting Western habits? Is a mass conversion acceptable in a collectivist culture? Can a person follow Jesus while venerating ancestors? Are some cultures more Christian than others? Generations of missionaries and converts have discussed questions such as these. In recent years, scholars of mission have emphasized the contextualization of the gospel into forms familiar to indigenous cultures. This was not the case at the peak of the modern missionary movement in the 1800s and early 1900s. During this period, many Western missionaries assumed that Christianity and "civilization"—becoming Western—were inseparable. They believed that privileged Western Christians, with their advanced culture and religion, had a duty to uplift the poor "heathens" living in primitive societies.

This was true for most missionaries sent out by the Foreign Mission Board of the Southern Baptist Convention (SBC), a large Baptist denomination in the southern United States. Southern Baptist missions publications spoke frequently of the need to help those living in the "bonds and superstitions of heathenism," who, as one report put it, "sit in the region and the shadow of death."[1] This attitude of superiority was especially evident in Southern Baptist mission efforts to Africa, which they and others considered the "dark continent."[2] The SBC's mission to the Yoruba people of present-day Nigeria, one of the first the denomination established, exemplifies the way Southern Baptist missionaries understood the relationship between

[1] "Notes," *Foreign Mission Journal* 49, no. 7 (January 1899): 250.

[2] "Report of the Foreign Mission Board," *Southern Baptist Convention Annual 1888*, XXXV. The Roman numerals are page numbers, but this is the style in which they were numbered in the FMB/HMB reports in the SBC annual.

gospel and culture around the turn of the twentieth century. In this chapter I analyze Southern Baptist missionaries' complicated and condescending attitudes toward African peoples and cultures and argue that these attitudes hindered their efforts to spread the gospel among the Yoruba between 1875 and 1905.

Birthed in Controversy

From the early days of the modern missionary movement, when William Carey and colleagues traveled to India, Baptists have played a significant role in global missions. In 1814, Baptists in the United States organized what came to be known as the Triennial Convention in order to work together to send domestic and foreign missionaries. But the growing sectional controversy in the United States made relationships between Baptists in the North and the South tenuous. Debates over slavery and abolition threatened to divide the Triennial Convention. Southerners deliberately nominated a slaveholder to serve as a missionary through the Convention's Home Mission Society. After the society declined to consider this application and stated their disapproval of slavery, delegates from throughout the South met in Augusta, Georgia, in May 1845, and formed the Southern Baptist Convention.[3]

The SBC, then, was founded in part to support the institution of slavery. South Carolinian Richard Fuller defended slavery in a debate with Frances Wayland in the *Christian Reflector*, a Boston Baptist newspaper. According to Fuller, "The condition of the African has been vastly improved, physically, intellectually, morally, and religiously, by his transportation to these shores"; slaves were thankful for "the great goodness of God in transferring them from the thick darkness of their own land to the privileges they enjoy in ours."[4] With such remarks, Fuller avowed that American culture was far superior to the cultures of Africa, without acknowledging the injustices involved in human slavery. In his view, and those of many other Southern Baptists of the time, white "Anglo-Saxons" who made up the majority of the American population had a superior civilization, religion, and culture to those of "primitive" societies that did not have the same history of Christianization and industrialization. Africans who had been transported to

---

[3] William Estep, *Whole Gospel—Whole World: The Foreign Mission Board of the Southern Baptist Convention, 1845–1995* (Nashville: Broadman & Holman, 1994), 54–55.

[4] Richard Fuller and Francis Wayland, *Domestic Slavery Considered as a Scriptural Institution*, ed. Nathan Finn and Keith Harper (Macon, GA: Mercer University Press, 2008), 98.

the United States against their will should not be unhappy with their enslavement, Fuller believed, but instead should be grateful that they had come to such a blessed land.

These sentiments are jarring to twenty-first-century interpreters but were common among southerners in the mid-nineteenth century. In their attempts to defend slavery, white southerners often assumed that African cultures were less advanced and peoples of African descent were less intelligent than themselves.[5] Yet Southern Baptists also believed that God had given them the responsibility to spread the message of salvation through Jesus Christ to all peoples of the world. In this view, even Africans deserved to hear the gospel, although they remained part of an inferior race. So it happened that Southern Baptists, who supported the enslavement of African Americans, began missionary efforts to liberate the souls of the peoples of Africa in 1850.

Sending Southern missionaries had been a primary goal in the organization of the SBC in 1845, and the denomination quickly formed Domestic and Foreign Mission Boards (FMB). The FMB appointed its first missionaries, serving in China, within a year. In their 1846 report FMB leaders discussed their next mission field: "Another important position, which the Board consider themselves as specially invited to occupy, is Africa.... Various considerations combine to urge upon our sympathies, her spiritual interests. Many of her sons are among us."[6] Because of their ties to African American slaves, these leaders implied, they had a special connection with the peoples of Africa. (Their slaves may have disagreed.) The first Southern Baptist missionary to Central Africa, Thomas Bowen, began serving among the Yoruba people of present-day Nigeria in 1850.[7] Other missionaries soon joined Bowen, but the work was slow. Disease claimed the lives of many missionaries, and the American Civil War resulted in a loss of funding and personnel for the FMB's efforts. Only around 1875 were Southern Baptists able to send new missionaries and reestablish most of their mission stations in what

---

[5] Many white northerners, while not advocating as vociferously for slavery, held similar views.

[6] "Fields of Labor," June 10, 1846, entry in *All Things "Ordered and Sure": Southern Baptist Missions in Central Africa, 1846–1880* (Richmond, VA: IMB Archives and Research Department, 2007) 1.

[7] Travis Collins, *The Baptist Mission of Nigeria, 1850–1993* (Ibadan: Nigerian Baptist Bookstores, 1993), 6.

they called Yorubaland, their most significant African mission field during this period.[8] This chapter focuses on that second wave of missionaries.

Racial Ideologies

In descriptions of their mission efforts in Africa, Southern Baptist missionaries and missions leaders repeatedly affirmed their own racial and cultural superiority while also claiming a biblical mandate for the Christianization of Africa. Multiple reports on Southern Baptists' African mission work alluded to Old Testament verses about Ethiopia (Cush), which they and other interpreters took to refer to the continent of Africa.[9] An 1886 FMB report claimed, "Never was that word of God which declares that Ethiopia shall stretch forth her hands unto God so thrillingly realized by the church of God as to-day."[10] This statement echoed the words of Psalm 68:31, which promised, "Princes shall come out of Egypt; Ethiopia shall soon stretch out her hands unto God."[11] Notably, this and related verses were also quoted by Africans and those of African descent who advocated African independence during this time as part of the movement called Ethiopianism. Ethiopianists hoped to return Africa to native rule, apart from foreign control.[12] Southern Baptist missionaries who eagerly quoted the same Bible verses about Ethiopia did not have this desire. Ironically, the missionaries used verses championed by advocates of African independence to justify the very foreign mission efforts that the Ethiopianists wanted to end.

Other biblical allusions that Southern Baptists made to Africa were not as positive. For example, in an 1876 letter, missionary W. J. David stated that he "beheld those sons and daughters of Ham…without God and hope."[13] This reference to Africans as descendants of Ham was familiar to

---

[8] I. A. Adedoyin, *A Short History of the Nigerian Baptist* (Ibadan: Nigerian Baptist Bookstores, 1998), 7. See also S. Ademola Ajayi, "The American Civil War of 1861–1865: A Major Challenge to the Survival of Early Baptists' Ventures in Nigeria," *Baptist History and Heritage* 43, no. 2 (Spring 2008): 86–95.

[9] This understanding was the result of a mistranslation in the Septuagint, which used the term "Aithiopia," a word that the Greeks used to refer to any land south of their known world (Ogbu U. Kalu, "West African Christianity," in Charles E. Farhadian, *Introducing World Christianity* [Malden, MA: Wiley-Blackwell, 2012], 44).

[10] *Southern Baptist Convention Annual 1886*, 24.

[11] King James Version (KJV).

[12] Kalu, "West African Christianity," 44.

[13] W. J. David, "Abeokuta and the Interior," June 19, 1876, entry in *All Things "Ordered and Sure,"* 81.

Southern Baptists. It alluded to the events of Genesis 9, where Noah's son Ham "saw the nakedness of his father" when Noah was drunk, with Noah subsequently proclaiming, "Cursed be Canaan [Ham's son]; a servant of servants shall he be unto his brethren."[14] Other biblical texts referred to Egypt as "the land of Ham."[15] Southern Christians often used these passages to justify slavery, claiming that contemporary Africans were the descendants of Ham, whom God had determined would forever be servants because of the way Ham dishonored Noah.[16] Multiple Southern Baptist missionaries referred to the African people among whom they served as children of Ham, thus implicitly approving of their subjugation.

Missionaries also at times spoke negatively of African peoples and cultures. P. A. Eubank detailed "obstacles to the gospel" among the Yoruba, including what he perceived as "the African's satisfaction with his condition," "his [the African's] lack of veracity and the consequent distrust of him," and "his [the African's] ignorance and superstition."[17] Such words demonstrated stereotypes of Africans as lazy, untrustworthy, and ignorant—some of the same stereotypes that white southerners had of African Americans. These ideas likely revealed the influence of southern prejudices on missionary thought. Rather than seeking to understand the Yorubas' relational culture and high-context communication, Southern Baptist missionaries tended to regard the Yoruba people and culture negatively. The missionaries believed that Africans needed to adopt Western habits in order to follow the gospel fully.

Southern Baptist mission leaders regularly discussed whether African Americans might serve as effective missionaries among the Yoruba, again demonstrating racial prejudice in their opinions. They clearly connected African Americans and Africans, with an SBC committee member chiding African Americans for not being more "interested in the salvation of their heathen brethren."[18] (Perhaps he had not considered that some African Americans were occupied with meeting their own basic needs in a challenging environment.) Although the United States had abolished the slave trade in 1808, meaning that only elderly African Americans in the late nineteenth

---

[14] Genesis 9:22, 25 (KJV).

[15] See Psalm 105:23, for example.

[16] See Stephen R. Haynes, *Noah's Curse: The Biblical Justification of American Slavery* (Oxford: Oxford University Press, 2007).

[17] "Report of the Foreign Mission Board," *Southern Baptist Convention Annual 1884*, V.

[18] J. K. Pace, "Work among Negroes," *Southern Baptist Convention Annual 1899*, 34.

century had been born outside of the country, Southern Baptists had no hesitation in identifying them as Africans, just like the Yoruba. African Americans, in Southern Baptists' view, had outsider status and were not true southerners. Southern Baptists sought to enlist African American missionaries to serve in Africa, their so-called homeland, while explaining that, as one white missionary put it, "a superior man of our own race is needed on the field as an enlightened instructor, a wise counselor, and a bold leader."[19] Such words clearly demonstrated the sense of racial superiority held by white southerners. While those of African descent could labor on the mission field, only a white man could be entrusted to serve as their leader.

Some white missionaries thought that Africans and African Americans would be the most effective at evangelizing the Yoruba (with proper supervision from a white leader, of course). Others agreed with C. E. Smith, who said, "If you can't get white [missionaries] send black ones."[20] In this view, African Americans were less desirable as missionaries, but could serve if not enough white men could be enlisted. If "field negroes" were appointed, a mission leader testified, "It will not be necessary for them to have the frequent vacations that white men have."[21] Apparently he believed that African Americans who worked the land were used to deprivations and acclimated to tropical diseases, and thus had no need for the periods of rest that were granted to white missionaries. With such sentiments from Southern Baptist leaders, is it any surprise that some black Baptists were hesitant to work together with them in their African mission?[22] While racial prejudice was common among white Americans during this time, this type of condescension was especially strong among Southern Baptists, with their recent ties to slavery. Such ideology hindered Southern Baptist missionaries from identifying with the people among (or alongside) whom they served, likely making them appear aloof and conveying the belief that Christianity, and the Christian God, favored white Westerners. This attitude and way of thinking did not attract large numbers of Yoruba people to the faith, to say the least.

---

[19] "Status of the Missions," May 8, 1873, entry in *All Things "Ordered and Sure,"* 69.

[20] "Report of the Foreign Mission Board," *Southern Baptist Convention Annual 1893*, XXX.

[21] "Report of the Foreign Mission Board," *Southern Baptist Convention Annual 1893*, XXXIV.

[22] See Sandy D. Martin, "The Debate over Interracial Cooperation among Black Baptists in the African Mission Movement, 1895–1905," *Journal of the Interdenominational Theological Center* 13 (Spring 1986): 291–303.

The Problem of Polygamy

One aspect of Yoruba culture that Southern Baptist missionaries found especially troubling was polygamy. Many Yoruba men married multiple wives, which missionaries believed was unbiblical and unacceptable for Christians. The Yoruba, however, viewed polygamy as part of their cultural traditions, a sign of wealth, and a way for women to have protection and provision. In addition, as one historian has noted, "The incidence of polygamy increased dramatically after colonization. New wealth gained from trade with European settlements enabled African men to afford the bridewealth required for additional wives."[23] Ironically, the presence of Westerners in Africa led to an increase in the very African practice that most Western missionaries were trying to prohibit.

Rather than viewing polygamy as an acceptable cultural practice, Southern Baptist missionaries (and those of most other denominations) believed that polygamy was sinful and incompatible with Christianity. FMB missionary P. A. Eubank, among others, felt strongly about this topic. He explained in an 1884 letter to supporters that he was "engaged in a civil war against polygamy and bigamy,"[24] using strong rhetoric to indicate the challenge that he believed polygamy presented to his ministry. Throughout this period, missionaries frequently commented on the difficulties that polygamy caused for their work. Many potential converts did not join the church because they were not willing to give up their polygamous marriages. Unlike the missionaries, not all Yorubas were convinced that polygamy was incompatible with Christianity. After all, they pointed out, weren't multiple Old Testament leaders polygamists?

Southern Baptist missionaries disagreed, asserting that the New Testament presented an ethic of monogamy. Yet there were differing opinions among them in the early years of their mission endeavors about how to deal with polygamists who confessed faith in Christ. The question was a complicated one. Eubank discussed this issue at some length in a letter to H. A. Tupper, corresponding secretary of the Foreign Mission Board:

---

[23] Timothy Willem Jones, "The Missionaries' Position: Polygamy and Divorce in the Anglican Communion, 1888–1988," *Journal of Religious History* 35, no. 3 (2011): 395.

[24] P. A. Eubank, "The Work in Yoruba," *Foreign Mission Journal*, March 1884, 3.

> 1. Shall we require polygamists, who have become such while heathen, to give up all their wives but one on their application for church membership?...
>
> 2. [If so,] What wife shall be retained?...
> 3. Should the wives who have been put away be taught to remain unmarried, or to marry another man?
> 4. Should the wives of a polygamist be required to leave him before being received?
> 5. If so, should they be allowed to marry again?[25]

As these questions demonstrate, prohibiting polygamy may have been simple in theory, but it was challenging in practice. Should missionaries really advocate divorce, which they also considered sinful, for those in polygamous marriages? If so, what would become of the wives who were forced to leave their family compounds? To some Yoruba Christians, these questions were unnecessary and troubling. Polygamy was a part of their social system, they believed, and breaking up families was in no way Christian. Surely men and women could follow Jesus without abandoning their spouses.

Yet missionaries persisted in their opposition to polygamy. By the turn of the twentieth century, the Southern Baptist mission was united in its stance on the topic as it related to church membership. In a strongly worded 1903 resolution, the missionaries expressed their opinion:

> Whereas polygamy is a great evil in this country, and whereas we believe it to be contrary to the spirit of the teachings of the New Testament, and whereas if allowed by the churches, we believe it will be their spiritual ruin, therefore be it resolved that, we advise against receiving polygamous persons into church membership, and further resolve that, we advise that the hand of fellowship be withdrawn from persons who go into polygamy.[26]

Polygamy was a "great evil" that led to "spiritual ruin," they insisted, leaving no doubt about the intensity of their conviction on the topic. Notably, their forbears had made no such statements about slavery. It was apparently easier for the missionaries to note the "evils" of another culture than of their own.

---

[25] P. A. Eubank, "A Hard Question," *Foreign Mission Journal*, October 1885, 3. Unfortunately, we do not have Tupper's reply.

[26] Minutes of the Annual Meeting of the African Mission, 1903, Southern Baptist Historical Library and Archives (SBHLA), Nashville, TN.

As missionaries preached and visited churches, they spoke against polygamy and monitored membership records to make sure that polygamists had not been admitted, demonstrating the power that they maintained over the congregations they had established. Missionary S. G. Pinnock described an 1895 church visit in this way: "I then gave them a statement of Scriptural evidence on the question of polygamy, urging upon them strict observance of God's law."[27] Among behaviors that the missionaries considered sinful, polygamy became one of the most significant when considering church membership. Gluttons and liars (and even slaveowners) might be admitted to the church; polygamists would not.[28] Unsurprisingly, this restriction kept membership numbers low, especially among middle-aged men. Missionaries repeatedly confessed that in their work in the region, "the obstacles have been great" and the results meager.[29] Their strong stance against polygamy hindered the effectiveness of their ministry efforts among the Yoruba.

The Rise of the Native Church

Not all Yoruba Christians agreed with the position of the missionaries against polygamy. In fact, some had begun to resent the missionaries' control and attempts at Westernization, influenced by Ethiopianism and its emphasis on African self-rule. Influential thinkers of African descent, such as Edward Blyden and James Holly, promoted ideas of African equality and independence, in contrast to the FMB's 1885 statement that "the brightest hopes for Africa seem now based upon European and American colonization."[30] Missionaries believed that they and their governments knew what was best for Africa; many Africans strongly disagreed. Some Africans relinquished the English names they had adopted at baptism and resumed using their indigenous names, or created them. David Brown Vincent, for example, became Mojola Agbebi. In an 1894 report to the SBC, missionary C. E. Smith remarked that "Bro. Murray has recently changed his name to L. O.

---

[27] "Africa," *Foreign Mission Journal*, August 1895, 401.

[28] In 1918 the mission created the category of "friends" of the church for polygamists. "Friends" were not allowed to participate in baptism or the Lord's Supper, but could profess their faith in Christ (Minutes of Called Meeting, Oyo, January 16, 1918, SBHLA).

[29] "Report of the Foreign Mission Board," *Southern Baptist Convention Annual 1887*, V.

[30] *Southern Baptist Convention Annual 1885*, 48. See also "Ethiopianism," blackpast.org, http://www.blackpast.org/gah/ethiopianism, and Ogbu U. Kalu, "Ethiopianism in African Christianity," in *African Christianity: An African Story* (Trenton, NJ: Africa World Press, 2007), 258–77.

Fadepe," adding, "I do not know his reason."[31] Smith was apparently puzzled by this shift—either unaware of its significance within Ethiopianism or feigning ignorance. Either way, he demonstrated the missionaries' distance from this movement.

Indeed, Southern Baptist missionary reports during this time lamented the "bitter race feeling" that had "swept over" the land and decried the "stinging severity" of Africans who "seem to favor the white man's extermination in Africa."[32] Such strong words demonstrated their displeasure and surprise at what they considered the disloyalty of some of their converts. Just as their ancestors had expected African American slaves to submit to their authority, the missionaries believed that the formerly "heathen" Yoruba Christians should gratefully assent to their leadership. The missionaries' implicit belief in their own racial superiority made it difficult for them to understand arguments for indigenous control.

Missionaries were distressed when, in 1888, their leading "native assistant," Moses Ladejo Stone, broke from the mission and began his own church. Of course, the missionaries' own Southern Baptist Convention had broken away from Northern Baptists just a few decades earlier, but the missionaries assumed that their group had the correct message and methods and should not split again. However, missionaries' failure to fully empower indigenous leadership resulted in a significant schism in the Yoruba mission. After disputes with missionary W. J. David over Stone's education and salary, Stone resigned from the First Baptist Church of Lagos. David did not inform the congregation of this matter, judging that the mission held sole authority over its employees. This inaction demonstrated David's belief in missionary superiority and control. When church members realized what had happened, sixty-three of them (a majority of the congregation) left and formed the Native Baptist Church, later named Ebenezer Baptist Church, demonstrating their own agency despite missionaries' attempts to maintain control.[33] Doctrinally, the new church was similar to missionary-founded churches; indigenous leadership was its distinguishing characteristic. Despite these similarities of belief, missionary P. A. Eubank lamented of Stone that "my son in the Gospel, the child of my tutelage, my trusted pupil on

---

[31] "Report of the Foreign Mission Board," *Southern Baptist Convention Annual 1894,* XXII.

[32] *Southern Baptist Convention Annual 1891*, 12; *Southern Baptist Convention Annual 1890,* XLI.

[33] Collins, *Baptist Mission*, 22–24; Adedoyin, *Short History*, 10–11.

whose head I laid my hands in ordination, has fallen."[34] In his view, Stone's resignation from the mission church and rejection of the missionaries' authority, as well as his establishment of a rival congregation, meant that he was no longer a virtuous Christian leader. A native church founded by a discontented African assistant was outside the realm of true Christianity.[35]

The mission suffered numerically as well as psychologically as a result of this split. By 1891, missionaries were seriously considering the possibility of turning over their church property to the native church—an idea that surely made them unhappy.[36] The Native Baptist Church and others like it were growing rapidly. Many such churches embraced traditional African customs, including polygamy, support of tribal chiefs, wearing traditional clothing, and worshiping in indigenous languages.[37] As Mojola Agbebi, who also led the schismatic Lagos congregation, put it, "To render Christianity indigenous to Africa, it must be watered by native hands, pruned with the native hatchet and tended with native earth."[38] These sentiments aligned with Ethiopianist thought but contrasted with missionaries' ideals of Western leadership and control. Unsurprisingly, they were more popular among Africans than were the missionaries' ways of thinking. Missionaries' frequent dismissal of indigenous culture and leadership hindered their own ministry efforts, but indirectly aided the growth of native congregations. Despite their efforts to direct the course of Yoruban Christianity, its future was African. Even after Stone and eventually Agbebi reconciled with mission leaders, independent, indigenous Baptist churches continued to flourish outside of missionary auspices.

Conclusion

In a sense, it is unsurprising that Southern Baptist missionaries in the late nineteenth and early twentieth centuries assumed that they and their culture were superior to the African peoples among whom they ministered. This

---

34 "Report of the Foreign Mission Board," *Southern Baptist Convention Annual 1889*, XX.

35 Not all missionaries agreed completely with Eubank; some were more sympathetic toward Stone.

36 "Report of the Foreign Mission Board," *Southern Baptist Convention Annual 1891*, XVI.

37 Kalu, "Ethiopianism in African Christianity," 272. Many of these churches went further than did the Native Baptist Church.

38 Mojola Agbebi, cited in Hazel King, "Cooperation in Contextualization," *Journal of Religion in Africa* 16, no. 1 (February 1986): 5.

attitude was common among Western colonizers and missionaries at the time; twenty-first-century interpreters must beware the temptation to judge historical actors by contemporary standards. Moreover, Southern Baptists in this period were steeped in southern culture, which included an understanding of white superiority; their denomination, in fact, had been formed in part to support slaveholders. In this context, it would be unexpected if they had not evinced racial prejudice. Still, it is remarkable to note the ways that Southern Baptist missionaries mixed ideologies of superiority and salvation as they worked among the Yoruba people. On the one hand, they professed an earnest desire to see Yoruba people accept the gospel and ensure their eternal bliss; on the other, they believed that Africans were inferior racially and culturally and should be subject to white leaders. Missionaries rejected Ethiopianism and traditional Yoruban cultural practices, while lamenting that few natives had converted to the faith they were attempting to spread. In their understanding, the gospel was closely associated with Western culture; "pagan" African cultures must be abandoned in order to follow Christ. Yet they seemed unaware that they imported the prejudices of their own culture to Africa alongside the gospel of Christ. These missionaries' negative views of the Yoruba people and culture ultimately hindered the very mission work in which they hoped to thrive. Emerging efforts by indigenous leaders proved to be more successful. Such contextualized approaches foreshadowed a more positive relationship that would develop between gospel and culture, alongside dramatic growth in African Christianity, in the decades that followed.

8

Zenana Missionaries and Cultural Constraints in Colonial Bengal, 1880s–1930s

Rosalind Gooden

Australasian Baptist single women missionaries started to arrive in Bengal, India in 1882, arriving there as the zenana mission movement was gaining momentum.[1] Serving as background to that event are three important earlier dates for the history of Baptist zenana missionaries: the establishment of the British Baptist Missionary Society (BMS) in 1792 with the work started by William Carey and the Serampore Trio, the successful attempts of later BMS missionary wives to visit Indian women in the *zenanas* or secluded quarters in the 1850s (particularly the efforts of Elizabeth Sale and Marianne Lewis), and the formation in 1867 of the Ladies Association for the Support of Zenana Work and Bible Women in India, in connection with the Baptist Missionary Society,[2] later known as the Baptist Zenana Mission (BZM).[3]

From 1867, leading British Baptist women, particularly wives of ministers, formed the committee of the BZM and were responsible for fundraising and finding suitable women for work in the zenanas of India. This committee responded to the requests of articulate missionary wives of BMS missionaries. Marianne Lewis's promotional paper (1866) was widely circulated among women's groups even as far away as Victoria, Australia, where an auxiliary to the BZM was formed.[4]

---

[1] The *zenana* was the portion of the house in a Hindu or Muslim household that was reserved for women, and the special constraint in this social context was that the missionary personnel must be women.

[2] BMS Zenana Mission Reports 1868–1880, Angus Archives, Oxford, UK.

[3] Brian Stanley, *The History of the Baptist Missionary Society, 1792–1992* (Edinburgh: T. & T. Clark, 1992), 150.

[4] Marianne Lewis, "A Plea for Zenanas," Baptist Zenana Mission papers (bound volume), Angus Archives, Oxford.

The BZM recruitment was aimed at women who were free to give more time to the work than the wives of missionaries. Single women, including widows, were accepted and financed by BZM. The missionary wives served as their supervisors. The wives reported to BZM and were carers of the single women. The BZM gradually built houses where a group of singles could live together as communities with the native Bible women.[5] The women's primary assigned role was to gain entrance to the women's quarters of the Indian homes. Regarding structures, Brian Stanley wrote,

> My conclusion that the BMS remained, even after the formation of the Baptist Zenana Mission, a predominantly male society, staffed and controlled almost entirely by men, reflected a view of the BZM as an important auxiliary to the work of the BMS but nothing more. Women had a specific but limited role to play on the field. In the BMS, as in other missionary societies, and as in church life, the assumption of male leadership and control remains inviolate. However, my impression was that the women who gained a substantial degree of independence of action in running the BZM were then reluctant to cede that independence when the BZM was absorbed into the BMS in 1914.[6]

The Indian culture determined the need for single women workers to become recognized as called of God for mission work rather than coming from the suffrage movement.

Colonial Initiatives

Practices for the Antipodean Colonial Baptist missions developed differently from those of the BMS/BZM. South Australian and Victorian Baptists, responding to BMS overtures, financed several Bengali agents (preachers), who were supervised from a distance by BMS missionaries. The South Australians centred their work in Faridpur District and the Victorians on Mymensingh. Faridpur was a new field of operation; Mymensingh had had BMS visitors. Eighteen years later, in 1882, the South Australian Baptist Mission Society (SABMS) sent their first missionaries, Ellen Arnold and Marie Gilbert, both single women. These two lived for their first year in

---

[5] The BZM zenana house was built in Calcutta in 1881 just before the arrival of Ellen Arnold and Marie Gilbert.

[6] Letter from Brian Stanley, Trinity College, Bristol, to Rosalind M. Gooden, January 5, 1994.

Calcutta with the Kerry family (BMS) and then moved to Faridpur. Their mentors there were Punchanon Biswas and his wife. Biswas was the first convert of the South Australian missionary efforts in Faridpur town who had visited South Australia in 1880 and was known and respected by the SABMS committee. SABMS seems to have had no hesitation in allowing their two women to move away from the care of the BMS into the newly built house at Faridpur. In fact, when Arnold had to be sent home for medical reasons, Gilbert was allowed to remain in Faridpur. SABMS extended their house so that the women from the other missions could live together for initial language learning and zenana work, thereby avoiding having to live in the metropolis of Calcutta for language instruction.

In the case of work in Mymensingh and Comilla, the BMS initially sent their own couples to these towns, but following a visit by the Reverend Alfred Baynes, BMS general secretary from London, in 1888, and consultation with the Australian missionaries, the BMS staff were withdrawn and those districts were left to the colonial societies to determine the work. Again, in both Mymensingh and Comilla single women were the first colonial workers for the Victorian Baptist Foreign Mission (VBFM) and the New South Wales Baptist Mission Society (NSWBMS).

Arnold, while on sick leave in 1884–1885, advocated a methodology for colonial societies.[7] In reporting the formation of the Queensland Baptist Mission Society, she wrote, "Two Zenana missionaries were to be sent out from this colony as soon as possible, with power to engage native agents as the work requires and as funds will permit."[8] She also recorded the following:

> As men missionaries cannot carry the gospel to the women of India whom it is so important to reach; as women missionaries can visit the homes of the people, conduct schools for girls and superintend the native preachers' work among the men of the country; as it costs less to support a European woman than a man; and as the work in these colonies is as yet young and funds are scarce it is advisable for each colony to send out zenana missionaries as speedily as possible, to accept the offer of housing and training them by South Australia, and to build a house for their occupation in their

[7] I have discovered that Arnold gave the identical proposal to the NSWBMS prior to visiting Queensland.

[8] *Queensland Freeman*, June 15, 1885, 5.

> own district as soon as may be. The option of engaging and dismissing native teachers and preachers, with the assistance of the secretary of the London Baptist Missionary Society, resident in Calcutta, should be allowed to these ladies, and they should be requested to use their own judgement in organising the work.[9]

Employing women to work in the zenanas was the initial plan. The women were also granted a supervisory role over native preachers: they could hire and fire preachers. The women were also to be trusted in choosing locations for establishing new work. Women missionaries were allowed to spearhead the initial phase in developing mission work in areas that were unevangelized. This option was not just a memorandum for Queensland but for the "work in the colonies" in general, providing significant backing of South Australia's offer of initial housing and guidance from the two women who had only been working there two years with the help of their "missionary," Punchanon Biswas.

The first eleven single women sent to Bengal from Australia arrived between 1882 and 1887, before any men were sent. The last of this Bengal group, Arnold, died there in 1931. But these were not the only women involved. In the period from 1882 to 1931, sixty-five single women were sent (compared with only twenty-eight men and eighteen married women), twenty-five of whom served for more than twenty years in Bengal, India.

Gender Marital Balance

	Men	Married Women	Zenana Missionaries	Total
1882–1891	2	1	19	22
1892–1901	8	3	13	24
1902–1911	5	3	10	18
1912–1921	7	7	13	27
1922–1931	6	4	10	20
	28	18	65	111

The first of these additional women to arrive were Iris Seymour (1888 VBFM) and Amy Parsons (1888 SABMS), who were already in Bengal by the time Baynes accepted the wisdom of allowing the colonials to work independently of the BMS. These two pioneers and also those who succeeded

[9] *Queensland Freeman*, June 15, 1885, 5.

them were part of the growing understanding of how zenana work needed to be conducted in the cultural context of Bengal.

With this general account as background, I now consider three aspects of the impact of the Bengali cultural context on the single zenana workers: bilingualism, biculturalism, and the constraints needed to become an "acceptable outsider" rather than being content to be accepted as an outsider.

Bilingualism

To be a Baptist missionary in Bengal in the nineteenth century was to be committed to bilingualism. Learning the Bengali language was viewed as essential for the sake of communicating the gospel.

Missionaries devoted considerable time to language study. Initially in Calcutta, Gilbert and Arnold arranged regular meetings with *pundits* (tutors), who taught them early each morning.[10] The system developed into two years of study with the requirements of passing formal exams and taking on no other responsibilities without permission. These two years of exams had to be completed in the first term of service. Rosalie Macgeorge,[11] just weeks after her arrival in Faridpur, described one of her methods of language learning:

> Yesterday I took my alphabet in the first book over to a house...and asked in dumb show [gestures without speech] for a lesson. Though I am reading little words, I cannot pronounce some of those dreadful letters the right way. The women were so amused at my mistakes, and four of them sat round me saying, Caw, caw,[12] till I felt in a regular rookery, and yet could not caw right at all. Then they called in a little fellow and told him to say caw, which he did as easily as you or I could say a.[13]

She was learning from ordinary users of the language and found children helpful. The educated language of the pundits and the *babus* of Bengali society was different from that of the average women. Abia Neville[14] noted that "the majority of the women speak a more or less corrupt form of the

---

[10] Arnold's diary of 1883 in Calcutta. The original is in the hands of Damien, a relative of her sister.

[11] Rosalie Macgeorge was the first missionary with the NZBMS.

[12] "Caw" is the first sound in the Bengali alphabet.

[13] Rosalie Macgeorge, *New Zealand Baptist*, April 1887, 62.

[14] Abia Neville was the second male missionary to arrive.

language that is difficult for an ordinary student of the vernacular to comprehend."[15] Importantly the Australian and New Zealand women were trying to learn to communicate with people, not just to read and write, although much of their examination was written rather than oral. However, training had to be more than bilingualism; there was also biculturalism, an understanding and willingness to live by the other culture.

Bengali Biculturalism: Impact on Zenana Missionaries

Noting reactions to differences in cultural practice is a useful method of tracing the level of impact of the culture on newcomers. Arnold and Gilbert's first letter to South Australian friends from Calcutta contained the following observations:

> How you would laugh if you could see how the people carry their babies. The poor little things have to sit straddle-legs on their mother's hip. Sometimes we long to take the poor little things and give them a good wash. The streets always seem to be swarming with poor, dirty, half-clothed men, women, and children, and as we walk amongst them, they jump out of our way as if they thought we were going to strike them....You know, only the rich women are shut up, and the poor women have to knock about and work very hard. Poor things, their faces look so miserable.[16]

Poverty ("poor" is used six times in that quote), dirt, lack of clothing, ambulant population, and misunderstood interactions interpreted as fear[17] are all items of note in this first letter. An invitation to a Christian wedding provoked comments on eating behavior and the issues of table fellowship:

> We all sat on the ground. I, being a guest, had a straw mat....In front of each was a large round brass dish with a good meal of rice and curry on it, and a brass vessel of water...and we began eating our rice with our fingers. The girls were immensely amused at my awkwardness...; but I felt I had greatly improved towards the end.[18]

---

[15] Abia Neville, *White unto Harvest: An Account of the Mission in Mymensingh, East Bengal* (Geelong: Victorian Baptist Foreign Mission, 1898), 61.

[16] *Truth and Progress*, March 1883, 30.

[17] This description represents a failure to recognizee their avoidance of contamination—a recognition of fear but a wrong interpretation of what was feared.

[18] *Truth and Progress*, March 1883, 30.

Similarly when the "five barley loaves"[19] arrived, they were invited to eat Bengali style. Fuller supplied the details:

> A table was spread...and chairs placed for each of us; when we sat down, a large brass plate was put before each one, containing rice and six different curries. A discussion arose, should we sit on mats or remain on the chairs; we soon decided in favour of chairs. Another point had to be settled, could we really manage to eat without spoons and forks? We resolved to try, and the gentleman of the house promised a prize to the one who disposed of the rice and curry in the neatest manner. It is a custom...in India not to sit down with the guests, but to remain standing; the servants may bring the dishes from the kitchen, but the lady and gentleman of the house esteem it a privilege to wait upon the guests. After dinner the host poured water over our hands, and we went into the women's apartment.[20]

Feeding guests was important; eating with them was not. As such, the concept of table fellowship had to be differently conceived in their culture. Using fingers to eat was not necessarily a result of poverty but of preference, and the missionaries struggled to overcome their assumptions that spoons were necessary. But they adjusted and later did not even comment on eating with fingers. To refuse food offered was unacceptable, as was the failure to serve food no matter the time of day.

The Aim to Be an Accepted Outsider: Living Arrangements

Single women missionaries needed to establish patterns for both living and working in Bengal that made sense to the Bengali community. In the colonial context of South Australia, Rev. Silas Mead had been a strong advocate of the selection of women deaconesses in Baptist churches, and Flinders Street Baptist Church had endorsed single women as missioners to the west and east ends of that city. Women's suffrage was granted in Adelaide in 1884. Thus, cognitively it was a relatively small step to commission women for ministry in Bengal—a logical extension of sphere, but it fundamentally removed the women from the protection and guidance of family and church leadership and gave them an experience of independent action. It was logical

[19] The women who came out in 1885 were Ellen Arnold (returning), Alice Pappin, Marion Fuller, Ruth Wilkin, and Martha Plested.

[20] Marion Fuller, *New Zealand Baptist*, September 1886, 144.

for Mead, from a colonial understanding of propriety, to arrange for the first two missionaries to board with the Kerry family in Calcutta on the BMS compound. They were thus under the protection of George Kerry, but once the women scattered to live in Comilla and Mymensingh there was a cultural clash regarding housing. Where ought the women live? VBFM had assumed that Fuller and Wilkin could share the house in Mymensingh with the Ellisons (BMS). The zenana women came to recognize a clash of worldviews caused by the proximity of living quarters for single women with others of the missionary team. The missionaries, as a group, believed that Bengalis thought that if single women moved in with married couples, they came as secondary wives or immoral sexual partners of married colleagues. The zenana missionaries therefore asked that they not have to share housing with couples or families and that their housing be a respectable distance from married couples. One of the reasons for the withdrawal of BMS staff from Mymensingh and Comilla was this cultural clash of perceptions regarding housing and sexual assumptions.

Another housing issue was the type of structure necessary to protect the life and health of missionaries in Bengal. The women often discussed the practical meaning of dwelling among the people, and one major issue for them was the compromises needed for foreigners to be able to cope with the enervating heat in India. In addition to standards of housing, diet and servants were also issues. Ellen Arnold, who was evacuated to Australia in 1884 and 1891, struggled with issues of *pukka* (a dwelling designed to be solid and permanent) housing and Western food. She envied Marie Gilbert's robust constitution that allowed her greater freedom to live closer to a Bengali lifestyle. Arnold and Gilbert arrived in India before the discovery of the link between mosquitoes and malaria. Early theories of the cause of malaria suggested that foreigners needed to sleep on raised platforms in *pukka* buildings.[21] However, Arnold ended her life living in a *kutcha* house with mud floors and a leaking thatched roof after forty-nine years of service, weak and ill, but still able to remain in Bengal. She preferred living with her Bible women to being cared for by Western colleagues.

---

[21] Mr. Lindeman addressed the meeting of the VBFM on the health of agents: "In view of malarious atmosphere of Bengal he recommended that a gallery about six feet from the floor be erected round the bedrooms" (VBFM, October 1895, 38). "The climate of India makes it imperative that the missionaries shall have the comfort and protection of masonry houses, and we cannot afford to risk the health and shorten the lives of our friends by residence in temporary structures" (*Australian Baptist*, April 21, 1914, 2).

Servants

The employment of help in the home was also an early and ongoing issue for most missionary newcomers, as were restrictions on women doing the household shopping. *Our Bond*, their locally published newsletter, contained long correspondence on whether it was acceptable to employ non-Christian servants or even servants at all. Multiple servants were common in foreign households in British India, and plenty of labor available in joint Bengali households. Wilkin had read an article that claimed that if missionary women could not find Christian servants, they should "serve themselves or go home."[22]

There was also the question of economics: living cheaply was another important issue. The women feared being thought rich. For a while, Marion Fuller and Ruth Wilkin gave up servants and did all the housework themselves, but found that consequently they had only limited time for visiting, and as their colleagues counseled productivity in the work, and the importance of their influence on the servants, they soon reverted to employing servants in the household.[23] There was also the considerable value of the servants' influence on the marketplace gossip, including spread of knowledge of the lifestyle of these outsiders to local residents, but at the expense of privacy.

Motivation

Motivation was another issue for the missionaries. They found galling the thought that they should either be working for a despised foreign government or earn religious merit. Even being paid by a foreign organization dissatisfied Macgeorge, and she took board with a family in return for schooling their children, much to the disapproval of her New Zealand Baptist Mission Society.

In general, many missionaries spent longer terms of service than their expatriate compatriots living and working in India. Arnold died in India in 1931—almost forty-nine years after her arrival; Gilbert died in India in 1926; Pappin (Mead) returned to Australia in 1920, having served for thirty-five years. Of the sixty-five zenana missionaries in this period, twenty-five served for more than twenty years. They made serious attempts at iden-

---

[22] Ruth Wilkin, "Is It Right to Employ Heathen as Servants in a Mission House?" *Our Bond*, June 1889, 46.

[23] Ellen Arnold, "Scraps from Comilla," *Our Bond*, July 1889, 49.

tification with the people. This, along with their length of service among them, makes these missionaries of interest in modern historical assessments of missions and imperialism.[24]

As Baptist missionaries they reacted not only to the specifics of life in Bengal but also to the patterns of British imperialism.[25] During the fifty years of their work in India, there was a strong movement from individualism to institutionalism. Under the pressures of anti-British political agitation, they sought settings where the missionaries were in control, living on their own properties or in compounds separate from colonial officials. Importantly these settings enabled the women to create supportive—even safe—social environments for their charges: boarders in hostels, pupils in schools, patients seeking medicine or advice, and care for the vulnerable perpetual widows, even to the extent of serving as matchmakers.

Zenana missiological practices demonstrate a clear progression in attitudes to mission work. Women had very limited opportunity for overt proclamation in public places. The inadequacies of the trickle-down hope that male converts would win their wives led to an effort to produce literature that might find its way directly into the hands of women. That in turn raised the question of the barrier of illiteracy and the need to teach reading to the female population. Several of the teacher-trained zenana missionaries sought to educate younger girls and establish schools.

Culturally Assigned Relationships in Bengal

In Bengali society, as in most of India, designated relationships for women were more important than their individual identity.[26] Bengali married women, following the birth of their first son, were usually known as his mother. In her early reports, Wilkin describes a visit made to a Bengali home:

> As the husband's surname is Mozumdar, we are accustomed among ourselves to speak of this lady as Mrs. Mozumdar, but that is incor-

---

[24] Stanley H. Skreslet, *Comprehending Mission: The Questions, Methods, Themes, Problems, and Prospects of Missiology* (Maryknoll, NY: Orbis Books, 2012), 62–63.

[25] Compare the argument in Martin P. Sutherland, *Conflict and Connection: Baptist Identity in New Zealand* (Auckland: Archer Press, 2011), of the struggle for New Zealand Baptist identity in the colonial conditions that were quite different from conditions in the British metropole. Of particular relevance for this study is chapter 7 on men's ways and women's ways (115–31).

[26] Sudhir Kakar, "We Are Caught between Extremes of Traditional and Western Perspectives on Women," *Times of India*, January 9, 2013.

> rect. A Bengali lady is always addressed and spoken of as so and so's mother. The highest aspiration of a Bengali woman's life is to be the mother of a son. Whatever she may have been called before the birth of her first son after that event she is just his mother....If she is unfortunate enough to have only girls, she must be content to take the name of the eldest. Should she have no children, sad indeed is her lot: in fact, she has no business to be in the world at all. In the first place she ought to have been a boy herself; and failing in that she ought to have redeemed her character by being the mother of a boy.[27]

Missionary wives accepted being identified by their children. For example, Pappin (Mead) was Dorothy's *ma*, and Wilkin (Neville) was Ernest's *ma* (not Emma's *ma*). The single women were often called *mashima* or maternal aunt, a sign of being accepted. Among the missionaries, the single women were called "Aunty" by the missionary children, an accepted surrogate role. Certainly, the Mead girls went boating with Aunt Nell (Arnold).

"Mother in the Lord" is a very rich label given to a single woman missionary from a Bengali Muslim male convert. Interestingly the context of the seminal scriptural reference of Carey in 1792 for rope holders to "lengthen your cords and strengthen your stakes" is that of children of the childless woman.[28]

On the other hand, in cultural contrast, within the British Raj, most married women were known as Mem Sahibs, while single women were called Miss Sahibs. Their identities were defined by their marital relationships (or lack of them). In an interesting early poem by Charlotte Marie Tucker (pen-name ALOE) written around 1876 during her second year with the Church of England Zenana Mission in India, she attempted to define the life of single women missionaries. The poem is written so early in her career it can be considered a reflection of some of the cultural stress she experienced in her early days in India. The poem, as published in her own biography, was titled "Rules and Regulations," and memorably depicted the life of single women missionaries as Mission Miss *Sahibs*. Arnold copied it out for her colleagues in 1890. I have found nothing in the Bengali or Garo

---

[27] Ruth Wilkin, *Gleanings from a Foreign Field* (Geelong, Victoria: Thacker, 1891), 11.

[28] This image is drawn from Isaiah 54:1–2: "Sing, O barren woman. You who never bore a child; burst into song; shout for joy, you who were never in labor; because more are the children of desolate woman than of her who has a husband," says the LORD. "Enlarge the place of your tent, stretch your tent curtains wide, do not hold back; lengthen your cords, strengthen your stakes."

culture that valued singleness in either men or women unless it be in relation to any idea of remarriage, but within missionary societies there did grow up a fear that single women missionaries would desert their call and marry at the first opportunity. Therefore, most missionary societies set conditions that demanded proportionate refunding of expenses if missionaries did not complete their first term of service. The one acceptable exception was a health breakdown. As ALOE put it at the conclusion of her poem,

> NB. Let all Mission Miss Sahibs single remain,
> For if not, they step out of their proper domain,
> And can never be Mission Miss Sahibs again.

Only nine women of the sixty-five of this period stepped "out of their proper domain" and married while on service. Four married male missionaries within the Australian missions; two married New Zealand missionaries; another found a husband who joined in her mission work. These seven couples provided very experienced, culturally aware wives, who had already given over thirty-five years of zenana service before marriage. Only two of the women married and resigned: Agnes Pearce and Bessie Bethell. After seven years of service, Bethell married a merchant from Darjeeling; they served the missionary community together with generous hospitality until his death, when she rejoined the VBFM and served for a further six years. Pearce was the only one lost to the Australian story of zenana missionaries. Hers is a story worth the telling in a different context. It is more the story of British Indian service: her husband served the maharajah of Mayurbhanj.

Dress

Finally, China Inland Mission's (CIM) principles for missions influenced the Australasian Baptist women significantly in their early years; therefore it is worth asking in response to the known practice of CIM missionaries in China of wearing national costume whether there needed to be some consideration of the clothes worn by zenana missionaries in Bengal. From limited early photos the evidence is mixed. There are pictures of the missionary women at outdoor baptismal services wearing Western dress. Similarly, photos of women at work inside the zenanas and views of them in school settings show *topees* (pith helmets) and high-necked, full-length gowns with long sleeves.[29] The photo in the Jubilee Edition of *Our Bond* (1932) shows Arnold on her last boating tour in Western dress.[30] However, in one photo of the Christmas Feast at Orakandi in 1914, a number of Bengali widows in white saris sat on mats and others were ready to serve the participants, and at the end of the room were Western women, also seated cross-legged on mats. The Mead daughters were dressed in bordered saris,[31] and zenana missionary Gladys Collins (a relative newcomer in India) was also dressed in a bordered sari; her mother, a visitor, wore an imposing hat and Western clothes; and Pappin (Mead) was dressed in Western clothes and a *topee.* This photo of Collins may well be an exception to her usual custom;[32] however, on occasions Australian missionaries wore national dress, particularly for festivals or worship sessions with the Christian community.[33] They sat cross-legged for the meal and ate with their fingers.

Marie Gilbert was a notable exception to the custom of wearing Western dress.[34] A photo of Gilbert, in a sari but with a typical long-sleeved Western blouse, was taken by W. Rossler in Calcutta, and another in a sari and a Western blouse is of Gilbert accompanied by an Indian prince, Ram Chandra Deo.[35] There is plenty of testimony to her cultural adjustments that had become her way of life. Her skin had so tanned that she was mistaken to be "non-white" by shipping officers on one of her trips to Australia.[36] As F. A. Marsh wrote of her,

> She became an independent missionary with special concern for the poor and destitute of the great centres of population. She identified

[29] *Our Indian Field*, April 4, 1915, 2, 7; May 1915, 4, 7; November 1916, 8. The photo of the convention at Rajbari shows the total staff in Western dress, March 5, 1916, 3.

[30] *Our Bond*, Jubilee Edition 1932, photographic section between pages 16 and 17.

[31] Widows always wore white saris and blouses; bordered saris were usually colored.

[32] *Our Indian Field*, March 1918, 7.

[33] Among much later missionaries after Partition, there was an understanding that within the Christian community national dress was encouraged by the national women, but the Australian High Commission suggested that such use was inappropriate for Australians in public.

[34] Her adaptation to Indian dress still conformed to her Western standards of decency. She did not follow their blouse style of tight short sleeves and bare midriff.

[35] This could well be one of the sons of the maharajah of Mayurbhanj (see http://members.iinet.net. au/~ royalty/ips/m/Mayurbhanj.html [accessed June 3, 2016]) who grew up with the Kiddell children. A copy of this photo appears in *Our Indian Field*, September 6, 1926, 3, although it must have been taken much earlier.

[36] "Thought She Was Indian: Lady Missionary's Experience," *The Advertiser*, May 4, 1910, 9.

> herself so completely with the people she served that she found it difficult to adapt herself to conditions in Australia when she returned for furlough. She had inured herself to hardship and privation and hostesses were often dismayed to find that she preferred the floor for a bed to the comfort which they had prepared for her.[37]

After her death in Calcutta in 1926 her colleague Pappin (Mead) wrote,

> She always ate native food and wore Indian dress. She had no regular times for meals, for getting up, for going to bed or for doing anything. She never slept on a bedstead. "Make your bed, Marie," meant getting a mat and a brick for a pillow. She was a great photographer but not in Mission work hours. She would soundly scold anyone being cruel to animals. Her great aim was that all should hear or read the Bible but specially the New Testament.[38]

Conclusion

Bengal, its language, its cultural relationships, its lifestyle, its attitudes, and even its timetable impacted the life, service, and habits of early zenana missionaries, some more than others. Most of them considered conforming to local customs worth the effort for the sake of winning the women of Bengal. They sought to be not just outsiders accepting of the Bengali culture in which they lived but also women who were willing to adjust their lifestyle to local practice in order to be more readily accepted by the Bengalis themselves. Thanks be to God that so many were given the grace to make the effort.

---

[37] F. A. Marsh, "Our Pioneer Missionaries," in *Churinga*, August 2, 1957, 8 (publication of the Australian Baptist Historical Society).

[38] Notes made by Alice Pappin (Mead) for memorial address after Gilbert's death, archives of Flinders Street Baptist Church, Adelaide, Australia..

9

Women in Ao Naga Society: The Nineteenth-Century Missionary Evaluation by Mary Mead Clark

Narola Imchen

Mary Mead Clark was an American Baptist woman missionary to Naga, influenced by the first wave of the woman's movement that developed in nineteenth-century America. The question as to how far the women missionaries who worked in North East India in the nineteenth century were influenced by the woman's movement is the subject of this chapter. I approach this question by focusing on the life and work of Mary Mead Clark as a case study, looking first at the origin of the woman's movement.

The "woman's movement" is a familiar term for many readers. Historians differ in their opinions as to what actually constituted what came to be called the "woman's movement." But its origins are generally traced to Olympe de Gouges's *Declaration of the Rights of Women*, 1791, which was modeled on *The Declaration of the Rights of Man and the Citizen*, published in France in 1789, on the eve of the French Revolution.[1] However, prior to this, changes in the status of women in society began to take place, particularly with the breakdown of feudalism and the rise of capitalism. Barbara MacHaffie believes that several factors contributed to the rise of the woman's movement in the 1830s and 1840s.[2] She says that women became more aware of their political and legal disabilities as more and more women participated widely in the democratic process. Further, as more women received secondary education, they became increasingly frustrated as they discovered that many professions and institutions of higher learning were closed to them.

---

[1] Frederick S. Downs, *The Impact of Christianity on the Status of Women of Northeast India* (Shillong: North Eastern Hill University, 1996), 17.

[2] Barbara J. MacHaffie, *Her Story: Women in Christian Tradition* (Philadelphia: Fortress, 1986), 101.

In the 1830s, just as the leadership of the evangelical crusades consolidated its institutions of regeneration and also the terms of their alliance with women, a new phase of religious reform announced that the millenarian impulse had escaped conservative control. The new reformers—abolitionists, temperance advocates, and campaigners against a host of social evils—built on the thought of earlier moral crusaders, but with a significant difference. In the United States the movement took shape as the woman's rights movement in the Declarations of the Convention held at Seneca Falls, New York, in July 1848.

The movement was given tremendous impetus by the Civil War in the early 1860s. During this conflict, women received what Helen Barrett Montgomery describes as a "baptism of power."[3] They were driven to organize and forced to cooperate by their passion of piety and patriotism; in raising and distributing resources to the soldiers, they discovered powers of which they themselves and the nation had been quite unconscious. It is thus no accident that in the decade following the Civil War, scores of organizations were launched.[4] During the Civil War, women were called upon to assume responsibilities traditionally reserved for men. They developed organizations for the purpose of securing rights traditionally denied to them, including the right to own property, the right to inherit, the right to keep their children in the event of divorce, and the right to vote.

All these developments—the woman's rights movement; the movement for women's education and literature; temperance; the formation of women's organizations, including women's missionary societies—constitute the "woman's movement" as it was popularly known.

The Beginning of American Baptist Mission in Northeast India

Twelve years before women gathered at Seneca Falls to issue their Declaration of Women's Rights, American Baptist women began to serve as missionaries in Northeast India, first as wives of missionaries and later as unmarried women serving under one of the newly formed women's missionary societies. Most of these women came from upstate New York or New England. This part of India came under British rule only when, in February 1826, the Treaty of Yandaboo at the conclusion of the First Anglo-Burman

---

[3] See Helen Barrett Montgomery, "What Our Mothers Have Told Us," in *Western Women in Eastern Lands: An Outline Study of Fifty Years of Women's Work in Foreign Missions* (New York: The Macmillan Company, 1910), 10.

[4] Downs, *Impact of Christianity*, 18–19.

War opened the area. Among the officers who served in the region in the early years of British rule, the most important was Francis Jenkins, the son of an English clergyman.[5] He played an important role in the entry of Baptist missionaries to Assam (the state of Northeast India). He invited what was then called the American Baptist Missionary Union to send missionaries to Assam, assuring them of protection and personal assistance. In response to this invitation, Nathan and Eliza Brown and Oliver and Harriet Cutter arrived at Sadiya in Upper Assam to undertake missionary work in 1836. They were sent for the purpose of work among the Khamti and Singpho tribes, with the aim of entering Upper Burma and the interior of China. The Khamtis and Singphos were believed to be closely related to the Shans of Burma, Thailand and China.[6]

During the nineteenth and early twentieth centuries the missionary women served among the Assamese people of the Assam plains and several different tribes resident in the surrounding hills. Among them were the Naga people of what is today the state of Nagaland but was then first unadministered territory and then called the Naga Hills district of the British province of Assam. The first American woman to work among the Nagas was Mary Mead Clark, the wife of Edward Clark. They both came from small farms in the Hudson Valley of upstate New York. The Clarks were appointed as missionaries of the Baptist Missionary Union and assigned to the Assam mission.

They arrived at Sibsagar on March 30, 1869, and Dr. Clark was put in charge of the mission press to relieve William Ward. But he and Mary Mead soon became interested in the Nagas who came down from their villages in the hills to trade in the weekly markets at Sibsagar. Eventually they persuaded the mission authorities to assign them to the Naga mission. The Home Board was hesitant as were their fellow missionaries because the Nagas were much feared by the plainsmen and the British government officials warned them that no protection could be given them because the Nagas lived outside of British jurisdiction. The government finally gave him permission but said that Clark would have to work at his own risk. As Mary Mead put it, the government advised them that they could expect no protec-

---

[5] Frederick S. Downs, *History of Christianity in India*, vol. 5: *Part 5: North East India in the Nineteenth and Twentieth Centuries* (Bangalore: Church History Association of India, 1992), 1.

[6] Frederick S. Downs, "The Establishment of the American Baptist Assam Mission, 1836–1841," *Indian Church History Review* 6, no. 1 (1972): 71–72.

tion from British arms. In addition to government permission he had to be reassigned to the Naga work by the Missionary Union. The Nagas in their turn were afraid that the British would annex their territory as they had annexed other areas in Assam. They therefore suspected that anyone from the plains, especially people who looked just like the British who entered their land, was suspect of being a spy, and not welcome. The Clarks learned that one of their Assamese colleagues at Sibsagar had already established contacts with people from an Ao Naga village. This man, Godhula Brown, and his wife, Lucy, prepared the way, first for Edward and then later Mary Mead to take up residence in the village.

The first time Clark visited the Naga Hills was when he went to Molungkimong with Godhula and baptized fifteen men in December 1872. The second visit was in February 1876 when he spent a week in the village.[7] He was determined to establish permanent work[8] and residence there but had to get the permission of the Missionary Union as well as the British government. The union was reluctant to start a new work when the missionaries who were already in Assam were too few. But eventually the government gave permission, and Clark took up residence in Malunions on March 2, 1876. Of this Mary Mead writes,

> Taking with him only the most necessary articles, he was soon settled in part of Naga house, the luxuriance of which demanded a rental of about thirty cents a month. His cook and general housekeeper was an orphan Bengali lad, who had been our ward for some time at Sibsagar. No inducement could have persuaded an Assamese servant to accompany him. There in a crowded village fortified by a heavy stockade, was begun the mining of this unwritten language and the necessary deeper delving to unearth the real character of these new parishioners.[9]

Clark was at Molungkimong for about eight months. During that time he began to learn the Ao language and translated the Lord's Prayer into Ao. He also translated some songs and taught them to the Christians. The village elders accepted his request to observe Sunday as a day of rest to worship

---

[7] S. W. Rivenburg, *Historical Sketch of the Ao-Naga Mission: The Assam Missionary Union Papers and Discussions of the Jubilee Conference Held at Nowgong, December 1829* (Calcutta: Baptist Mission Press, 1889), 81.

[8] Edward Gait, *A History of Assam* (Calcutta: Tacker Spink & Co., 1906), 355.

[9] Mary Mead Clark, *A Corner in India* (Philadelphia: American Baptist Publication Society, 1907), 15–16.

God. On Sundays he taught not only the Christians but also other villagers on the streets.[10] However, he soon discovered that it was difficult to maintain Christian discipline in the village. For one thing, there were constant raids or rumors of raids. Either the warriors of the village were attacking other villages, or their village itself was under attack. It was therefore in a state of constant alert, which disrupted daily routines. The Christians were expected to participate in the defense of the village as well as its raids. Their reluctance to do so as well as their refusal to participate in village festivals that involved drinking made them increasingly unpopular and objects of persecution. Clark therefore decided that the Christians should join a group of dissidents from Molungkimong who had decided to establish a new village. Though all the inhabitants were not at first Christians, Clark believed that it offered an opportunity to establish a community where the spirit of Christianity rather than of war should reign.[11] Thus on October 24, the move was made to a site not too far from the old village, and the work of clearing the forests and constructing houses began. The new village eventually came to be called Molungyimsen (New Molung), shortened in mission reports simply to Molung.

The Clarks were unique among the American Baptist missionaries serving in Northeast India at that time. All the other missionaries lived in British bungalow-style houses located either on mission compounds or areas inhabited by British officials. Most lived in district headquarter towns. But Clark lived in a village most of the years, except for a few years at the end of his career when he lived in the newly established mission compound at Impur near the district headquarter town of Mokokchung. Even then he moved under protest and on condition that a Naga-style house be built for him at Impur. He refused to live in a mission bungalow. Thus, Mary Mead Clark, except for times when for health reasons she had to return to the United States, lived in an Ao village, in an Ao-style house. No missionary woman was in a better position to understand the condition of women in Ao Naga society than was Mary Mead. And yet…more of that later.

---

[10] Molungkimong Baptist Arogo, *Mulungkimong Baptist Arogo Centennial Otsu* [Mulungkimong Church Centennial History], (Molungkimong, 1972), 22.

[11] Frederick S. Downs, *The Mighty Works of God: A Brief History of Council of Baptist Churches of North East India, the Mission Period, 1836–1950* (Guhati: Christian Literature Centre, 1971), 66.

Mary Mead Clark (1832–1924)

Mary Mead was born in July 1832 at Amenia, New York. She married Edward Winter Clark on September 29, 1858. Mary and her husband worked among the Nagas from 1872 to 1911. She was the author of the book *A Corner in India,* one of the early writings on the Ao Naga tribe of Northeast India, published by the American Baptist Publication Society. She wrote this book in 1907, after she had left the Naga Hills; her husband continued his work for four more years.[12]

While Mary was on medical leave, on March 2, 1876, Clark went into the Naga Hills to live in Molungkimong. In 1878, two years after Clark chose to settle among the Ao people, Mary joined him. A daughter of the woman's movement, the first thing she did was start a school. While she taught both boys and girls, her first love was her female students. According to Bendangyapang, an Ao historian, this further hastened the development of Ao literature.[13] The Clarks served in the Ao field and ministered to all Naga tribes in general as evangelists, mediators, Christian administrators, translators, writers, organizers, and printers for about forty years. While each had their own special interests and responsibilities in times of sickness or absence, each would take up the work of the other.

In 1885 Mary Mead and her husband went home on medical leave, and when they returned two years later, they resumed the various lines of work, reducing the Ao language to writing, translating portions of the Scriptures, and composing and translating hymns, schoolbooks, and Sunday school literature. In 1901 they were obliged to return to America again for health reasons. But in 1903 Clark returned alone as Mary Mead's health did not permit her to accompany him.[14] Clark retired from active service in 1911 and died at St. Augustine, Florida, on March 18, 1913, at age eighty-three. Following the death of her husband, Mary Mead spent her winters in Florida and her summers in her girlhood home of Amenia, New York, where she died on November 23, 1924, age ninety-two.[15]

---

[12] Clark, *Corner in India,* 15, 60.

[13] A. Bendangyapang Ao, *History of Christianity in Nagaland: A Source Material* (Mokokchung: Shalom Ministry, 1998), 150, 240.

[14] A. Bendangyapang Ao, *History of Christianity in Nagaland,* 240-41.

[15] L. Kijung Ao, *Nokinketer Mongchen* [The genesis of the Ao Naga Church history], (Gauhati: Christian Literature Centre, 1972), i.

Mary Mead Clark and the Woman's Movement

We now look briefly at the main emphasis in the ministry of Mary Mead Clark and identify how much she was influenced by the nineteenth-century American woman's movement. The two most important emphases of the woman's movement introduced into her "agenda" in Molung were the importance of education for the advancement of women, and the organization of women into societies that could advance their welfare and, through them, the welfare of families, churches, and societies.

Education

Education was the area where the women missionaries made the greatest contribution. This was also the area that most clearly showed the influence of the woman's movement upon them. The woman's movement saw education as the primary means of improving the situation of women, the main agency through which everything else that they tried to do could be achieved. Dana L. Robert describes the goals that women on the mission field sought to achieve through education:

> First: In a setting where there was little interest in Christianity on the part of the people, starting schools for girls would be the best way to gain access to the female half of the population for the purpose of evangelization.
>
> Second: Teaching females to read would prove to the men of the society that women were capable individuals and should not spend their life in darkened seclusion.
>
> Third: A pool of educated Christian women was needed to provide wives and co-laborers for the male clergy and Christian workers who would emerge.
>
> Fourth: Finally, and most importantly, for the overall mission of the church, the education of women would subvert the very foundations of "heathen" society and would catalyze the profound social changes needed to accompany broad conversion to Christianity. All of these reasons were given by missionaries at various times to justify the expense of founding schools for women and girls.[16]

---

[16] Dana L. Robert, *American Women in Mission: A Social History of Their Thought and Practice,* (Macon, GA: Mercer University Press, 1996), 38.

The study of the work of American Baptist women missionaries in Northeast India certainly indicates that all these reasons for promoting female education were at work there. Thus, in almost all the mission stations, the first work on which the missionaries concentrated was starting schools and offering some kind of education.

Before the missionary could think of beginning her school, she herself must be a pupil in order to learn the language. It was often difficult, within the cultures concerned, to find a person willing to teach a woman missionary—and those who were willing might not be competent. Mary Mead faced this problem as she started her mission.

Mary had not accompanied her husband when he moved into the hills because of the ill health that had made it necessary for her to return to America for treatment. But early in November 1878, she was able to join him at Molung. Within a few months she had started a school for girls.[17] This was the first formal school for children of either gender in Nagaland. It is significant that it was for girls. Though it was difficult to teach the children at first, the school steadily developed and in due course began to admit boys as well as girls.[18]

With reference to their everyday life at Molung, years later Mary Mead wrote,

> Bringing the gospel to these savaged hill tribes taxed to the utmost the resources of the missionary. A good knowledge of their language, habits and character is absolutely essential for gaining their confidence and winning their souls. We were alert to show this people that we were not among them for the benefit of a single village, but for the best good of all.[19]

To begin their work, they needed to learn the language. They chose from the men of the village two persons whom they judged to be the most intelligent to come to their residence each morning to talk with Mary and her husband, or rather to permit them to pick from their mouths, or throats, it seemed, their unwritten language. These two men were paid one rupee each for their lessons.

---

[17] E. W. Clark, "Naga Mission and Church Record" (1894) in "A History of Ao Baptist Churches: Source Materials," ed. Renthy Keitzar and L. T. Maja (1985, unpublished), 2.

[18] *Platinum Jubilee Souvenir* (Impur: CMI, 1970), 11.

[19] Clark, *Corner in India*, 68.

For reducing the language to writing they used Roman characters. The expense of printing the primer was borne by Mr. Godby's Bible class of the First Baptist Church, Newark, New Jersey. Regarding her first attempt to teach the people, Mary Mead writes,

> On opening our first school the children came pouring in as if for a holiday; but as soon as they understood that quiet and attention were the rule, all was changed. Then, to get them in at all, it was necessary to hold our session in the early morning, before the day's work in the field began and even then, we were never certain whether they would be in the school room or like monkeys, in the trees, on the roofs of the houses or some other place. But gradually there came to be some appreciation of what educated boys and girls might be and do.[20]

Mary Mead named some but not all of the girls in the first batch at the Molung School. Those she mentions were Tongpangkokla, Noksangla, Jongmayangla, Purla, Punayula, and Taripisu.[21] According to the Molungkimong Baptist Women's Centenary publication, Taripisu was from the old village. When Mary Mead started the school for girls, Taripisu went from the old village to attend. After that it is said that some more women also went to study there—and were eventually baptized by Clark. Interestingly, it is said that the main reason the girls were sent to school was not to learn but to get the one paisa that was given to all who attended. Later, of course, they began to understand the importance of education.[22]

Mary Mead writes that those older girls whose work would not permit their attendance in the mornings would come each evening to the missionaries' home. They spent an hour learning to read, sewing, and discussing the new religion and other matters. Tongpangla was the first Naga woman to become a Christian. Soon Tongpangla and Noksangla, another schoolgirl, were baptized. Tongpangla became a valuable helper for Mary Mead—teaching in the day school and visiting in the village homes. She and her husband were also the first to be married as Christians.[23]

The school opened the eyes of Ao women in an entirely new way. Through this school, many women developed religious belief and learned to

---

[20] Clark, *Corner in India,* 84–85.

[21] A. Olemkilep, *Laishir Mongchen: Nagaland Mezungbuba Arogo Otsu* [History of the First Naga Church](Mokochung: Molungyimsen Baptist Church, 1976), 60.

[22] *Molungkimong Baptist Arogitsur Centenary Otsu* [History of Molungkimong Baptist women: 1885–1985] (Dimapur: Molungkimong Baptist Arogo, 1985), 3.

[23] Clark, *Corner in India,* 85–86.

sing gospel songs, besides learning to read and write. Because of this school—which admitted girls before boys—Ao women were the first among their people to be able to read and write, to sing gospel songs, or to read the Bible.

Starting a Women's Fellowship

An important part of the nineteenth-century woman's movement in America, especially after the Civil War, was the phenomena of women's organizations. Evidence of the influence of the woman's movement is found in the fact that similar organizations began to be established by women missionaries in the latter part of the century. This took the form of organizing women's meetings at the local church level and in conjunction with the meetings of associations, when they began to be held in various fields from the 1870s onward. Like the other women missionaries, Mary Mead gave importance to organizing the women for prayer and fellowship.

Thus, once women began to join the church, the missionaries decided that special attention needed to be given to women's participation in its affairs. Hence, in 1880 Mary Mead started a women's fellowship that met once each week. It had several objectives. First, it sought to teach the women how to manage family affairs in a Christian way, and second, to teach them the importance of stewardship. In due course the women began to bring their offerings to the church at the time of Sunday worship.[24] These were the beginnings of the women's fellowship that was to develop considerably through the years.

Through the women's fellowship the number of Christian women increased. The earliest women leaders among the Aos were Tongpangkokla, Noksangla, Jongmayangla, Chubasenla, Punayula, Impangkokla, and Sentikumla. They were courageous women with great faith. It is sometimes said that they showed greater interest than did many men in church affairs. From the time of the Molung fellowship onward, the women kept separate funds of their own, out of which they paid the salaries of women leaders. This was in keeping with the traditional rights of the women to do "private" trading with their own moveable property, which they, not the men, possessed and administered. But traditionally this had been an individual affair. Now it was done collectively for the benefit of projects chosen by the women, which gave them an influence in church affairs that women would not otherwise

[24] Kijung, *Nokinketer Mongchen,* 44.

have had. Meeting regularly with the women in this way, Mary Mead must have gained insights into the position of women in Ao society. She also introduced the women of Molung to the practice of planting kitchen gardens with new and nutritious vegetables.

When the Clarks left for furlough in 1885, Tongpangkokla was entrusted with the leadership of the fellowship. She was also given responsibilities as a teacher in the school. After teaching at Molung for three years, in 1888 she went down to Yajang village to teach in the mission school established there and also to serve as village pastor. This was the first time that an Ao woman served either as schoolteacher or pastor.[25] After Tongpangla left Molung, Zilli's wife Jainty was chosen as leader of the fellowship. Sometimes she too, in the absence of the pastor assumed that role.[26]

The Molung women's fellowship became the model for other churches as they were formed. In 1897, when the first Ao Baptist Association meeting was held at Molung, a collection of two or three rupees was given by the women's fellowship to be used for starting women's fellowships in other villages. A. Temjen says that this was the first women's group collection.[27] Thus, as Christianity spread throughout the Ao area, more churches were established. Whenever a church was established in any village, it was encouraged to start a women's fellowship immediately. As noted above, Mary Mead first took the initiative in this matter, and the other missionary women who followed her had similar interest in it.

This is how the nineteenth-century American woman's movement was mirrored in the work of women missionaries, including Mary Mead Clark, in the areas of female education and the beginning of the establishment of women's organizations.

The Status of Ao Women

Looking at the status and role of Naga women, people come to different conclusions and have a variety of opinions. One group says that women were

---

[25] It is surprising that at that time a woman was given the job of a pastor. Today it is exclusively for men only.

[26] Olemkilep, *Laishir Mongchen,* 75.

[27] A. Temjen Ao, "Aotsur Jenjang" [The status of Ao women] (1991, unpublished), 2–4.

esteemed and of equal status with men. This group includes some British administrators and missionaries like Mary Mead,[28] who wrote,

> There is no degradation of women among the Naga. Although not sharing directly in civil or military administration, yet in both of these they exert a strong, subtle influence, and emulate the lover's and husband's pride in war medals.[29]

As previously noted, this was not the opinion of a casual visitor, but rather the opinion of someone who had lived and worked among Ao Nagas for nearly forty years. She was fluent in their language and worked closely with women in their village context.

Yet Ao Naga scholars today paint quite a different view of the traditional status of Ao women, and their conclusions are briefly summarized here. Ao Nagas refer to women as *Sungolang* (a bunch of leaves) or as *tetsur-tanur* (women-children). This is clearly indicative of the fact that in Ao society women have been assigned a lower status than men.[30] Women were not given any role in the political sphere, though in other spheres of life they enjoyed some privileges. The status of women may be better understood by looking at the traditional Ao society and the role of women in it.

Political System

The male inhabitants of the village were regarded as citizens of the republic, and they performed the role of citizenship. Women inhabitants were not regarded as citizens. As Tajen Ao writes, "every citizen contributes his share of duties and services for the common welfare of the republic."[31] Women were not seen as having political responsibility. The village was run by the elected male elders from each clan. A woman had no place at all in the village council. No woman could be elected as a councilor even though she

---

[28] Limatula Longkumer, "Christianity and Naga Women," in *Transforming Theology for Empowering Women: A Theological and Hermeneutical Reflection in the Context of North East India*, ed. R. L. Hnuni (Jorhat, Assam, India: Women's Studies Eastern Theological College, 1999), 53.

[29] Clark, *Corner in India*, 49.

[30] M. Akang, "Akidang Ao Yimli nung tetsurtem jenjang meyipa reprangshiba" [Looking back at the status of women in the old Ao society], in Ruth and Chubala, ed. *Shisa Lemsa Kaket* (Mokokchung:Watsu Rogo Mungdang, 1989), 2.

[31] Tajen Ao, *Ao Naga Customary Law* (Mokokchung: Tribal Gospel Publisher's Shoppe, 1984), 14.

might be the eldest person in the village. She could not participate in any public debate or discussion.[32]

An *arichu*[33] was an institution where boys normally above twelve years of age were trained and learned under older boys. They stayed there until they were married. An *arichu* was a place where war expeditions were planned and weapons were made. Every enemy head was also brought there after a successful raid. Even after the British prohibited intravillage warfare, the *arichu* long remained the center of the men's social life. Women were not permitted to enter the *arichu* on any occasion.[34] As Mills wrote, "It is of course forbidden for a woman to enter it."[35] Hence, women were excluded from one of the community's most important social and cultural institutions.

Headhunting was a part of everyday life for the Ao Nagas, as it was for other Naga tribes. It was a man's activity. A modern Naga scholar, Wati Longchar, suggests that headhunting had the effect of giving women an inferior status. He writes,

> Head-hunting involves many risks. It was purely a man's game. One's social status was solely dependent upon the success in head-hunting. Since women folk could not participate in it, they were excluded from all kinds of decision-making processes. Their voice was not heard by the society, and so they were given no status in society but treated as subordinate to men.[36]

Social System

The family is the smallest unit of the clan. It consists of the father, his wife, and their children. Sometimes it also includes children of relatives whose parents are dead. The family is patriarchal. The father is the head of the family, and family descent is through the male. When a daughter is married, she leaves her father's family and comes under the authority of her husband.

---

[32] Imti Aier, *Ao Naga Social and Customary Geneology* (Mokokchung: Pioneer Book Stall, 1967), 4.

[33] The popular name used is Morung. This is a term used for the institution as found among all the Naga tribes. Aos call it *arichu*, Lothas call it *champo*, Angamis call it *kichüki*. In English it is referred to as bachelor dormitory.

[34] Milanda Ganguli, *A Pilgrimage to the Nagas* (Calcutta: Oxford and I. B. H. Pub. Co., 1884), 115.

[35] J. B. Mills, *The Ao Nagas* (London: Macmillan & Co., 1926), 73–74.

[36] "Head-Hunting: A Socio-Religious Factor for Oppression of Women in North East India," *North East India Religious Review* (September 1990): 37.

The children of the daughter are considered the children of her husband's family—a different family and clan from their mother. Therefore, the daughter and her children have no further place in her father's family once they are married. Thus, in the father's family, the daughters are regarded as subordinate members. They do not become co-owners with the sons and do not inherit family property. The status of women is clearly below that of men in the Ao family.

Analysis of Mary Mead's View on Ao Naga Women

Mary Mead must have been familiar with all of this. How then was she able to make the statements she did about the high status of Ao women? From our perspective, women's status was clearly not equal with that of men. Why did Mary Mead Clark not see this reality? After all, by the time she wrote her book she had lived among Ao Nagas for decades. She lived right in the village, working among girls and women in her school and the church. How could she not understand the true situation—that the women were subordinate to men in that culture? Here several hypotheses come to mind.

Being an outsider, Mary Mead might have thought that free movement and free mixing of men and women meant that women had the same social status and roles as men. Without actually understanding the sociocultural context of the people, she might have drawn a premature conclusion about women's status. Given her experience of living on a daily basis in an Ao Naga village for so long, this explanation is not likely.

In a lecture on the Christian impact on the status of women in tribal societies of Northeast India, F. S. Downs advances another hypothesis. He suggests that those who agreed that the status of Northeast India tribal women was high based their judgment on comparisons with the status of women in other societies. In his own words, "[For] those who agree that the status of women was high, one needs to understand that their judgements are not based on any analysis of the societies themselves but upon comparisons with other societies."[37] If so, in attributing a high status to Ao women Mary Mead simply meant that Ao women were much better off than the Hindu and Muslim women of India and were in a situation similar to that of American women who, like Ao women, were free to move about in public

---

[37] Frederick S. Downs, *The Christian Impact on the Status of Women in NEI* (Shillong: NEHU, 1996), 10.

and mix with men. All that was being said was that Ao women were better off or equal to other women, not that they had equal status with men.

The life of the tribal people is best expressed in their relationship with one another. They lived in an interrelatedness that molded a person to be a member of a close-knit community. The traditional tribal worldview portrayed an egalitarian society that spoke of an equal relationship between men and women. However, despite these assertions, one cannot deny that the tribal society was based on and ruled by patriarchy. One can certainly identify factors that hinder the people from living a life promoting equal participation for everyone.

Patriarchy was very apparent when the missionaries established the formal education process in Naga soil. When the missionaries opened schools, many parents strongly opposed the education of their daughters. Parents thought that the education of girls was a waste of time and domestic labor. Thus, they preferred educating only the boys.[38] This was true even in the early stages of Christianity when women were not favored with early baptism.

In fact, in one of her letters Clark wrote, "There are some women who deserve baptism, but due to some reason their baptism is refused. This feeling will soon be over from them."[39] That is why she wrote, "There was difficulty in early persuading the women that this new religion was for them as well as for their husbands and sons."[40] But the conversion of Aos to Christian faith brought about radical changes in the tribal society. The Christian missionaries brought social transformation and made many positive contributions toward the liberation of women in the church and society.[41] The conservative attitude soon vanished, and less than ten years after the coming of Christianity, baptism among women took place. The first women to be baptized were Noksangla and Tongpangkokla,[42] on August 15, 1880.[43] Mary

---

[38] Limatula Longkumer, "Naga Women in Theological Education: Problems and Prospects," in *Side by Side: Naga Women Doing Theology in Search of Justice and Partnership,* ed. Limatula Longkumer and Talijungla Longkumer (Jorhat: CCA-EGY and NWTF, 2004), 19.

[39] L. Kijung Ao, *Nokinketer Mongchen,* 41.

[40] Clark, *Corner in India,* 72.

[41] A. Wati Longchar, "A Liberated Woman in Captivity," in *Women's Issues in the 21st Century,* Women Study Series 1, ed. Narola Imchen (Jorhat: WSCETC, 2001), 117.

[42] Clark, *Corner in India,* 85.

[43] L. Kijung Ao, *Nokinketer Mongchen,* 51.

Mead wrote, "Tongpangkokla became a valuable helper, teaching in our day-school, and visiting with me from house to house."[44]

However, missionaries who themselves came from the patriarchal culture and a male-dominated church kept a patriarchal mind-set. However much she worked for the welfare of Ao women, Mary Mead's own cultural conditioning did not lead her to seek equality of status with men. In her native America such goals did not become a central part of the woman's movement until well into the twentieth century. One sees this limitation in her description of the objectives of the training school to be started at the newly established mission station at Impur. Its purpose was to be a "training school, preparing young men for pastors, evangelists, and day-school teachers, and young women to be suitable wives for such men."[45]

Mary Mead's own personal experience clearly shows how Christianity reinforced a male-biased theology. The whole Christian tradition is interpreted from the perspective of a male's experience and has resulted in belief in a male deity, inferior status for women, and an exclusive male Christian ministry.

Concluding Remarks

Although the American Baptist missionary women working in Northeast India did not overtly use the language of the woman's movement, they were nevertheless influenced by it. This is evident in the ministry of Mary Mead Clark, although she and the other missionaries, while working for the welfare of girls and women, did not seek equality with men. In this, they reflected the patriarchal assumptions of the American churches and, perhaps, the limited goals of the nineteenth-century woman's movement itself.

But sometimes things that are begun for one reason end up serving different ends. Among the Aos and throughout Northeast India, the schools that were started to teach girls how to be good wives and mothers developed a life of their own. An increasing number of Christian schools requiring teachers and training departments for girls were opened. The next step was to prepare them for other professions and for responsible citizenship. In due course the great-granddaughters of Mary Mead's students became university professors and college presidents. Women who had been excluded from village councils became actively involved in government. However limited the

[44] Clark, *Corner in India,* 85.

[45] Clark, *Corner in India,* 148.

vision of Mary Mead may have been because of her own patriarchal culture, in time schools were to become the main instrument for raising the status of Ao women.

10

The Baptist Mission in Myanmar

Wado Kawthoolei

The Republic of the Union of Myanmar is a Southeast Asian country of approximately 55 million people that borders India, Bangladesh, China, Laos, and Thailand. Myanmar is a land of mountains, jungles, rice fields, lakes, rivers, and seashores. Its inhabitants comprise eight major races—Kachin, Kaya, Karen, Chin, Mon, Burmese, Rakhine, and Shan—and some 135 ethnic groups. It is an agricultural country, and most of the people are peasants who live in rural areas. Myanmar has become one of the poorest countries in the world, but the country is rich in its ecosystem and biodiversity, with valuable and beautiful natural resources. It is the land of the golden pagoda and one of the strongest enclaves of Theravada Buddhism in all Asia.[1]

On May 26, 1989, the military regime changed the name of the country from the European word "Burma" to "Myanmar." The regime also changed the names of several cities and divisions. Rangoon became Yangon; Iraeaddy became Ayerwaddy; May Myo became Pyin Oo Lwin; Karen State is now called Kayin State; and the Karen Baptist Convention was named the Kayin Baptist Convention. Throughout its independent years, since 1947, the country has suffered rampant strife and war: many ethnic groups have been involved in one of the world's longest-running ongoing civil wars. During this time the United Nations and several other organizations have reported consistent and systematic violations of human rights and religious freedom in the country. General Ne Win formally took power in 1962 and declared, "When a soldier shoots, he does not shoot in the air, he shoots the target."[2] He then did what he had pledged. Thousands of people were

---

[1] Andrew Boyd, *Baroness Cox: A Voice for the Voiceless* (Oxford: Lion Publishing, 1998), 217.

[2] This was an "off-the-cuff" comment reported by the late Reverend Dr. Simon, a firsthand witness of General Ne Win's coup d'état. Ne Win actually said, "As for the control of civil disturbances, I have to inform the people throughout the country that when the army

gunned down when soldiers fired their automatic weapons into crowds of unarmed demonstrators.[3] It was a blood massacre. The White Bridge in the area became the Red Bridge. All Christian missionaries were kicked out of the country by 1966. American Baptists represented the main Protestant presence from 1813 to 1966. The church they established was called the Karen (later Kayin) Baptist Convention.

In the 1970s the people of Burma suffered another severe persecution called the "four-cut operation," which resulted in widespread displacement, establishment of internationally displaced persons camps, relocations to towns under military control, and construction of refugee camps in Thailand. In 2005 the government started a resettlement program. Mass migration of refugees departed for several destinations, including the United States and Canada; some European countries, including Norway, Sweden, Denmark, and Finland; and New Zealand and Australia in the Asia-Pacific region. Japan and Korea also took some refugees as part of the resettlement program. The people of Burma were hard hit by the regime's four-cut operation. The intention of the policy was to deprive the ethnic resistance movements of their food, money, intelligent leadership, and recruits. Along with this operation came widespread displacement and the refugee crisis. Thousands of refugees flooded into Thailand, and thousands more became displaced and re-displaced in the eastern jungle of Myanmar. Thus, many Karen churches in eastern Burma were cut off from the mainstream Karen Baptist Convention headquartered in Insein, Rangoon. Now the need for strengthening and nurturing the churches along the Thai-Burma border has become an urgent priority. For this reason, the Kawthoolei Karen Baptist Church was established on June 9, 1983.

Following a 2010 general election, the military junta was officially dissolved, and a nominally civilian government was installed in 2011. This, along with the release of Aung San Suu Kyi and other political prisoners, has improved the country's human rights record and foreign relations, and has led to the easing of trade and other economic sanctions. There is, however, continuing criticism of the government's treatment of ethnic minorities, and its response to the ethnic insurgency and religious clashes. In the landmark 2015 election, Aung San Suu Kyi's party won a majority in both houses. However, the Burmese military remains a powerful force in politics.

---

shoots, it shoots to hit; it does not fire into the air to scare." See Robert H. Taylor, *General Ne Win: A Political Biography* (Institute of Southeast Asian Studies, 2015), 529.

[3] Taylor, *General Ne Win*.

The government is actively involved in promoting Theravana Buddhism, the religion practiced by the majority of the Burmese population, particularly among members of ethnic minorities.

The Baptist Mission in Myanmar

Over two hundred years ago, a simple small-town English shoemaker named William Carey (1761–1834) became convicted by the realization that thousands of people around the world had never heard the gospel, and he became convinced that it was the responsibility of the church to do something about it. He mentioned this at a Baptist meeting in Northampton in 1786, asking if Matthew 28:18 was still relevant for the church today: "Is not the commission of our Lord still binding upon us? Can we not do more than now we are doing?" William Carey received a sharp rebuke when he first proposed the idea of foreign mission endeavor: "Young man. Sit down! You are an enthusiast. When God pleases to convert the heathen, he will do it without your help or mine," said the moderator, Dr. Ryland.[4] Carey did not sit down. He came to India with his son Felix Carey, who introduced Burma to the Judsons.

Felix Carey

In 1802, at eight years of age, Felix Carey traveled to India with his father, William Carey, who helped start the Serampore Mission in India. While living in India, Felix became a scholar in the languages of Bengali, Pali, and Sanskrit. The missionary printer William Ward came to India, and under his ministry Felix was saved. Ward taught Felix how to operate the printing press at the Serampore Mission. It was there that Felix printed portions of his father's newly translated Bengali New Testament.

In 1807 Felix traveled to Burma and mastered the Burmese language. Realizing the need for literature in many languages, Felix began preparing and translating many materials, including the Gospel of Matthew, the first dictionary in the Burmese language, a Bengali-English dictionary, a Pali grammar book, and many others. In 1814 Felix was requested to begin a mission in Ava, Burma. While en route, the boat sank, and Felix lost everything, including his family, a printing press, and a translated manuscript of the Gospel of Matthew. Distraught from losing his wife and children, he

---

[4] M. Thomas Starkes, *God's Commissioned People: A Fresh History of Christian Missions* (Nashville: Broadman Press, 1984), 155.

resigned from all mission work and translation and became an ambassador to Calcutta. He soon accumulated much debt, began drinking heavily, and eventually lost his ambassadorship. For three years Felix wandered aimlessly until longtime friend William Ward persuaded him to return to the Serampore Mission. Back in India and once again under the influence of Ward, Felix returned to mission translation and work. On November 10, 1822, at the age of thirty-seven, Felix died of cholera. He was among the first missionaries to work in translation and printing. He paved the way for others, such as Adoniram Judson and Henry Martyn. It was Felix Carey who introduced mission work in Burma to the Judsons.

Adoniram Judson (1788–1850)

Myanmar has long been known as the Golden Land because of the Shwedagon Pagoda, the oldest, the largest, and the grandest pagoda in Myanmar. This pagoda is a symbol of how deeply Buddhism is rooted in the lives of the Myanmar people. Into this context the U.S. Baptist missionaries Adoniram Judson and Ann Hasseltine Judson were sent. They landed in Rangoon on July 13, 1813, and started learning the Burmese language immediately. Additional missionaries later came to support the work, and therefore the gospel spread from Yangon to Kyaikame, Molamyine, and Dawai, where the good news reached the Karens, Mons, and Burmese people. Then the mission proceeded to the north of the Rakhine area and then to many other hill tribes. After two years of preparation, the Judsons and George H. and Phebe Hough (who arrived in October 1816) were able to begin the work for which they had come to Burma, including translating, printing, and distributing the Holy Scriptures; preaching the gospel; circulating religious tracts; and promoting the instruction of native children. The Judsons learned Burmese very efficiently and used many contextualized ways to share the gospel. The Zayat,[5] not a Western church, was used for preaching, and the robes were a different color from those used by the Buddhists.[6] Judson studied Buddhism in such a way that he understood the worldview of Burmese Buddhists and used that understanding in translating the Bible into Burmese. Because of his skill in the Burmese language, Judson was used as an

---

[5] The Zayat was a Burmese building found in almost every village; it was primarily used as a shelter for travelers and as an assembly place for meetings.

[6] Maung Shwe Wa, "Genevieve Sowards and Erville Sowards," *Burma Baptist Chronicle* (Rangoon: Board of Publications Burma Baptist Convention, 1963), 12.

interpreter by the Burmese king in the peace treaty made between the Burmese and the British.

After six years of Baptist work in Burma (1819), Maung Naw, the first Burmese convert, was baptized and received into the Christian fellowship. "He had been told plainly that he had nothing to expect in this world but persecution and perhaps death; but he thought it better to die for Christ and be happy hereafter, than to live a few days and be forever wretched."[7] "In the history of the church in Burma, Maung Naw was the first fruit and will always be honored for his courageous faith and unselfish obedience."[8] Within a year the young church had grown to ten members. The church was beginning to grow as surely as seeds in a paddy nursery.[9] During the war between Britain and Burma (1824–1825), Judson was imprisoned for seventeen months. He would have his feet shackled and his shoulders barely touched the ground. Once when asked by a prisoner about their future and his faith, Judson replied, "The future is as bright as the promise of God."[10]

Adoniram Judson survived prison only through the sacrifices of his wife, Ann, who attempted to visit him daily. Ann's struggle while Adoniram was imprisoned was so great that she became impoverished and sick, so much so that she could not produce milk to breastfeed their child. She sought Burmese women, begging them to help feed her child. The missionaries had to suffer untold agonies for the nation to receive the gospel. However, by 1860 there were seventy-four churches with 3,904 baptized members in the country. By 1900 the Baptist mission reached the Burmese people (who are the majority ethnic people) in Phyi and Mandalay. Since then, churches have grown in number, and Christianity has been established with strength and vitality. The Baptist mission kept functioning through its established institutions, including schools, colleges, hospitals, vocational training schools, orphanages, agricultural projects, development programs, and so on. Through the efforts and leadership of American missionaries and the local Burmese leaders, the Burma Baptist Missionary Convention was organized on October 15, 1865. In 1954 the word "missionary" was dropped, and the name was changed to the Burma Baptist Convention.

---

[7] Wa, "Genevieve Sowards and Erville Sowards," 17.

[8] Ibid., 19.

[9] Ibid., 21.

[10] https://www.preceptaustin.org/adoniramjudson (accessed January 5, 2019).

Karen: Ko Tha Byu

Upon seeing the Karens, the Burmese guide told Judson, "They are Karens, wild cattle from the mountain. They are unattainable. Be careful; they are just wild hill people given to stealing and fighting."[11] In fact, the Karens were pioneers in "one of the most remarkable Christian movements of modern times."[12] Ko Tha Byu was converted through the ministry of Judson and later asked for baptism on a trip to Dawei with George Dana Boardman, the first American Baptist missionary to the Karens. Ko Tha Byu was baptized at Dawei on May 16, 1828, at the age of fifty. After his conversion he traveled throughout Burma as a flaming evangelist. One missionary described him as "an ignorant man; yet he did more good than all of us, for God was with him." Missionary Francis Mason described him as a "drill" in his evangelism work. The American missionaries gave him the title "The Karen Apostle."[13] By the time of his death at age sixty-two on September 9, 1840, there were 1,270 Baptist church members among the Karens.

Karen: Saw Quala

Saw Quala was also a well-known Karen evangelist, translator, and leader. In 1857, when Francis Mason became ill and had to retire, Saw Quala took over Mason's work and supervised an entire district. Within two years Saw Quala increased the number of assistants under him from three to eleven and established twenty-seven new churches. He wrote, "I dare not rest, neither in the rains nor in the hot season. God has shown me my work and I stop not. I go hither and thither, up the mountains, down in the valley, one night or two nights [in each place]. Some come to me from a distance...saying, 'Teacher, thou sayest thou comest to exhort men and thou has never been to our streams....Dost thou not love us? Then I feel unable to open my mouth....Brethren, teachers, teacheresses, pray for me....When I think of my inability to do the work, I weep."[14] Work with the Karens is

---

[11] Don Richardson, *Eternity in Their Hearts: The Untold Story of Christianity among Folk Religions and Ancient People* (Ventura, CA: Regal Books, 1981), 73.

[12] Ian Morrison, *Grandfather Longlegs: Gallant Death of Major H. P. Seagrim* (London: Faber and Faber, 1946), 27.

[13] https://Wikipedia.org/wiki/Myanmar, accessed May 14, 2017.

[14] Maung Shwe Wa, *Burma Baptist Chronicle*, 187.

deemed as one of the more successful efforts in Southeast Asia in modern Christian missionary history.[15]

Baptist Mission among the Kachin

The Swedish American Baptist woman missionary Minnie Johnson Hanson (1869–1957), together with her husband, Ola Hanson (1864–1929), along with sixteen Karen missionaries started mission work among the Kachins, a marginalized hillside ethnic group in northern Burma. The king of Burma once addressed the missionaries who came to work with the Kachins, telling them, "So you are to teach the Kachins! Do you see my dogs over there? I tell you, it will be easier to convert and teach these dogs. You are wasting your life."[16] When the missionaries came to Kachin land, they discovered that these people possessed an extensive mythology that had been passed from generation to generation. There were stories dealing with creation, death, resurrection, and even a flood. They also told of a book that they lost. The Kachin version states that God gave each race a book. The Chinese book was on paper; the Burmese book was written on parchment. On their way home from their meeting with God, the Kachins became hungry and ate their copy. The Kachins also had a prophecy stating that one day a foreigner would bring the copy of the book back to them. When he heard the story of the lost book, Hanson determined that he would restore the book to the Kachins: he would give the Kachins the Bible in their own tongue. Today there are four hundred thousand to five hundred thousand Kachin Christians, and three hundred thousand of them are Baptists. Ola Hanson is greatly revered even today as the father of the Kachin church.[17] The Kachins were 100 percent illiterate in 1890, and now virtually all Katchins can both read and write in Katchin as well as in Burmese, which is the national language.[18]

Baptist Work among the Chin

Eighty-six years after Adoniram Judson arrived in Burma, Christianity came to Chin state through American Baptist missionaries. In 1899 the Chin

---

[15] Kenneth Scott Latourette, *The Christian World Mission in Our Day* (New York: Harper & Brothers, 1954), 52, 115.

[16] https://www.hopeingod.org/document/ola-hansonstory, accessed June 14, 2018.

[17] https://www.hopeingod.org/document/ola-hansonstory, accessed June 14, 2018.

[18] https://www.hopeingod.org/document/ola-hansonstory, accessed June 14, 2018.

Mission in Burma began with establishment of the station at Thayetmyo by American Baptist missionaries Arthur and Laura Carson. Additional American Baptist missionaries, along with Karen missionaries, helped to establish this work. Today about 80 percent of the Chin people are Christian. Carson described the Chins as follows: "The people have no religion, being like the Karens, Ka Chins, and other Chins who are propitiators of evil spirits. They are very drunken, exceedingly savage, being headhunters living in villages, but otherwise much like the North American Indian."[19] The Carsons worked in Chin state for twenty-one years, and their priority was to open a mission compound. They started work on the Chin language, and in 1907 they introduced the Chin-Roman alphabet. On April 1, 1908, Arthur died of appendicitis at the Haka mission station. During his short stay he baptized one hundred converts and formed two churches. Mrs. Carson stayed in Chin until 1920 when she was compelled to return home due to ill health. Karen missionaries contributed much to the evangelization of the Chin state. Dr. J. H. Cope rightly commented,

> We owe everything to the Karens. We do not know what we would do without them. When Mr. Carson first came up, he brought three or four Karens with him, and from that time on, with a few exceptions, they have proven splendid men on whom one could place no end of responsibility. For a long time they were the only evangelists here. They went out to strange villages where no preparation had been made for them and where they were direly threatened. The first Chin Christians came seven days' journey from Haka where a Henzada Karen, Thra Shwe Zan, worked alone, seeing the missionaries only once a year. The Chin preachers went out under the Karens and some of our finest workers were trained by them. They learned the language, learned the ways of the people, and won their confidence. In the first literary work I did, it was the Karens who helped me. In the schoolwork as well, we have Karen Headmasters, and they have proved as valuable there as in the evangelistic work.[20]

---

[19] Jeffrey Lian and Bianca Son, "Conversion of the Chin in Burma: The Creation of an Elite, https://www.academia.edu/22663096/conversion_of_the_Chin_in_Burma_the_Creation_of_an_Elite (accessed January 5, 2019).

[20] Robert G. Johnson, "The Church in the Chin Hill," *Burma Baptist Chronicle* (Rangoon: University Press, 1963), 388.

Karens did not preach to the Burmese: first, because Burmese "bullied the Karen and regarded him as slave."[21] Second, the ethnic groups more readily embraced the gospel than the predominately Buddhist Burmese. Third, people like the Karens, the Kachins, the Lahu, the Wa, the Shan, and the Palaung from time immemorial had prophetic expectations of the coming of the Bible and the gospel within their religion. Don Richardson called this expectation "eternity in their hearts."[22]

Conclusion

For more than sixty years Myanmar has been ruled by a succession of brutal military regimes that ranked among the worst dictatorships in the world. They waged genocidal war against ethnic minority groups, successive regimes having used torture and rape as weapons of war, as well as forced labor—using people as mine sweepers and children as soldiers—and inflicting religious persecution. In fact, Milbrandt reported in 2012, "Based on the significant data collected in the field over the past decade…the forced displacement of the Karen ethnic group does rise to the international standard of genocide."[23]

In October 2015 eight of Myanmar's twenty-one ethnic groups/ organizations signed a nationwide ceasefire agreement (NCA) with the government of Myanmar and the army (Tamadaw), but there have been clashes between the Tamadaw and the Shan and the Karen Army.[24] Myanmar has continued to launch attacks on groups that did not sign the NCA (such as the Kachin-Independent Organization [KIO]), including large-scale offensives that have forced civilians to flee and deepened humanitarian crises across conflict-afflicted parts of northern Burma. Across much of the rest of the country, ethnic nationality communities are concerned about widespread violence; for example, the stateless Muslim Rohinjans in Northern Rakhine state have suffered genocidal abuses and marginalization with heavy-handed crackdown by the military.[25]

---

[21] Morrison, *Grandfather Longlegs*, 21.

[22] Richardson, *Eternity in Their Hearts.*

[23] Jay Milbrandt, "Tracking Genocide: Persecution of the Karen in Burma," *Texas International Law Journal* 48, no. 1 (Fall 2012): 63.

[24] In my opinion, the NCA is a fragile deal because the military occasionally violates the agreement in many areas.

[25] Free Burma Rangers, "Peace Process in Crisis," *Global Day of Prayer for Burma*, 2017, 5, https://www.freeburmarangers.org/wp-content/uploads/2017/01/2017-DOP-LowRes.pdf.

The fate of the Rohinja, the Muslim minority in Arakaine's state in western Burma, and that of Karen refugees in Thailand (and, for that matter, the fate of the internally displaced people in the eastern jungle of Myanmar) is similar. The Rohinja Muslim minorities are unwanted in Myanmar and Bangladesh. The Karen refugees are seen as oddballs in Thailand and Myanmar. The regime's attitude to non-Burman and non-Buddhist ethnic and religious groups is shaped by a fascist mentality that echoes Adolf Hitler and the German Nazi Party. In Burmese, this is summed up in the phrase "Amyo, Batha, Thathana" (One race, one language, one religion).[26]

The Chin also face religious persecution in its starkest form. A common Chin practice, as an expression of their faith and their culture, is to construct crosses on hillsides and mountaintops. In the past years the Tamadaw have torn down almost all of the crosses. In many instances, Chin Christian villagers have themselves been forced at gunpoint to destroy their crosses, which are so closely associated with their faith, and to build Buddhist pagodas in their place. Additionally, they are forced to contribute labor and resources for the construction of Buddhism, the religion of their oppressors.[27] Their churches and Bibles were burned, and Chin Christians were forcefully converted to Buddhism. In certain places Christians are offered food and educational opportunity for their children if they convert to Buddhism.

In conclusion, Burma remains today perhaps one of the most repressed countries on earth. The dominant influences on Baptists of Myanmar today are a hostile government and a hostile Buddhist majority. Myanmar Baptists must work and worship in the face of persecution. Baptists do not enjoy freedom of worship, a right deeply cherished in the West. Rosalie Hall Hunt recognizes that

> Among those hardest hit by the nation's woes is the community of faith. Often Christians are deliberately targeted, especially the ethnic minorities, where the percentage of Christians is impressively high....[But there is hope] along with thousands of pagodas, the spires of churches dot the landscape.[28]

---

[26] Benedict Rogers, *Burma: A Nation at the Crossroads* (London: Rider Books, 2012), 104.

[27] Rogers, *Burma*, 108.

[28] Rosalie Hall Hunt, *Bless God and Take Courage: The Judson History and Legacy* (Valley Forge, PA: Judson Press, 2005), 353.

Epilogue

Hunt is right. Sometimes I want to ask, "Lord, is this how you build your church?" The answer will be invariably, "Yes." This is how he builds his church—among the weak and the oppressed, amid severe persecution and zero tolerance. Yes, he will continue to build his church among the refugees, the displaced, and the persecuted, and the gates of hell will not overcome it. The religious freedom for Christians in Burma is fragile. But the fragile freedom can be a solid ground upon which Christ will build his church. To this I am a witness, a messenger, and a cheerleader.

PART III

BAPTISTS AND CULTURE IN THE MODERN WORLD (20TH–21ST CENTURIES)

Baptists in the United States

11

The Big Shift in the Twentieth Century: When God Became a Minority Object of Corporate Worship among Southern Baptists

Stuart Sheehan

The theological functions of corporate worship among Baptists in America, particularly those who were predecessors of Southern Baptists, were surprisingly consistent from the seventeenth century until the first half of the twentieth century. For nearly 250 years, these Baptists structured their worship around both doxology and communality. In more than 50 percent of all psalm and hymn texts they spoke vertically to God and horizontally to one another. This changed in the first half of the twentieth century. Southern Baptist worship assumed a strong communal focus in which congregants spoke predominantly to one another and mostly about themselves. By mid-century, God became a minority object of the people's worship.[1]

Evidence of this change was found during a detailed analysis of over 17,000 psalm and hymn texts published between 1638 and 2008 and used by Southern Baptists and their predecessors. This paper focuses on one segment of this data gathered from 2,710 texts contained in six hymnals used by Southern Baptists between 1892 and 1955.[2]

Prior to 1892, 54 percent of all psalm and hymn texts addressed God directly, and 59 percent of texts addressed fellow converts. Between 1882 and 1955, the average number of texts to God dropped below 40 percent, while texts to fellow converts rose to nearly 66 percent (see Figure 11.1). This was unprecedented among Southern Baptists and their predecessors in America.

---

[1] The complete study is in Stuart Lee Sheehan, "The Changing Theological Functions of Corporate Worship among Southern Baptists: What They Were and What They Became (1638–2008)" (PhD diss., University of Aberdeen, 2017).

[2] A list of the hymnals used for the analysis is located in the appendix for this chapter.

Doxology and Communality:
Average Allocation, 1638–1881 and 1892–1955

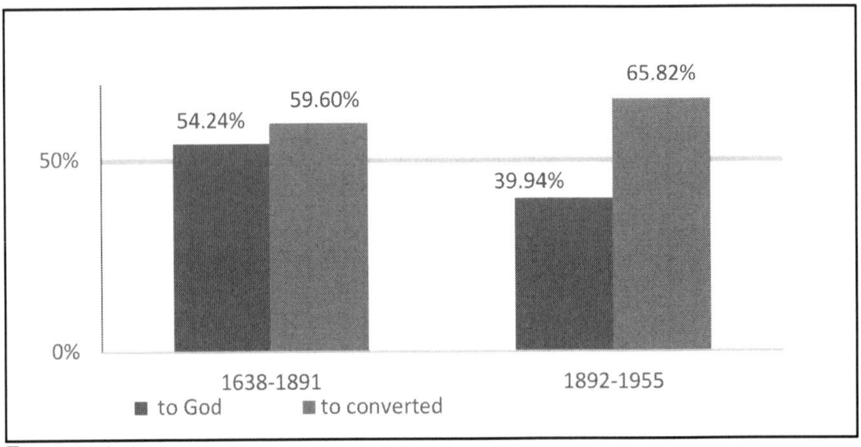

Figure 11.1.

In this chapter I provide a bit of context for this change and look more closely at how and when it progressed.

Influencers

Such a shift in corporate worship did not happen in isolation. Various denominational and cultural changes influenced Southern Baptists (large-scale societal change, denominational expansion, etc.). A large part of this change, however, occurred concurrently with significant shifts in Southern Baptist theology. We look briefly here at two men at the forefront of these theological changes: E. Y. Mullins (1860–1928) and W. T. Conner (1877–1952), and two men who implemented these changes in corporate worship: Robert Coleman (1869–1946) and B. B. McKinney (1886–1952).

The Influential Theologians

In the first half of the twentieth century, Southern Baptists were a homogenous group. In 1920, "About 80 percent of Baptist church members were farmers; 35 percent of these were tenants." They were mostly rural people who lived and believed similarly.[3] As late as 1941, 63.3 percent of all South-

[3] See Paul Harvey, *Redeeming the South: Religious Cultures and Racial Identities among Southern Baptists: 1865–1925* (Chapel Hill: University of North Carolina Press, 1997), 86.

ern Baptist churches were still located in rural areas.[4] Southern Baptists, however, existed in a growing environment of theological and cultural upheaval, typical of the fundamentalist-modernist controversy.[5] While the impact of the fundamentalist-modernist controversy was much stronger among Baptists in the North,[6] it did propel Southern Baptists to affirm their own beliefs, which they published in the first version of *The Baptist Faith and Message* (1925).[7]

The chief architect of this doctrinal statement was E. Y. Mullins. Mullins served as president of Southern Baptist Theological Seminary from 1899 to 1928. He and his protégé, W. T. Conner, were the most influential theologians among Southern Baptists in the twentieth century.[8] Their theological views reshaped the way Southern Baptists understood the significance of the individual. R. Stanton Norman has observed,

> Baptist distinctive writings prior to the twentieth century all shared the core distinctive of biblical authority. A shift in this expression occurred early in the twentieth century. Although many Baptists continued to assert biblical authority as the primary distinctive, others began to argue for the authoritative role of the individual, autonomous, religious experience prior to the authority of the Bible. The first major work to argue for a "redefining" of the primary distinctive of Baptists was E. Y. Mullins's *The Axioms of Religion*.[9]

The Axioms of Religion was broadly influential, impacting Baptists throughout North America.[10] The greatest influence was within his own denomination.

---

[4] Nancy Tatom Ammerman, *Baptist Battles: Social Change and Religious Conflict in the Southern Baptist Convention* (New Brunswick, NJ: Rutgers University Press, 1995), 53.

[5] James Leo Garrett Jr., *Baptist Theology: A Four-Century Study* (Macon, GA: Mercer University Press, 2009), 442–43.

[6] Barry Hankins, *Evangelicalism and Fundamentalism: A Documentary Reader* (New York: New York University Press, 2008), 39.

[7] Jerry Sutton, *A Matter of Conviction: A History of Southern Baptist Engagement with the Culture* (Nashville: B&H Publishing Group, 2008), 94.

[8] Walter B. Shurden, *Not an Easy Journey: Some Transitions in Baptist Life* (Macon, GA: Mercer University Press, 2005), 82.

[9] R. Stanton Norman, "Southern Baptist Identity: A Theological Perspective," in *Southern Baptist Identity: An Evangelical Denomination Faces the Future*, ed. David S. Dockery (Wheaton, IL: Crossway Books, 2009), 53.

[10] David W. Bebbington, *Baptists through the Centuries: A History of a Global People* (Waco, TX: Baylor University Press, 2010), 259.

Mullins's theology has been described in various ways. Gregory Wills wrote that Mullins "reconstructed Christian doctrine on the basis of experience."[11] This was a radical shift, one that David Dockery described as moving away "from a hermeneutic of divine sovereignty...to one of personal revelation and experience."[12] Mullins's approach was structured around two themes: soul competency and Christian experience.[13] To him, soul competency was, as Elizabeth Newman wrote, a "competency under God, one that excluded all human interference."[14] Walter Droughton opines that Mullins's view of acquiring spiritual knowledge "called for testing the facts until truths become valid....Only human experience could verify these truths."[15] Timothy George has stated that Mullins's view of soul competency so strengthened the focus on the individual that it rendered the Reformation ideal of congregational priesthood meaningless.[16] Mullins's views, owing much to individualism and personalism, became fundamental to the way Southern Baptists understood their faith.[17]

W. T. Conner served as professor of systematic theology at Southwestern Baptist Theological Seminary for nearly forty years (1913–1952). He studied under Mullins and "may have exceeded his old professor in trumpet-

---

[11] Gregory A. Wills, *Southern Baptist Theological Seminary: 1859–2009* (Oxford: Oxford University Press, 2009), 242.

[12] David S. Dockery, *Christian Scripture: An Evangelical Perspective on Inspiration, Authority, and Interpretation* (1995; Eugene, OR: Wipf & Stock, 2008), 186.

[13] Anthony L. Chute, Nathan A. Finn, and Michael G. Haykin, *The Baptist Story: From English Sect to Global Movement* (Nashville: B&H Academic Publishing Group, 2015), 418.

[14] Elizabeth Newman, "The Priesthood of All Believers and the Necessity of the Church," in *Recycling the Past or Researching History?*, Studies in Baptist Historiography and Myths, ed. Philip E. Thompson, Anthony R. Cross (Eugene, OR: Wipf & Stock, 2005), 51.

[15] Walter D. Droughton III, "The Atonement," in *Has Our Theology Changed: Southern Baptist Thought since 1845*, ed. Paul A. Basden (Nashville: Broadman and Holman Publishers, 1994), 85.

[16] Timothy George, "Toward an Evangelical Future," in *Southern Baptiusts Observed: Multiple Perspectives on a Changing Denomination*, ed. Nancy Tatom Ammerman (Knoxville: University of Tennessee Press, 1993), 290. For his exposition of this subject, see Timothy George, "The Priesthood of All Believers," in *The People of God: Essays on the Believers' Church*, ed. Paul Basden and David S. Dockery (Eugene, OR: Wipf & Stock, 2009), 85–95.

[17] Mullins's theology was a derivative of Schleiermacher (individualism) and Bowne (personalism). See William E. Ellis, *A Man of Books and a Man of the People: E. Y. Mullins and the Crisis of Moderate Southern Baptist Leadership* (Macon, GA: Mercer University Press, 2003), 76–77.

ing the competency of the individual before God."[18] Like Mullins, his theology linked biblical authority to personhood. Almer Jesse Smith has observed, "Conner subordinated the Scriptures to other factors in his consideration of the doctrine of revelation. His understanding of persons as spiritual beings found its basis in the philosophy of personalism rather than biblical teaching."[19] His long tenure made his impact on Southern Baptist pastors and missionaries undeniable.[20]

Mullins and Conner moved the Southern Baptist understanding of theology toward a horizontal plane, from one based on biblical authority toward one dependent on personal ratification. In this construct, the people and their experiences were paramount in understanding their faith. So great was the change that occurred under Mullins's watch that Harold Bloom described him not as the founder of modern Southern Baptists "but as their refounder, the definer of a creedless faith."[21] Thus, theologies previously constructed around propositional truth required validation by personal experience. This was a portent of significant upheaval in the construct of corporate worship.

The Influential Practitioners

Changes during this period were largely implemented in Southern Baptist worship by Robert Coleman and his protégé, Baylus Benjamin McKinney. These men stood watch for more than forty years over the content of hymnals that Southern Baptists used. David Music and Paul Richardson state that Robert Coleman was "the most important shaper of congregational song among Southern Baptists during the first four decades of the twentieth century."[22] He was a Baptist—an active member of the First Baptist Church of Dallas (Texas) during the tenure of George W. Truett.[23] His greatest influence was as a publisher. He produced dozens of hymnals and songbooks,

[18] Shurden, *Not an Easy Journey*, 83.

[19] Almer Jesse Smith, *The Making of the 1963 Baptist Faith and Message* (Eugene, OR: Wipf & Stock, 2008), 109.

[20] Garrett, *Baptist Theology*, 455.

[21] Harold Bloom, *The American Religion: The Emergence of the Post-Christian Nation* (New York: Simon & Schuster, 1992), 199.

[22] David W. Music and Paul Akers Richardson, *"I Will Sing the Wondrous Story": A History of Baptist Hymnody in North America* (Macon, GA: Mercer University Press, 2008), 350.

[23] Keith E. Durso, *Thy Will Be Done: A Biography of George W. Truett* (Macon, GA: Mercer University Press; Atlanta, GA: Baptist History & Heritage Society, 2009), 85.

many advancing the revival/gospel style beloved by Southern Baptists. So strong was Coleman's influence among Southern Baptists that they preferred his hymnals to those offered by their denomination. For example, Baptists from both the northern and southern United States combined forces to issue the *New Baptist Hymnal* in 1926. It was widely received in the North, but Southern Baptist churches were not receptive. In the same year Coleman released *The Modern Hymnal.* Baptist churches across the South embraced Coleman's hymnal rather than the *New Baptist Hymnal.*[24]

B. B. McKinney was a Southern Baptist luminary. He served as professor of church music at Southwestern Baptist Theological Seminary from 1919 to 1931.[25] Concurrently, he served as Robert Coleman's editor from 1919 to 1935. Thereafter, McKinney became the first person to hold the position of music editor at the Sunday School Board of the Southern Baptist Convention.[26] In 1941 he was named the first director of the Convention's newly formed Church Music Department, a position he held until his death in 1952.[27] McKinney's long tenure with Coleman, his teaching position at Southwestern Baptist Theological Seminary, and his leadership with the Sunday School Board gave him a grand platform from which to influence the corporate worship of Southern Baptists.

It is interesting that Coleman and McKinney shared various connections with Mullins and Conner. McKinney served on the faculty at Southwestern Baptist Theological Seminary with Conner for eleven years. Coleman and Mullins worked closely together in denominational activities.[28] The intermingling of the professional and denominational lives of these men lasted for decades. Through men such as Mullins and Conner, changes oc-

---

[24] Music and Richardson, *"I Will Sing the Wondrous Story,"* 410.

[25] "Biographies: Baylus Benjamin McKinney," Southern Baptist Historical Library and Archives, http://www.sbhla.org/bio_bbmckinney.htm (accessed September 1, 2017).

[26] William H. Brackney, "McKinney, Baylus Benjamin," *Historical Dictionary of the Baptists*, 2nd ed. (Lanham, MD: Scarecrow Press, 2009), 380.

[27] Music and Richardson, *"I Will Sing the Wondrous Story,"* 355.

[28] In 1922 Mullins preached and Coleman led music in the plenary sessions of the Southern Baptist Convention when it met in Jacksonville, Florida, and again the next year at the Southern Baptist Convention in Kansas City. See *Annual of the Southern Baptist Convention, 1922: Sixty-Seventh Session, Seventy-Seventh Year, Jacksonville, Fla., May 17–22, 1922* (Nashville: Marshall & Bruce, n.d.), 9; and, *Annual of the Southern Baptist Convention, 1923: Sixty-Eighth Session, Seventy-Eighth Year, Kansas City, Missouri, May 16–20, 1923* (Nashville: Marshall & Bruce, n.d.), 46. Coleman also held leadership positions in the Convention during the time of Mullins's tenure as president. For his committee assignments, see *Annual of the Southern Baptist Convention, 1922*, 16.

curred in the way Southern Baptists understood themselves and how they viewed God. Southern Baptists were moving from a theocentric understanding of faith to one that was more anthropocentric.

Data

Texts Addressed to God and Texts Addressed to Other Believers

Figure 11.2 shows how the axis of corporate worship tilted away from God. In the first and second volumes tested during this period (1892 and 1904), direct address to one or more persons of the Triune God held at levels that were consistent with previous centuries of practice. In the third volume tested, which was the first in the sample edited by Coleman (1918), the number of texts addressing God plummeted to 30.83 percent.

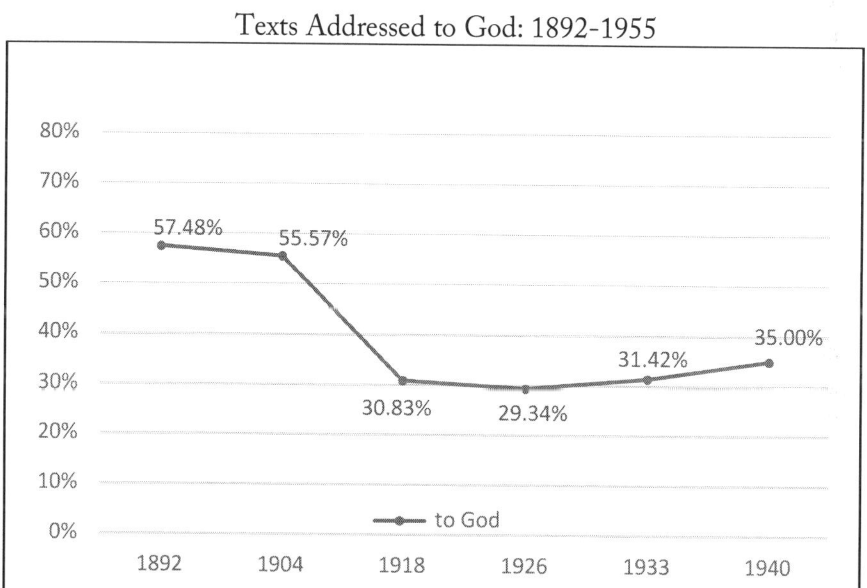

Figure 11.2.

Coleman's next two volumes stayed at similar levels and recovered only slightly in 1940. In McKinney's *The Broadman Hymnal*, still only 35 percent of texts contained a vertical or doxological orientation.

As congregants addressed God less, they also addressed him less in terms of his transcendence. The image of a holy and transcendent God was giving way to a closer, gentler one—a father who welcomed his children to live near him. Surprisingly, the closer God became in the minds of worshipers, the less they spoke to him. Apart from examining any other feature in this period, the change in the fundamental structure of corporate worship away from a vertical, doxological orientation was an extraordinary development.

Figure 11.3 shows that as texts addressing God declined, congregants addressed each other more often. In 1892 and in 1904 the allocation of direct addresses to fellow converts remained consistent with historical practice. Thereafter, it rose to 72 percent in 1918 and remained high in the last volume (67.50 percent). Clearly, Baptists turned their attention away from God, speaking to one another about their shared experiences in the faith.

Texts Addressed to the Converted, 1892–1955

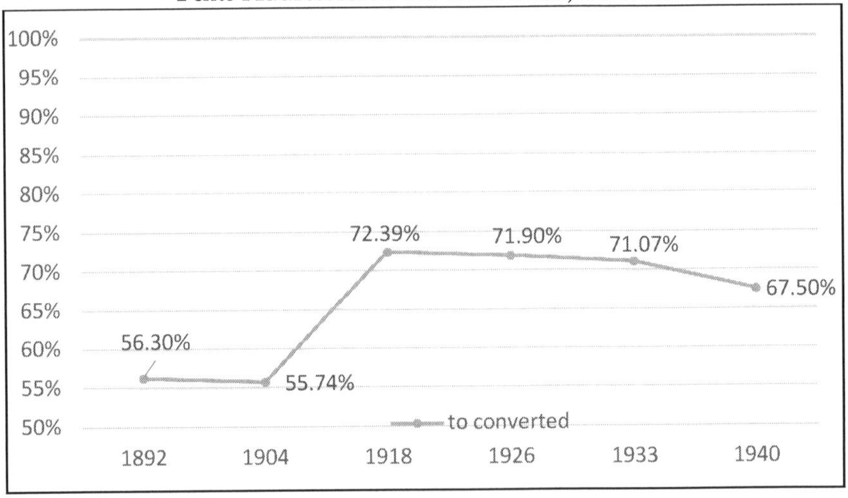

Figure 11.3.

The remarkable difference from 1918 forward demonstrated the degree to which Coleman and McKinney affected Southern Baptist worship. Both men were working from a paradigm where the horizontal axis in worship was significantly more important than the vertical axis. The rise of texts in which congregants spoke to one another was concurrent with a proportionate decrease in texts that addressed God.

The graph of Figure 11.4 shows that as congregants spoke less to God, there was a change in what they said. The answer reveals McKinney's great contribution to the profound change that occurred in Southern Baptist worship. McKinney placed an unusually high value on reflexive texts, those in which worshipers spoke about themselves. His allocation of reflexive texts evidenced an extraordinary increase. In the first five volumes tested in this period published between 1892 and 1933, the average number of texts in which worshipers spoke about themselves was about 54 percent. In McKinney's *Broadman Hymnal*, over 72 percent of all texts were reflexive. McKinney followed Coleman in reducing texts to God, but he went far beyond Coleman in creating a worship environment in which congregants were most concerned about themselves.

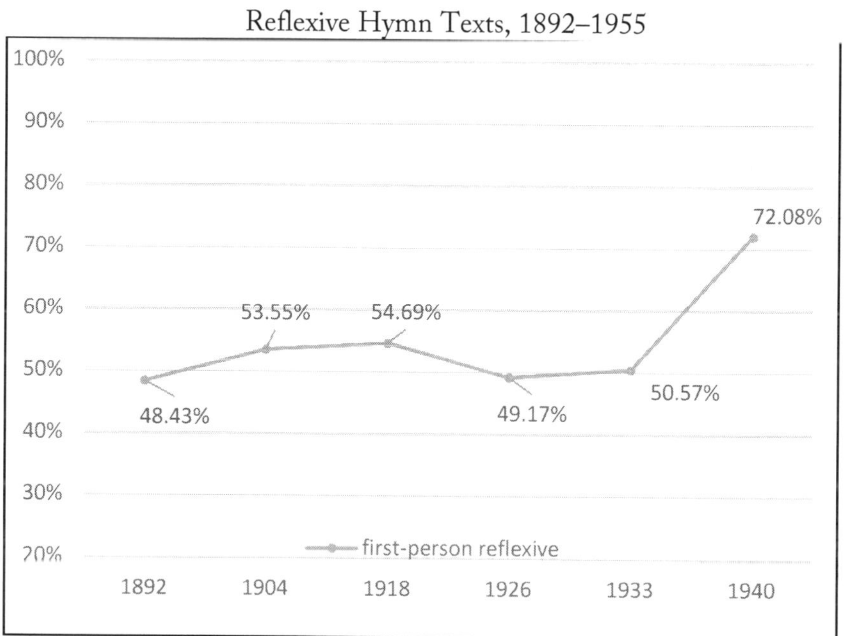

Figure 11.4.

By 1940 the self-focus was dominant. McKinney's own words provide an explanation of this strong self-orientation. In the foreword to the *Broadman Hymnal*, he wrote that hymns are a medium "through which all devout souls may join in giving expression to their deepest emotions."[29] Such a notion of corporate worship was well suited to individualism and the fascination with personal experience so prevalent in the theologies of Mullins and Conner. Figures 11.5 and 11.6 create a striking picture of how texts ad-

[29] B. B. McKinney, foreword to *The Broadman Hymnal* (Nashville: Broadman Press, 1940).

dressed to God, texts addressed to fellow converts, and the use of reflexive texts changed during this period.

Texts Addressed to God, Texts Addressed to Other Converts, and Reflexive Texts, 1892–1955

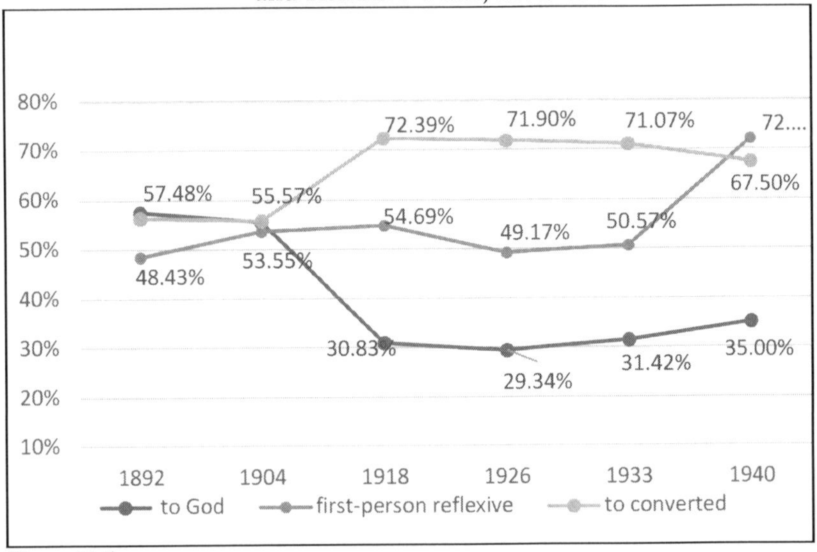

Figure 11.5.

Doxology and Communality: Average Allocation, 1638–1881 and 1918–1955

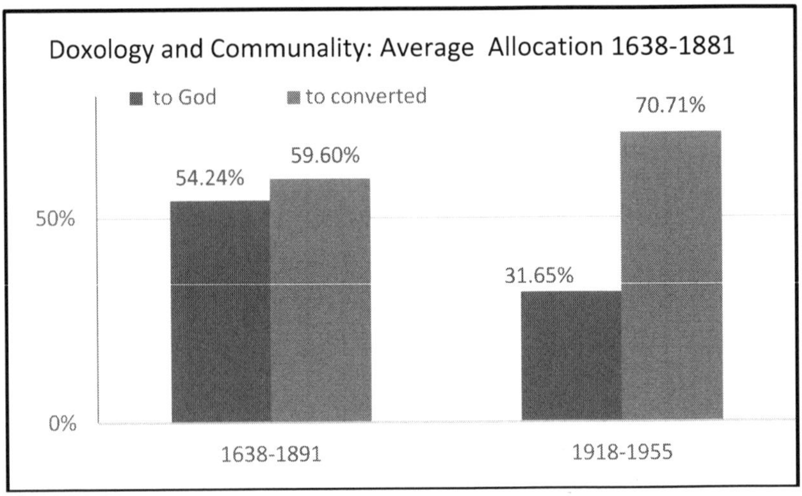

Figure 11.6.

Speaking to one another largely replaced speaking to God. As we have seen, this trend reached its zenith with McKinney as he provided a supermajority of texts for worshipers to speak through the lens of their personal emotion and experience. Congregations spoke of God less in terms of his transcendence and less *to* him in general. Certainly, texts that spoke about God had some doxological function, if only in a secondary sense. To talk about someone, however, does not have the same effect as speaking to them directly. The preference was leaning more toward an obsession with personal testimonies and mutual encouragement. Worship services in this construct no longer served a primarily doxological function.

Conclusion

Timothy George has observed that, by the mid-1920s, Southern Baptists had "imbibed freely of the spirit of 'rugged individualism,' attenuating fixed norms of doctrine to a theology of radical subjectivism."[30] The data from Southern Baptists' most used hymnals confirms this subjective focus, not only in the way influential theologians wrote and thought but also in the way Southern Baptist people practiced their worship.

Speaking less to God resulted, in the end, in an increased focus on people. This was particularly evident in the *Broadman Hymnal*, the first hymnal uniquely published by the Sunday School Board of the Southern Baptist Convention. By 1940, the maturation of corporate worship among Southern Baptists had spanned nearly one hundred years. The fruit of that process was surprising. By the mid-twentieth century, Sunday gatherings among Southern Baptists were not shaped for doxology. This was indicative of a reordering in their fundamental understanding of spiritual life. In theological terms, this transition bore the imprint of Mullins and Conner, who argued that personal experience was the basis of spiritual truth. A measurable connection was evident between the trajectory set by Mullins and Conner and the implementation wrought by Coleman and McKinney. There was an undeniable irony that a more immanent God, who revealed himself through personal experience, was also one to whom congregations gave less attention. Undeniably, the Creator and Savior was no longer the primary object of the

---

[30] Timothy George, "Toward an Evangelical Future," in *Multiple Perspectives on a Changing Denomination*, ed. Nancy Tatom Ammerman (Knoxville: University of Tennessee Press, 1993), 289.

people's worship, at least not in terms of speaking to him through their hymns.

Appendix

Hymnals Analyzed Used between 1892 and 1955

Burrows, Lansing. *The Baptist Hymn and Praise Book.* Nashville: Sunday School Board of the Southern Baptist Convention, 1904.

Coleman, Robert H. *The American Hymnal.* Dallas, TX: Robert H. Coleman, 1933.

———. *The Modern Hymnal.* Dallas, TX: Robert H. Coleman, 1926.

———. *The Popular Hymnal.* Dallas, TX: Robert H. Coleman, 1918.

Manly, Basil. *Manly's Choice: A New Selection of Approved Hymns for Baptist Churches with Music.* Louisville, KY: Baptist Book Concern, 1892.

McKinney, B. B. *The Broadman Hymnal.* Nashville: Broadman Press, 1940.

12

Walter Rauschenbusch on Baptists, Gospel, and Culture

Bill Pitts

Walter Rauschenbusch (1861–1918) was a Baptist minister and professor who believed that the biblical message to the church had been misunderstood. Properly interpreted, it included the mandate to transform society. In this chapter I explore why and how he reached this conclusion. I proceed by discussing his Baptist identity, his understanding of the gospel, and his view of the relationship of Christianity to culture.

The Shaping of Walter Rauschenbusch as Baptist Leader

Family Inheritance

Who was Walter Rauschenbusch? Religious and educational influences were crucial factors in his life. Rauschenbusch's father, Augustus, was a particularly strong influence. The sixth of a line of Lutheran pastors in Germany, Augustus came to the United States in 1846 to minister to German immigrants. After extended discussions with Baptists, Augustus joined their ranks. His German Pietism readily adapted to American Protestant conversionism.[1] Highly qualified academically because of his superb education in Berlin and Bonn, Augustus accepted the call to move to Rochester, New York, where he taught in the German Department of the Baptist Rochester Theological Seminary. Augustus was the chief educator for German-speaking Baptist ministers in the United States for thirty years (1858–1888).[2] Walter was born in Rochester in 1861. He admired his father's pas-

---

[1] This theme is developed in Carl E. Schneider, "The Americanization of August Rauschenbusch," *Church History* 24 (September 1953): 3–14.

[2] See the autobiography *Life and Ministry of August Rauschenbusch,* completed by Walter Rauschenbusch, trans. Donald H. Madvig (Sioux Falls, SD: North American Baptist Heritage Commission, 2008), 146–95.

sion for Baptists and excellence in education, as well as his devotion to German culture. Walter credits his mother for teaching him to pray when very young, and she was his single parent during Augustus's extended absences.

Convinced of the superiority of German education, in June 1865 Augustus moved the family to Germany for four years. Walter began his schooling there. Upon returning to Rochester in August 1869 Walter continued his education, and the family attended the First German Baptist Church. In this church Rauschenbusch made his profession of faith at age seventeen. He reported that this was a turning point in his life because in that experience he determined to become more serious about life and seek a way to turn others toward God and work to redeem humanity. This commitment was foundational for him. He said that he "wanted to do hard work for God."[3] Augustus sent Walter to Germany again to complete his high school education at the Gymnasium at Gütersloh. Bright and hardworking, Rauschenbusch finished at the top of his class. Following his work at Gütersloh, Rauschenbusch returned to Rochester and simultaneously entered the university to earn his AB degree and the Baptist seminary to prepare for church leadership. The seminary curriculum included biblical, theological, historical, and practical studies. He particularly favored New Testament and historical studies. The Baptist home, church, and training shaped his early religious and vocational outlook.

A New Theology

Protestant theology during the 1880s was undergoing changes of immense proportions. The idea of development was applied to understanding everything. Life was understood to be dynamic, not static. The new interpretation of Christianity emphasized God working through the process of history rather than from above it. Optimistic about human capacity, the newer theology stressed the possibility of human progress. Called at the time simply the "New Theology," this outlook embraced changes in cultural outlook and sought to adapt Christian theology to shifting understandings of the world, human beings, and God. The New Theology accepted the findings of science regarding the theory of evolution. Moreover, it embraced the historical

---

[3] Walter Rauschenbusch, "The Kingdom of God," *Cleveland's Young Men*, January 9, 1913.

approach to Scripture and to creeds, affirming the human and historical character of both.

Conservative Protestants reacted to the liberal New Theology by affirming traditional ideas about God, the creation of humanity, and the divine character of Scripture. Professors at Rochester held differing opinions about the New Theology. Rauschenbusch's Old Testament professor, Howard Osgood, taught traditional views, whereas his New Testament professor, William Arnold Stevens, accepted historical-critical studies. The youthful student experienced intense struggles over these contrasting approaches to Scripture. Rauschenbusch followed the counsel of his professors who held to the ideal that students should always seek the truth. He believed that the New Theology reflected honest pursuit of the truth much better than traditional theologies. He reported that this intellectual shift "cost him a great struggle."[4] He declared that this shift was the second conversion in his life.[5] By 1900 the New Theology had been adopted by most northern Protestant seminaries in America, including the Baptist seminaries.[6]

The Economic Challenge of Society

After completing his seminary training, Rauschenbusch accepted a call to become pastor of the Second German Baptist Church near Hell's Kitchen in New York City. Here he dealt with people living in the midst of persistent poverty. Immigrants searching for work took unskilled jobs in factories and lived in tenement housing that required one-fourth to one-half of their wages.[7] Disease, alcoholism, and despair were rampant in New York City. Although academically he had finished at the top of his class, Rauschenbusch was overwhelmed when he realized that seminary had not prepared him at all to minister to the pressing daily needs of his people.[8] It is fair to say that,

[4] Walter Rauschenbusch to C.E. Smith, March 21, 1912, cited in Paul M. Minus, *Walter Rauschenbusch: American Reformer* (New York: Macmillan Publishing Company, 1988), 40.

[5] Lemuel Call Barnes, "Walter Rauschenbusch—His Personal Testimony," *Watchman Examiner*, August 1, 1918: 985.

[6] LeRoy Moore Jr., "The Rise of American Religious Liberalism at the Rochester Theological Seminary, 1872–1928" (PhD dissertation, Claremont Graduate School, 1966), and Moore, "Academic Freedom: A Chapter in the History of Colgate Rochester Divinity School," *Foundations* 10 (January–March 1967). 64-79.

[7] Jacob Riis, *How the Other Half Lives* (New York: Dover, 1971), 190–200 passim.

[8] For a recent comprehensive history of New York City in the 1880–1898 period, see Edwin G. Burrows and Mike Wallace, *Gotham* (New York: Oxford University Press, 1999).

for Rauschenbusch, the social gospel began when he encountered suffering humanity. What was a minister to do?

Response: A Social Gospel

Rauschenbusch was deeply moved in 1886 when he heard a speech by Henry George, author of *Poverty and Progress.* In this book George asked why poverty was rampant if the nation was making progress.[9] This book introduced Rauschenbusch to social analysis of the nation. Rauschenbusch took a summer sabbatical during his first year as pastor to read analyses of changing American society. He was drawn to a moderate form of socialism. Socialism in Europe had connotations of revolutionary politics, atheism, and sexual license. Rauschenbusch wanted none of this, and he refused to join the American Socialist Party. But by definition the overall goal of socialism is to create a society that looks out for the well-being of all of its members. Rauschenbusch believed that this goal was compatible with the Christian teaching of love, service, and cooperation with others, whereas the structure of unrestrained capitalism was clearly not Christian because it was built on competition and hurt other people. How might the nation be made more Christian? What should change? Rauschenbusch advocated public or city ownership of essential utilities used by everyone, including water, electricity, and public transportation. Prices for coal should be fixed at a low rate. In this way all of society, including the poorer, would benefit from low, regulated costs for the essentials of daily life. Does this goal of benefitting everyone have anything to do with Christianity? Rauschenbusch soon began to believe that it did. He met on Sunday afternoons with two like-minded young Baptist ministers, Leighton Williams and Nathaniel Schmidt. They discussed Christian devotional classics, prayed, and took Communion together.[10] They agreed that they must minister outside the walls of their churches. Soon Rauschenbusch and colleagues started a journal called *For the Right*, which gave Rauschenbusch a platform for articulating his views regarding the plight of American workers. The paper was short-lived, but Rauschenbusch continued to publish his views in newspapers and religious journals, advocating changes for the common good in American society.

---

[9] Henry George, *Progress and Poverty* (New York: D. Appleton and Co., 1879).

[10] Winthrop S. Hudson, ed., *Walter Rauschenbusch: Selected Writings* (New York: Paulist Press, 1984), 17.

What Is the Gospel?

Rauschenbusch believed that the gospel had been misinterpreted. Modern biblical studies opened the way to a fuller understanding of Jesus's message.

The Biblical Message: Two Levels of Redemption

Rauschenbusch served as a Baptist pastor in New York City from 1886 to 1897. In 1891, halfway through his ministry, Rauschenbusch determined to take a sabbatical in Europe. He visited England to see how socialism was implemented in major cities, finding mixed results. In his view socialism had failed in Liverpool but succeeded in Birmingham. In Germany he spent time in libraries reading theology and analyses of society, and also writing a long analysis articulating his views. He called the work "Christianity Revolutionary."[11] When he returned to the United States, his typescript was left unpublished due to pastoral duties. It contained many of his essential ideas. In 1897 Rauschenbusch moved back to Rochester, where he served as professor for the remainder of his life (1897–1918), training Baptist ministers. There he produced a more succinct and compelling version of his 1891 manuscript, which he published in 1907 as *Christianity and the Social Crisis.* This book is his manifesto and perhaps the single most influential statement of the social gospel. Reflecting on his life, Rauschenbusch judged that discovery of the social gospel was his third major conversion, and he credited Henry George with pointing him toward social Christianity.[12] It was a radical view since it proposed that the church should work for systemic change in the economic order of society rather than simply providing charity to the poor. Critical skeptics would deny that this is the goal of the gospel. More liberal interpreters would affirm it.

In this book Rauschenbusch began by demonstrating the biblical evidence for concern for society. He pointed out that the prophets demanded justice in their moral message: religion and ethics were not separated in their thought. Their primary interest was the welfare of the nation, and they were outraged at the rich's treatment of the poor. Likewise, in his announcement of his mission Jesus emphasized that he came to liberate the poor and oppressed (Luke 4). Rauschenbusch anchored his argument firmly in Scrip-

---

[11] Max Stackhouse published the typescript as *The Righteousness of God* (Nashville: Abingdon Press, 1968).

[12] Walter Rauschenbusch, *Christianizing the Social Order* (New York: Macmillan, 1912), 394.

ture. He realized that his proposal was revolutionary, and he often took the opportunity to remind readers how radical Jesus was and how he challenged the prevailing religion of his day. Baptists had become traditional in their outlook. He called on them to change their thinking and become radical, like Jesus.

Rauschenbusch read deeply into current New Testament and theological studies. There he learned that the core teaching of Jesus was his proclamation of the kingdom of God, which was a proposal to transform society, not just the individual. Rauschenbusch declared that there are two great realities of humanity—the individual and the social—and both, he said, need redemption.[13] The idea of the kingdom of God was comprehensive in Rauschenbusch's view. It included all the goals, teachings, and practices of Christianity. So why was the church not living by the guidance of Scripture? He said that unfortunately this broad understanding of God's kingdom was lost during the second century, and the church soon settled on offering individuals eternal salvation through sacraments, liturgies, and creeds, while failing to advocate for justice in the social dimensions of the kingdom.

Social Redemption: Lost and Recovered

How could Rauschenbusch make such a bold claim? In his view, Adolph von Harnack was the most significant church historian of his era. Harnack famously taught that Jesus's message had been obscured by church fathers who sought to explain the Christian message by introducing Hellenistic categories such as *hypostases* and *homoousion*, terms foreign to the Bible. Early Christian theology thereby created a shell around the original teachings of Jesus and obscured his original thought. Harnack believed his task as church historian was to peel back these layers of dogmatic interpretations and reclaim Jesus's original teachings.[14] Rauschenbusch asked ironically, "What would Jesus have said to the symbol of Chalcedon or the Athanasian Creed if they had been read to him?"[15] Like Harnack, Rauschenbusch proposed to

---

[13] Walter Rauschenbusch, *Christianity and the Social Crisis* (New York: Macmillan, 1907), 307.

[14] Adolph Harnack, *History of Dogma*, 3rd ed., vol. 4 (New York: Dover, 1894); also, Adolph Harnack, *What Is Christianity* (New York: G. P. Putnam's Sons, 1901).

[15] Donovan Smucker, *The Origins of Walter Rauschenbusch's Social Ethics* (Montreal: McGill-Queen's University Press, 1994), 99. Historical understanding of doctrinal development was crucial to Rauschenbusch's interpretation. Smucker is citing Rauschenbusch, *Theology for the Social Gospel*, 25.

restore the full meaning of the kingdom of God to guide the church. He noted, for example, when Jesus offered a model prayer, it began, "Our Father," not "My Father." Jesus's major message centered on the kingdom of God—a social, not an individual concept.[16] Rauschenbusch gave much attention to studies of Jesus, and he himself wrote a life of Jesus, *Das Leben Jesu.*[17] He believed that recent biblical scholarship had recovered Jesus's true meaning of the kingdom of God. Rauschenbusch did not like the phrase "social Christianity" because in his view there is no other kind of Christianity. For him, original Christianity was both individual and social. It always includes both dimensions of life. At the heart of his thought was the affirmation of a two-level Christianity.[18] When Rauschenbusch later wrote a book on Jesus's teachings, he titled it *The Social Principles of Jesus,* and when he took on the task of writing a theology, he called it *A Theology for the Social Gospel.*[19] In his view, genuine Christianity always addresses the culture of society as well as the individual. It should include individual conversion, but the gospel proclaimed by Jesus reached beyond the personal to the transformation of society.

The Kingdom of God

During his 1891 sabbatical Rauschenbusch studied social theory and recent New Testament studies, especially the lives of the historical Jesus. What was becoming clear in the scholarship of this era was that Jesus's central message was the kingdom of God or kingdom of heaven. By employing comparisons, Jesus's parables repeatedly pointed to the kingdom of God as the goal of life. Similarly, Jesus's Sermon on the Mount centered on this kingdom. It was important, then, to understand what this meant. For Rauschenbusch, the kingdom appears as people accept the will of God for their lives. As he studied this idea, the comprehensive nature of the kingdom became clear to him. It was an inclusive idea that involved the messages and practices of the

---

[16] Walter Rauschenbusch, *Prayers of the Social Awakening* (Boston: The PilgrimPress, 1910), 17.

[17] Walter Rauschenbusch, *Das Leben Jesu* (Cleveland: P. Ritter, 1895).

[18] Richard Ely, *Social Aspects of Christianity* (New York: Charles Scribners Sons, 1889), had clearly affirmed this notion of two levels of Christianity, and Ely's thoughts influenced Rauschenbusch on this point.

[19] Walter Rauschenbusch, *The Social Principles of Jesus* (1916; New York: Association Press, 1927), and *A Theology for the Social Gospel* (1917; Louisville, KY: Westminster John Knox Press, 1997).

church but also extended to the will of God beyond the institutional church. Jesus's message of the kingdom of God included redemption of the political and economic life in the cities and the nation.

The implication of this understanding of the gospel is clear. The task of the church is to get beyond its own walls with its focus on individual salvation and morality. Does the church have relevance for the larger society? Rauschenbusch's answer was yes, and at the point it engages the culture, it seeks redemption for all aspects of life. How can people tell if they are on the track to the kingdom? Rauschenbusch's formulation for the kingdom of God is "the will of God in the hearts of men," a phrase drawn from Henry Scougel's *The Life of God in the Soul of Man* (1648). In practice Rauschenbusch appeals to justice as the criteria for creating orders of society that promote the well-being of all citizens. If this analysis of the kingdom is accurate, then the church has a much larger task before it than previously conceived. Jesus preached that all of society needed renewal and redemption.

The Churches and Culture

Rauschenbusch believed that Christians should create a better world. This idea was implicit in the teaching of the Kingdom of God. He believed this meant that Jesus taught the rule of God not merely in lives of individuals but also in the structures of the society which shaped their lives.

The Churches' Historic Response to Poverty

The church has always recognized its social obligation. Three patterns emerged in church history. The first response was charity. The earliest recorded narrative of the church—the book of Acts in the New Testament—offers clear evidence that followers of Christ were attentive to the physical needs of others. The office of deacons was created to assist fellow Christians. Likewise, Paul collected an offering for poorer Christians. Jesus himself taught us to pray, "Give us this day our daily bread."[20] Physical well-being is essential. Since the days of the New Testament, the church has taken responsibility for the poor, and for centuries the church has offered relief through the giving of alms, sharing of tithes, and distributing part of life

[20] Matthew 6:11.

savings through wills.[21] The motivation for Christian care for others is embodied in the primary ethic of Christians—the practice of love, or charity.[22]

The Industrial Revolution caused Christians to look closely at the problems that economic upheaval caused. People were drawn to cities for work. Crowded together, the social problems of poverty—poor housing, disease, insufficient wages, and loss of dignity—created a large, economically marginalized class of factory workers and the unemployed. Because alms were insufficient, Christians initiated a second level of response. The response of society in England and the United States created an unprecedented number of humanitarian movements designed to relieve human struggles—the Salvation Army and YMCA/YWCA, Factory and Prison Reform, the Anti-Slavery Campaign, and so on. The multiplication of relief institutions doubtless provided reliable and welcome assistance for thousands of people in scores of industrial cities of Europe and America. Yet the financial position of the lower classes did not change: chronic economic insecurity persisted, producing anxiety and hardship for millions. A more radical solution was needed.

Turn-of-the-century social critics analyzed the economic order and proposed a systemic overhaul of the capitalist system, whose very structure produced poverty and suffering for generation after generation. Some church leaders adopted this approach and named their new proposals "social Christianity" (F. D. Maurice [1805–1872] in England) or "social gospel" (Washington Gladden [1836–1918] in the United States). Walter Rauschenbusch did not create this third approach to addressing poverty, but he became its most eloquent and persuasive voice and thereby made a signal contribution to Christianity that has lasted to the present day.

---

[21] On wills, see Christopher Haigh, *English Reformations: Religion, Politics and Society under the Tudors* (Oxford: Clarendon Press, 1993). Haigh cites wills extensively, showing how funds were to be distributed.

[22] This outlook on life permeates the Bible. The Old Testament admonishes care for widows, orphans and strangers—the marginalized of society; the concern for care of others is evident in the New Testament. Throughout church history, a variety of church charities have aimed to relieve individuals from their suffering. The study of the church and economics has generally been neglected. See, however, serious attention developed on the topic in *The Church and Wealth,* ed. J. Shiels and Diana Wood (Oxford: Basil Blackwell, 1987). This volume explores many dimensions of the church and wealth.

Rauschenbusch's Proposal for Social Redemption

Reader response to *Christianity and the Social Crisis* was overwhelmingly positive. Ministers wrote to Rauschenbusch with gratitude for rearticulating their task. Many had felt the need to work for redemption of society. Now they had clear justification.[23] The book was the best seller in religion for the next three years.[24] It had struck a responsive chord. Appreciative ministers wanted their churches to be relevant, to be involved in constructing a better society. The kingdom of God included not merely individual personal conversion or healthy churches; it would also strive to create a more just nation. What would a Christian nation look like? In 1907 Rauschenbusch published an article titled "What Is a Christian Nation?" Here he identified six characteristics. A Christian nation would: (1) render help to the suffering, (2) punish with purpose to save [in the criminal justice system], (3) support development in every personality, (4) value spiritual over material wealth, (5) create a community of love modeled on the family, and (6) be conscious of God in national affairs.[25] These are general ideas, but he is clearly proposing striving for a society that values the lives of every person in the culture. This vision of the rule of God in society clearly demands of the church efforts to improve the culture of society guided by the value of justice for all as well as love to all.

In his longest book, *Christianizing the Social Order*,[26] Rauschenbusch offered further proposals on the Christian nation. He deeply valued American society, especially its emphasis on democracy, liberty, and justice. Rauschenbusch added a strong emphasis on solidarity. In this book his optimism reached its greatest height. He believed that major "orders" (institutional dimensions of life) had been Christianized: the home, where democracy prevailed more fully than in previous societies; the churches, which

---

[23] Providence, Rhode Island, resident Samuel Bottomley's sentiments are typical: "I want to express my hearty appreciation of *Christianity and the Social Crisis*. I consider it the most valuable contribution toward solving the many social and industrial problems of the world....It should be placed in the hands of every minister....The church can never repay the debt it now owes you" (Samuel Bottomley to Walter Rauschenbusch, December 6, 1907, in Rauschenbusch Family Papers, Box 25, American Baptist Historical Society Archives, Atlanta, Georgia).

[24] Robert D. Cross, "Introduction to the Torchbook Edition," *Christianity and the Social Crisis* by Walter Rauschenbusch, ed. Robert D. Cross (New York: Harper and Row, 1964), viii.

[25] Rauschenbusch, "What Is a Christian Nation," *The Standard*, January 23, 1907, 757–58.

[26] The Macmillan edition published in 1926 runs to 493 pages.

were increasingly democratic; public education, which did not limit access as did the selective German social structure; and finally, even politics. To be sure, politics were readily corrupted, but at least the design included a separation of powers and possibility of reform—unlike the traditional hierarchical political structure of many European regimes.

Despite all these notable advances, Rauschenbusch pronounced American society only semi-Christian. The one sector that fell short in its structure as well as in practice was the economic system. Rauschenbusch declared that unbridled capitalism was driven by greed and hence antithetical to Christian teaching. Instead, he proposed a system of cooperatives that would serve the needs of the masses.

Although Rauschenbusch offers a proposal for creating a better society, the mechanism he calls on is merely the goodwill of Christian Americans to cooperate in this effort. Critics since his day have seen this as a hopelessly naïve sentiment. People do not freely surrender their advantages. Yet he did offer a vision. Moreover, Americans did implement much of what he advocated. Regulating the economy would have to be done by law. The Progressive Party reached its peak at the same time as the influence of the social gospel (c. 1912), and legislation it supported proved to be the instrument of change in society—regulating work to forty hours per week, ending child labor, establishing safety regulations in factories, adding pure food and drug regulations, extending voting rights to women, adopting the direct election of senators, and so on. These changes in the law were driven by reformers who desired to extend participation and justice for all citizens. Rauschenbusch wanted the churches to at least serve as the conscience of the nation and work for its salvation.

The Churches Accept the Social Gospel

The churches did not give up on this task of creating a better society despite their lack of power to make actual legislative changes. They could continue to advocate for these changes, and they did precisely that. Methodist ministers, driven by conscience, proposed that the churches make efforts toward justice, and they prepared a social creed (1907), offering guidance for this. The Federal Council of Churches of Christ in America (1908) adopted a social platform that embodied Rauschenbusch's ideas.[27] Rauschenbusch's

[27] This most influential ecumenical structure was renamed The National Council of Churches of Christ in the U.S.A. in 1950.

persuasive writings brought the church to consciousness of its responsibility to reach beyond its own walls and work for human flourishing. The National Council of Churches has kept its commitment to social responsibility to the present day. In Shelton Smith's words, "Rauschenbusch was perhaps the foremost molder of American Christian thought in his generation....He was undoubtedly the major architect of American Protestant social thought."[28] As for its success, C. C. Morrison, editor of the *Christian Century,* observed that by the 1920s, study of the social gospel was included in the curriculum of all major North American seminaries except the Lutheran.[29] Gary Dorrien argues that Rauschenbusch's legacy was continued by Reinhold Niebuhr and then by liberation theologies.[30] While conservative Baptists rejected Rauschenbusch's proposals, insisting on changing individuals one by one to change society, mainline churches, including the Northern Baptist Convention, adopted the social gospel as an essential component of the gospel, message. Rauschenbusch was a Baptist who understood the gospel in a new way and empowered churches to work for the transformation of the culture around them in order to benefit all members of society. The social gospel finds its motivation in love of God; it also declares that Jesus's message of the kingdom is not complete without attention to the welfare of neighbors. In his classic *Christ and Culture*, Richard Niebuhr identifies five major patterns of relationship between Christ and culture that have emerged in the history of Christianity. These include "Christ against Culture," "The Christ of Culture," "Christ above Culture," "Christ and Culture in Paradox," and "Christ the Transformer of Culture." In Niebuhr's analyses, social gospel advocates fall into the category of the Christ of Culture.[31] Donovan Smucker appears to be close to the mark when he argues that Rauschenbusch is best understood as belonging to the category of Christ as transformer of cultural traditions.[32] This clearly was Rauschenbusch's intent.

---

[28] Shelton Smith, *Changing Conceptions of Original Sin* (New York: Charles Scribner's Sons, 1955), 198–206, 199.

[29] C. C. Morrison, *The Social Gospel and Christian Culture* (New York: Harper and Row, 1933), 15.

[30] See Gary Dorrien, *Soul in Society: The Making and Renewal of Social Christianity* (Minneapolis: Fortress, 1995).

[31] H. Richard Niebuhr, *Christ and Culture* (New York: Harper and Brothers, 1951), 100, 112.

[32] Smucker, *Origins of Walter Rauschenbusch's Social Ethics*, 87-91.

Rauschenbusch's Legacy

Rauschenbusch's legacy is broad. This chapter has focused on three aspects of his work: his Baptist legacy, gospel legacy, and social/cultural legacy.

Baptist Legacy

Rauschenbusch was a successful Baptist minister and professor. His sermons and publications, along with the reflections of friends and former students, attest to his intellect, his piety, his integrity, and his compassion. Rauschenbusch contributed to Baptist life not only as minister and teacher of ministers but as a denominational activist, seeking to guide the denomination to better practices. He was also a denominational loyalist who was proud of Baptist accomplishments and simply wanted fellow Baptists to do more.

How did Rauschenbusch understand Baptist identity? He made the effort to articulate Baptist principles in a series of articles he called "Why I Am a Baptist." The series, which became very popular, developed Baptist identity along four major themes.

First, Rauschenbusch said that Baptists call each person to conscious repentance from sin to faith in Christ. If someone wants to enter a Baptist church, said Rauschenbusch, the only criterion is evidence of such experience. Rauschenbusch explained that the point of religion is to put people in contact with God.[33] He drew on his knowledge of church history to draw contrasting claims among Christian traditions. He noted that the Catholic Church emphasized sacraments and rituals and the Lutherans stressed catechism and confirmation to make this connection. But Baptists relied on experience as the bedrock of their faith. For Baptists the essential point of religion is that it be experienced by each individual.[34] Rauschenbusch clearly embraced voluntary personal experience as the foundational Baptist principle that for him makes religion true and vital. This belief is, of course, the historic basis for Baptists rejecting infant baptism. Rauschenbusch's first reason for embracing the Baptist path is that true religion is personal and experienced.

Second, Rauschenbusch organized his argument around Baptist social expression and organization. Baptist churches admit only people "who deliberately apply" for membership and who seek to distinguish themselves

---

[33] Walter Rauschenbusch, "Why I Am a Baptist: My First Reason," *Rochester Baptist Monthly* 20, no. 4 (December 1905): 85–86.

[34] Rauschenbusch, "Why I Am a Baptist: My First Reason," 87.

from "the world."[35] Baptist churches are "Christian democracies." The congregation is the locus of authority, and it confers power on its ministers and officers. He thought the apostolic churches were democratic, and in modern Baptist life, "each church is sovereign in its own affairs."[36] Baptists accept no dictation from the State in their spiritual affairs, and "they ask no favors from the State."[37] He affirmed the importance of having democratic principles "in their very constitution in all of these many levels of social arrangements."[38]

In developing his third category of reasons for being a Baptist, Rauschenbusch focused on worship. He said that Baptists are radical Protestants when it comes to an understanding of baptism and the Lord's Supper.[39] Moreover, Rauschenbusch concluded that real worship, "the only kind that God cares for, is a Christ-like life." Jesus's prayer, Rauschenbusch declared, was meant to teach "utter simplicity."[40] He rejected sacramentalism as the essence of the meaning of worship and instead emphasized living out the Christian life.

Rauschenbusch's fourth and final article on Baptist identity addressed the intellectual component of religion, affirming that "religion appeals to the whole of man and...there is an intellectual element in all religions" because people seek answers to the eternal questions of how the world originated, why there is suffering, and what comes after death.[41] Baptists, he said, have no creeds; they do have statements of faith, but these are nonbinding.[42] In Rauschenbusch's view, Baptists have always recognized the Bible as their sole authority.

Rauschenbusch was careful not to discount the faith of Christians in fellow Protestant denominations. Although a loyal Baptist, his spirit transcended that commitment, and he considered himself part of a much larger company of Christians.

---

[35] Walter Rauschenbusch, "Why I Am a Baptist: My Second Reason," *Rochester Baptist Monthly* 20, no. 5 (January 1906): 107.

[36] Rauschenbusch, "Why I Am a Baptist: My Second Reason," 107.

[37] Rauschenbusch, "Why I Am a Baptist: My Second Reason," 107–8.

[38] Rauschenbusch, "Why I Am a Baptist: My Second Reason," 108.

[39] Walter Rauschenbusch, "Why I Am a Baptist: My Third Reason," *Rochester Baptist Monthly* 20, no. 6 (February 1906): 135.

[40] Rauschenbusch, "Why I Am a Baptist: My Third Reason," 136–37.

[41] Walter Rauschenbusch, "Why I Am a Baptist: My Fourth Reason," *Rochester Baptist Monthly* 20, no. 7 (March 1906): 156.

[42] Rauschenbusch, "Why I Am a Baptist: My Fourth Reason," 158.

Gospel Legacy

Biblical studies during the late nineteenth and early twentieth centuries experienced enormous change. Historical-critical methodologies, linguistic studies, and archaeological knowledge gleaned from Near Eastern discoveries brought innovation, creativity, and variety in interpretations of the biblical text. Rauschenbusch was immersed in the new approaches to biblical interpretation. He was well prepared for careful biblical studies. He was competent in New Testament Greek and was deeply influenced by his New Testament professor, who introduced him to modern methods of biblical study. Rauschenbusch's sermons, books, and especially the numerous Sunday School lessons he wrote and his seminary lectures reveal his appropriation of newer interpretative approaches. Rauschenbusch often noted that each book of the Bible had its own context that must be taken into account in order to arrive at legitimate interpretations; the Bible should not be interpreted by simply selecting a verse here and another there. Such an approach leads to misinterpretation. Rauschenbusch also sought out principles in the Bible that could be applied to the present. Thus, the prophets' messages were addressed to the nation of Israel, and their theme was God's demand for justice in people's dealings with one another. Recent scholarship had focused on producing lives of the historical Jesus, and these in turn found that his central theme was the kingdom of God. Albrecht Ritschl, the leading theologian of the era, and Adolph Harnack, the leading church historian, both adopted the current findings from New Testament studies. Rauschenbusch also accepted the centrality of the kingdom of God as the heart of the gospel. However, his creativity and his chief legacy in understanding the gospel were to interpret the kingdom as social as well as individual. The new tools of interpretation stimulated scholars to recover the original meaning of the gospel, obscured by centuries of church practice. Rauschenbusch's enduring legacy was to show that the original Christian good news included a message of salvation for the nation as well as for the individual.

Social/Cultural Legacy

Rauschenbusch's emphasis on the kingdom of God created a context for a broader interpretation of Christianity. He anchored his view not simply in his own compassion for the poor but in his belief that Scripture revealed a God who cares deeply for the poor. He sought principles in the Bible that could be applied to current life. For him the gospel addressed good news for all of life—body, mind, and soul. In his view the individual quest for salvation to escape hell and gain heaven was in the end a rather selfish, self-centered goal for religion. This was apparently not the model of relationship with God that Jesus taught. The Christian churches themselves had often slipped into being self-serving rather than servants. The church's existence was not meant to be an end in itself. Its task was to help to bring in the kingdom of God.

Conclusion

"Culture" is a broad term with many meanings. For Rauschenbusch it in cluded multiple human organizations, such as family relationships, educational institutions, political arrangements, and the economic structures of life. He was an optimist about many of the institutions and was grateful for all the nation had achieved, but he was appalled at the suffering of the lower classes of workers. He identified problems and proposed reforms meant to address inequities. He was deeply concerned that the church apply its energies to the reform of society. He understood that it was an institution and was interested in its own self-preservation and privileges. But he called on the church to seek to serve the larger society, to move beyond its own self-interest. Baptists and others divided over Rauschenbusch's proposal. Much of the church resisted his call, while much of it responded favorably.[43] But the struggle between greed/self-aggrandizement and benevolence/compassion for others is never ending. As Rauschenbusch said, "The kingdom is always but coming."[44] At a minimum he helped us think what Jesus's kingdom of God might look like in the world today.

[43] For analysis of the positive reception of Rauschenbusch during the past century, see William L. Pitts Jr., *The Reception of Rauschenbusch: The Responses of His Earliest Readers* (Macon, GA: Mercer University Press, 2018), chap. 12.

[44] Rauschenbusch, *Christianity and the Social Crisis*, 421.

13

The Gospel and the City: Four Baptist Churches in Twentieth-Century New York City

George Hancock-Stefan

If there is a city that considers itself in superlative terms, it is the city of New York, New York. If one listens to the classical or the most avant-garde contemporary radio stations; if one talks about Broadway or Wall Street; if one looks for an address that the world will know, or just says, "The City" without mentioning the name, it must be New York. From its beginnings under the name New Amsterdam to the changed name of New York, the city has always considered itself the leading city of the nation and of the world.

During his brief stay at Union Theological Seminary in New York, Dietrich Bonhoeffer's assessments of the seriousness of the students at Union, as well as the theological studies both of professors and students, were not generally flattering. What stands out very positively amid his negative assessment of his time in New York were his recollections of the Abyssinian Baptist Church in Harlem. In this Baptist church Bonhoeffer learned black hymnody and observed a depth of spirituality and relationship with God that he did not find in other churches in New York nor in Germany.[1]

My selection of the four churches is subjective, even though I think that my criteria of eliminating and choosing are valid. I have decided not to include Riverside Church because it has never identified itself as an exclusively Baptist church, even though it is associated with the ABC-USA. I also decided not to include the First Baptist Church of New York because,

[1] Bob Smietana, "Sunday Morning in America Still Segregated—and That's OK with Worshippers," *Lifeway Research,* last modified January 15, 2015, https://lifewayresearch.com/2015/01/15/sunday-morning-in-america-still-segregated-and-thats-ok-with-worshipers/.

even though it has deep historical roots, having been started by John Gano in 1762,[2] it is not currently an overly prominent church.

I have chosen four New York City Baptist churches that have been influential in the twentieth and twenty-first centuries: Abyssinian Baptist Church in Harlem, the Concord Baptist Church in Brooklyn, Calvary Baptist Church in Manhattan, and Judson Memorial Church in Manhattan. Since there is not any particular way to define influence in preaching the gospel, I seek to allow each individual church to tell its story and define its influence in the city and beyond.

The Abyssinian Baptist Church is one of the oldest black churches in New York City. It was started in 1808 after six African Americans were told they had to stay in the balcony of First Baptist Church, and it boasts a proud history of preacher-politicians. The Powells (father and son) represented their district in Congress for over forty years. From 1930 to 1931, Dietrich Bonhoeffer worshiped there and, as aforementioned, later wrote that one of the things that strengthened him during his imprisonment in a Nazi camp were the spirituals that he learned at the Abyssinian church.[3] Currently, the pastor of the church, Dr. Calvin Butts, is also the president of the State University of New York at Old Westbury.

The Concord Baptist Church was established in 1847. Under the leadership of Dr. Gardner Taylor (considered by many to be the dean of black preaching), the church was influential in the formation of the Progressive National Baptist Convention, the establishment of a private bank for black businesses, and the creation of opportunities for hundreds of preachers to hone their skills. Taylor's abilities were so influential that the current pastor, Dr. Gary V. Simpson, in cooperation with Dr. Edward L. Taylor, has collected and edited the sermons of Dr. Gardner Taylor in five volumes titled *The Words of Gardner Taylor*.[4] These sermons currently contribute to shaping the writing and preaching skills of many pastors.

---

[2] Kenneth T. Jackson, "Baptists," in *The Encyclopedia of New York City* (New Haven, CT: Yale University Press, 2010), 87; Robert G. Torbet, *A History of the Baptists*, 3rd ed. (Valley Forge, PA: Judson Press, 1973), 226.

[3] Eric Metaxas, *Bonhoeffer: Pastor, Martyr, Prophet, Spy: A Righteous Gentile vs. the Third Reich* (Nashville: Nelson, 2010 . Also described in Genna Rae McNeil et al., *Witness: Two Hundred Years of African American Faith and Practice at the Abyssinian Baptist Church of Harlem, New York* (Grand Rapids: Eerdmans, 2014), 143–45.

[4] Gardner C. Taylor, *The Words of Gardner Taylor*, vol. 1: *The NBC Radio Sermons, 1959–1970;* vol. 2: *Sermons from the Middle Years, 1970–1980;* vol. 3: *Quintessential Classics,*

Calvary Baptist Church was considered a bastion of conservative theology from the time of the modernist-fundamentalist controversy, through the stellar days of Stephen Olford. Contemporary church historian Philip Jenkins writes that the liberals won in the United States but the fundamentalists won globally; in many denominations the liberals are the Americans and the conservatives are the internationals.[5] Additionally, Calvary is located within a hotel that belongs to the church and provides huge financial resources for the church's ministry.

Judson Memorial Baptist Church, started in 1901, prides itself on being the leader of liberal causes in Baptist life, and one of the few churches wherein spirituality and the arts have collaborated successfully. The pastors represent liberal agendas primarily within the ABC-USA, but they have also been very influential in the city as a whole.[6]

All four churches are connected to the political and cultural life of the city and have influenced people nationally and internationally as leading musicians, politicians, educators, and diplomats have worshiped in their sanctuaries. Each church also has trained a vast cadre of preachers and church leaders who were sent out to work in other churches, as well as in education and politics.

In this chapter, I present a historical chronological history of the churches, an account of the leaders and events that have caused each church to become influential, and ways in which preaching of the gospel at each of the four churches has advanced the kingdom of God in the city.

The Abyssinian Baptist Church

The Abyssinian Baptist Church, established in 1808 as the fifth black Baptist church in the United States, is the mother of Concord Baptist Church, the first African American Baptist church in Brooklyn, built in 1847. The Abyssinian church was established by freed colored individuals who deeply

---

1980–Present; vol. 4: *Special Occasion and Expository Sermons;* vol. 5: *Lectures, Essays, and Interviews,* comp. Edward L. Taylor (Valley Forge, PA: Judson Press, 2000).

[5] Philip Jenkins, *The New Faces of Christianity: Believing the Bible in the Global South,* (New York: Oxford University Press, 2006), 2–12. See also Jenkins, *The Next Christendom: The Coming of Global Christianity*: "The North would be secular, rational, and tolerant, the South primitive and fundamentalist. The North would define itself against Christianity" (New York: Oxford University Press, 2002), 162.

[6] "Judson Memorial Church: Overview," Classic Judson.Org, last revised 2015, http://classic.judson.org/historical-overview.

treasured their connection with their ancient roots in Ethiopia, also known as Abyssinia. Until 1864 the church was located on 44 Worth Street; at that time they moved to 166 Waverly Place. Then, in 1902 they moved to 242 West 40th Street. During the Harlem Renaissance, the church built a new sanctuary on West 138th Street between Lenox and Seventh Avenues. In addition to this historic building, dedicated in 1928, the church bought additional land in order to build homes for the retired and aged.

While the Abyssinian Baptist Church has had a number of pastors for short periods, their stellar pastors stayed for a long time. Rev. William Spellman was pastor of the church from 1856 to 1885, during which time the congregation grew to sixteen hundred members. During the pastorate of Robert Wynn (1885–1902), the congregation moved to Greenwich Village, which became the hub for the African American community in New York. During the centennial celebration in 1908, Rev. Dr. Adam Clayton Powell Sr. became the pastor and started the so-called Powell Years, continued by the pastorate of his son Rev. Dr. Adam Clayton Powell Jr. The father served from 1908 to 1930 and the son served from 1930 to 1971. In 1971 Samuel DeWitt Proctor became the pastor until 1989, when the current pastor, the Reverend Dr. Calvin Butts succeeded him. These four pastors have served the Abyssinian Baptist Church for a period of 110-plus years.

The membership of the church had phenomenal growth, from two thousand members when the church's new sanctuary was built in the 1920s to fourteen thousand members in 1941 during the tenth anniversary of the Powell Jr. pastorate. The elder Powell set the tone of the ministry of the Abyssinian church as social activism blended with spiritual leadership. He established the standard for missions through community service, which the Abyssinian Baptist Church still upholds today.[7]

In 2017 it was announced that the current pastor, Dr. Butts, was considering running for the office of the mayor of New York. Currently he is president of SUNY (State University of New York) College at Old Westbury. If successful, it would represent the blend of religion and politics that was previously maintained by the Powells, who represented their district in the U.S. Congress for forty years. The uniqueness and the impact of the

---

[7] McNeil et al., *Witness*; "A Legacy of Leadership: Keeping Faith: A Historical Timeline of Abyssinian Baptist Church Dedicated to 'the Worship of God and the Service of Humanity," *Abyssinian Baptist Church*, http://abyssinian.org/about-us/history/ (accessed July 9, 2018).

Abyssinian Baptist Church stems from their members' and leaders' ability to combine politics, theology, education, arts, and real estate.[8]

According to the *Real Deal: New York Real Estate News*, the Abyssinian Development Corp., the development arm of the Abyssinian church, "is believed to be the third largest landlord in Harlem, steadily adding properties since the 1980s. The company eventually owned $172 million in properties and assets and was responsible for more than $600 million in residential and commercial development in Harlem."[9] Butts is the leader of both—the Abyssinian Baptist Church and the Abyssinian Development Corporation. Although the real estate activity has garnered the finances necessary to perform mission work, it has received much criticism from members of the New York press,[10] as did the increasingly lavish lifestyle that Adam Clayton Powell Jr. maintained during his political involvements, while claiming that he was a representative of the Harlem poor.[11]

The Abyssinian Baptist Church pastors have shown an unsurprisingly expansive and multidimensional range in their preaching as well. In a sermon preached on "If anyone is in Christ, he is a new creation," Butts had eight main points. The first four could have been preached in any evangelical church (including Calvary in Manhattan), while the last four points were vintage social gospel. While Powell Sr., like Butts, was homiletically very conservative, Powell Jr. showed his capabilities for straying very far from tradition when he wrote,

> We do not believe in the Bible as the Word of God. It is too filled with contradictions. We believe in the Thomas Jefferson Bible. Carefully that brilliant Founding Father cut from the New Testament only

---

[8] "Abyssinian's Fire Sale Sets Off Legal Spat," *The Real Deal: New York Real Estate News*, March 13, 2017, https://therealdeal.com/2017/03/13/abyssinians-fire-sale-sets-off-legal-spat/.

[9] "Abyssinian Will Continue Selling Properties to Cover Shortfalls," *The Real Deal: New York Real Estate News*, November 23, 2015, https://therealdeal.com/2015/11/23/ abyssinians-will-continue-selling-properties-to-cover-shortfalls/.

[10] Timothy Williams, "Powerful Harlem Church Is Also a Powerful Harlem Developer," *New York Times,* August 17, 2018, https://www.nytimes.com/2008/08/18/nyregion/ 18abyssinian.html.

[11] William H. Brackney, *A Genetic History of Baptist Thought* (Macon, GA: Mercer University Press, 2004), 464.

> the words that Jesus spoke. Then in a logical order he put them together until he created a new Bible, a new Bible of old words.[12]

Thus, Powell Jr. mainly preached on what he considered to be the authentic words of Jesus. Also he moved beyond one of his favorite theologians, Walter Rauschenbusch, believing that the kingdom of God is achievable here on earth.[13]

The historic Abyssinian church hosts many visitors. Thinking logistically, the church has multiple services on the weekend, with one at 11 a.m., specifically reserving seats for visiting tourists.[14] Throughout its history, the church not only has had excellent preachers but has also been involved in the arts. The pipe organ is a five-manual, sixty-seven-rank instrument that was installed during the time of Reverend Proctor, and artists such as Leontyne Price, Billy Taylor, Andre Watts and others have contributed to the worship services. In addition, the church regularly lists all of its artists who are involved on and off Broadway. Commissioned for the two hundredth anniversary of the church, Wynton Marsalis composed "The Abyssinian 200: A Celebration," which was performed both at Lincoln Center and at the church.[15] Internationally known athletes are also regular attendants of the church's worship services.

The Abyssinian Baptist Church is involved in education through its own schools that span from kindergarten through high school—the Thurgood Marshall Academy Lower School and the Thurgood Marshall Academy for Learning and Social Change.[16] In 2014 the church published *Witness: Two Hundred Years of African American Faith and Practice at the Abyssinian Church of Harlem, New York*, detailing the life and the impact of this great congregation.[17]

---

[12] Adam Clayton Powell Jr., *Adam by Adam: The Autobiography of Adam Clayton Powell Jr.* (New York: Kensington, 1971), 43.

[13] Brackney, *Genetic History*, 464–65.

[14] The author visited the church on a Sunday when Dominique Dawes was the person in the audience. I went to the early service but was gently told by a deacon/usher to come to the tourist service at 11 a.m.

[15] "Legacy of Leadership."

[16] " Legacy of Leadership," and McNeil, *Witness.*

[17] *Witness* was a collaboration among Genna Rae McNeil, a professor at the University of North Carolina at Chapel Hill, who specializes in African American history and U.S. social movements of the twentieth century; Houston Bryan Roberson, who was a history professor at the University of the South in Sewanee, Tennessee, for twenty years; Quinton Hosford Dixie, historian and author of other works such as *This Far by Faith: Stories from the*

The Concord Baptist Church

Many people think that in the 1960s, the members of the African American Baptist Conventions all supported the ideas of Martin Luther King Jr. and voted for the Democratic Party. However, the leadership of the largest African American Convention, the National Baptist Convention, USA Inc., actually supported Nixon in his political battle with John F. Kennedy. Martin Luther King Jr. knew that although he had great ideas and many young African American leaders behind him, he also needed someone who came from a large church and was regarded as a seasoned leader. That church was Concord Baptist Church, and that seasoned leader was Gardner Taylor.[18]

How did this daughter church of the Abyssinian church of Harlem become such a leader in the sixties? The short answer is the combination of superb preaching by Gardner Taylor (preceded by other homiletical greats) and the fact that this Brooklyn church followed a unique trajectory. In 1847, four members from the Abyssinian church and the church's pastor, the Reverend Sampson White, moved across the bridge to Brooklyn. As the membership grew, the congregation moved to larger facilities, first on Adelphi Street in 1917 and then to Marcy Street, where they were able to purchase a large edifice that satisfied the needs of the growing congregation. However, on October 2, 1952, the entire edifice burned to ashes, with the exception of the church membership roll, which was miraculously protected by a fallen sheet of roofing tin. Remarkably, within a period of eight years the congregation rebuilt a sanctuary that seats 2,250 people at a cost of $1.7 million.[19]

From 1847 until 1863 when President Lincoln signed the Emancipation Proclamation, Concord had six pastors with Samson White serving twice. Thus in 1863, the sixth pastor was William T. Dixon (1863–1909), followed by Dr. William Moss (1909–1921). He was succeeded as eighth pastor by Rev. Dr. James B. Adams (1921–1946), who died suddenly as the

---

African-American Religious Experience; and Kevin McGruder, associate professor of history at Antioch College in Yellow Springs, Ohio. Two other excellent examples of well-written Baptist church history are H. Leon McBeth's *The Baptist Heritage: Four Centuries of Baptist Witness*, (Nashville: Broadman Press, 1987), and McBeth's *Texas Baptists: A Sesquicentennial History* (Madison: University of Wisconsin and Baptistway Press, 1998).

[18] Brackney, *Genetic History*, 430–66; Taylor, *Words of Gardner Taylor;* Wallace C. Smith, "Progressive National Baptist Convention: The Roots of the Black Church," *American Baptist Quarterly* 19, no. 3 (September 2000): 245–59.

[19] "The Concord Baptist Church of Christ History," ConcordCares.org, http://www.concordcares.org/about-us/history (accessed July 9, 2018).

congregation prepared to celebrate its centennial. In the midst of their grief and centennial celebration the church invited Dr. Gardner Taylor from Baton Rouge, Louisiana, who served from 1949 to 1990, when he was made the Senior Pastor Emeritus. In 1990 Concord invited one of its own preaching sons, Dr. Gary V. Simpson, to become the church's pastor.

When one looks at the history of Concord, one is reminded of the prayer of a deacon at an installation of their young pastor. "Lord, we thank you for sending us a good pastor. We promise that with your help we will make him so much better." The church hired young pastors who stayed for a long time: William T. Dixon was barely twenty-two when he became the pastor; James B. Adams was a young army chaplain; Gardner Taylor was twenty-nine when he came from his beloved Louisiana; Gary Simpson was twenty-seven when he stepped up to succeed the inimitable Taylor.[20]

These five were the major pastors of Concord, but they were much more than that. Pastor Dixon was called Father Dixon and regarded as the pastor of all of Brooklyn. William Moss, who served the shortest time of the last five pastors, was one of the founders of the National Urban League. Cornel West described Moss as an "organic intellectual."[21] Dr. James Adams increased the size of the congregation and also enabled the congregation to adopt a broader vision. He transformed the church into a national model for the training of laypeople in an enlightened program of Christian discipleship. Dixon and Taylor were both known as the deans of black preaching during their pastorates. Additionally, the current pastor has called his congregation to become a tithing congregation with 10 percent of their giving going to missions, making the church involved not only in Brooklyn but throughout the world.[22]

I have also had my own amicable experiences with the Concord Baptist Church. As a professor of Baptist history and polity for the past twenty years I have helped my students learn how to baptize in many different Baptist churches' baptistries. I fondly recall the superb reception given to eighteen students and me at Concord. Dr. Simpson greeted each one of us at the door. The congregation prepared dinner for us and invited us to have a word for those who came to see this group of students, after which we learned how to baptize in this place where thousands had preceded us.[23]

---

[20] "Concord Baptist Church of Christ History."

[21] "Determination," in "Concord Baptist Church of Christ History."

[22] "The Power of Love," in "Concord Baptist Church of Christ History."

[23] I taught this class at New Brunswick Theological Seminary.

Many years ago, I heard Gardner Taylor preach in celebration of Martin Luther King's life. I record here a short portion of this sermon that illustrates the historical incisiveness of Taylor and his superb articulation of the past working in the present:

> God comes at us in strange ways and from such unexpected and, to many of us, apparently awkward angles. What is the clue to this? Well, let me cite another example which may help to set this in its proper context. That is this word recorded in the Gospel of Luke: "In the fifteenth year of the reign of Tiberius Caesar, Pontius Pilate being governor of Judea, and Herod being tetrarch of Galilee, and his brother Philip tetrarch of Ituraea and of the region of Trachonitis, and Lysanias the tetrarch of Abilene, Annas and Caiphas being the high priests, the word of God came unto John the son of Zacharias in the wilderness" (Luke 3:1–2).
>
> When you start calling these names, it sounds like a roll call of the people who really mattered and on whose side the future lay and to whom the coming generations belonged. Tiberius Caesar, and one thinks of purple and high-ceilinged palaces. Courtiers, screaming eagles of the legions, standing sentinels at the farthest outposts of empire, at the very extreme borders which civilized men counted it worthy to rule. Tiberius Caesar, successor to Augustus, with the Forum in Rome there at one end and over at the other the Coliseum. All roads leading to and from Rome with its seven hills of imperial glory. "In the fifteenth year of the reign of Tiberius Caesar, Pontius Pilate being governor to Judea"—and one thinks of the second line of command, prouder usually in the colonies than even at home, the representation of all the grandeur and glory of Rome. "Pontius Pilate, being governor or Judea, and Herod being tetrarch of Galilee"—the splendor of the court of an oriental monarch—"Annas and Caiaphas . . ." Annas, banished in the intricacies and turbulence of Judean politics from its own place as high priest, but having had the resourcefulness and shrewdness to introduce his son-in-law, Joseph Caiaphas, as chief priest. The glory of ecclesiastical authority, "Annas and Caiaphas being the high priests," and you begin to think that all that can be said about where power was and where influence lay had already been uttered. "In the fifteenth year of the reign of Tiberius Caesar, Pontius Pilate being governor of Judea, and Herod being tetrarch of Galilee...Annas and Caiaphas being the high priests, the word of God came unto John...in the wilderness."

> Does that explain it? God comes at us at strange angles and from unexpected sources, establishing new bridgeheads in history, in places where we scarcely expect them. John did not fit the bill of somebody as a deliverer. He had an awkward, angular personality. His diet was the wrong diet. He ate the old desert food of the poor—locusts and wild honey. He dressed not in the refined cloth that we call camel's hair but in the roughly textured hair of the camel. And there were strange wheels in his head; somewhere in the crooning of the desert winds he believed that he had heard the voice of God. There was a strange light in his eyes and a frown in his countenance. His words were cutting and sharp. They were not compromising, they were not honeyed, but "in the fifteenth year of the reign of Tiberius Caesar, Pontius Pilate being governor of Judea, and Herod being tetrarch of Galilee,...Annas and Caiaphas being the high priests, the word of God came unto John...in the wilderness." Dwight D. Eisenhower, being president of the United States, and John Patterson, the governor of Alabama, J. Edgar Hoover, the omnipotent autocrat of the FBI, Billy Graham and Norman Peale, the high priests of middle America. The Word of God came to Martin King in the wilderness of America.[24]

Assessing the many activities of the Concord Baptist Church over the years, one observes that the church functions with a "thy kingdom come" definition versus a congregational preparation definition. Many Baptist congregations operate with the mind-set of earthly salvation as a preparation for the eternal abode, while churches such as Concord are striving to bring the kingdom of God on earth as it is in heaven. During the time that Taylor was at Concord, he realized the fact that blacks were not able to take loans as easily as whites; thus, Concord established the Concord Credit Union in 1950. In connection with the bank, Concord created the Concord Christ Fund for individuals as well as organizations in Brooklyn. Concord is also involved in education and in 1960 opened an elementary school as a part of the church. For the aged, Concord has the Concord Home Services for the Elderly and the Concord Nursing Home and Rehabilitation Center. Addi-

---

[24] Gardner Taylor, "The Strange Ways of God," Martin Luther King Jr. Memorial Service, Harvard University, Cambridge, Massachusetts, January 1972, in *The Words of Gardner Taylor,* vol. 4: *Special Occasion and Expository Sermons,* comp. Edward L. Taylor (Valley Forge, PA: Judson Press, 2000), 101–3.

tionally, Concord also runs the Concord Family Service and the Concord Clothing Exchange.[25]

The 1960s presented new challenges to the black community. Many pastors and congregations were satisfied with what they had accomplished so far and were reluctant to accept new ideas. The largest of the African American Conventions was the National Baptist Convention USA Inc., and the president of that Convention, Dr. J. H. Jackson, attacked black theology and the younger preachers who wanted to make changes. The older leadership voted to change the terms of the presidency, while the younger generation proposed Gardner Taylor as the new president. The president of the National Baptist Convention USA Inc. was, for all intents and purposes, the ex-officio president of black America and was elected almost for a lifetime.[26] He favored gradualism in social changes and was not very much in favor of King. After attempts at two Conventions, the Taylor/King faction saw that changes were not possible, and they formed the Progressive National Baptist Convention in 1961.[27]

The Progressive National Baptist Convention became a center of ideas that have shaped the United States in regard to civil rights. Names that have become familiar internationally were a part of this breakaway from the National Convention. Gardner Taylor arguably shaped this movement as much as King did.[28]

Yet in addition to all his involvements in the social upheavals of American society, Taylor also preached on some well-known texts, such as "Ye Must Be Born Again,"[29] turning to the book of Revelation for revival sermons. When he preached funeral sermons, he opened the glories of the heavens and touched Jesus together with the departed who had joined in his presence.[30]

---

[25] "Justice," in "Concord Baptist Church of Christ History."

[26] Smith, "Progressive National Baptist Convention," 247.

[27] Smith, "Progressive National Baptist Convention," 245–59.

[28] "Justice," in "Concord Baptist Church of Christ History."

[29] Gardner C. Taylor, "What 'Born Again' Really Means," in *The Words of Gardner Taylor*, vol. 3: *Quintessential Classics, 1980–Present*, comp. Edward L. Taylor (Valley Forge, PA: Judson Press, 2000), 202–8.

[30] Taylor, *Words of Gardner Taylor*, 4:135–38.

Calvary Baptist Church

Calvary Baptist Church of Manhattan maintains that its unique influence is due to the continued evangelistic voice that it has provided for the city of New York. Many would agree that the apex of this church's impact was the long ministry of Stephen Olford, pastor from 1959 to 1973, who largely shaped the preaching style of the conservative Baptists, but he was preceded and followed by preachers committed to the same evangelistic style.

The church started under the name of Hope Chapel Baptist Church in 1847 (the same year that Abyssinian church started its daughter church Concord in Brooklyn). The church migrated geographically and changed its name to Calvary Baptist Church in 1854. Since 1931 the congregation has been in the same place, in addition to becoming one of the few churches that has a hotel and a sanctuary in the same building. The purchase of this location was a fantastic investment that has paid huge dividends that have been used for the ministry of the church.[31]

During the modernist-fundamentalist controversy, Calvary became a center of conservative theology and supplied multiple counterarguments to liberal theology. In fact, the answer to Harry Emerson Fosdick's well-known sermon "Shall the Fundamentalist Win" was given by Calvary's pastor John Roach Straton with the title "Shall the Liberals Win." Contemporary historian Philip Jenkins writes that the liberals like Fosdick have won in the United States, but the fundamentalists have won globally.[32] In global denominations such as the Anglicans and Methodists, there has been a resurgence of conservative/fundamentalist theology that has stopped these denominations from becoming even more liberal and even reverted some of them to more conservative positions. Calvary also is proud of the many international diplomats who attend its worship services, another indication that Calvary's conservative Baptist theology is appreciated and practiced outside the United States.

Calvary has a substantial history of preachers who have been deeply involved in the life of the city, including Straton, who created Calvary into a bastion of conservative theology; William Ward Ayer, who started the radio broadcasting ministry from Calvary and was considered in his day to be the third most popular person in New York behind Eleanor Roosevelt and

[31] "Our History, Beliefs, Vision: Calvary Baptist Church, NYC," CBNYC.org, revised 2010, http://www.cbcnyc.org/our-history.

[32] Jenkins, *New Faces of Christianity,* 2–8.

Bishop Fulton Sheen; and Stephen Olford, who was a mentor to evangelists like Billy Graham, Southern Baptist pulpiteers like Charles Stanley and Adrian Rogers, and missionaries like the martyred missionary Jim Elliot. The current pastor, David Epstein, has been there for over twenty years and has continued the conservative tradition. Calvary is one of the few churches in New York that posts its conservative statement of faith and its position on traditional marriage.[33]

The preaching tradition of Calvary has been expository preaching. In the 1970s, when books like Phil Barnhard's *Don't Call Me Preacher*[34] were published and when seminaries were teaching that the best sermon is eighteen minutes long, Stephen Olford continued to preach a full hour. In fact, his style became so popular with many conservative preachers that Olford left Calvary in 1973 and devoted the rest of his life to the Olford Institute for Biblical Preaching in Memphis, Tennessee.[35]

Calvary purposes that everything they do is Bible-centered. The church has over thirty mission posts outside the United States and countless ministries in Manhattan, from children's clubs to diplomatic gatherings, but has also stayed away from having those church activities labeled as parts of social movements.[36]

Judson Memorial Baptist Church

If Calvary is Bible-centered, Judson can be described as a sociocentric, issues-driven church. Judson was started by Edward S. Judson as a memorial to Adoniram Judson, the first American Baptist missionary to Burma. Due to the fact that, at the turn of the twentieth century, lower Manhattan had attracted both rich elites and poor Italians, Edward Judson envisioned the church as an outreach in the ethnic community by mission-minded people. In addition to vibrant worship and religious instruction, the church operated as a center of health, nutrition, education, and recreational programs. However, the finances did not materialize as planned, and the church remained the property of the New York Baptist Society from 1912 until 1973.[37]

---

[33] "Our History, Beliefs, Vision."

[34] Phil Barnhart, *Don't Call Me Preacher: For Laymen and Other Ministers* (Atlanta: Forum House, 1972).

[35] Olford Institute for Biblical Preaching, "A Brief History: How We Got Started," https://olford.org/what-we-do/ (accessed September 19, 2018).

[36] "Our History, Beliefs, Vision.".

[37] "Judson Memorial Church: Overview."

Judson Memorial Baptist Church prides itself on being the leader of liberal causes in the Baptist life. The church's pastors carry a liberal agenda primarily in the ABC-USA, but they have been and still are also very influential in the city. This agenda also prompted the church to align itself with the liberal United Church of Christ. In the early 1920s, under church auspices, Dr. Eleanor A. Campbell cofounded the Judson Health Center, which became one of the largest health-care facilities in the nation.[38]

During the Depression era and World War II, the congregation reverted to services in Italian and was mostly served by seminary students. The pastoral team of Robert Spikes (1949–1955) and Dean Wright (1948–1952) started to create a new vision for the church. The new and subsequently longtime pastor, Howard Moody (1956–1992), led the church in every avant-garde program that appeared in the United States. Moody was flamboyant, eloquent, persuasive, and bigger than life. His definition of church was a faith-based institution that responds to the societal issues of its time and place by working and advocating for progressive changes—with special attention to the needs of the people that many mainstream churches tend to overlook or find "undeserving." Thus, from 1949 to 1968, the church sponsored an interracial, international residence for students, and opened the first drug treatment center in Greenwich Village in 1960–1962. Furthermore, in the 1960s, before *Roe v. Wade*, the church had an abortion counseling and referral service.[39] Moody also hired associates who had developed specialized emphases in their ministries: Arlene Carmen, in addition to running the abortion and the referral service, had a ministry of presence with New York prostitutes. In the early 1980s Lee Hancock was involved with the AIDS ministry before AIDS was recognized as a health crisis.

Judson also has an art gallery in which many avant-garde artists, including Claes Oldenburg, Allen Caprow, and Yoko Ono, first exhibited their works. Al Carmines, a prolific musician, was hired to bring the arts into the mainstream of worship. Judson became one of the "Off-Off Broadway" venues—Judson Dance Theater was formed, and Carmines's choral groups won awards for their stellar performances. In the late sixties the Baptist format of worship went through an experimental phase that resulted in a much more agape-style worship—more relaxed, more artistic, and with more food served at the end of the worship service.[40]

---

[38] "Judson Memorial Church: Overview."
[39] "Judson Memorial Church: Overview."
[40] "Judson Memorial Church: Overview."

The long pastorate of Moody created for the church a special place in the life of New York that was difficult to maintain after he left. Peter Laarman (1994–2004) continued the traditions of the church but was saddled with the burden that the buildings needed major repairs, which the church completed in 2006. The recent and current pastoral team of Donna Schaper (2006–present), Michael Ellick (2007–2014), and Micah Bucey (present) initiated new programs—such as a community ministry for people in the neighborhood, and the Bailout Theater, which addresses the recession that is affecting the arts. Judson has also taken a leading role in the New Sanctuary Coalition of NYC.[41] While the three other churches described have membership in the thousands, Judson still manages to be extremely influential with a current membership of about 250.

Baptists, Gospel, and Culture

Baptists in New York have engaged with gospel and culture at many levels. When consulting the periodic list of the ten best preachers in the United States, Baptists can be very grateful because often about half of the preachers listed are Baptists.[42] Good preaching is vital to the success of Baptists. As the saying goes, in the black church a preacher can be missing lots of gifts, but if he cannot preach, he does not last long. These four churches each have had some great pulpiteers who, in season and out of season, have raised their voices to proclaim the gospel. Their preaching has challenged the city's culture.

The emphasis on the gospel certainly has differed from church to church. At Judson, Carmines created music that invited everyone to praise God even when they thought they could not sing; Steve Olford's exegesis brought spiritual depths that one had not fathomed; Gardner Taylor was a master homiletician, where every word was another doxology to the Lord Jesus Christ; Adam Powell Jr. showed the viciousness of Satan, who infiltrated every crevice of the city life.

---

[41] "Judson Memorial Church: Overview."

[42] Kate Shellnutt, "Tim Keller, John Piper, and Andy Stanley Among the 12 'Most Effective' Preachers: Baylor's Seminary Asked Homiletics Experts to Pick the Top English-Speaking Sermon Givers of Today's Generation," *Christianity Today*, May 2, 2018, https://www.christianitytoday.com/news/2018/may/tim-keller-john-piper-andy-stanley-most-effective-preachers.html; Michael Duduit, "The 25 Most Influential Preachers of the Past 25 Years," *Preaching*, http://www.sermoncentral.com/content/michael-duduit-25-most-influential-preachers?ac=true (accessed September 20, 2018).

It is not only the preaching of the gospel that identifies Baptists but also the fact that Baptists celebrate public baptisms. It is impressive to read that the Abyssinian, Concord, and Calvary churches have regularly scheduled baptisms where people come to be baptized and become a part of the body of Christ. People are converted and give testimony of their faith by being baptized in obedience to the command of Jesus Christ.

Some Baptists are emphatic in their claim that churches should be separate from the government, while others are equally insistent that the so-called separation of church and state is not a part of their theological beliefs. For example, Marvin McMickle feels that black churches should be involved in every facet of the government and argues that the whole concept of the separation of church and state has never been a part of African American churches (Baptist or other denominations).[43] On the other side, Olford did not have time for such political involvement. He preached expository sermons and trusted that the Holy Spirit would guide his audience to the appropriate practical application. Thus, Concord and Abyssinian are involved in the fabric of their community and in the politics of their community, state, and nation, while Calvary is not.[44] The relationship with culture varies.

Another differing characteristic is that Concord, Abyssinian, and Calvary are involved in real estate. Concord occupies a whole block and has real estate elsewhere in Brooklyn; Abyssinian reportedly owns one-third of Harlem, while Calvary owns a large hotel where celebrated performers such as Van Cliburn have chosen to stay.[45]

Throughout their history, Baptists have been congregational in their polity, as is apparent, at least in theory, in local churches and large Baptist Conventions.[46] No one will dispute the greatness of Samuel DeWitt Proctor, as is clear from the eulogizing words of Gardner Taylor:

> Something vast and noble has passed from among us. It is like a mighty oak has fallen, leaving an empty and gaping and glaring space against the sky where he stood.[47]

---

[43] Marvin A. McMickle, *Pulpit and Politics: Separation of Church and State in the Black Church* (Valley Forge, PA: Judson Press, 2014).

[44] Brackney, *Genetic History.*

[45] "Our History, Beliefs, Vision."

[46] H. Leon McBeth, *The Baptist Heritage: Four Centuries of Baptist Witness* (Nashville: Broadman Press, 1987): "Whoever fails to grasp the differences between society and convention methods will never understand Northern and Southern Baptists," 347.

[47] Taylor, *Words of Gardner Taylor,* 4:144.

Nevertheless, when he was voted in as the pastor of his church, fewer than five hundred members voted out of over fifteen thousand members in good standing. This is clearly an example of a Baptist congregation choosing to remain uninvolved in shaping the direction of the church, which was also a problem at the national level for Baptists.

Wallace Smith, the pastor of the prestigious Shiloh Baptist Church in Washington, DC, identified some potential issues involving the combination of politics and religion when he reflected on King's and Gardner Taylor's newly formed Progressive National Baptist Convention:

> Another, and perhaps most devastating challenge facing the Convention is the one of leadership authority and control. Tenure in office has been rigidly maintained. But there is a perception among many of the younger pastors and members that decisions are still made by cabal, not too dissimilar from the style of National Baptists.[48]

One aspect from the past that Abyssinian, Concord, and Calvary have maintained, even though modified over the centuries, is their emphasis on teaching the Bible in various forms of Sunday school classes. Looking at the weekly schedules of these churches, one can see that classes for children, youth, and adults are constantly occurring between worship services or simultaneously with these worship services. The Word of God is still central for Baptists.

After listening to a Yale lecture given by acclaimed *New York Times* columnist and best-selling author David Brooks, Russ Dean wrote an article for *Opinion*, April 13, 2018, titled "No Prophets in Today's Society? Maybe We're Just Not Listening."[49] In the article Dean excerpts a part of the speech and a brief conversation: "As David Brooks was offering his critique which was intellectually sound, academically rigorous and theologically sophisticated he opined that our country is missing the great prophets of bygone eras. 'Where are the Abraham Joshua Heschels, the Martin Luther King Jrs., the Reinhold Niebuhrs?'[50] he asked. 'We need those voices of moral clarity and courageous spirituality.'

---

[48] Wallace C. Smith, "Progressive National Baptist Convention: The Roots of the Black Church," *American Baptist Quarterly* 19, no. 3 (2000): 256.

[49] Russ Dean, "No Prophets in Today's Society? Maybe We're Just Not Listening," *Baptist News Global,* April 13, 2018, http:// https://baptistnews.com/article/no-prophets-in-todays-society-maybe-were-just-not-listening/#.W6qhrHtKipo.

[50] Dean, "No Prophets in Today's Society."

> At the wine-and-dine after the event I asked the speaker about his critique: "You say there are no prophets among us these days. Are there not?" His response was quick, "Whom would you nominate?"
>
> I nominate David Brooks—and I also invite him to listen more carefully. Voices of prophetic warning and social critique and spiritual conviction are being spoken. I read them every day. If our culture wasn't so shallow and so consumed with trying to make what's mine great again, we might hear them again.[51]

This topical exchange between the elites of the *New York Times* and the students of Yale was considered by a well-known Baptist, Marvin McMickle, in his book *Where Have All the Prophets Gone? Reclaiming Prophetic Preaching in America.*[52] One of the felicitous aspects of this book is that McMickle expands on the group of prophets who worked with Martin Luther King (James Lawson, Ralph Abernathy, Wyatt T. Walker, C. T. Vivian, Andrew Young, Fred Shuttlesworth, Walter Fauntroy, Jesse Jackson, James Bevel, Kelly Miller Smith, Thomas Kilgore, C. K. Steele, and many more) and brings it all the way to the end of the twentieth century. Yet he too is reluctant to name the people of the twenty-first century who may serve as an answer to the question of David Brooks.

As one who grew up in Detroit and completed high school there, who worked in Chicago and pastored a bilingual church in the downtown area for eight years, and who lives across the Sandy Hook Bay from New York City, I have always been aware of Jeremiah's injunction and Jacques Ellul's book *The City.*[53] The prophet Jeremiah tells the captives to seek the welfare of the city for their welfare depends on the city's welfare.[54] Jacques Ellul writes that while many people are still pining for a return to the garden of Eden, the Lord is building the glorious city and current cities should seek to be mirrors, albeit imperfect ones, of that reality.

Keeping that in mind, when I visit our city churches, I am always looking at how they attempt to mirror the Celestial City, particularly on racial acceptance. Thus, I must confess that when the Abyssinian deacon/usher told me that I was at the wrong service because tourists come for the later

---

[51] Dean, "No Prophets in Today's Society."

[52] Marvin A. McMickle, *Where Have All the Prophets Gone? Reclaiming Prophetic Preaching in America* (Cleveland: Pilgrim Press, 2006), 119–54.

[53] Jacques Ellul, *The Meaning of the City* (Eugene, OR: Wipf & Stock), 2011.

[54] Jeremiah 29:7 NIV.

service, I felt that we have not been achieving celestial race integration, even in our big cities. The Abyssinian and the Concord Churches continue to be predominantly black congregations, and Calvary and Judson continue to be predominantly white.

Considering Baptist churches and attempts to achieve racial equality and integration, we may recall the statement of Martin Luther King: "The most segregated hour of Christian America is eleven o'clock on Sunday morning."[55] Despite difficulties and failures, these four New York City Baptist churches have sought to communicate the gospel and redeem society according to their vision.

---

[55] Smietana, "Sunday Morning in America Still Segregated."

14

For the Sake of the Gospel: Theological Education for Women at the Southern Baptist Theological Seminary, Louisville, Kentucky, 1907–2007

T. Laine Scales

In the fall of 1908, twenty-four-year-old Jewell Leggett boarded a train in her hometown of Port Lavaca, Texas, and headed for Louisville, Kentucky, to begin classes at the Southern Baptist Theological Seminary. The all-male seminary was founded in 1859 with its primary purpose to prepare white Southern Baptist men for the preaching ministry. Jewell's father was an itinerant horseback preacher and her mother a missions-minded nurse sacrificing financially for their eldest daughter to attend coeducational Baylor University. Jewell had been a member of the Foreign Mission Band, a group of college men and women supporting one another's interest in sharing the gospel overseas. After a year of teaching school and a broken marriage engagement to another teacher, Jewell enrolled in the Woman's Missionary Union Training School, which had been cooperating with the seminary for nearly one year to offer missionary training for white Southern Baptist women. In her second semester the principal asked Jewell if she would like to leave her program early with another student, Jane Lide, because two missionary women were urgently needed to work with the famed Charlotte (Lottie) Moon. The decision was a difficult one, and as the days unfolded Jewell wrote many pages in her diary, prayed often, and talked with Jane. "If God is in it, I know He will show me," she wrote in her diary, "but it's hard to know just how far to trust my human judgment."[1] Jewell concluded that it was indeed God's will for her to go to China, and after a commissioning

---

[1] Jewell Legett, unpublished diary, January 3, 1909. The Texas Collection, Baylor University, Waco, TX, Jewell Legett Daniel papers, Box 1. (This copy of the diary was placed in the Texas Collection in 2019.)

service with the Southern Baptist Convention (SBC), she sailed there a few months later with Jane and a group of returning missionaries.

Sharing the gospel worldwide was a primary motivation for Southern Baptist churches to cooperate in support of the missionary enterprise. Initially SBC missionaries were men only, though wives often evangelized other women and children. In the latter part of the nineteenth century, as single women were appointed, the need for women's training became more urgent and led to seminary courses being opened to women at the turn of the twentieth century.

To explore the themes of gospel and culture, I recount here the stories of four women students across one hundred years at the Southern Baptist Theological Seminary in Louisville, Kentucky. Rather than progressing along a line of increasingly wider opportunities for women, as did American mainstream culture, Southern Baptists drew a circle. If we imagine a linear progression of opening opportunities at first, but then suddenly taking the end of that line and drawing it back around to where we started, we have a visual representation of the seminary's relationship with women students. To explain the formation of this circle, I use oral histories along with student diaries and archival research, supplemented with secondary sources on higher education.

A Separate "Curriculum for Ladies"

The idea that evangelistic motives were important to opening higher education for women has been explored thoroughly by historian Andrea Turpin in her book *A New Moral Vision*. Although her analysis addresses colleges in the North, her observations may be applied cautiously to denominational schools in the South. Turpin argues that the founding of religious colleges in the mid- to late-nineteenth century was motivated by "evangelical pragmatism"—"the desire to educate as many people as possible, both male and female, as cheaply as possible, in order to equip them to evangelize the world and thus speed the coming of the millennial Kingdom of God, a golden age of righteousness."[2] This pragmatism would drive colleges established in the nineteenth century to make some compromises. For example, Oberlin College, founded in 1833 by two Presbyterian ministers, pioneered in coeducation not for egalitarian reasons but practical ones, according to

[2] Andrea Turpin, *A New Moral Vision: Gender, Religion, and the Changing Purposed of American Higher Education, 1837–1917* (Ithaca, NY: Cornell University Press, 2016), 24.

Turpin. Also, among Turpin's "evangelical pragmatists" was Mary Lyon, founder of Mount Holyoke in 1837 in Massachusetts. Lyon designed a prototype women's missionary training school that emphasized combining school and home into one building and keeping a strict daily schedule. The Mount Holyoke model influenced Jewell's experience even seventy years later.[3]

Pragmatism motivated Southern Baptists as well, and they built an impressive network of colleges beginning in the mid-nineteenth century. Meanwhile, the women organized the Woman's Missionary Union (WMU) in 1888 to raise funds and educate young people like Jewell to support missions. In accordance with the conservative cultural norms of the American South, the women indicated that their WMU was *auxiliary* to the convention—supplemental to and not competing with the all-male SBC. Embracing the ideology of "woman's work for woman," a phrase used by the broader women's missionary movement, the WMU followed the pattern set by other denominations and Northern Baptists when, in 1907, one year before Jewell arrived, the women established their missionary training school in cooperation with Southern Seminary.

Women had been visitors in the Southern Seminary lecture halls from as far back as the 1880s, primarily wives of seminary students and a few single women living locally.[4] In 1902 the seminary officially opened classes to women.[5] As they joined seminary classes, a public relations problem arose: How would the seminary ensure Southern Baptists that women students would stay in their own sphere and would not be preparing as preachers, a practice that had begun in some other Protestant denominations and among Baptists of the North? The faculty set guidelines for the women students, requesting that women "take no public part" in classes, but instead silently audit them. In addition, the women would be confined to the lecture halls and not given access to the cafeteria or sitting rooms so it was clear that they were not mingling inappropriately with men between classes.[6] Seminary

---

[3] Turpin, *New Moral Vision*, 24.

[4] Carrie Littlejohn, *History of Carver School of Missions and Social Work* (Nashville: Broadman Press, 1958), 8–9; Isla May Mullins, *House Beautiful* (Nashville: Sunday School Board of the Southern Baptist Convention, 1934), 11. An unnamed woman from Virginia studied biblical languages of Greek and Hebrew, and a Mrs. Steinmetz took the homiletics (preaching) course.

[5] Littlejohn, *History of Carver School*, 14.

[6] Faculty minutes, Southern Baptist Theological Seminary (hereafter SBTS) Archives, December 10, 1903, Louisville, KY

president E. Y. Mullins appointed a faculty committee to create a "curriculum for ladies," which spelled out that survey courses would be open to women, but language courses such as Greek and Hebrew, or any courses related to preaching (homiletics and pastoral duties) would be off limits.[7] In addition the faculty created a special course for women called "Practical Work" taught by the seminary's young missions professor W. O. Carver.[8] The course emphasized a particular way of evangelizing for women's sphere; it did not include preaching but instead emphasized women's own special type of evangelism coupled with social services to individuals and families. The WMU promoted this method, called "personal service," and women students in Louisville experimented with these methods in their own settlement house after 1912.[9]

For the next forty years, the women students of the WMU Training School followed this pattern of taking some courses at the seminary, six blocks away, coupled with practical courses at their own school, such as personal service, music, domestic science, and elocution.[10] They earned degrees: a two-year bachelor of missionary training or a three-year master of missionary training. Single women lived in the school's building while married women attended classes as day students.[11] They practiced music and elocution skills in the daily women's chapel services. One student recalled in later years that students "were always reminded to step to the side of the pulpit when we spoke publicly, for no lady would stand behind the sacred desk."[12]

When the seminary moved to the suburbs in 1926, the women were alone downtown for about a decade until they purchased an adjacent property to rejoin the seminary classes in 1942. As the century progressed, the im-

---

[7] Southern Baptist Theological Seminary, *Catalogue 1904–05* (Louisville, KY: Southern Baptist Theological Seminary, 1904); faculty minutes, SBTS, April 25, 1904.

[8] Faculty minutes, SBTS, April 25, 1904.

[9] This was true among women missionaries of multiple denominations. See Patricia Ruth Hill, *The World Their Household: The American Woman's Foreign Mission Movement and Cultural Transformation, 1870–1920* (Ann Arbor: University of Michigan Press, 1985), 4, 125. The WMU Training School's Goodwill Center provides another early example of this development.

[10] Faculty minutes, SBTS, May 27, 1907.

[11] Catherine Allen, *A Century to Celebrate: History of Woman's Missionary Union* (Birmingham, AL: Woman's Missionary Union, 1987), 271.

[12] G. R. Ferguson, "A Tribute to Mrs. James H. Anderson," Address to Carver School of Missions and Social Work, October 2, 1959, typescript, 1, SBTS archives, Louisville, KY. See also Maud McLure, *Is It Worthwhile?* (Baltimore, MD: Woman's Missionary Union, 1908), 3.

age of ideal womanhood promoted by the women's school gradually began to change; women embraced a new professionalism. In addition to mission work, two new professions of religious education and social work would become part of an expanding women's curriculum. In addition, a few women students at the dawn of a new decade, the 1950s, grew dissatisfied taking some of the same courses as male students but not being able to enroll in the seminary to earn its degrees. A few protested against the "little study courses at the Training School," pushing for the women's school to be fully merged with the seminary.[13] In similar ways to what they had experienced as widening opportunities for women in American culture after World War II, these students found the idea of a separate women's curriculum to be too constricting.

Enrolling Women Seminary Students

These students' agitation led to the next point on the line of progression, drawn in 1948 when the board of trustees authorized the seminary "to admit qualified women who are wholly committed to an educational ministry and who have completed the Master of Religious Education at the Training School as candidates for the B.D. [Bachelor of Divinity] and Th.D. [Doctorate of Theology] degrees."[14] Two important clarifications in this statement reinforced women's limited roles: first, women were to prepare for educational ministry, not pastoral ministry; second, they could only enroll after first earning a master's degree from the women's training school. In other words, the criteria for admission were higher for the women; male students would not be required to have earned a prior master's degree to be admitted. These criteria limited the pool of eligible women, but after completing her work at the training school, Helen Armstrong was the first woman to enroll directly into the seminary's School of Theology and became Southern Seminary's first woman graduate in 1950. Later recalling her motivations, she mused, "My two years at the Training School had opened some doors, but I wanted to know more....'Brother Armstrong' (as I was kiddingly called by some) was not preparing for a pastorate but perhaps to teach or do counseling or both."[15] Southern Baptists of this era still were not open to women in

---

13 Carrie Littlejohn to Training School Trustees, May 1, 1950, Littlejohn File, Woman's Missionary Union Archives, Birmingham, AL.

14. SBTS, *Catalogue,* 1950, 20.

15. Helen D. (Armstrong) Wright to Marilyn Helton, April 23, 1978, SBTS Archives, Louisville, KY.

the pulpit, though some other Protestant denominations as well as American Baptists in the North had opened those doors.

In the 1950s as the seminary allowed women to matriculate without attending the training school, the enrollment of the training school declined, never to recover. WMU tried to modify the original purposes of the training school in response to financial strain, changing admissions policies in 1953 to admit African Americans into the previously all-white female environment. Curricular reform focused on professionalism for educators and social workers, leaving behind the earlier emphasis on domesticity. The school's name became the Carver School of Missions and Social Work, both honoring beloved missions professor W. O. Carver and emphasizing the professionalization of social work for the church. In spite of these experiments, the school failed to achieve the needed accreditation to offer a master of social work (MSW) degree.[16] Unable to support the school financially, the WMU turned over its assets and leadership to the SBC in 1957, and President Emily Lansdell resigned explicitly to make way for a male president. The Carver School never regained sufficient enrollment, and in 1963 the SBC closed the school, merging its courses with the Southern Seminary's School of Religious Education.

Church Social Work and Other Pathways to Ministry

The mid-century message was clear. New freedoms that allowed women to earn degrees from the SBC's flagship seminary diminished students' interest in a separate women's school. The 1960s and 1970s would lead to further expansion of roles for women in SBC churches and denominational agencies, with a few women adopting the title of "minister" for their roles in church music, religious education, or social work. A handful of women seminary students of the 1970s explored courses in preaching, which was unusual, but no longer forbidden. A few Southern Baptist women were ordained to pastoral ministry.[17] Cora Anne Davis, who grew up preaching from the

---

[16] Allen, *Century to Celebrate*, 283; T. Laine Scales, *All That Fits a Woman: Training Southern Baptists Women for Charity and Mission: 1907–1926* (Macon, GA: Mercer University Press, 2000), 253.

[17]. See Susan M. Shaw, "I Am Woman: Southern Baptist Women and Feminism," *Baptist History and Heritage* 45, no. 2 (Spring 2010): 6–19; Shaw, *God Speaks to Us, Too: Southern Baptist Women on Church, Home, and Society* (Lexington: University Press of Kentucky, 2008), 148–55; Pamela Robinson Durso, "She-Preachers, Bossy Women, and Children of the Devil: Women Ministers in the Baptist Tradition, 1609–2012," *Review & Expos-*

age of seventeen at her family's rural Virginia church, was instrumental in organizing the Southern Baptist Women in Ministry group for these women in the early 1980s.[18]

Davis was a gifted preacher and would use this skill throughout her career, but her true calling was in social work. In her junior year at Westhampton College, a Southern Baptist college for women, Davis took an introductory course in social work and found her calling. "It was like someone was singing my song," she recalled in later years.[19] After graduating from the Carver School, she worked with several congregations in Kentucky through the 1960s until she returned to teach social work classes, which had been moved from the defunct Carver School into the seminary's School of Religious Education. Davis held on to a dream throughout the 1970s to revive professional social work as a means of serving the church and supplying the denomination with an army of MSWs—preparing graduates to serve its churches and agencies, such as the vast network of children's homes, soup kitchens, and community centers operated by the Home Mission Board. These agencies employed good-hearted church workers, but they had no professional knowledge of social work. Davis worked with seminary president Roy Honeycutt to create the Carver School of Church Social Work, opened in 1984.[20]

Social work brought both men and women to the seminary, and the next point along our line of opening opportunities may be drawn in this period. Although women also were found in religious education, music, and even preaching, Patty Villareal exemplifies women social work students of the 1990s. She had been working in child welfare at a Baptist agency in San Antonio and studying for the MSW part time but was not inspired by the education she was receiving. Unlike the young Jewell, Patty was in her thirties and had already been living out her calling to minister to vulnerable populations. She recalls, "I already knew that my calling was in the social work ministry. I already knew that there was no misgivings [*sic*], no doubt in

---

itor 110, no. 1 (Winter 2013): 33–47; Leon McBeth, *Women in Baptist Life* (Nashville: Broadman Press, 1979), 153–72.

18. Michael Tutterow and Anita Bowden, "Women in Ministry Group Draws 250," *Baptist Press*, June 11, 1984.

19 For a complete biography of Davis, see T. Laine Scales, "C. Anne Davis (1938–2006): Shaping an Ethic of 'Doing the Word,'" in *Twentieth-Century Shapers of Baptist Social Ethics*, ed. L. Allen and L. McSwain (Macon, GA, Mercer University Press, 2007), 226–43.

20 Cora Anne Davis, interviews by author, March 15 and 23, 2005, transcript at Baylor Institute for Oral History, Baylor University, Waco, Texas. .

my mind that this is what the Lord called me to; I received such joy serving in that capacity."[21] Her need was to further her education, and after learning about Carver's emphasis on church social work she resigned from her job and moved to Kentucky to become a full-time graduate student. Patty experienced the seminary of 1990 as a place of openness in terms of her gender and her Hispanic (or Latina) cultural background. She recalled in an interview, "The atmosphere of the school at the time it was, it truly was scriptural, in that, God saw no gender.... There was encouragement for women to develop their ministry calling, Not only ministry calling, but leadership skills."[22]

The Circle Turns Back: "Women's Ministry"

Patty Villareal graduated from Southern Seminary in May 1993, a few months before the line that had been progressing forward was radically turned back as the seminary returned to cultural understandings of gender roles reminiscent of a hundred years earlier. The line was becoming a circle. R. Albert Mohler, emerging leader of the conservative resurgence, arrived in 1993 to assume the presidency of the flagship SBC seminary. Gender became an immediate issue, and in an interview with Dr. Mohler in 2002, he described the seminary's stance thus: "The one issue we try to be very clear about is we believe a Biblical normativity to the relationships between men and women and a certain order of authority and responsibility in the church and in the home, but in particular the issue here is in the church."[23]

Within two years of Mohler's arrival, controversy erupted over the direction of social work, leading to the firing of the school's dean, Diana Garland, and the closing of the Carver School in 1997. Opponents of the decision believe that gender issues were central to the closing. However, Mohler stated that gender was not the source of the conflict. He believed that social work could have offered a place for women, like education, that was "theologically nonproblematic," he reflected. Mohler and the trustees were expecting that the Carver School would develop what he called "Christian social work" that took place "in a confessional environment and a clear understanding of the doctrinal framework and moral framework in which

[21] Patty Villareal, interview with Mark Menjivar, October 18, 2001, San Antonio, TX. The interview is on a cassette in the author's possession.

[22] Villareal, interview with Menjivar,.

[23] R. Albert Mohler, interview with the author, February 28, 2002, Louisville, KY, Baylor Institute of Oral History.

that sits."[24] Instead, professional gatekeepers challenged the seminary's conservative stance, and according to Mohler, the central disagreement that led to the closing was about "the codification, and I guess the professionalization" of social ministry.

At the same time that the Carver School was closing in the late 1990s, the seminary cleared out from its School of Theology women faculty and any men supporting women in pastoral roles. These were replaced with new faculty who would agree in interviews that women should not be pastors. The seminary's stance was bolstered by the 2000 SBC revision of the *Baptist Faith and Message,* which reaffirmed a 1998 mandate for wifely submission and added a clause stating that only men should serve as pastors.[25] Thomas Kidd and Barry Hankins, in their analysis of these troubled years at Southern Seminary, point out the countercultural nature of these positions on women's roles in home and church from SBC leaders who "seemed to relish the opportunity to take a stand against the secular mainstream."[26] Kidd and Hankins note that these seemingly anachronistic mandates symbolize

> the larger SBC conservative view that Christians today live in a hostile culture, a Babylon, where they must actively dissent from the mainstream. As such, Southern Baptists seek to recapture the outsider status of their forebears in the seventeenth and eighteenth centuries. Back then, Baptists played the role of free-church dissenters in a culture dominated by other Protestants. Today, SBC conservatives position themselves as dissenters against a secular culture.[27]

The new conservative faculty who had endorsed limited roles for women in home and church would teach women students like Monica Merrifield who enrolled at the turn of the twenty-first century. Monica's experiences, gleaned from an interview with a reporter in 2003, have a great deal of similarity to Jewell's experiences and indicate that the seminary experience had come full circle for these women enrolled about one hundred years apart. After launching her career teaching children, Monica felt called to church

---

[24] Mohler, interview with the author.

[25] For a comparison of the different versions, see "Comparison of 1925, 1963 and 2000 Baptist Faith and Message," The Baptist Faith and Message, Southern Baptist Convention, http://www.sbc.net/bfm2000/bfmcomparison.asp (accessed December 7, 2019).

[26] Thomas S. Kidd and Barry Hankins, *Baptists in America: A History* (New York: Oxford University Press, 2015), 243.

[27] Kidd and Hankins, *Baptists in America*, 244.

work and moved to Southern Seminary to pursue the master of Christian education degree. She arrived with her husband, David, also a seminary student, but earning the master of divinity degree. Monica had several important commonalities with Jewell. Both women were baptized at about age twelve, and both women used the opportunity of seminary study to refine their callings. Monica explained that while "she was not certain what post-seminary life would mean for her, she hopes to use the gift of teaching she believes God has implanted within her."[28] Both Jewell and Monica were schoolteachers prior to enrolling and only could imagine their future selves working with other women and children, not with adult men.[29]

What may be a surprising commonality is that both women shared similar views on women's roles in church life, despite coming from different eras, including what we would now call a "complementarian view of gender roles," in which women were to submit to the authority and leadership of men in their families and their churches. That term was not used in Jewell's day, but most of the people she encountered in the American Southwest would probably have endorsed a complementarian view. In Monica's day, however, the word "complementarian" was offered up regularly as the only correct biblical view of gender roles. Her SBC of the twenty-first century had fought and won this battle to reinstate conservative views on gender.

Presented with a remarkably similar women's curriculum, Jewell and Monica illustrate clearly that instead of progressing along a linear journey toward ever widening opportunities, this journey has become circular, as women students of the new millennium returned back to the roles, expectations, and even similar courses to where they started a hundred years prior.

Today, Southern Seminary's website describes separate curricula for men and for women on its "Women at the Seminary" webpage. The sanctioned degree for women like Monica is the master of Christian education. Women are not completely excluded from the master of divinity (MDiv), but they are not allowed to participate in certain concentrations, such as Pastoral Studies, which the website tells us is "primarily designed to prepare men who are called to serve in the office of pastor in local congregations."[30]

---

[28] Jeff Robinson, "Student Focus," *Southern Seminary Magazine* 71, no. 4 (Winter 2003): 20-21, 21.

[29] Robinson, "Student Focus."

[30] See "Master of Divinity in Pastoral Studies," Southern Baptist Theological Seminary, http://www.sbts.edu/theology/degree-programs/mdiv/pastoral-studies (accessed December 7, 2019).

Within the other MDiv concentrations, three course titles are followed by a footnote to indicate these are for men only: Christian Preaching, Preaching Practicum, and Pastoral Ministry. These are "reserved for, but not required of, men."[31]

Just like one hundred years ago, the seminary has more recently created new women's courses reminiscent of the seminary's "curriculum for ladies" of the early twentieth century. The Seminary Wives Institute was initiated by seminary first lady Mary Mohler in 1997 when she gathered a few wives in her home to plan the curriculum. Survey courses address similar topics to those seminary husbands study, such as a survey of biblical studies, Baptist polity, and church history. In addition, the wives may take electives in areas considered women's responsibility: Ministry of Hospitality, Biblical Parenting, and Playing Hymns. A certificate may be earned after completing seventeen credits, and by 2017, over three hundred women had graduated from the program. Rather than sitting in on lectures with their husbands, as women did at the turn of the twentieth century, the seminary wives of the new millennium gather in their own courses taught by seminary faculty and with child care provided.[32] While women students one hundred years ago did not dare use the word "ministry" to describe their work, it is interesting that women of the twenty-first century embrace a broadened view of "ministry of the laity" as the role of all Christians and regularly use the term "women's ministry." In SBC culture it is well understood that this does not mean preaching ministry, teaching men, or leading men. It means roughly the equivalent to what the early WMU called "women's work for women."

Conclusions

Some sociological approaches for discussing culture may be helpful in conclusion. According to Ann Swidler, "Culture influences action not by providing the ultimate values toward which action is oriented, but by shaping a repertoire or 'tool kit' of habits, skills, and styles from which people construct 'strategies of action.'"[33] She differentiates a process for "settled" or "unsettled" times. In "settled" times, action proceeds along the lines of con-

[31] "Master of Divinity in Pastoral Studies."

[32] Annie Courser, "Seminary Marks 20 Years Nurture of Minister's Wives," *Baptist Press*, May 22, 2017, http://www.bpnews.net/48906/seminary-marks-20year-nurture-of-ministers-wives.

[33] Ann Swidler, "Culture in Action: Symbols and Strategies, " *American Sociological Review* 51 (April 1986): 273–86, 273.

vention and even habit, and we can imagine here the women leaders of the early twentieth century literally establishing habits for their students, such as stepping to the side of the podium when they spoke so as not to appear to be preaching. However, says Swidler, in unstable times we may experience the "bursts of ideological activism in periods when competing ways of organizing action are developing and contending for dominance."[34] During the instability of the 1990s, competition among ideas led to intense battles among Southern Baptists, with the reformers ultimately winning control of the seminary and steering it back toward restrictive roles for women in Baptist life. In Swidler's model the views that win dominance will lead to establishment of new habits and conventions. We can see this in the Seminary Wives Institute of the twenty-first century as the women's curriculum establishes particular habits of daily living related to parenting, hospitality, and modesty that shape women's learning how to submit to and support their husband's ministries.

In this comparative analysis I have presented stories about four women students attending Southern Seminary between 1907 and 2007. Each of these women was motivated to share the gospel message in a variety of contexts and time periods. It is not surprising that the progression of ever-widening opportunities for women follows the same thread as American culture but only until we arrive at the tail end of the twentieth century. The unexpected part of the story is that, after a century of increasingly widening opportunities, a sudden and radical change of direction occurred. Under new leadership, the seminary proudly proclaims its stance as countercultural when it comes to women in leadership roles.

What might the future hold for women at Southern Seminary? One might predict that women's enrollment directly might decline as the denomination continues to hire only men in leadership positions. The Seminary Wives Institute may grow as more women embrace this role and find practical use in the courses. On the other hand, conservative women may have ideas of their own. In May 2018 we witnessed instability within the SBC as conservative women challenged SBC leaders along the lines of a Me Too movement, prompted by the downfall of denominational giant Paige Patterson.[35] The next hundred years may bring about some interesting changes for

[34] Swidler, "Culture in Action," 278–79.

[35] Sarah Pilliam Bailey, "'We Are Shocked': Thousands of Southern Baptist Women Denounce Leader's 'Objectifying' Comments, Advice to Abused Women," *Washington Post*, May 7, 2018, https://www.washingtonpost.com/news/acts-of-faith/wp/2018/05/07/we-are-

the women students of Southern Seminary as they navigate the complexities of gender, theological education, and practical service, for the sake of the gospel.

---

shocked-hundreds-of-southern-baptist-women-denounce-leaders-objectifying-comments-advice-to-abused-women/?utm_term=.398e37f4d015; Kate Shellnut, "Southern Baptist Women Launch Petition against Paige Patterson," *Christianity Today*, May 6, 2018, https://www.christianitytoday.com/news/2018/may/paige-patterson-swbts-letter-southern-baptist-women-sbc.html.

15

A Baptist at Yale: Kenneth Scott Latourette, Faith, and the Culture of the American Academy, 1921–1953

Samuel J. Kelley

In his controversial 1951 book, *God and Man at Yale*, the emerging conservative leader William F. Buckley Jr. famously leveled serious charges against his alma mater. The thesis of his book was that Yale College was founded as a Christian institution but had deviated from its educational mission of "fostering…a belief in God" among its students.[1] "I propose," Buckley said in his foreword, "simply to expose what I regard as an extraordinarily irresponsible educational attitude that, under the protective label 'academic freedom,' has produced one of the most extraordinary incongruities of our time: the institution that derives its moral and financial support from Christian individualists and then addresses itself to the task of persuading the sons of these supporters to be atheistic socialists."[2] In the book's first chapter, Buckley conceded the presence of some genuinely religious faculty members. Among them he mentioned "most notably Mr. Latourette, a staunchly pro-Christian minister who teaches mostly at the Divinity School."[3]

This Mr. Latourette was Kenneth Scott Latourette, a prolific church historian and an early historian of Christian missions. Latourette was born in Oregon City, Oregon, in 1884 and was descended from the state's earliest white settlers. He earned his doctorate in history at Yale in 1909 and joined the faculty of the Yale Divinity School in 1921, where he remained until his retirement in 1953. When he died in 1968, he had been, at various points in

[1] William F. Buckley, Jr., *God and Man at Yale: The Superstitions of "Academic Freedom"* (1951; South Bend, IN: Gateway Editions, 1977), lviii.

[2] Buckley, *God and Man at Yale*, lix–lx.

[3] Buckley, *God and Man at Yale*, 9.

his career, the president of the American Historical Association, the Association for Asian Studies, the American Society of Church History, and the American Baptist Convention, with some of these being honorary roles.

Unsurprisingly, given the breadth of his institutional affiliations, historians attach different degrees of significance to Latourette. For church historians and historians of Christian mission, Latourette is a giant and known especially for his *A History of the Expansion of Christianity,* a multivolume global history of Christianity since the first century. Many of these scholars also recognize him as a formidable and articulate defender of the American ecumenical movement.[4] Although he was considered an authority on East Asia before the growth and maturation of Asian studies programs in the United States, scholars of China and Japan have understandably mostly forgotten him.

This brief chapter suggests a different perspective on Latourette, one that joins historiography with an appreciation for the man himself as he navigated his way through a tumultuous phase of American religious and intellectual history. Latourette had a reputation as a prolific writer. One of his students remarked that he was "almost ascetic in his consistent reading

---

[4] There is no published, full biography of Latourette, but he is the subject of several dissertations, articles, and chapters in edited volumes. For dissertations, see William Allen Speck, "The Role of the Christian Historian in the Twentieth Century as Seen in the Writings of K. S. Latourette, Christopher Dawson, and Herbert Butterfield" (PhD diss., Florida State University, 1965); William Lee Pitts Jr., "World Christianity: The Church History Writing of Kenneth Scott Latourette" (PhD diss., Vanderbilt University, 1969); Patricia C. Neils, "China in the Writings of Kenneth Scott Latourette and John King Fairbank" (PhD diss., University of Hawaii, 1980); and Juhani Lindgren, *Unity of All Christians in Love and Mission: The Ecumenical Method of Kenneth Scott Latourette* (Helsinki: Suomalainen Tiedeakatemia, 1990). Articles and chapters include William Richey Hogg, "The Legacy of Kenneth Scott Latourette," *Occasional Bulletin of Missionary Research* 2, no. 3 (July 1978): 74–80; Norman Kutcher, "'The Benign Bachelor': Kenneth Scott Latourette between China and the United States," *Journal of American-East Asian Relations* 2, no. 4 (Winter 1993): 399–424; William L. Pitts, "Kenneth Scott Latourette," *Baptist History and Heritage* 37, no. 1 (January 2002): 52-70; and Dana L. Robert, "The Giants of 'World Christianity': Historiographic Foundations from Latourette and Van Dusen to Andrew Walls," in *Understanding World Christianity: The Vision and Work of Andrew F. Walls*, ed. William Burrows, Mark Gornik, and Janice McLean (Maryknoll, NY: Orbis Books, 2011), 141–53. A Festschrift for Latourette, which includes a bibliography of his work through 1960, is Wilber C. Harr, ed., *Frontiers of the World Christian Mission since 1938: Essays in Honor of Kenneth Scott Latourette* (New York: Harper and Row, 1962).

and writing."[5] But he was also an observer of and participant in broader shifts in the relationship between Protestantism, academic disciplines, and American culture.

Viewing Latourette from this vantage point can help historians think at a biographical level about two different historical problems: the secularization of the American academy and the influence of mainstream Protestantism in the twentieth-century United States. The scholarship on the secularization of American institutions of higher education has followed many and various themes, but virtually all scholars agree that, beginning in the 1870s, processes or agents of secularization gradually displaced and eroded the privilege of religious perspectives in the creation of knowledge.[6] Latourette's minority status at Yale, which William F. Buckley noted, supports this interpretation, but his career also allows historians to see, at the level of particular disciplines, that the story of academic secularization is distorted if it is limited to what happened on university campuses. Factors operating independently of academic institutions also contributed to but sometimes worked against secularization within disciplines. Latourette's career also bears reexamination given fresh reinterpretations of mainstream American Protestantism.[7] Recent scholarship has tested and generally supported the thesis that America's Protestant establishment experienced "cultural victory

---

[5] Searle Bates, "Christian Historian, Doer of Christian History: In Memory of Kenneth Scott Latourette, 1884–1968," *International Review of Mission* 58, no. 231 (July 1969): 317.

[6] See George M. Marsden and Bradley J. Longfield, eds., *The Secularization of the American Academy* (New York: Oxford University Press, 1992); George M. Marsden, *The Soul of the American University: From Protestant Establishment to Established Nonbelief* (New York: Oxford University Press, 1994); Julie A. Reuben, *The Making of the Modern University: Intellectual Transformation and the Marginalization of Morality* (Chicago: University of Chicago Press, 1996); Jon H. Roberts and James Turner, *The Sacred and the Secular University* (Princeton, NJ: Princeton University Press, 2000); and Christian Smith, ed., *The Secular Revolution: Power, Interests, and Conflicts in the Secularization of American Public Life* (Berkeley: University of California Press, 2003).

[7] By "mainstream American Protestantism" I mean the churches, institutions, and ecumenical organizations led by the seven major denominations in the United States in the period in question: the white Baptist and Methodist denominations, Congregationalists, Presbyterians, Episcopalians, the Disciples of Christ, and the United Lutherans. This definition is derived from William R. Hutchison, *Between the Times: The Travail of the American Protestant Establishment in America, 1900–1960* (Cambridge: Cambridge University Press, 1989).

and organizational defeat" over the course of the twentieth century.[8] Latourette's career shows how this process played out at an individual level. A mainstream Baptist who retained the evangelical sympathies of his early life, Latourette was adaptable to the shifting fate of Protestantism in the American academy, but he adapted without surrendering his commitment to a traditional Protestant view of the meaning of Christian faith. At times this made him seem like a relic of late Victorian Protestantism, but at others it equipped him to speak to his current cultural moment.

Latourette's background is important for understanding why he responded as he did to changes in American Protestantism after 1920. His faith was shaped early in life and changed little itself despite the many intellectual storms through which he lived. The best way to describe his religious perspective is as a hybrid of the nondenominational evangelicalism of Dwight L. Moody and establishment Protestantism. In the decades before the fundamentalist controversies of the 1920s, many Protestants drew from both of these streams in their tradition without a sense of the tensions or contradictions between them.[9]

Latourette grew up a Northern Baptist and remained part of that denomination throughout his life. In his autobiography, published in 1967, he described his childhood church as "in the Moody tradition."[10] That tradition's emphasis on the importance of individual faith and its ethic of Christian voluntarism were especially influential on Latourette. He attended college in Oregon at the Baptist McMinnville College. There he was active in the YMCA and pledged with the Student Volunteer Movement to become a foreign missionary.

The decision to become a foreign missionary was what led Latourette to Yale, where he hoped to further his education in preparation for a life abroad. Continuing participation in student activities at Yale was an im-

---

[8] The literature on this subject is too vast to cite here. However, much of it is a response to and refinement of N. J. Demerath III's argument in an older but still important article, "Cultural Victory and Organizational Defeat in the Paradoxical Decline of Liberal Protestantism," *Journal for the Scientific Study of Religion* 34, no. 4 (March 1995): 458–69.

[9] George M. Marsden, *Fundamentalism and American Culture*, rev. ed. (New York: Oxford University Press, 2006); Grant Wacker, "The Holy Spirit and the Spirit of the Age in American Protestantism, 1880–1910," *Journal of American History* 72, no. 1 (June 1985): 45–62.

[10] Kenneth Scott Latourette, *Beyond the Ranges: An Autobiography* (Grand Rapids: Eerdmans, 1967), 17. The sketch of Latourette's early life provided in the following three paragraphs is based largely upon the autobiography.

portant part of his experience. With the unknown horrors of the Great War still almost a decade in the future, these were the years when student volunteers like Latourette still hoped for "the evangelization of the world in this generation."[11] He was particularly active in the Yale University Christian Association, for which he organized Bible studies and spoke to undergraduates about joining the foreign missionary movement.[12] Such leaders of early twentieth-century Protestantism as Henry Sloane Coffin and Robert Speer were also active in the Christian Association during their time at Yale in the late nineteenth century. Although Latourette was part of a younger generation of Yale men, the religious culture he participated in during his student days was much the same as that of the younger men.

Latourette's doctoral studies in history and his missionary aspirations were closely related. He expected to work as a missionary and teacher in China, so he studied the history of China and Japan and wrote his dissertation on the early history of U.S.-China relations. Latourette's adviser, Frederick Wells Williams, son of the Sinologist Samuel Wells Williams, was also the chair of the executive committee of Yale-in-China, the student missionary organization that eventually sent Latourette to China in 1910.[13] Like most missionaries of his day, Latourette was thoroughly convinced of the need of reforming China through education. "We must seek to combine the new education to the old [education in China]," he wrote in his diary. "To do this we must understand the old, and it is this I intend to make my specialty."[14] He had barely gotten started in China when he became ill with dysentery—right on the eve of the Revolution of 1911. In early 1912 he sailed for his home in Oregon to convalesce, but he never fully recovered. He tried for several years to convince the board of Yale-in-China to allow him to return. Meanwhile, he shuffled between several teaching posts at colleges and universities. Those early forays into teaching and writing—not the mission field—were to set the pattern for the rest of his life.

---

[11] For the history of the Student Volunteer Movement, see Michael Parker, *The Kingdom of Character: The Student Volunteer Movement for Foreign Missions (1886–1926)* (Lanham, MD: University Press of America, 1998).

[12] Latourette, *Beyond the Ranges*, 34–35.

[13] Latourette, *Beyond the Ranges*, 30–33.

[14] Kenneth Scott Latourette, October 19, 1910, diaries and ledgers, Kenneth Scott Latourette Papers, Box 133, Record Group No. 3, Special Collections, Yale Divinity School Library, New Haven, CT.

In September 1921 Latourette began at Yale as the D. Willis James Professor of Missions. In his autobiography he described his first ten years at Yale as "very difficult." He explained why: "To many on the Yale faculty and elsewhere in academic circles, missions seemed associated with propaganda and valid scholarship in the field was deemed unlikely."[15] On its face, this comment about the growing unpopularity of the missionary movement among Yale academics would seem to uphold a standard secularization thesis for American higher education. Contemporary debates over the relationship between religion and the academic enterprise certainly lay behind this suspicion of scholarship on missions. Earlier in the century, scholars like Harlan Page Beach—whom Latourette replaced in the divinity school—and Frederick Wells Williams were both unapologetically devout and considered first-rate scholars. Their student, Latourette, even though he shared their religious convictions, did not inhabit the same pro-missionary atmosphere that they enjoyed.[16]

Although shaped by internal factors at the university, the sidelining of the academic study of missions at Yale and elsewhere also had numerous external causes. The crisis of American Protestantism in the years following the Great War had a profound, depressive effect on denominations, churches, and the missionary movement.[17] Latourette was regularly involved with two institutions that suffered in the crisis of missions. The Student Volunteer Movement, which Latourette had long supported, was one. He describes the students at the SVM's 1919 quadrennial convention as "restive," with some claiming that the chair, John R. Mott, "did not understand either the world situation or the student mind."[18] According to Latourette, the 1923 convention had an "electric" atmosphere in which some student groups dissented from the convention's traditional presentation of missions and

[15] Latourette, *Beyond the Ranges*, 63.

[16] On Beach, see Parker, *Kingdom of Character*; Latourette, *Beyond the Ranges*, 30. For a more critical view of these scholars, see David A. Hollinger, *Protestants Abroad: How Missionaries Tried to Change the World but Changed America* (Princeton, NJ: Princeton University Press, 2017), 236.

[17] A classic statement of this thesis is Robert T. Handy, *A Christian America: Protestant Hopes and Historical Realities,* 2nd ed. (New York: Oxford University Press, 1984), chapter 7, "The Second Disestablishment (1920–1940)." For the impact of World War I on the missionary movement, see John C. Barrett, "World War I and the Decline of the First Wave of the American Protestant Missions Movement," *International Bulletin of Missionary Research* 39, no. 3 (July 2015), 122–26.

[18] Latourette, *Beyond the Ranges*, 70.

sought to voice their special concerns about them.[19] "In the student temper of the 1920s and 1930s," he says, "the traditional appeals [to foreign missions] had little force."[20] Besides the SVM, Latourette was also in the thick of the conflict between fundamentalists and liberals over the policies of the American Baptist Foreign Mission Society during the 1920s. Part of the large moderate party in the Northern Baptist Convention, Latourette described the annual Baptist Conventions as growing "more peaceful" in later years of his involvement. However, this peace came only after the fundamentalists withdrew from the Foreign Mission Society and the Convention itself.[21] During Latourette's first decade at Yale, the mainstream Protestant foreign missionary enterprise was not only suspect from an academic standpoint but was also suffering from a crisis of identity in its supporting institutions.

The missions crisis deepened in the later 1920s and 1930s. Criticisms of foreign missions mounted, and there were calls from some quarters for the missionary movement to recognize its culpability for the problems of Western imperialism and then quietly fade away.[22] Articles dedicated to defending foreign missions against these criticisms appeared in a special issue of the missionary periodical *The Missionary Review of the World* in 1929. "The conclusions I draw from this barrage of hostile comment," wrote one author, "are that we are in living in an age which is not only critical, but superficial, when people, even church people, are prone to take up with almost any opinion which appears to be the stamp of neutrality, breadth, and the desire to overthrow existing ideals and institutions."[23] In his article Latourette acknowledged that, of course, missionaries had made mistakes and at times had been hypercritical of non-Western cultures and uncritical of their own. But after making this concession he said, "It must also be admitted...that the Gospel is revolutionary. The early disciples were accused of turning the world upside down—and this has always been the result where the Gospel has been consistently preached and lived."[24] There was no good

[19] Latourette, *Beyond the Ranges*, 70.

[20] Latourette, *Beyond the Ranges*, 100.

[21] Latourette, *Beyond the Ranges*, 122.

[22] William R. Hutchison, *Errand to the World: American Protestant Thought and Foreign Missions* (Chicago: University of Chicago Press, 1987), esp. chapters 5 and 6.

[23] Cornelius H. Patton, "Who Are the Critics?" *Missionary Review of the World* 52, no. 5 (May 1929): 330.

[24] Kenneth Scott Latourette, "Do Missionaries Cause Trouble?" *Missionary Review of the World* 52, no. 5 (May 1929): 342.

cause, argued Latourette and others, for drawing down the Western missionary program, because, notwithstanding the minority of troublemaking missionaries, it was still necessary to preach the true gospel. If the gospel unsettled foreign cultures, that was a mark of its success, not its failure.

There was also the question of whether the missionary project should be substantially altered to better deal with the global crises of the interwar years. In 1932 the Rockefeller Foundation–funded Laymen's Foreign Missions Inquiry published *Re-Thinking Missions: A Laymen's Inquiry after One Hundred Years.*[25] The "Report," as it came to be called, landed like a bombshell in the missionary community. The book's introduction was composed not by a missionary or clergyman but by the Harvard philosopher William Ernest Hocking, writing as a layperson. This simple fact of authorship is evidence that missionary activity was increasingly subject to the scrutiny of scientific-minded academics. The book famously called for missionaries to cut back or terminate their evangelistic efforts and instead engage in cooperative social service efforts abroad with indigenous peoples of all faiths. Undergirding this perspective was the view that Christianity and other world religions differed in degree rather than kind. In his sober review published in *Re-Thinking Missions*, Latourette never railed against its prescriptions for modern missions. In fact, he agreed with many of its findings and said that missionaries should be concerned with social service. Nevertheless, he left plenty of space for sharing his reservations about the book's liberal outlook. He called the book a "partisan document"[26] and lamented that

> the Report's statement of the unique contribution of Christianity has in it little or nothing of the cross, the Atonement, the Resurrection, and the Holy Spirit—doctrines which historically have meant much in the life of the Church and to-day are cherished by large groups of Christians in the United States as well as elsewhere in the Protestant world.[27]

He also complained about the report's exclusion of Catholic missionary efforts, "from which Protestants can learn much."[28] Latourette remembered in

---

[25] The Commission of Appraisal, *Re-Thinking Missions: A Laymen's Inquiry after One Hundred Years* (New York: Harper & Brothers, 1932).

[26] K. S. Latourette, "The Laymen's Foreign Missions Inquiry: The Report of Its Commission of Appraisal," *International Review of Missions* 22, no. 86 (April 1933): 158.

[27] Latourette, "Laymen's Foreign Missions Inquiry," 160.

[28] Latourette, "Laymen's Foreign Missions Inquiry," 160.

his 1967 autobiography that *Re-Thinking Missions* "seemed...to undercut the theological convictions on which foreign missions were based."[29] The author of the novel *The Good Earth* and the most famous missionary in the United States, Pearl Buck, gave hearty approval to the book, however, and many other Protestant leaders and intellectuals in the United States agreed with her.[30] The fracas over *Re-Thinking Missions* signaled a deeper reality: the missionary consensus of the late nineteenth and early twentieth centuries had splintered during the 1920s.[31]

In the bleak international context of the 1930s and 1940s, Latourette and other moderate denominational evangelicals who shared his view of missions appeared naïve. Besides the liberal critique of missions, a growing neo-orthodox movement in American Protestantism also challenged those, like Latourette, who remained optimistic about the prospect of missions and the staying power of the church. Reinhold Niebuhr, the leading American neo-orthodox thinker and admired by many in the academy, dismissed Latourette as a "layman in theology."[32] In his recent work *Protestants Abroad*, American intellectual historian David Hollinger also casts Latourette as a backward-looking holdout. By supporting Western missions in an era when the world seemed ready to burst at its seams, Latourette, according to Hollinger, was "putting a good face on the situation" and "thinking positively."[33] Leaving aside Hollinger's broader argument about Protestant missionaries in the United States, he is right that the Yale professor was increasingly in the minority. The mainline missionary project came to cite its efforts to promote international peace and goodwill—not the spread of the Christian gospel—as the justification for its existence. From the decline of student missionary organizations and Baptist denominational struggles in the 1920s, to divisions within the missionary community and the neo-orthodox critique, it is clear that the academic study of missions became marginal partly because of the global and institutional factors that challenged missionaries and those who trained them. In other words, there is more to the story than

---

[29] Latourette, *Beyond the Ranges*, 102.

[30] See Hutchison, *Errand to the World*, chapter 6.

[31] James Alan Patterson, "The Loss of a Protestant Missionary Consensus: Foreign Missions and the Fundamentalist-Modernity Conflict," in *Earthen Vessels: American Evangelicals and Foreign Missions, 1880-1980*, ed. Joel A. Carpenter and Wilbert R. Shenk (Grand Rapids: Eerdmans, 1990), 73–91.

[32] Hogg, "Legacy of Kenneth Scott Latourette," 76, 79.

[33] Hollinger, *Protestants Abroad*, 77, 78.

the doubts circulating among university faculty at Yale about whether missions-minded scholars could also be fair-minded scholars.

Developments impacting the community of scholars of East Asia in the United States also led to the declining influence of traditional faith perspectives like Latourette's. As noted above, earlier in the century Latourette's professors at Yale were highly esteemed as Christian scholars. As one of a handful of advocates for scholarship on East Asia in the United States in the 1920s and early 1930s, Latourette simultaneously advanced and limited the scholarly discussion. Certainly he drew attention to a region of the globe that American historians had barely begun to notice. However, Latourette read no Asian languages, so virtually all of his sources represented the Western perspective. With these limitations in mind, his scholarship was nevertheless impressive. He produced multiple volumes on the histories of China, Japan, and Korea. His most famous accomplishment in this field was his 1929 work *A History of Christian Missions in China*.[34]

The paradigm for Asian studies was on the verge of a significant shift as Latourette wrote these histories, though. Again, David Hollinger's recent work on the domestic influence of American Protestant missionaries is instructive. Hollinger documents how several institutions and individuals professionalized the study of East Asia in the United States during the interwar period and distanced it from its roots in foreign missions. One of the examples he gives is the Institute of Pacific Relations (IPR), founded in 1925. The IPR "emerged directly from the YMCA," but it came to be more of a political think tank.[35] In its earliest days, missionaries supported the institute and directed it, but it came to focus on international politics in the Pacific region rather than anything resembling missions or philanthropy. Latourette was a founding member of the IPR and in 1952 published a book under its auspices describing the causes of the Chinese Communist Party's victory in China.[36] Nevertheless, in his autobiography Latourette noted his distance from the institute, saying he "had never been active in [the institute's] affairs."[37] He suggested that one of the leaders of the IPR, Edward Carter, was concerned that his "missionary conviction" would be an obstacle to the

---

[34] Hogg, "Legacy of Kenneth Scott Latourette," 78.

[35] Hollinger, *Protestants Abroad*, 143.

[36] Kenneth Scott Latourette, *The American Record in the Far East, 1945–1951* (New York: Macmillan, 1952).

[37] Latourette, *Beyond the Ranges*, 130.

purposes of the institute.[38] Other institutions like the Harvard-Yenching Institute at Harvard University and the Association for Asian Studies had similar early missionary or church-related connections, however short-lived.[39] The evolution of the purposes and constituencies of such organizations demonstrate the shift away from a religious focus in the study of East Asia.

Even more than institutions, a generational shift altered Asian studies in the United States. New work produced by younger scholars—not to mention the changing geopolitical relationship between the East and West—quickly dated Latourette's religious perspective on this part of the world. Especially important were historians John King Fairbank and Edwin O. Reischauer, the son of missionaries to Japan.[40] Often working together, both men pioneered Asian studies at Harvard University in the postwar period. Fairbank's and Reischauer's differences with Latourette are telling. In the first place, both scholars had mastery of the languages of the cultures they studied, and they made such mastery a requirement for their graduate students. Second, neither scholar approached history from the standpoint of Christian missions, although they acknowledged the importance of missionaries in shaping American involvement in China and the East. Fairbank, for example, came to his interest in China by way of diplomatic history rather than missions history. Third—and this is especially true of Fairbank—neither scholar worked from or personally held to a traditional religious faith. In his autobiography, Fairbank described his religion with one word: Harvard.[41] Reischauer, for his part, described his own religious outlook as follows:

---

[38] Latourette, *Beyond the Ranges*, 130.

[39] Latourette was well aware of Asian studies' debt to missionaries. See his short book *Missions and the American Mind* (Indianapolis, IN: National Foundation Press, 1949), 34–35. For the history of the Harvard-Yenching Institute, see Paul Daniel Waite and Peichi Tung Waite, "China's Christian Colleges and the Founding of the Harvard-Yenching Institute," in *China's Christian Colleges: Cross-Cultural Connections, 1900–1950*, ed. Daniel H. Bays and Ellen Widmer (Stanford, CA: Stanford University Press, 2009), 241–66. For the history of the Association for Asian Studies, see Charles O. Hucker, *The Association for Asian Studies: An Interpretive History* (Seattle: Published for the Association for Asian Studies by the University of Washington Press, 1973).

[40] The following sketch of Fairbank and Reischauer relies on their respective memoirs: Edwin O. Reischauer, *My Life between Japan and America* (New York: Harper & Row, 1986); and John King Fairbank, *Chinabound: A Fifty-Year Memoir* (New York: Harper & Row, 1982).

[41] Fairbank, *Chinabound*, 5.

> It never once occurred to me to follow my parents in Christian missionary work, and I easily slipped into a very different attitude toward organized religion than they had, but I have always respected their beliefs and have taken pride in their accomplishments. Without doubt, I drew many of my ideals as well as personal traits from my missionary background.[42]

Hollinger makes bold conclusions about the differences between the early American student of East Asia, Latourette, and the generation that nurtured Asian studies to maturity after World War II. For him, the central figures in the story of Asian studies in the United States are scholars—whether of missionary background or not—who oriented their work toward a cosmopolitan, secular outlook. He describes Fairbank as intellectually "more capacious" than the missionary-minded Latourette, whose "narrowness"[43] and interest in foreign missions prevented him from enjoying influence in Asian studies in his later career. The point is well taken: the future of Asian studies in the United States did indeed follow the model of Fairbank and Reischauer at Harvard, not Latourette at Yale. However, another way to understand Latourette is not as a historian whose ambitions had shrunk, but as one whose interests were formed in a very different religious and cultural atmosphere and who was now (on the eve of World War II) working in an academic setting where religious commitments and motivations had less purchase. Intellectual capaciousness and intellectual interest are different qualities. The new generation of scholars, represented by Fairbank and Reischauer, were indeed more secular in their outlook, but their scholarly interests and training also account for why Asian studies became detached from missions history.

A third academic discipline also shifted around Latourette: the American historical profession itself. The change in the relationship between Protestant missions and the academy and especially the professionalization of Asian studies in the United States were closely connected to changes in the guild of historians in the United States, which naturally encompassed historians of missions and East Asia. However, because Latourette identified as a Christian historian and presented his work this way, his place in the American historical profession is worth discussing separately. Quite unlike his experiences in missiology and Asian studies, Latourette's career as a his-

[42] Reischauer, *My Life between Japan and America*, 18.

[43] Hollinger, *Protestants Abroad*, 234.

torian saw new, unexpected opportunities arise, especially during World War II and the 1950s.

From the time Latourette became a historian to his retirement in the early 1950s, the American historical profession experienced a profound series of shifts in its conception of historical knowledge and historical reasoning. When Latourette earned his doctorate, the American Historical Association (AHA) largely considered itself the steward of a value-free, objective discipline. By the early 1930s, "That mood [was] passing," as one historian, Carl Becker, noted at the time.[44] Leading historians like Becker held that all historians have interpretative biases that guide those historical facts they do or do not emphasize, and even how they construe those facts in broader historical patterns. "However 'hard' or 'cold' they may be," said Becker in his 1931 address to the AHA, "Historical facts are after all not material substances which, like bricks or scantlings, possess definite shape and clear, persistent outline. To set forth historical facts is not comparable to dumping a barrow of bricks."[45]

Even though Latourette was trained in the scientific-objective school of historiography, he agreed with Becker that historians must adopt a perspective in their work.[46] "History cannot be written without some basis of selection, whether artificial and purely subjective or inherent in man's story," he said in his own presidential address to the AHA in 1948.[47] For Latourette, this basis of selection—also the title of his address—was "The Christian Understanding of History." This point of view "centers upon historical occurrences"[48] such as the incarnation, crucifixion, and resurrection of Jesus and the outpouring of the Holy Spirit. Although historians hotly debate the historicity and significance of those events, those arguments are "evidence of the struggle of the human mind and spirit to comprehend what Christians hold to have been a quite unique event." Since the first century, Latourette continued, the Holy Spirit has "remade" men in God's image and gathered them in a fellowship, the church, which is united in and motivated by love

---

[44] Carl L. Becker, "Everyman His Own Historian," *American Historical Review* 37, no. 2 (January 1932): 233.

[45] Becker, "Everyman His Own Historian," 233.

[46] Latourette discussed his historical training in *Beyond the Ranges*, 30–33. See also Hogg, "Legacy of Kenneth Scott Latourette," 76.

[47] Kenneth Scott Latourette, "The Christian Understanding of History," *American Historical Review* 54, no. 2 (January 1949): 261.

[48] Latourette, "Christian Understanding of History," 264. All the quotations from the address in this paragraph are taken from 264–66.

for all of humanity. The church for Latourette was expansive indeed, embracing Protestantism but also Catholicism, Eastern Orthodoxy, the Coptic Church, and the ancient sects of the early church. And the purpose of history? It was "God's search for man," a quest to "save him and transform him." Latourette's eschatology—which would have been the most shocking feature of the address for his fellow historians—posited extrahistorical time. "God has always been sovereign, and in the cross and the resurrection He signally triumphed, but beyond history His sovereignty is to be seen as complete." The address was bold, if not very theologically refined. The transcript of the address contained twenty-five footnotes, all but one a Scripture reference. It "disgusted" many in his audience. "Some said," Latourette later recalled, "that if they wanted to hear a talk on the subject they would go to church."[49] To hold, like Becker, that historians must make interpretative decisions regarding evidence was one matter; to claim the historical progress of the Christian gospel as a guide to interpretation was quite another.

If the guild would no longer tolerate an explicit Christian perspective in the work of a historian, the marketplace would. As one of Latourette's students noted in an obituary for him, his writings sold over a million copies.[50] Furthermore, as this student noted with surprise, many of those books were published not by religious or academic presses, but by popular publishing houses like Harper & Brothers and Macmillan. These houses "carried almost all of Latourette's books, even those with strongly Christian titles and contents....These channels aided witness to the larger world, and entry into thousands of public and school libraries."[51] Historian Matthew Hedstrom has carefully studied this growth in popular religious literature in the twentieth century. In response to the crises of institutional Protestantism that followed World War I, Hedstrom argues, liberal Protestants embraced books and reading as a means for promoting religious values among the American people. The trend gained traction during the Depression and World War II.[52] A market for religious books printed by secular publishers would not have surprised Latourette. Indeed, his former student, Eugene Exman, was the director of the Religious Book Department of the Harper & Brothers publishing house. That department's aim was "to publish books that repre-

---

[49] Latourette, *Beyond the Ranges*, 115.

[50] Bates, "Christian Historian," 319.

[51] Bates, "Christian Historian," 320.

[52] Matthew S. Hedstrom, *The Rise of Liberal Religion: Book Culture and American Spirituality in the Twentieth Century* (New York: Oxford University Press, 2012).

sent important religious groupings, express well-articulated thought, combine intellectual competence and felicitous style, add to the wealth of religious literature irrespective of creedal origin, and aid the cause of religion without proselyting for any particular sect."[53] Exman began working with his old professor in the late 1930s, publishing his *A History of the Expansion of Christianity*. The multivolume work, while scholarly, also fit well with Harper & Brothers Religious Book Department's religious mission. Latourette called his association with the publisher "unqualifiedly happy, with a valued friendship with Exman and his staff."[54] Throughout the 1940s and 1950s, Latourette published several other smaller, single-volume works on Christian history. Some of these described the two-thousand-year story of Christianity beginning in the first century and followed it through the present—a moment, Latourette candidly told readers, when the fate of Christianity was uncertain. Others dealt only with the contemporary situation of Christianity in the world. All, however, strived to give American Christian readers a sense of the historical relationship between their faith and the cultures in which it took root.[55]

The trend toward popular literature affected historians as well as authors of religious books. Latourette's church histories reflect this popular turn in historical writing as much as they demonstrate the rise of popular religious literature. In one of the popular, middlebrow periodicals of the day, the *Saturday Review of Literature*, journalist-turned-historian Allan Nevins famously called academic historians "pedants."[56] The guild historians, as opposed to literary or popular historians such as himself, he said, were "so preoccupied with the scholarly values of historical work—with laborious thoroughness and extreme accuracy—that they totally neglect all literary values. Most of them are also hostile to ideas as distinguished from facts."[57] In the 1930s, 1940s, and 1950s, new institutions like Nevins's Society of American Historians (founded in response to the AHA's lack of interest in starting its

---

[53] Eugene Exman, *The House of Harper: One Hundred and Fifty Years of Publishing* (New York: Harper & Row, 1967), 287–88.

[54] Latourette, *Beyond the Ranges*, 110.

[55] These works include, in order of publication, *Anno Domini: Jesus, History, and God* (1940); *The Unquenchable Light* (1941); *The Christian Outlook* (1948); and *Challenge and Conformity: Studies in the Interaction of Christianity and the World of Today* (1955). All were published by Harper & Brothers.

[56] Allan Nevins, "What's the Matter with History?" *Saturday Review of Literature*, February 4, 1939, 3.

[57] Nevins, "What's the Matter with History?" 4.

own popular historical organization) and periodicals like *American Heritage* stood for a popular form of history directed toward a broad reading public.[58] Although Latourette had none of the literary flair of this genre's big-name authors, his books cast the story of Christianity in a narrative that was remarkably like Bruce Catton's and Allan Nevins's histories of the Civil War or Bernard DeVoto's trilogy on the American West. Latourette's numerous popular or semipopular writings on religion and Christian history demonstrate that he was not limited by the standards or demands of his historian peers. While the academy may have been suspicious of Latourette's Christian perspective on the past, new markets for religious literature and popular history were eager to absorb and distribute books like his that treated big historical themes in a sweeping narrative style.

Conclusion

In closing, it is helpful to take an image of which Latourette was fond and apply it reflexively to his own historical situation: a tide as it ebbs and flows. Latourette used this image in many of his books on Christian history to describe the advances and retreats of Christian influence that he discerned in the history of the faith. The nineteenth century was, for him, a great age of advance, especially considering the global reach of Western missionaries. However, Latourette wrote in 1940, starting in "A.D. 1914" (the "A.D." added to emphasize the central importance of the incarnation),

> What may prove to be another major recession in the Christian tide came upon the world. Many would declare unequivocally that a major recession is upon us. Some would have us believe that Christianity is suffering the greatest reverse in its history, and that the ebb is eliminating the influence of Jesus from human affairs. That, however, is too early and rash a verdict.[59]

Eighty years on, we are in a better place to assess whether Latourette was living amid an ebb or a flow. A single life—whether Latourette's or any other historical figure's—admittedly provides a limited amount of historical

---

[58] For background on Nevins, see Gerald L. Fetner, *Immersed in Great Affairs: Allan Nevins and the Heroic Age of American History* (Albany: State University of New York Press, 2004). For an academic historian's critical take on the origins of popular historical writing in the United States, see Sean Wilentz, "America Made Easy," *New Republic*, July 1, 2001.

[59] Kenneth Scott Latourette, *The Unquenchable Light* (New York: Harper & Brothers, 1940), 133.

evidence, but Latourette's involvement in so many fields of intellectual and religious life makes him useful for probing the influence of American Protestantism in the decades following World War I. On one hand, as William F. Buckley noted, Latourette was emblematic of the attenuation of religious influence at Yale and in American academic life in general. Developments largely beyond the control of the academy challenged the mainstream Protestant foreign missionary movement and those who considered it worthy of academic study and support. Owing partly to that decline but also to new geopolitical realities, the study of East Asia secularized. By the end of Latourette's career, the academy had little to no interest in his traditional view of foreign missions, and new, better-trained scholars had surpassed him in expertise on East Asia. On the other hand, however, Latourette's life shows that Protestant influence in American thought and culture could flourish in less formally academic environments. If he was in the minority at the American Historical Association, his books on Christian history were very well suited to the mid-century trend in popular religious and historical literature. To use the man's own terms, Latourette demonstrates that Protestant influence in American intellectual life was both ebbing and flowing in this period. His traditional Protestant beliefs and commitment to foreign missions limited his formal academic influence at times, but they also enabled him to speak forcefully about the grand story of Christian history to other audiences.

16

The "Noblest Career of All:" Housekeeping and the Ideal of Southern Baptist Domesticity, 1945–c. 1960

Adina Kelley

In and out of water
A dozen times a day,
Testing a hot oven,
Or wiping tears away.

Never still a minute,
Pulling weeds or hoeing,
Always tending pot plants,
Hours of careful sewing.

Mother's hands are aged and worn,
From tasks of love and duty,
But she would not exchange them
For idle hands of beauty.[1]

This poem was published in 1956 and, at first glance, seems to perfectly embody the ideal that second-wave feminist Betty Friedan later labeled "the feminine mystique" by praising a woman for performing the roles of housewife and mother.[2] However, this poem was not published in a U.S. women's magazine such as *Good Housekeeping* or *Ladies' Home Journal.* Instead, it appeared in *Home Life*, a magazine published for families by the Southern Baptist Convention. Poems like this raise the question: Were Southern

---

[1] Violet M. Roberts, "Working Hands," *Home Life*, May 1956, 22.

[2] Betty Friedan, *The Feminine Mystique* (New York: W. W. Norton, 1963).

Baptist norms for women in the postwar period any different than those of mainstream periodicals?

The 1950s were a period of rhetorical domesticity in mainstream women's magazines in the United States such as *Ladies' Home Journal* and *Good Housekeeping*. Circulations skyrocketed, and the issues themselves were extremely long.[3] For example, the May 1954 issue of *Good Housekeeping* contained 298 pages of advice columns, profiles, and advertisements. The editors also profited from maturing technology, and photographs and full-color spreads became the norm. However, the message of 1950s' magazines has been under scrutiny since Friedan first published *The Feminine Mystique*, critiquing them for enforcing gender stereotypes that kept women out of the marketplace and subjected to their husbands.

Many historians have argued that the postwar magazines were not nearly as domestic as Friedan claimed. In *A Strange Stirring*, Stephanie Coontz posits that *The Feminine Mystique* "made claims about women's history that I knew were oversimplified, exaggerating both the feminist victories of the 1920s and the antifeminist backlash of the 1940s and 1950s."[4] Joanne Meyerowitz's article "Beyond the Feminine Mystique" goes a step further and samples popular literature from the postwar period in order to gauge if the rhetoric was as domesticity-centered as Friedan claimed it was. She finds that the literature "did not simply glorify domesticity or demand that women return to or stay at home. All of the magazines sampled advocated both the domestic and the nondomestic, sometimes in the same sentence."[5] In fact, Meyerowitz claims that 60 percent of nonfiction articles focused on the achievements of individual women outside of the home. Delving even deeper into Friedan's rhetoric, Eva Moskowitz argues in her article "'It's Good to Blow Your Top'" that women's periodicals were even discussing the negative aspects of domesticity in the postwar period. She writes, "Indeed, far from imagining the home as a haven, the women's mag-

---

[3] *Good Housekeeping*'s circulation grew from just over 3 million in 1950 to almost 4.5 million in 1960. *Ladies' Home Journal* saw a similar rise, from 4,473,630 in 1950 to 5,755,317 in 1960. See William F. McCallister, ed., *N. W. Ayer & Son's Directory: Newspapers and Periodicals 1950* (Philadelphia: N. W. Ayer & Son, 1950), 671, 863; McCallister, ed., *N. W. Ayer & Son's Directory: Newspapers and Periodicals 1960* (Philadelphia: N. W. Ayer & Son, 1960), 714, 909.

[4] Stephanie Coontz, *A Strange Stirring: The Feminine Mystique and American Women at the Dawn of the 1960s* (New York: Basic Books, 2011), xix.

[5] Joanne Meyerowitz, "Beyond the Feminine Mystique: A Reassessment of Postwar Mass Culture, 1946–1958," *Journal of American History* 79, no. 4 (March 1, 1993): 475.

azines often rendered it as a deadly battlefield on which women lost their happiness, if not their minds."[6] Moskowitz argues that magazines used personal testimonies, not unlike that of Friedan herself, in order to "document unhappiness."[7] However, these studies, focused only on the postwar period, do not test for change over time. They also minimize the impact of the larger cultural turn toward domesticity identified by historians such as Elaine Tyler May and Lizabeth Cohen.[8] Though Coontz affirmed Moskowitz's findings, arguing that people in the larger media were already addressing the housewife problem prior to *The Feminine Mystique*, she also acknowledged that, indeed, "There was no name for the guilt, depression and sense of hopelessness many housewives felt.[9] Perhaps women's magazines in the 1950s were more nuanced than Betty Friedan claimed, but they did present a particularly domestic and homeward-focused ideal for women that was different than any other time in the twentieth century, before or after.[10]

This chapter evaluates Southern Baptist magazines' rhetoric about gender from 1945 to 1960, asking two specific questions. First, were Southern Baptists during the postwar period uniformly extolling the value of domesticity, or were their magazines, like mainstream women's periodicals, quietly offering more nuanced perspectives on the idea of femininity? Second, were Southern Baptists debating what role women should play in the new U.S. Cold War society, or were they holding fast to conservative, traditional ideals of femininity? Historians such as Melody Maxwell and Betsy Flowers also seek to answer these questions in their work.[11] Maxwell in particular argues that periodicals reflected the domestic culture of the 1950s before becoming more moderate in the late 1960s and 1970s.[12] My work differs

---

[6] Eva Moskowitz, "'It's Good to Blow Your Top': Women's Magazines and a Discourse of Discontent, 1945–1965," *Journal of Women's History* 8, no. 3 (1996): 481.

[7] Moskowitz, "'It's Good to Blow Your Top,'" 484.

[8] Elaine Tyler May, *Homeward Bound: American Families in the Cold War Era* (New York: Basic Books, 2017); Lizabeth Cohen, *A Consumers' Republic: The Politics of Mass Consumption in Postwar America* (New York: Knopf—distributed by Random House, 2003).

[9] Coontz, *Strange Stirring*, 21.

[10] Adina Kelley, "The Evangelical Mystique: Conservative Protestant Femininity from 1940 to 1966" (dissertation, Baylor University, forthcoming).

[11] Melody Maxwell, *The Woman I Am: Southern Baptist Women's Writings, 1906–2006* (Tuscaloosa: University of Alabama Press, 2014); Elizabeth Hill Flowers, *Into the Pulpit: Southern Baptist Women and Power since World War II* (Chapel Hill: University of North Carolina Press, 2012).

[12] Maxwell, *Woman I Am*.

from hers in a crucial way, however. While Maxwell uses mostly Southern Baptist Woman's Missionary Union sources, this chapter primarily focuses on two magazines she does not survey, *Home Life* and *Baptist Student*, both published by the Sunday School Board. *Home Life* in particular was an influential magazine during the postwar period and beyond. In 1960 it boasted a circulation of eight hundred thousand and featured articles written by both sexes, but the majority by women.[13] The content of *Home Life* in particular reflected the concerns of an average Southern Baptist woman.

Even taking into account work such as Flowers's and Maxwell's, homemaking was by far the most prominent ideal for Southern Baptist women during the postwar era. Homemaking consisted of three primary roles: wife, mother, and housekeeper, and in this article I focus on the third of these. This emphasis on homemaking closely mirrored the broader mainstream ideals of the 1950s Betty Friedan would later describe, however hyperbolically, as the feminine mystique.[14] Furthermore, during this period, more than any other in the twentieth century, evangelical gender norms aligned with those of the broader culture. In doing so, however, they also engaged with the difficulties of being a housewife, and even offered alternatives to women on a limited basis.[15]

Southern Baptists are representative of this conservative Protestant trend. To illustrate this claim, I divide this chapter into three sections. First, I evaluate the ideal of the Christian home and its homemaker. Second, I trace discussions that compared housekeeping with careers outside the home. Finally, I show that, in some cases, periodicals demonstrate that Southern Baptists were open to women pushing the boundaries of the "evangelical mystique" and exploring opportunities for hobbies and work outside the home.[16]

The Ideal Christian Home and Its Homemaker

At the conclusion of World War II, the ideal of home was on the mind of many Americans. Soldiers looked forward to returning home to see parents, wives, and sweethearts. Young couples anticipated buying their own homes and raising families for the first time. The mainstream desire for home was

---

[13] McCallister, *N. W. Ayer & Son's Directory: Newspapers and Periodicals 1960*, 967.

[14] Friedan, *Feminine Mystique*.

[15] Kelley, "Evangelical Mystique."

[16] The "evangelical mystique" is defined as the evangelical domestic gender norms for women from 1945 to 1970.

largely consumerist and individualistic.[17] Conservative Protestants were sometimes caught up in the consumerist and suburban fever of late 1940s. In fact, one author, Helen Laura Renshaw, wrote for such mainstream magazines as *Parents* while also writing for *Home Life*.[18] In general, conservative Protestants had a more holistic view of the Christian home and its value for society than mainstream authors. They argued for its moral impact on culture and saw the Christian home as essential to the health of the Christian religion. Still, their attraction to postwar consumerism married well with their views of marriage and motherhood. During the postwar years, Southern Baptists synthesized this focus on the Christian home into a particular ideal of homemaking that centered on the physical home as well as the homemaker, who was always a woman.

Southern Baptists were not immune to the rush for comfortable housing after World War II fueled by a booming economy and the G.I. Bill. J. R. Grant, president of Ouachita Baptist University, wrote that the goal of marriage should be "a happy home in a peaceful, prosperous community."[19] This kind of goal was evident in the way Southern Baptists wrote about physical houses in the postwar years. Each issue of *Home Life* magazine featured a profile of a family that started off with the description of the family's house. For instance, the profile of the Sewell family began by portraying their house as "a small white clapboard dwelling, unpretentious in design, housing a rather small, close-knit family."[20] Other articles featured tours of beautiful homes built and landscaped by Southern Baptist families. One such family was quoted as saying, "We feel that we have been more than amply repaid for all work, money, and time spent in making our home attractive."[21]

Southern Baptists were certainly caught up in the postwar housing boom, but they also attached spiritual significance to the quest for a physical

---

[17] "Dream House," *LIFE*, May 6, 1946; "LIFE Presents: A Portfolio of Ideas for Home Planning," *LIFE*, May 28, 1945; "Some Veterans Get Temporary Homes as Fight over Permanent Solution Rages," *LIFE*, April 15, 1946.

[18] Editor, "Woman's Work," *Home Life*, January 1952, 48.

[19] J. R. Grant, "College Marriage: Good or Bad?," *Home Life*, May 1947, 5–7.

[20] David Ragan, "The Sewells: A Courageous Christian Family," *Home Life*, January 1947, 8–11.

[21] Adelaide Blanton, "Laurel Oaks Is Our Haven," *Home Life*, April 1948, 31. See also Roy E. McFee, "YOU and Your Books," *Better Home*, April–May–June 1946, 6–8; Sam W. Scantlan, "Hungry for a Home," *Home Life*, April 1950, 5–6; Ruth Anne Grisso, "We Wanted to Be Different," *Home Life*, February 1953, 17, 19.

home. One poem featured in *Home Life* honored a woman's attachment to her former houses. Its author imagined a woman's heart wandering back to her previous dwellings in order to pray at the kitchen window and remember where her children used to play.[22] For a woman, the poem proposes, a house and home were intrinsically linked. Another female author praised the value of a kitchen to the spiritual identity of the home. Her article exclaimed, "From our kitchens come a love for home and the joy of taking good care of our families, delight in doing a task well, development of patience and serenity, a spirit of gaiety in daily living, and a trust in an all-wise God."[23] A physical house could be the locus of spiritual growth and identity for the whole family. The 1952 article "Wanted: Secretary" seemed at first to reaffirm this Southern Baptist romance with suburbia. At the beginning of the story, the protagonist, Anne, complained about her family's small living quarters. She wailed, "If we could only get out of this war-bride's paradise," and wished "for the hundredth time she could think of a way to earn some money so they could save enough to put a down payment on a nice six-room house at the edge of town." As a solution, Anne decided to pursue an opportunity to become a secretary; however, by the end of the story she realized that her presence at home was far more important than the size of the house.[24] This narrative illustrates that, for Southern Baptists, the heart of the postwar Christian home was its homemaker, while also showing the unease Southern Baptist periodicals expressed toward women working outside the home. But what of the work of a homemaker on a daily basis? Did Southern Baptist periodicals acknowledge the daily grind of the housewife, or did the Southern Baptist mystique ignore what Friedan called "the problem that has no name"?[25] While many articles promoted the ideal of homemaking, it was also common for authors to recognize the difficulties housewives faced while still emphasizing the need to look on the bright side and embrace the high calling of housework, all without neglecting their families. The articles acknowledging the struggle of homemakers usually had a happy ending. Still, they defied Friedan's assumption that postwar periodicals provided no recognition of the difficulty housewives experienced. Some articles

[22] Virginia Moran Evans, "A Woman's House," *Home Life*, August 1947, 26.

[23] Ruth Boon Fusselle, "Your Kitchen Is What You Make It," *Home Life*, September 1948, 30–31.

[24] Virginia B. Novinger, "Wanted: Secretary," *Home Life*, January 1952, 24–27, 33.

[25] Friedan used this to describe the feeling of loneliness and boredom many housewives felt (Friedan, *Feminine Mystique,* 57 [chapter 1 title]).

openly attested to the despondency one could feel from the repetitive duties of housework and motherhood. Kathleen Blake asked readers, "Do you have the housework blues? There's always the same old round confronting you: dishwashing, beds, cleaning, mending, and laundry, and no matter how hard you work today you have to do it all over again tomorrow."[26] Blake's solution to the housework blues was simple: she sang to herself a variety of songs in order to lift her spirits.[27]

Ellen Mercer's fictional character, Janet, prayed that God would "help me to get through this day without screaming from weariness. I must do the laundry and the shopping and the ironing and mending."[28] The main character in Kathleen Collins's story, Abby, experienced this discontentment after her husband left for work and her children for school. "When the last child had bolted for the school bus, Abby turned to the sink and broke a plate, not quite by accident. 'Dear God,' she whispered in reverent supplication, 'today let me do something *different*. If life begins at forty, let's get the show on the road.'"[29] Edna B. Hawkins told of her frustrations rising to the surface when her cheerful neighbor asked if she could go to town. "'Goodness, no!' In precise words I told Mrs. Johnson I had a half-dozen crinolines to starch, a birthday cake to bake, a Brownie's uniform to let out, a dozen calls to make for the P.T.A., and no telling what else the day would demand that I hadn't dreamed of."[30] Each of these women was expressing the problem that had no name. Sometimes the protagonists shared their feelings with their husbands or friends; sometimes they did not. In a particularly memorable exchange, Abby tried to explain her discouragement to her husband, Harry, who responded, "Your blood sugar may be low, are you dieting again?"[31] As Friedan observed, this dissatisfaction was not one that men understood, and the *Home Life* articles reflected this fact.

The inability of a man to understand the problem that has no name meant that each protagonist had to seek out a solution on her own. Janet sought hers by reading a newspaper article titled "Psychologist Says College

---

[26] Kathleen Blake, "You Can Sing Yourself Happy," *Home Life*, January 1952, 18–19.

[27] Others found hope in new washing machines or even simply a new, more positive frame of mind. Jessie Merle Franklin, "The Miracle," *Home Life*, May 1956, 24–28; Lydia Lion Roberts, "Adding Spice to Housekeeping," *Better Home*, April–May–June 1938, 17.

[28] Ellen Mercer. "College Wife," *Home Life*, January 1961, 58.

[29] Kathleen Collins, "The Daily Bread of Love," *Home Life*, February 1961, 16.

[30] Edna B. Hawkins, "House with a View," *Home Life*, May 1961, 33.

[31] Collins, "Daily Bread of Love," 16.

Marriages in Danger."[32] Abby decided to answer a classified ad and get a job against her husband's wishes, only to eventually quit and return home. Barbara, Ellen Kerr's character, spent a day alone with a friend.[33] Except for Lorrie, each of these women sought a solution outside the home, but each ultimately found peace back in their positions as housewife.[34]

However all-consuming this housework was, these periodicals reminded readers that they should never neglect their first duties: their husbands, children, and faith. Some articles reminded women that even if they felt like they were wonderful homemakers, they may actually be achieving such a status via the wrong motivations. One such article published in 1949 was titled "For Whom Do You Wear Yourself Out?" It began by telling homemakers that they should check their egos if they felt tired and then asked if readers were wearing themselves out for their neighbors or for their families. The author illustrated her point by telling the story of Mrs. Freeling, who kept cleaning an already spotless home and would not allow her husband to set foot on her newly cleaned rug. "It did not occur to her that the most important person in her life had just dropped in. He was trying to enjoy the home he had provided for his family. Such false values may make an otherwise good homemaker a homewrecker."[35] Mrs. Fleta Harris, in the *Baptist Student* in May 1959, made an explicitly theological argument for staying at home, stating that "Woman was created to fulfill a need of man which God himself could not fulfill. Because God created me for this purpose, I have dedicated my life to homemaking."[36] Ultimately, the role of Christian homemaker was dignified and justified through a particular form of spiritual rhetoric that endowed housework and motherhood with eternal value. In doing so, the Southern Baptist mystique ultimately diverged from the femi-

---

[32] Mercer, "College Wife," 59.

[33] Hellen V. Kerr, "Everything at Once," *Home Life*, March 1961, 34–35.

[34] Mercer, "College Wife," 59.

[35] Loise G. Morrison, "For Whom Do You Wear Yourself Out?" *Home Life*, August 1949, 15. For a similar argument, but focusing on children rather than a husband, see Margaret Evans, "Are You a Robot Mother?," *Home Life*, February 1952, 22–23; Violet M. Roberts, "Housework Can Wait," *Home Life*, March 1957, 7; Cozette Holmes, "I Didn't Marry a House," *Home Life*, April 1956, 38–40.

[36] Mrs. Fleta Harris, "The Sacred Privilege of Womanhood," *Baptist Student*, May 1959, 36–37. Other articles that emphasized that homemaking should be gendered female include Anne Alexander, "Cook's Holiday," *Home Life*, June 1955, 7–8; Josephine Stone Breeding, "Heirloom Cookbook," *Home Life*, February 1952, 43; Billie Eckert Martin, "Little Girls Are Little Women," *Home Life*, November 1950, 12–13, 15.

nine mystique, despite their apparent similarities. By acknowledging the repetitive, difficult work housewives had to endure and simultaneously spiritualizing its value, Southern Baptist periodicals urged women to keep quiet and accept their roles within the evangelical mystique.[37]

Housewife Versus Career Woman

In order for women to accept the evangelical mystique, the option of working outside the home as a "career woman" had to be undermined.[38] *Home Life* ran an article that demonstrates this effort, perfectly titled "I Was a Working Wife." In it, Elisabeth C. Cunkle recounted her experiences as a wife working outside the home. She explained that her primary goal in working outside the home was not to gain independence herself but to do her best to help her husband "get ahead." Eventually, though, she realized that her efforts to help her husband outside the home were only undermining his masculine need to provide, and her feminine duty to create "an attractive home background" and enlarge "their circle of acquaintances," through her "club work and social activities." Interestingly, her reasoning for returning to homemaking was purely social, not spiritual. The positive results that she claimed were also entirely temporal. Cunkle exclaimed at the end of her article, "The happy postscript to this little tale of a modern wife who decided that her place is in the home is that my husband's earnings have almost doubled, I have learned to bake a lemon pie, my husband has gained ten pounds, and we have acquired a home."[39] It was not spiritually

---

[37] There were many other articles that presented a neutral perspective on careers for women. *Descriptive:* Barbara Dupree Yarbrough, "Airline Stewardess—Ten Years Later," *Home Life*, November 1957, 7–9; Catherine May, "Career Girl at Seventy-Two," *Home Life*, October 1956, 40; Ella Wiebe, "Secret to Being an Ideal Mother," *Christian Life*, March 1962, 39; "Full-Time Service, Dorothy G. Mann," *Home Life*, April 1957, 5–6.

Prescriptive: H. C. Brearley, "New Roles of Women and Children," *Home Life*, July 1955, 6–7, 42–43; Marjorie Moore Armstrong, "She's Crusading for Her Children inside Her Home and Out," *Home Life*, June 1957, 9, 43–44; Joe W. Burton, "Women Know Their Place," *Home Life*, October 1955, 48.

[38] Such discussion was not new, though it increased in intensity in the postwar years. Articles published in the years before World War II in the predecessor to *Home Life*, *The Better Home*, included Azalete Bolger Wells, "Ambition," *Better Home*, April–May–June 1940, 27; Editor, "A Profession for Women," *Better Home*, April–May–June 1938, 2; Elise R. Glover, "Artists Will Paint," *Better Home*, April–May–June 1940, 26–27.

[39] Elisabeth C. Cunkle, "I Was a Working Wife," *Home Life*, February 1948, 9. For more on the importance of putting energy toward family rather than a career, see Johnnie Lee Bounds, "American Mother," *Home Life*, November 1949, 4, 18.

disobedient for Cunkle to work outside the home, but practically unhelpful in reaching the goals of a happy home. "I Was an Airline Stewardess" made a similar argument, though added the twist of asserting that the author's time as a flight attendant would actually help the author become a better mother.[40] Similarly, Elna Worrel Daniel decided to go to work to try to pay for her daughter's speech therapy, only to discover that the stutter could only be cured when Daniel learned to pray and trust God rather than try to earn extra money.[41] Each of these articles has a clear moral: to be a career woman is to take something vital away from the family.[42]

"Why Joyce Quit Work," demonstrates a man's perspective on the importance of homemakers, as John Alden wrote about his experience when his wife decided to work outside the home. Alden concluded, "It was costing us too much for her to work. We were only fooling ourselves, actually cheating ourselves. I wonder how many other parents are doing the same thing."[43] Other articles by men were much blunter, such as the 1956 article by Frank Howard Richardson that stated women were likely to work "because of the belief that a business or professional career is more desirable than the humdrum task of being 'only a mother' and 'merely a housewife.'" Indeed, he goes as far as to say, "Unless it is absolutely unavoidable, no young mother should deprive her family of a wife and mother's loving care and attention when they need it so badly."[44] Many other articles published in this time period made similar arguments as to why women should stay home.[45]

---

[40] Barbara Dupree Yarbrough, "I Was an Airline Stewardess," *Home Life*, June 1949, 8–10. See also Nell Dunkin, "She Lives with Them," *Home Life*, July 1949, 18; Jacqueline Compere Boyd, "Just a Housewife," *Home Life*, July 1961, 58–59.

[41] Elna Worrel Daniel, "Someone to Lean On," *Home Life*, August 1956, 24–27.

[42] Elaine Bierbauer, "Mother, Do You Really Have to Work?" *Home Life*, September 1961, 37; Blossom Bennet, "Can We Stand This Prosperity?" *Home Life*, November 1956, 10–13; Mrs. W. D. Kendall, "It Could Happen to You," *Baptist Student*, February 1955, 6–8.

[43] John Alden, "Why Joyce Quit Work," *Home Life*, March 1958, 44–45.

[44] Frank Howard Richardson, "Are Mothers Expendable?" *Home Life*, October 1956, 38–40; Olin T. Binkley, "Parenthood as a Vocation," *Home Life*, June 1954, 5, 18–19.

[45] Ross L. Holman, "Part-Time Mothers," *Home Life*, May 1957, 5–7; N.A. "Second Pay Check: What It Means to Church and Home," *Christian Life*, February 1957, 68–71; Joe W. Burton, "Which Will It Be—Mother or Maid?" *Home Life*, January 1959, 48; An Old-Fashioned Father, "Mother Stay Home," *Moody Monthly*, August 1961, 11–13; "The Cost of Missing Mothers: Editorial," *Moody Monthly*, June 1962, 15; Clyde Merrill Maguire, "Homemaking: The Forgotten Art," *Baptist Student*, February 1958, 46–49; O. K. Armstrong, "She's Neglecting Her First Duty," *Home Life*, June 1957, 8, 42.

Even female college students who were pursuing nondomestic degrees sometimes had to frame their ambitions as to fit the postwar evangelical mystique. In a profile of Margaret titled "Among the Professionals," the author made clear that Margaret did not intend to continue working outside the home despite her three years of nursing training. The author explained,

> She is a math major, but don't let that frighten you. She is not cold and calculating, for in a calm, reverent way, Margaret simply says, "My ambition in life is to make an ideal Christian home." Don't doubt she can use her three years of nursing...as well as the talents...toward accomplishing the highest ambition a girl can have.[46]

According to this author and many others, being a Christian homemaker was the highest ideal for a Southern Baptist woman. Even Christian vocations did not measure up to the calling of wife and mother. *Baptist Student*'s profile of Lieutenant Elizabeth Hardy emphasized this point. Although she had been a missionary prior to the war, and a nurse in the military during the war years, Hardy's only desire at the conclusion of World War II was to "settle down and have a Christian home."[47] In another article in *Home Life*, John L. Hill tells the story of three college-age girls he interviewed. The first, he remembered, wanted to go to China for foreign mission service. The second wanted to be a nurse on the mission field. Hill honored their self-sacrificing piety, but then wrote about his reaction to the third girl. He wrote, "The third was not as ready in response as the other two. 'Young lady,' I finally said, 'what's on your mind?' 'Oh,' she said, 'I want a Christian home!' 'Bless your heart,' I said, 'yours is the highest ambition of the three.'"[48] Missionary work for women was certainly a valuable calling, but not as valuable as creating a Christian home.

Pushing the Boundaries of the "Evangelical Mystique"

Thus far I have shown that the Southern Baptist discourse surrounding gender did in fact discuss the problems housewives dealt with, but each example ultimately reaffirmed a woman's place in the home. But there was also literature in these magazines that found, outside of the domestic sphere, solutions to the problem that has no name. The two solutions found in these

[46] Frances Barbour, "Among the Professionals," *Baptist Student*, December 1947, 22.

[47] William Hall Preston, "A Missionary Goes to War," *Baptist Student*, October 1945, 27–28.

[48] John L. Hill, "The Highest Ambition," *Home Life*, July 1948, 30.

periodicals were an individual woman's pursuit of a hobby or, in very limited cases, a career outside of the home. These solutions were offered before Friedan's work was published, and hobbies and paid work were both part of her new life plan in *The Feminine Mystique.*

Friedan suggested that in order to overcome the feminine mystique, a woman should pursue some sort of hobby, preferably for pay. Several Southern Baptist articles also proposed hobbies as a solution to the problem of the housewife. Gertrude A. Rae, in her autobiographical story "How I Found Myself," recounted how her dedication to writing freed her from the "major hazards to the well-being of the young wife and mother." These dangers included "monotony, a sense of inadequacy to the demands made upon her, loneliness for adult companionship, and a feeling of negative personal accomplishment." The release Rae felt after dedicating time to writing seems to be precisely the kind of self-discovery Friedan was hoping housewives would experience. Rae wrote, "My hobby has many advantages, the greatest being that it has freed me of frustrations....To discover that talent and develop it is the simple answer to chronic frustration. I know!"[49] Continuing, she explained that between a career and a hobby, "The results are the same: to release the mother from a too dedicated domesticity; to give her something to achieve, apart from her round of duties; to make her feel individual. I saw that there is nothing negative about a housewife's accomplishments—that she is a distinct person in her own right."[50] This discovery of selfhood could easily be assumed to be a result of reading the book *The Feminine Mystique*, had she not published two years before Friedan.

Finally, a few articles in Southern Baptist periodicals defended women who worked full-time outside the home.[51] One of the most prominent careers for women to appear in the pages of conservative Protestant magazines was, perhaps unsurprisingly, nursing. This makes sense, as nursing could prepare one for motherhood or a career. A 1958 article by Annette Franks Walker made this exact point when she explained the motivations of her fellow students: "Several of the girls admitted that the main reason they chose nursing was to prepare themselves for marriage and motherhood. 'Hey, don't forget us career women!' a pretty, energetic junior chimed in.

---

[49] Gertrude A. Rae, "How I Found Myself," *Home Life*, September 1961, 16–18.

[50] Rae, "How I Found Myself," 18.

[51] There were also rare articles that argued that women could also work in the case of family need, such as David R. Mace, "The Wider Scope of Marriage," *Home Life*, December 1953, 16–19, 31.

She is strictly dedicated to the nursing profession, and marriage is not her dream." Nursing was a feminine, flexible career choice for a woman seeking a career or needing to work but wanting to stay within the bounds of acceptable domestic femininity.[52] Another article, titled "Open Doors to Ambitious Women," was even clearer in its support of career women: "No longer can it be said that this is a 'man's world.' It isn't! It definitely is a 'woman's world.' The hand that rocks the cradle today may also belong to a career woman." The author then goes on to list occupations that may have interested her female readers, who would have been Southern Baptist college students: jobs such as teaching, journalism, nursing, government, and/or radio and television. But true to her time, Agnes Ford, the author, also spilled a significant amount of ink explaining that, "At least 80 percent of all women choose marriage and homemaking as an occupation. This vocation is the highest to which any woman can aspire."[53]

In conclusion, Southern Baptists in the postwar years were discussing the problem of the housewife before Friedan ever published *The Feminine Mystique*. Moreover, they did not present a monolithic solution to this problem but offered a range of possibilities for female fulfillment that both contradicted and agreed with Friedan's prescriptions for a "new life plan." But this flexibility did not outweigh their overwhelming push for domesticity, which closely aligned with the mainstream postwar ideals of suburban housewives in houses with white picket fences. The Southern Baptist, and evangelical, ideal did differ from the mainstream rhetoric in one essential way, however. The role of housewife, or homemaker, was spiritualized as a woman's calling and duty before God. The article "It Could Happen to You" in the February 1955 issue of *Baptist Student* serves as great final example of this rhetorical phenomenon. The author, Mrs. W. D. Kendall, reminded and exhorted women considering full-time Christian work that "Maybe God needs you for a homemaker. No career offers more opportunities for a rich, full, happy life. God in his wisdom created woman, and he provided for her this richly satisfying and worth-while career."[54] The feminine mystique and the evangelical mystique were not too far apart during the postwar years. Those who advocated for

---

[52] Annette Franks Walter, "Calling Student Nurse Jones," *Baptist Student*, October 1958, 36–37, see also Estelle Slater, "It Could Be You," *Baptist Student*, December 1959, 50–51.

[53] Agnes Ford, "Open Doors to Ambitious Women," *Baptist Student*, January 1954, 15–17, 31.

[54] Kendall, "It Could Happen to You."

domesticity within the Southern Baptist Convention in the 1950s clearly presented it as a calling—and as "the noblest career of all."[55]

[55] Doris Garst, "Noblest Career of All," *Home Life*, May 1949, 32.

17

Evangelical by Conviction, Baptist by Tradition: David Dockery's Vision for Southern Baptist Higher Education

Nathan A. Finn

On February 1, 2018, the Council of Christian Colleges and Universities (CCCU) awarded David S. Dockery the 2018 John R. Dellenback Global Leadership Award. According to the CCCU, the annual award "is presented to an individual who has made outstanding contributions to Christian higher education through scholarship, writing, and public influence."[1] In many ways, Dockery was an obvious choice for this award. The CCCU press release noted that Dockery had served as president of two prominent Christian universities: Union University (1996–2014) and Trinity International University (2014–2019). Dockery authored or edited several influential books related to Christian higher education, in addition to writing numerous journal articles and contributed essays on the topic. Dockery previously served as chair of the board of directors for both the CCCU and the Consortium for Global Education, and at the time his reception of the Dellenback Award was announced, he was serving as board chair of the Christian College Consortium and president of the Evangelical Theological Society.[2]

Despite his accomplishments in evangelical higher education, Dockery's reception of an award from the CCCU would have been unlikely a generation ago. He is a lifelong Southern Baptist who has written widely on

---

* I would like to thank David Dockery for his comments on an earlier draft of this chapter. He helped correct some factual errors and provided some additional information that strengthened several sections. However, the interpretations advanced in this chapter remain my own.

[1] "Dockery to Receive 2018 Delleback Award," Council of Christian Colleges and Universities, November 21, 2017, https://www.cccu.org/news-updates/david-dockery-dellenback-award/.

[2] "Dockery to Receive 2018 Delleback Award."

topics related to Baptist historical theology and Southern Baptist identity, most notably in his coedited volume *Baptist Theologians* and the treatise *Southern Baptist Consensus and Renewal: A Biblical, Historical, and Theological Proposal*.[3] Union University, where Dockery spent the bulk of his career, is a Baptist institution affiliated with the Tennessee Baptist Mission Board, which in turn is a state convention that cooperates with the Southern Baptist Convention. Prior to his tenure at Union, Dockery taught at Criswell College, a small Baptist-related college in Texas; served as a professor and chief academic officer at Southern Baptist Theological Seminary, the oldest SBC-related seminary; and was the academic editor for the Baptist Sunday School Board (now LifeWay Christian Resources), the Southern Baptist denominational publishing house. Not surprisingly, based on his distinguished Baptist pedigree, Dockery—in addition to the CCCU honor in 2018—was also honored that year by the International Association of Baptist Colleges and Universities (IABCU). Dockery had previously served on the board of the organization, and in June 2018 he delivered the distinguished Hester Lecture for the IABCU annual meeting for the second time. Tellingly, his three lectures focused on the future of Christian higher education in the evangelical tradition and educating leaders for the Baptist future.

Throughout his career, Dockery's influence has been felt in the oft-overlapping worlds of Southern Baptist higher education and evangelical higher education—but these worlds have not always shared ground. In fact, it has not been uncommon over the past couple of generations for Baptist scholars to periodically ask whether Southern Baptists should even be considered evangelicals, and if so, what type.[4] These discussions have been

---

[3] Timothy George and David S. Dockery, eds., *Baptist Theologians* (Nashville: Broadman, 1990); Dockery, *Southern Baptist Consensus and Renewal: A Biblical, Historical, and Theological Proposal* (Nashville: B&H, 2008). Much of the information related to Dockery's career used in this chapter has been taken from his personal curriculum vitae, which is in the author's possession.

[4] For example, see James Leo Garrett Jr., E. Glenn Hinson, and Jame Tull, *Are Southern Baptists "Evangelicals"?* (Macon, GA: Mercer University Press, 1982); David S. Dockery, ed., *Southern Baptists and American Evangelicals: The Conversation Continues* (Nashville: B&H, 1994); Malcolm B. Yarnell III, "Are Southern Baptists Evangelicals? A Second Decadal Reassessment," *Ecclesiology* 2, no. 2 (2006): 195–212; William H. Brackney, "Are Baptists Evangelicals? The Question Revisited," *Perspectives in Religious Studies* 33, no. 1 (Spring 2006): 105–21; Nathan A. Finn, "Southern Baptists and Evangelicals: Passing on the Faith to the Next Generation," in *Southern Baptists, Evangelicals, and the Future of Denominationalism*, ed. David S. Dockery, Ray Van Neste, and Jerry Tidwell (Nashville: B&H Academic, 2011), 231–60; C. Jeffrey Robinson Sr., "Evangelicals from the Beginning: English Baptists

fueled by the inerrancy controversy in the Southern Baptist Convention, and postcontroversy efforts by conservative and moderate Baptists in the American South to refine and commend their respective understandings of Baptist identity.[5] Not surprisingly, Dockery has weighed in on this discussion frequently, editing a book on the topic and regularly weaving the theme into numerous other writings.[6] Throughout his career, Dockery has positioned himself as a self-consciously evangelical Baptist, with both of those terms enriching the other.[7]

In this chapter I seek to make a small contribution to two discussions: the relationship between Southern Baptists and evangelicals, as well as the nature of higher education in the Baptist tradition. David Dockery's career, particularly his time at Union University, is used as a window into these larger discussions. During his tenure at Union, Dockery helped popularize heretofore evangelical emphases among Baptist-related colleges and universities. In so doing, he served as a bridge figure between Southern Baptists and the wider evangelical world as the former moved increasingly into the orbit of the latter in the years following the inerrancy controversy. Dockery offered Baptist universities that were sympathetic to the conservative faction of that controversy an intellectual identity that was distinctive from the moderate vision that predominated among most of the oldest and most prestigious Baptist-related institutions, many of which were renegotiating or even severing their denominational ties.

---

of the Seventeenth Century," in *Ministry by His Grace and for His Glory: Essays in Honor of Tom Nettles*, ed. Thomas K. Ascol and Nathan A. Finn (Cape Coral, FL: Founders Press, 2011), 59–75.

[5] For more on how the inerrancy controversy and its aftermath have been shaped by competing visions of Baptist identity, see Nathan A. Finn, "Debating Baptist Identities: Description and Prescription in the American South," in *Mirrors and Microscopes: Historical Perceptions of Baptists*, ed. C. Douglas Weaver (Bletchley, Milton Keynes, UK: Paternoster, 2015), 173–87.

[6] See Dockery, *Southern Baptists and American Evangelicals.*

[7] Dockery's identity as an evangelical Baptist was noted by several contributors to a 2015 festschrift published in his honor. See especially James Leo Garrett, "David Samuel Dockery: Evangelical Baptist and the Doctrine of the Bible," in *Convictional Civility: Engaging the Culture in the 21st Century: Essays in Honor of David S. Dockery*, ed. C. Ben Mitchell, Carla D. Sanderson, and Gregory Alan Thornbury (Nashville: B&H Academic, 2015), 3–10, and Timothy George, "With David Dockery among Baptists and Evangelicals," in Mitchell et al., *Convictional Civility*, 11–18.

Evangelical Higher Education: Two Key Concepts

Historians and theologians are constantly debating the origins, doctrinal identity, and future prospects of American evangelicalism; I don't rehash those debates in this chapter. But for the most part, scholars agree that the modern evangelical movement emerged in the years following World War II; that it was a transdenominational movement that coalesced around individuals, institutions, and parachurch ministries rather than traditional denominational structures; and that evangelical leaders self-consciously positioned their movement as the healthy middle between separatist fundamentalism on the right and mainline Protestantism on the left.[8] By and large, evangelicals avoided discussions of ecclesiology, since those differences divide denominational traditions, and instead focused their attention on a broad commitment to Protestant orthodoxy, missions and evangelism, and faith-motivated cultural engagement.[9] Of course, all of those commitments have been fiercely contested by self-confessed evangelicals and studied by scholars of evangelicalism: note the ongoing debates about David Bebbington's justly famous "evangelical quadrilateral" and the periodic intra-evangelical discussions about whether "authentic" evangelicalism is more Reformed or Wesleyan in its emphases.[10]

---

[8] This consensus has reflected George Marsden's influence on the field. See especially George M. Marsden, *Understanding Fundamentalism and Evangelicalism* (Grand Rapids: Eerdmans, 1990), which offers his mature reflections on evangelicalism. The consensus interpretation of twentieth-century evangelical history has recently been challenged by Matthew Avery Sutton, *American Apocalypse: A History of Modern Evangelicalism* (Cambridge, MA: Harvard University Press, 2014). Sutton argues for greater continuity between fundamentalism and evangelicalism and suggests that efforts to focus on postwar discontinuities have been driven by evangelical historians with a vested interest in protecting their self-identification.

[9] Bruce Hindmarsh, "Is Evangelical Ecclesiology an Oxymoron? A Historical Perspective," in *Evangelical Ecclesiology: Reality or Illusion?*, ed. John G. Stackhouse Jr. (Grand Rapids: Baker Academic, 2003), 15–37.

[10] For the original distillation of the Bebbington Quadrilateral, see David W. Bebbington, *Evangelicals in Modern Britain: A History from the 1730s to the 1980s* (London: Unwin Hyman, 1989), 3–19. For recent discussions of the ongoing utility of Bebbington's summary, including responses by Bebbington, see the relevant essays in the Winter/Spring 2015 issue of *Fides et Historia*, which includes contributions from Kelly Elliott, Thomas Kidd, Amanda Porterfield, Darren Dochuk, Mark Noll, and Molly Worthen. The Reformed/Wesleyan debate about evangelical historical interpretation has been most clearly represented in the periodic debate between George Marsden and Donald Dayton, in response to each other's respective works, between the mid-1970s and mid-1990s. The debate is ably summarized in

Despite this diversity, in 1976 a group of about forty evangelical colleges founded the Coalition for Christian Colleges, which later became the Council for Christian Colleges and Universities (CCCU). Among the CCCU's founding institutions, only three were related to Baptist traditions—Bethel University, Eastern University, and Campbellsville University—and only the last is historically Southern Baptist in its identity. This should not be surprising to students of Southern Baptist history. The same year the CCCU was getting off the ground, Southern Baptist leader Foy Valentine was quipping that *evangelical* is a "Yankee word."[11] Yet evangelicalism was culturally ascendant. That same year, self-confessed evangelical Jimmy Carter was elected president of the United States and Watergate conspirator-turned-evangelical-activist Charles Colson's spiritual memoir *Born Again* was a bestseller, leading *Newsweek* to dub 1976 "The Year of the Evangelical."[12] Of note is that Carter and Colson were not only evangelical luminaries, but they were also both Southern Baptist laymen. This shared evangelical and Southern Baptist identity was a portend of the two movements drifting closer to each other during the 1980s and 1990s. By 2018 at least twenty-five institutions with historic ties to Southern Baptists had become members of the CCCU, while two others were collaborative partner institutions of the council.[13]

Douglas A. Sweeney, "Historiographical Dialectics: On Marsden, Dayton, and the Inner Logic of Evangelical History," *Christian Scholar's Review* 23, no. 1 (September 1993): 48–52.

[11] See Kenneth L. Woodward, "Born Again! The Year of the Evangelicals," *Newsweek*, October 25, 1986, 76.

[12] See Charles W. Colson, *Born Again: What Really Happened to the White House Hatchet Man?* (Grand Rapids: Chosen Books, 1976). The full cover story about evangelicalism's cultural ascendancy in 1976 can be found in Woodward, "Born Again!" 68–78.

[13] The list of institutions historically related to Southern Baptists that are currently members of CCCU as of December 2018 includes the following: Anderson University, Bluefield College, California Baptist University, Campbell University, Campbellsville University, Carson-Newman University, Charleston Southern University, Dallas Baptist University, East Texas Baptist University, Hannibal-LaGrange University, Hardin-Simmons University, Houston Baptist University, Howard Payne University, Judson College, Louisiana College, Mississippi College, Missouri Baptist University, North Greenville University, Oklahoma Baptist University, Ouachita Baptist University, Palm Beach Atlantic University, Southwest Baptist University, University of Mary Hardin–Baylor, University of Mobile, and Williams Baptist College. Baylor University and Samford University are two historically Southern Baptist schools that are collaborative partner institutions of CCCU. Collaborate partners are sympathetic to CCCU and its initiatives but do not have employment policies requiring all faculty members to be professing Christians. Incidentally, Union University, as well as a few other non–Southern Baptist–related schools, withdrew from CCCU in 2015 due to concerns

Schools in CCCU circles often emphasized two key concepts in shaping their distinctively evangelical vision for Christian higher education. The first is the importance of a Christian worldview. According to Philip Ryken, "A worldview—or 'world-and-life view,' as some people call it—is the structure of understanding that we use to make sense of our world. Our worldview is what we presuppose. It is our way of looking at life, our interpretation of the universe, our orientation to reality."[14]

Worldview language has its origins in nineteenth-century German idealism, and it was imported into Christian circles around the turn of the twentieth century.[15] Theologians including Abraham Kuyper and James Orr first promoted the idea of a Christian worldview, though in the 1970s and 1980s, scholars such as James Sire, Brian Walsh, Richard Middleton, and Albert Wolters popularized worldview language in evangelical higher education. Sire, a former English professor and longtime editor for InterVarsity Press, provided a list of basic questions for discerning one's worldview.[16] Wolters, a Dutch Reformed theologian, offered an influential framework for Christian worldview that is built around the so-called grand narrative of Scripture: creation, fall, and redemption.[17] Walsh, a Reformed theologian, and Middleton, a Wesleyan scholar, contrasted the biblical world with the modern world, attempting to bridge the gap for the sake of faithful cultural engagement.[18] Building on these thinkers, evangelical scholars also focused

---

that the organization was opening its membership to institutions that have adopted a welcoming and affirming stance toward homosexuality. This withdrawal took place after David Dockery was no longer Union's president. See J. C. Derrick, "CCCU Loses Union," *World Magazine*, August 12, 2015, https://world.wng.org/2015/08/cccu_loses_union_university.

[14] Philip Graham Ryken, *Christian Worldview: A Student's Guide*, Reclaiming the Christian Intellectual Tradition (Wheaton, IL: Crossway, 2013), 19.

[15] For a history of worldview thinking, see David K. Naugle Jr., *Worldview: The History of a Concept* (Grand Rapids: Eerdmans, 2002).

[16] James Sire, *Naming the Elephant: Worldview as Concept*, 2nd ed. (Downers Grove, IL: IVP Academic, 2015), 20–21. Sire's list of worldview questions includes the following: (1) What is prime reality—the really real? (2) What is the nature of external reality, that is, the world around us? (3) What is a human being? (4) What happens to a person at death? (5) Why is it possible to know anything at all? (6) How do we know what is right and wrong? (7) What is the meaning of human history? (8) What personal, life-orienting core commitments are consistent with this worldview?

[17] Albert M. Wolters, *Creation Regained: Biblical Basics for a Reformational Worldview*, 2nd ed. (Grand Rapids: Eerdmans, 2005).

[18] Brian J. Walsh and J. Richard Middleton, *The Transforming Vision: Shaping a Christian Worldview* (Downers Grove, IL: IVP Academic, 1984).

on matters such as philosophical foundations for a Christian worldview, the influence of Christian worldview thinking on higher education, and the place of Christian worldview analysis in an increasingly pluralistic context.[19]

A second key concept championed within evangelical higher education is the integration of faith and learning. The conversation about faith-learning integration has its roots in Dutch Reformed thought, although, as with the emphasis on Christian worldview, it has been embraced by a variety of evangelical institutions. Longtime Wheaton College philosopher Arthur Holmes popularized this terminology in his 1975 book, *The Idea of a Christian College*, which has become a modern classic in Christian higher education. Holmes suggested at least four different approaches to the integration of faith and learning, but argued that all of them recognize that "the Christian faith can touch the entire range of life and learning to which a liberal education exposes students."[20] The reason so many evangelicals believe integration is needed relates to the separation of faith and learning that has accompanied the secularization of higher education, even in schools that began as church-related institutions, a process documented in the influential works of George Marsden and James Burtchaell, among others.[21] Though not all evangelicals have been enthusiastic about the concept of faith-learning integration, colleges and universities affiliated with the CCCU have widely embraced this language.[22]

---

[19] David S. Dockery and Gregory Alan Thornbury, eds., *Shaping a Christian Worldview: The Foundation of Christian Higher Education* (Nashville: B&H Academic, 2002); J. P. Moreland and William Lane Craig, *Philosophical Foundations for a Christian Worldview*, 2nd ed. (Downers Grove, IL: IVP Academic, 2017); Tawa J. Anderson, W. Michael Clark, and David K. Naugle, *An Introduction to Christian Worldview: Pursuing God's Perspective in a Pluralistic World* (Nashville: B&H Academic, 2017).

[20] Arthur F. Holmes, *The Idea of a Christian College*, rev. ed. (Grand Rapids: Eerdmans, 1987), 45.

[21] See George M. Marsden, *The Soul of the American University: From Protestant Establishment to Established Unbelief* (New York: Oxford University Press, 1994), and James Tunstead Burtchaell, *The Dying of the Light: The Disengagement of Colleges and Universities from Their Christian Churches* (Grand Rapids: Eerdmans, 1998).

[22] The nature and utility of the faith-learning integration model is regularly debated in the pages of disciplinary journals such as *Christian Scholars Review*, *Faculty Dialog*, *Journal of Education and Christian Belief*, and *Christian Higher Education*. For attempts to move beyond the model, see Douglas Jacobsen and Rhonda Hustedt Jacobsen, eds., *Scholarship and Christian Faith: Enlarging the Conversation* (New York: Oxford University Press, 2004), and Todd C. Ream, Jerry Pattengale, and David L. Riggs, eds., *Beyond Integration: Inter/Disciplinary Possibilities for the Future of Christian Higher Education* (Abilene, TX: Abilene Christian University Press, 2012).

Evangelical by Conviction, Baptist by Tradition

David Dockery became president of Union University in 1996.[23] At the time, Union's identity was closely identified with the West Tennessee region, and though the school was arguably more conservative than its sister Tennessee Baptist schools Belmont University and Carson-Newman University, many of Union's administrative leaders and religion professors had been sympathetic to the moderate faction in the inerrancy controversy. Union's Religion Department had periodically experienced controversy over professors' views of the Bible between the 1960s and 1980s. By the mid-1990s, the department included both inerrantists and non-inerrantists, though the more recent hires held to inerrancy.[24]

Dockery also held to biblical inerrancy, and throughout the 1980s and 1990s he published widely on the nature of biblical inspiration and authority, as well as hermeneutics, emerging as arguably the leading conservative Southern Baptist scholar of bibliology.[25] James Leo Garrett suggests that

---

[23] In his dissertation examining Dockery's presidential administration at Union University, Tanner Hickman looks at Dockery's approach to Christian higher education in relation to Jesus's Great Commandment based on Deuteronomy 6:4–9; Matthew 22:37–39; and Mark 12:29–31. My own argument is narrower, focusing on the evangelical/Baptist dynamic in Dockery's thought. Nevertheless, Hickman's work remains the most extensive study of Dockery's views to date. See Tanner Franklin Hickman, "The Integration of Jesus' Great Commandment Within Christian Higher Education: An Analysis of the Leadership Praxis of Dr. David S. Dockery" (EdD diss., Southeastern Baptist Theological Seminary, 2010).

[24] In his institutional history of Union University, James Alex Baggett discusses how controversy in the Religion Department over progressive theology led to a sharp decline in majors prior to conservative George Guthrie's appointment as department chair in 1993, shortly before Dockery became president. See James Alex Baggett, *So Great a Cloud of Witnesses: Union University, 1823–2000* (Jackson, TN: Union University Press, 2000), 224–29.

[25] Major works include David S. Dockery, *The Doctrine of the Bible* (Nashville: Convention Press, 1991); David Alan Black and David S. Dockery, eds., *New Testament Criticism and Interpretation* (Grand Rapids: Zondervan, 1991); David S. Dockery, *Biblical Interpretation Then and Now: Contemporary Hermeneutics in the Light of the Early Church* (Grand Rapids: Baker, 1992); Robison B. James and David S. Dockery, eds., *Beyond the Impasse? Scripture, Interpretation, and Theology in Baptist Life* (Nashville: Broadman, 1992); David S. Dockery, *Christian Scripture: An Evangelical Perspective on Inspiration, Authority and Interpretation* (Nashville: Broadman & Holman, 1995); David S. Dockery, Kenneth A. Matthews, and Robert B. Sloan, *Foundations for Biblical Interpretation: A Complete Library of Tools and Resources* (Nashville: B&H, 1999); David Alan Black and David S. Dockery, eds., *Interpreting the New Testament: Essays on Methods and Issues* (Nashville: B&H Academic, 2001); David S. Dockery, "Special Revelation," in *A Theology for the Church*, rev. ed., ed. Daniel L. Akin (Nashville: B&H Academic, 2014), 103–54.

Dockery's writings on the doctrine of Scripture, including his expertise in hermeneutics, represented the "more reflective aspects of the SBC inerrancy controversy."[26] However, unlike some conservative SBC theologians, Dockery was more irenic in his demeanor, was willing to find ways to cooperate with (and in some cases employ) Baptists who were less theologically conservative than himself, and was interested in more closely intersecting with the wider evangelical movement.[27] All these themes became identified with what might be called the Dockery Vision for Union. Dockery attempted to position the school as a national Christian university on par with a Wheaton College or Calvin College, deeply rooted in its Baptist identity and aligned closely with conservative Southern Baptist thought, but also more broadly evangelical in its ethos and priorities than many other similar institutions. Dockery summarized his vision with the phrase "evangelical by conviction, Baptist by tradition."[28]

Dockery implemented his vision through a number of initiatives. Like other Baptist schools, Union had already joined the CCCU in the early 1990s, so Dockery was able to build on some initial evangelical engagement in promoting his evangelical Baptist vision for higher education. One of his earliest acts was to establish a Center for Faculty Development that was tasked with helping professors to think about their disciplines from the perspective of a Christian worldview and to integrate their faith into their teaching and research.[29] The center sponsored workshops and reading groups that fostered discussions about the same books that were being read throughout CCCU circles. Dockery's particular approach to worldview and faith-learning integration was not simplistically biblicist, but rather sought to frame these concepts in dialog with what he called the Christian Intellec-

---

[26] James Leo Garrett, *Baptist Theology: A Four-Century Study* (Macon, GA: Mercer University Press, 2009), 708.

[27] Baggett notes that faculty were pleased that Dockery was a convictional conservative, but not a fundamentalist, a comment that seems to suggest Dockery was a theological conservative, but not as militant as some moderate faculty members feared. See Baggett, *So Great a Cloud of Witnesses*, 240–41.

[28] David S. Dockery, *Renewing Minds: Serving Church and Society through Christian Higher Education*, rev. and updated ed. (Nashville: B&H Academic, 2008), 29. Dockery also addresses the relationship between Baptist identity and evangelical theology in his essay "Blending Baptist with Orthodox in the Christian University," in *The Future of Baptist Higher Education*, ed. Donald D. Schmeltekopf and Dianna Vitanza (Waco, TX: Baylor University Press, 2006), 83–97.

[29] See the website for the Center for Faculty Development, Union University, http://www.uu.edu/centers/faculty/ (accessed September 20, 2018).

tual Tradition and what others sometimes refer to as the Great Tradition.[30] In so doing, Dockery, along with his longtime friend and collaborator Timothy George, was seeking to articulate evangelical Baptist identity as a particular expression of classical Christian orthodoxy, reflecting what might be called an evangelical Baptist ecumenism that stands to the theological right of, but in some ways complements, the Bapto-Catholic movement among moderate Baptists.[31]

Dockery also invited strategic guest lecturers from the world of evangelical higher education to champion evangelical concepts among Union's faculty and students. Most notably, in 2000 he established a Scholar-in-Residence program that included a public lectureship, guest teaching in classes, and consulting with faculty.[32] Early Scholars-in-Residence included Holmes and Sire, two scions of evangelical higher education; as well as ethicist David Cook, then of Wheaton College; and British evangelical theologian Anthony Thiselton. Dockery showed a particular affinity for other Baptists who also identified with the wider evangelical movement. Two of

---

[30] Dockery borrowed the phrase "Christian Intellectual Tradition" from the Roman Catholic historian Robert Louis Wilken. See Robert Louis Wilken, "The Christian Intellectual Tradition," *First Things*, June 1991, https://www.firstthings.com/article/1991/06/the-christian-intellectual-tradition. Both Wilken and Dockery mean something like the consensus of Christian thinking about such foundational issues as the Trinity, Christology, human nature, and the canon of New Testament writings. This tradition was codified in the ecumenical creeds of the patristic era, was affirmed by the most well-known premodern theologians, and continue to represent commitments widely shared among traditional Catholics, conservative Protestants, and Eastern Orthodox believers. Dockery represents a growing number of Baptist and evangelical scholars interested in more deeply engaging with church tradition. For a recent study of this trend, see Kenneth J. Stewart, *In Search of Ancient Roots: The Christian Past and the Evangelical Identity Crisis* (Downers Grove, IL: IVP Academic, 2017).

[31] Space precludes a thorough discussion of this theme, which deserves a chapter unto itself. Both men have evidenced their interest in Baptist engagement with the Great Tradition through a variety of relationships and initiatives, including a book series discussed below. Both men are also fellows of the Center for Baptist Renewal, which describes itself as "a group of conservative, evangelical Baptists committed to a retrieval of the Great Tradition of the historic church for the renewal of Baptist faith and practice." See the Center for Baptist Renewal, http://www.centerforbaptistrenewal.com/ (accessed September 20, 2018). For the best introduction to the moderate Bapto-Catholic movement, see Cameron H. Jorgenson, "Bapto-Catholicism: Recovering Tradition and Reconsidering the Baptist Identity" (PhD diss., Baylor University, 2008).

[32] A list of Scholars-in-Residence, as well as related press releases and audio recordings of some of the lectures, is available at https://www.uu.edu/events/scholarinresidence/ (accessed September 20, 2018).

the early Scholars-in-Residence were James Leo Garrett, a Southern Baptist theologian who was the most influential advocate for the notion that Southern Baptists are evangelicals, and Millard Erickson, a Baptist theologian who was more identified with the wider evangelical movement rather than the Baptist General Conference of which he was a part. Incidentally, Garrett and Erickson were two Baptist theologians who had profoundly shaped Dockery's own thought, and he edited Festschriften for both men.[33] In 2000 Dockery established the Carl F. H. Henry Center for Christian Leadership at Union. The center's namesake was a Baptist—and at periods in his life a Southern Baptist—though Henry was far more identified with postwar evangelicalism than any particular Baptist group.[34]

Dockery's hiring practices also reflected his vision of an evangelical Baptist university. Cabinet-level administrators and faculty members in what became known as the School of Theology and Missions were all required to be members of Tennessee Baptist churches in "friendly cooperation" with the Southern Baptist Convention. And, as with many other Baptist institutions, a majority of the faculty across the university were Southern Baptists. However, Dockery also intentionally recruited evangelical professors from other denominational traditions and from nondenominational backgrounds, sometimes placing them in strategic leadership positions such as academic deans, department chairs, and directors of academic institutes and centers. Dockery also took the unusual step, at least for a Baptist institution, of drafting a confessional statement that all professors needed to verbally affirm as part of the interview process. However, the statement was not explicitly Baptist, but rather summarized what might be called "mere evangelical Christianity."[35] This approach to confessional identity was unlike both the generally nonconfessional approach of more moderate Baptist

[33] See Paul A. Basden and David S. Dockery, eds., *The People of God: Essays on the Believers' Church* (Nashville: Broadman, 1991), and David S. Dockery, ed., *New Dimensions in Evangelical Thought: Essays in Honor of Millard J. Erickson* (Downers Grove, IL: InterVarsity, 1998).

[34] See Carl F. H. Henry, "Fifty Years a Baptist," in *Why I Am A Baptist*, ed. Tom J. Nettles and Russell D. Moore (Nashville: B&H, 2001), 209–17; R. Albert Mohler Jr., "Carl F. H. Henry," in *Theologians of the Baptist Tradition*, ed. David S. Dockery and Timothy George (Nashville: B&H Academic, 2001), 279–96; Russell D. Moore, "God, Revelation, and Community: Ecclesiology and Baptist Identity in the Thought of Carl F. H. Henry," *Southern Baptist Journal of Theology* 8, no. 4 (Winter 2004): 26–43.

[35] The statement of faith is available at the Union University website, http://www.uu.edu/about/what-we-believe.cfm (accessed September 20, 2018).

schools, as well as the strict confessionalism of more conservative schools that were adopting the Baptist Faith and Message of 2000 and requiring some or all professors to sign the document.

During Dockery's tenure Union also hosted a number of conferences that promoted his vision for an evangelical Baptist identity. Three examples will suffice. In 2004 and 2007 Union held conferences on the topic of Baptist identity. The proceedings of these meetings were subsequently published in 2009 as *Southern Baptist Identity: An Evangelical Denomination Faces the Future*.[36] The title of the book is noteworthy, but so is the publisher—Crossway, an evangelical publishing house, rather than LifeWay or a Baptist-related university press. In 2009 Union hosted a conference titled "Southern Baptists, Evangelicals, and the Future of Denominationalism." Two years later, the proceedings were published under that title.[37] Whereas this second book was published by LifeWay imprint B&H Academic, it is noteworthy that the contributors included Michael Lindsay of Gordon College and Duane Litfin of Wheaton, both of whom served in evangelical contexts. Furthermore, Southern Baptist contributors such as Dockery, George, Albert Mohler, and Nathan Finn contributed essays that addressed the intersection of Southern Baptist and evangelical life.

Disseminating the Dockery Vision

Dockery's Union University became a role model for other Baptist institutions interested in cultivating an evangelical Baptist identity that is more conservative than most moderate Baptist institutions, but more cosmopolitan than Baptist institutions influenced by fundamentalism. Dockery championed his evangelical Baptist vision for higher education in a variety of different ways. Shortly after arriving at Union, he began receiving invitations to lecture on higher education at other Baptist institutions, including over half the schools affiliated with the IABCU, plus the six Southern Baptist seminaries.[38] Many of these lectures were dedicated to the heretofore evangelical

---

[36] David S. Dockery, ed., *Southern Baptist Identity: An Evangelical Denomination Faces the Future* (Wheaton, IL: Crossway, 2009).

[37] Dockery, Neste, and Tidwell, eds., *Southern Baptists, Evangelicals, and the Future of Denominationalism*.

[38] The list includes Anderson University, Baptist College of Florida, Baylor University, California Baptist University, Campbellsville University, Charleston Southern University, East Texas Baptist University, Hannibal-LaGrange University, Houston Baptist University,

topics of Christian worldview and/or faith-learning integration, though applied to other emphases Baptists often cherish, such as biblical inspiration and authority, global missions, and close partnership with local churches. In 2004 Dockery delivered the Hester Lectures for the International Association of Baptist Colleges and Universities for the first time, a sign of the esteem with which he was held among his fellow Baptist educators. He also lectured periodically in non-Baptist contexts such as Asuza Pacific University, Biola University, Wheaton College, the CCCU, and even the Southern Association of Colleges and Schools.

In addition to his widespread lecturing opportunities, Dockery promoted his vision through a raft of publications, many of which originated as lectures. In 1999 he coedited *The Future of Christian Higher Education*, a compendium that emerged from a conference at Union.[39] The contributors included several Southern Baptist educators as well as evangelical scholars such as Joel Carpenter, Erickson, and Holmes. Three years later, Dockery coedited *Shaping a Christian Worldview: The Foundation of Christian Higher Education*.[40] In this book, all the contributors were faculty and staff at Union who were applying a Christian worldview to their respective academic disciplines and university departments. In 2012 a similar edited volume took the same approach with faith-learning integration.[41] Yet another coedited work, *Christian Higher Education: Faith, Teaching, and Learning in the Evangelical Tradition*, was published in 2018, addressing these same topics, though this time with contributors from a variety of Southern Baptist and evangelical institutions.[42]

In 2008 Dockery published his most noteworthy volume on higher education: *Renewing Minds: Serving Church and Society through Christian Higher Education*. The book drew together themes that Dockery had written and lectured on widely since the mid-1990s, synthesizing them into a coherent manifesto. Though B&H Academic published *Renewing Minds*, and though Dockery regularly referenced his own Baptist convictions and context, the

---

Louisiana College, Mississippi College, Oklahoma Baptist University, Palm Beach Atlantic University, Southwest Baptist University, and University of Mobile.

[39] David S. Dockery and David P. Gushee, eds., *The Future of Christian Higher Education* (Nashville: B&H, 1999).

[40] Dockery and Thornbury, *Shaping a Christian Worldview*.

[41] David S. Dockery, ed., *Faith and Learning: A Handbook for Christian Higher Education* (Nashville: B&H Academic, 2012).

[42] David S. Dockery and Christopher W. Morgan, eds., *Christian Higher Education: Faith, Teaching, and Learning in the Evangelical Tradition* (Wheaton, IL: Crossway, 2018).

book was written for a broadly evangelical readership. The fact that it was endorsed by a variety of evangelical and Southern Baptist scholars and educators demonstrates the way Dockery had become a bridge figure between these two increasingly overlapping worlds. Capitalizing on this broad appeal, in 2012 Dockery and George launched a series of short books with Crossway titled Reclaiming the Christian Intellectual Tradition.[43] The purpose of the series is to introduce key academic disciplines from the perspective of a Christian worldview, putting each discipline in dialog with the Great Tradition of Christian orthodoxy. The series editors coauthored the lead book, which introduces students to the Christian Intellectual Tradition and its role in the history of higher education.[44] Additional series contributors include Southern Baptists and non-Baptist evangelicals who teach at institutions as diverse as Baylor University, Union University, North Greenville University, Wheaton College, Biola University, and Grove City College.

A final way Dockery exported his vision was through directly mentoring other Baptist educational leaders. During his years at Union, Dockery frequently invited new or aspiring administrators from other Baptist institutions to shadow him and his leadership team. Some of these individuals later took up leadership roles in Baptist-related schools, and over the years Dockery delivered inaugural addresses or related lectures for several of the Baptist presidents whom he had formally or informally mentored.[45] More broadly, he also mentored non-Baptist evangelical leaders through a CCCU program for new presidents.[46] Several of Dockery's administrative protégés at Union became presidents or provosts at other institutions—some Baptist-related, some evangelical, and some nonsectarian.[47] Not surprisingly, considering his

---

[43] A full list of the books in the series can be found at the Crossway website: https://www.crossway.org/books/?newnotable=All&series=Reclaiming+the+Christian+Intellectual+Tradition (accessed October 2, 2018).

[44] David S. Dockery and Timothy George, *The Great Tradition of Christian Thinking: A Student's Guide*, Reclaiming the Christian Intellectual Tradition (Wheaton, IL: Crossway, 2012).

[45] Dockery delivered inauguration-related speeches for Evans Whitaker (Anderson University), David Whitlock (Oklahoma Baptist University), Anthony Allen (Hannibal-LaGrange University), Gene Fant (North Greenville University), and Stan Norman (Williams Baptist University).

[46] Dockery's CCCU mentees were Jon Wallace (Azusa Pacific) and John Senyony (Uganda Christian University).

[47] Examples include Barbara McMillan of Blue Mountain College; Kina Mallard of Rheinhardt University; Greg Thornbury, formerly of King's College; Gene Fant of Palm Beach Atlantic and then North Greenville University; Tim Smith of Anderson University

mentoring experiences, in 2011 Dockery edited a leadership book.[48] Once again, nearly all the contributors worked in the context of Christian higher education, several of them were Dockery protégés, and the list included Southern Baptists and representatives from the broader evangelical tradition. Dockery was not only modeling his vision at Union and speaking and writing about it for a wider audience, but he was also equipping others to lead their respective institutions to adopt a similar approach in their particular contexts.

Conclusion

In 2014 Dockery stepped down as president of Union University and became president of Trinity International University, where he served until his retirement in 2019. Trinity International University, most famous for its widely respected Trinity Evangelical Divinity School, is a broadly evangelical institution with historic ties to the Evangelical Free tradition. Dockery, who had spent much of his adult life as a convictional Baptist engaging with and learning from non-Baptist evangelicals, now found himself the Southern Baptist president of an evangelical university. Dockery eventually took four administrators with him from Union to Trinity, while a fifth became a Trinity regent, thus exporting elements of the Dockery vision to his new institution. However, Dockery also continued to be active in Southern Baptist life, attending the SBC annual meeting and speaking widely at Baptist institutions.

After Dockery's departure for Trinity, the leadership at Union University made a strategic decision that guaranteed his evangelical Baptist identity would long remain part of the latter university's DNA. In 2017 Union established the David and Lanese Dockery Lectureship in Baptist Heritage and Thought.[49] The purpose of the lectureship was to invite renowned scholars of Baptist studies to deliver public lectures that reflected serious scholarship but remained accessible to a more general audience. The desire was for many of the lecturers to reflect the sorts of evangelical and Baptist

---

and then University of Mobile; and Carla Sanderson of Chamberlain College of Nursing. This list does not include Dockery protégés who took other vice president positions or deanships in various universities.

[48] David S. Dockery, ed., *Christian Leadership Essentials: A Handbook for Managing Christian Organizations* (Nashville: B&H Academic, 2011).

[49] For a list of past lecturers, see https://www.uu.edu/events/dockerylectures/ (accessed October 2, 2018).

emphases that Dockery championed in his own work. The lectureship also included a plan to publish the lectures in book form every few years, under the editorship of the dean of Union's School of Theology and Missions.[50] Appropriately, Dockery himself delivered the second annual lectures in 2018. It was only fitting that the titles of the two lectures encapsulated the heart of the Dockery vision: "Southern Baptists and Evangelicals: Why Southern Baptists Needed Evangelicals" and "Evangelicals and Southern Baptists: Why Evangelicals Need Southern Baptists." Though no longer Union's president, Dockery remained evangelical by conviction, Baptist by tradition.

[50] I was serving as dean of Union's School of Theology and Missions at the time the Dockery Lectureship was established, and I invited the first three lecturers to the Union campus.

18

Toward and away from an Electric Church: Baptists in America and Radio, Film, and Television

Jake Raabe

In his 1979 book *The Electric Church*, Presbyterian minister and National Religious Broadcasters' president Benjamin Armstrong spoke in nearly millenarian terms about the rise of technology in the twentieth century.[1] Armstrong was convinced that radio, film, and television were returning the church to its golden age described in the book of Acts: "In this vision I saw the electric church as a revolutionary new form of the worshiping, witnessing church that existed twenty centuries ago....Radio and television have broken through the walls of tradition we have built up around the Church and have restored conditions remarkably similar to the early Church."[2]

Armstrong would surely not have made the same statement a decade later, following a decade famously marked by high-profile scandals involving popular Christian television personalities. The 1990s would be a well-documented retreat from the "electric church" and a shift toward sentimentality and self-help for those already Christian and much quieter, more internally aimed productions that largely sought to ensure Christians of the veracity and utility of their faith rather than serving the evangelistic agenda I discuss in this chapter.[3]

The question of Christians and technology in the twentieth century is massive and impossible to capture in even a single book-length treatment.[4]

[1] Benjamin Armstrong, *The Electric Church* (Nashville: Thomas Nelson, 1979).

[2] Armstrong, *Electric Church*, 9.

[3] An especially helpful overview of this phenomenon can be found in Todd M. Brenneman's *Homespun Gospel: The Triumph of Sentimentality in Contemporary Evangelicalism* (New York: Oxford University Press, 2014).

[4] The three-volume series *Evangelicals and Popular Culture: Pop Goes the Gospel*, ed. Robert J. Woods (Santa Barbara: Praeger, 2013), is a fantastic resource for entering into this field of study. Despite the title, sufficient attention is also given to mainline interaction with

It is, as such, better treated from a variety of subgroups of Christians and their interactions with subgroups of technology. In this chapter I endeavor to do so, examining the response of evangelical Baptists in America to the most important advances in communication technology of the greater twentieth century: radio, film, and television.

How did Baptists, a decentralized denomination with strong tendencies toward pragmatism and nonprofessionalism, adapt to the rapid and complicated changes in communication technology that came about in the twentieth century? To answer this question, I examine how twentieth-century Baptists in the United States used radio, film, and television for evangelistic purposes.

Radio

The twentieth century's revolution in broadcast communication technology began with radio, which exploded into prominence in American life shortly after its inception. The first broadcast of voice over radio occurred in 1906, and the first known broadcast station began operating just three years later.[5] The proliferation of radio broadcasting and broadcast consumption grew rapidly. By 1922, 537 known radio stations were in operation, and at least one hundred thousand radio receiving sets were produced in the United States; the next year half a million sets were produced, and by the year after that over 3 million radio receiving sets were in operation in the United States, with at least 1,400 radio stations broadcasting throughout the country.[6]

Up to 10 percent of radio broadcasts were religious in nature during the first three decades of the twentieth century. During this time, which historian Mark Ward Sr. has playfully dubbed the "wildcat years" due to its almost total nonregulation, conservative Christians were among the fastest adopters of this growing technology.[7] Low-quality broadcasting stations were easy to

---

technology in the twentieth century. Little attention, unfortunately, is given to Roman Catholic use of technology.

[5] Robert C. Reinehr and Jon D. Swartz, *Historical Dictionary of Old-Time Radio* (Lanham, MD: Scarecrow Press, 2008), xvii.

[6] Reinehr and Swartz, *Historical Dictionary of Old-Time Radio*, xviii.

[7] Mark Ward Sr., "Air of the King: Evangelicals and Radio," in *Evangelicals and Popular Culture: Pop Goes the Gospel*, vol. 1: *Film, Radio, Television, and the Internet* (Santa Barbara, CA: Praeger, 2013), 105.

build, with the cost low enough that individual churches or even particularly technologically astute individuals could afford to operate them.

Baptists were a key part of this movement, often broadcasting entire services live rather than producing content specifically intended for radio. First Baptist Church of Dallas was among the first churches in the United States to do so in 1921, under the leadership of George W. Truett, who relied on a metal salad bowl placed upon the pulpit to catch and amplify his voice into the broadcasting microphone.[8] The practice of broadcasting services over the radio was frequent among individual churches and occasionally sponsored by state conventions, though unorganized at any larger level.

The lack of regulation and the ease of operating low-quality broadcasting stations led to a cacophony for radio owners of sectarian evangelistic voices airing over the nation's radio waves. Even a decade after the wildcat years, one mainline minister would remark, "While most of [the evangelicals'] programs are sincere, many of them are cheap and tawdry and tend to bring Protestant radio into disrepute."[9] This frustration with the large number of poor-quality transmissions and aggressive sectarian voices would lead to several changes in the structure of U.S. radio broadcasting.

The first of these changes that directly targeted evangelical programs came in 1928, when the Federal Radio Commission (FRC), supported by several mainline denominational bodies, mandated radio broadcasters to attain licenses that required meeting quality specifications that were unattainable for most churches and individual broadcasters.[10]

This crackdown on private and small radio broadcasters struck Baptists particularly hard, as Baptist radio broadcasting had not utilized larger secular broadcasting networks in the same way other denominations tended to do. Baptists adapted to new broadcasting regulations in a variety of ways. Following the FRC's adoption of broadcasting standards, the National Broadcasting Corporation set aside regular airtime to be filled by the Federal Council of Churches, of which the Northern Baptist Convention and National Baptist Convention were participating members. Most of the more conservative Baptists purchased airtime from local stations; popular shows in

---

[8] H. Leon McBeth, *The First Baptist Church of Dallas: Centennial History 1868–1968* (Grand Rapids: Zondervan, 1968), 151–52.

[9] Alfred Grant Walton, "Reconsider Religious Radio!," *Christian Century*, September 10, 1947, 1047.

[10] Ward, "Air of the King," 105.

this category included *Songs in the Night* hosted by Youth for Christ founder Torrey Johnson and *Old-Time Gospel Hour* hosted by Charles Fuller.

The most successful Baptist radio ventures were those that were able to purchase airtime through national broadcasting bodies despite not being affiliated with the Federal Council of Churches. Two of these programs are particularly noteworthy.

The Hour of Decision, a joint venture first organized and managed by Cliff Barrow and recorded by Billy Graham, was the most successful Baptist radio venture of the twentieth century. This thirty-minute program featuring gospel music and a sermon from Graham proved immediately popular, with approximately 20 million weekly listeners at the height of its popularity in 1951.[11]

The largest Baptist radio network not directly associated with Billy Graham was the Southern Baptist Convention's Radio Committee, founded in 1938 and in operation until 2008.[12] The Radio Committee produced a weekly hourlong preaching program called *The Baptist Hour*. The show was recorded for its first eighteen years by Herschel Hobbs and subsequently by Frank Pollard. In the latter half of the twentieth century, *The Baptist Hour* developed numerous non-English programs. The Spanish-language *La Hora Bautista* began production in 1958, and later programs were developed in Polish, Portuguese, Chinese, Navajo, and other languages by the late 1980s.

Radio's dominance as Americans' preferred method of media content consumption began to give way to television in the 1950s. Most popular radio broadcasts, including religious programming such as *The Hour of Decision* and *The Baptist Hour*, began reformatting for television by the end of the decade. Radio use by religious broadcasters persists to this day, but changes in social preferences caused most Baptist denominational bodies (including, most notably, the Southern Baptist Convention) to turn their attention nearly exclusively to television.

Film

Film developed along a similar timeline as radio, with motion picture companies arising in the 1890s and the first theater dedicated specifically to showing motion pictures opening in Pittsburgh in 1905, with over two

---

[11] See Billy Graham, *Just ss I Am: The Autobiography of Billy Graham* (San Francisco: HarperSanFrancisco and Zondervan, 1997), 176–81.

[12] H. Leon McBeth, *The Baptist Heritage: Four Centuries of Baptist Witness* (Nashville: Broadman), 659–60.

thousand such theaters opening worldwide within the next two years. By 1908 there were over nine thousand theaters in the United States, and a surprising 65 percent of the U.S. population attended a cinema on a weekly basis.

High production and distribution costs as well as the array of skills necessary to produce a film kept the medium from being a viable evangelistic tool for most of the first half of the century. Biblical stories were common cinematic material from the inception of the theater but were almost exclusively produced by secular studios.[13] Early "passion plays" such as Sidney Olcott's especially well-received 1912 film *From Manger to Cross* proved popular with Christian audiences of all denominations, but were seen as novelties during first two decades of the twentieth century rather than the dominant technology that film would become.[14] Increasingly risqué material becoming prominent in film and high-profile scandals surrounding popular Hollywood personalities in the late 1920s caused a general deflation in Christian interaction with film, especially among conservatives feeling increasingly spurned by the culture of the larger society during the fundamentalist/modernist debates ongoing at the time. The consensus among Protestants regarding film was summarized well by an anonymous Christian writer in the *Literary Digest* in 1920: "The motion-picture can either be made of assistance to the Church...or it may be left as an opposing weapon for satanic mischief....As the case stands now, the motion picture is regard ed by some church papers in this country and abroad a more potent influence for evil than for good."[15]

Early Baptist use of film mostly consisted of footage of missionary endeavors produced to assist in fund-raising. Baptist use of film as its own evangelistic media, though, began with the efforts of Billy Graham. In 1950 a documentarian named Dick Ross requested permission to film and produce a documentary about Graham's upcoming Portland crusade. Intrigued

---

[13] See Terry Lindvall, *Sanctuary Cinema: Origins of the Christian Film Industry* (New York: New York University Press, 2007), 55–117, for films based on biblical stories in the first half of the twentieth century.

[14] See Lindvall, "A History of Evangelicals in North American Film Culture" in Woods, *Evangelical Christians and Popular Culture*, 1: 1-20..

[15] "The Church's Duty to Movies," *Literary Digest*, February 21, 1920, 38. Interestingly, Roman Catholics were much faster to adopt film as a media. As early as 1898, Pope Leo XVIII allowed cameramen working with Thomas Edison to film pontifical blessings to convey them to American congregants. See Lindvall, "History of Evangelicals in North American Film Culture," 2–3.

by the possibility of evangelistic films since college, Graham agreed.[16] Soon after, he established Billy Graham Films, later renamed World Wide Pictures (WWP), with Ross's assistance. The studio's first film, *Mr. Texas,* was produced in 1951. The film told the story of a West Texas rancher injured in a rodeo accident who is brought to Christ by his sister, who had been converted at a Billy Graham rally. The premiere drew a crowd of twenty-five thousand, the most-attended film premiere in history at that time.[17] Unfortunately, the premiere showing was plagued with technical difficulties involving both the speakers and projectors, and the film's low budget and rushed production were evident. Graham was highly unsatisfied with the final product. When Graham showed the movie to Arthur Rank, a filmmaker friend, Rank said, "It's not technically a good film, but the message comes across."[18]

The technical shortcomings of *Mr. Texas,* however, did not dissuade Graham or World Wide Pictures from continuing to experiment with film. Early World Wide Pictures productions were typically screened in churches or church-sponsored venues for free, with a strict policy of screening films only to unsegregated audiences. The 1963 film *The Restless Ones* was both a major gamble for World Wide Pictures and its first major breakthrough into cultural acceptance. Controversially, WWP decided to charge an admission price to screenings. While this change met resistance from individual congregations, it allowed for a higher production budget that translated into significantly greater cultural relevancy and greater praise from critics than previous WWP films had attained. *The Restless Ones* regularly sold out in the many venues in which it was shown, due in large part to grassroots marketing campaigns initiated by local Baptists and other evangelical groups.[19] The film is likely WWP's most viewed film, with an estimated 4.5 million people seeing it by 1968.[20]

Shortly after this, World Wide Pictures began to experiment with traditional theater distribution. Around this time, Graham and Ross were approached by Robert Moses, the chief architect of the 1964–1965 New York's World Fair, who offered them a pavilion space for the entire two-

[16] Graham, *Just as I Am,* 174–76.

[17] Religion: "First Christian Western," *TIME*, October 8, 1951, 109.

[18] Graham, *Just as I Am*, 176. It is perhaps noteworthy that *Mr. Texas* is the only World Wide Pictures films no longer distributed by the organization.

[19] Martin, *Prophet with Honor*, 307.

[20] Martin, *Prophet with Honor*, 308.

year duration of the event, which was expected to see at least 50 million total visitors.[21] The film, which would involve a high-quality production shot and projection onto cutting-edge technology would need to be staffed for two full years. Graham initially told the board of the Billy Graham Evangelistic Association that he thought the endeavor was unattainable. However, Graham was persuaded of the project's viability by Wheaton University president Raymond Edmond, who convinced Graham that this was "a great challenge put before us by our Lord," and reminded Graham of Dwight L. Moody's massive evangelism campaign at the 1893 Chicago World's Fair.

Graham, World Wide Pictures, and the Billy Graham Evangelistic Association rose to the challenge, producing a thirty-three-minute film titled *Man in the Fifth Dimension.* Filmed with a unique wide-screen capability meant to project onto curved screens, *Man in the Fifth Dimension* made extensive use of cutting-edge cinematography and editing developments to match the technological innovation of the screening area. The film ended with a call to accept the word of Jesus by visiting one of the on-site "decision counselors." The film was shown hourly in both the original English format and in translated versions in six languages offered in separate screening areas. The projects' ambition paid off, with an estimated 1 million people attending the exhibit across its two-year run.

Graham's greatest film success both commercially and critically was *The Hiding Place*, a dramatization of the life of Corrie ten Boom. At the film's premiere in 1975 at the Beverly Theater in Beverly Hills, a swastika-marked canister of tear gas was thrown into the theater, forcing an evacuation.[22] The international attention garnered by this incident, along with the very positive reviews the film received, helped lift the film to a cultural acceptance unmatched by any previous World Wide Pictures production.

Despite the success of *The Hiding Place*, it would be World Wide Picture's last self-produced and -distributed film of the century, with only a few joint productions appearing in the 2000s. The rising production cost of films was increasingly requiring heavy subsidization from the Billy Graham Evangelistic Association, eventually proving too high a resource cost to continue making full theatre-release movies. Though he made the decision to end full production and distribution of films following *The Hiding Place*, Graham considered World Wide Pictures a successful venture. World Wide Pictures,

---

[21] Graham, *Just as I Am*, 435–37.

[22] Graham, *Just as I Am*, 434.

despite limiting itself largely to distribution for the last twenty years, remains the most prolific Christian film studio in the world. At the height of its popularity, one analyst calculated that "at any hour of the day or night, a WWP film is being shown somewhere in the world."[23]

Television

The rise of television marked both the most optimistic and excited view of technology among evangelical Baptists in its early years and a collapse of interest in broadcast media in later years. Radio technology was cheap and simple to use, and the production of a film incurred a onetime, set cost. Television stations, by comparison, were substantially more expensive to operate than radio stations, and television programs incurred regular production costs. As evidenced by books such as *The Electric Church*, television was seen as a challenge to rise to, with an expotentially increased potential for bringing the gospel to every person.

Both *The Hour of Decision* and *The Baptist Hour* had developed televised versions of their programs by the 1980s. Since television stations were costly to operate, most specifically evangelical Baptist broadcasting was done by producing independent shows and purchasing time from local stations, or by participating in already existing secular programs.

In 1955, under director Paul Stevens, the Southern Baptist Convention's Radio Commission moved its headquarters from Atlanta, Georgia, to Fort Worth, Texas; approved the construction of a state-of-the-art production and broadcasting facility; and became the Radio and Television Commission.[24] In 1956, in addition to a new televised version of *The Baptist Hour*, the commission began producing a new television program called *This Is the Answer* in 1956. *This Is the Answer* would prove popular also, and the Radio and Television Commission would quickly begin to expand into additional new programming (as well as adapting existing programming into different languages), and "by January, 1961, the Commission was producing 1,100 programs per week."[25] By 1970 the combined radio and television programming outputs were such that original programming and church services were broadcasting "somewhere in the world on the average of every

---

[23] Graham, *Just as I Am*, 436.

[24] Jesse C. Fletcher, *The Southern Baptist Convention: A Sesquicentennial History* (Nashville: Broadman & Holman, 1994), 198–99.

[25] Fletcher, *Southern Baptist Convention*, 199.

three minutes," and much of the programming broadcast through the commission's stations had become self-sustaining through viewer donations.[26]

In 1984, under the leadership of commission director Jimmy Allen, the committee made the ambitious decision to launch its own dedicated television satellite network, the American Christian Television System (ACTS). Though expensive, the station would help the commission continue to secure broadcasting time despite fewer stations giving free air time to religious organizations. The project would be short-lived and financially disastrous, as its operation required the commission to borrow several million dollars within its first few years.[27] By 1988 the commission found it necessary to merge ACTS with another network, which in turn reduced the number of hours available for Southern Baptist broadcasting, leading to a decline in financial support for the expensive ministry.[28] In 1997 the Radio and Television Commission folded and became a part of the North American Mission Board; the final remaining ACTS resources were sold in 2003, dissolving the project completely.

More successful than ACTS in Baptist television programming was Pat Robertson's Christian Broadcasting Network, one of the most important religious television ventures of the twentieth century. Robertson began CBN in 1960, with its flagship show *The 700 Club* beginning in 1966 and greatly increasing the network's popularity and volume of donations. Despite the massive cost of operation, CBN was successful enough to operate entirely through viewer funding until the early 1990s, when a series of scandals damaged its reputation and jeopardized its financial viability.[29]

CBN had been instrumental in the rise to prominence of Jim and Tammy Bakker in the late 1960s, with both having their own successful recurring segments on *The 700 Club*. The Bakkers' association with Robertson would damage the latter's reputation by proxy when the Bakkers were implicated in a high-profile series of financial and sexual improprieties. A similar scandal involving Jimmy Swaggart and, toward the end of the decade, in-

---

[26] Fletcher, *Southern Baptist Convention*, 232–33.

[27] "ACTS TV Network Refinanced, Business Plan Announced," *Religious Broadcasting* 18, no. 1 (January 1886): 44, 48.

[28] Sam Hodges, "Baptists Sell Famed Broadcast Unit," *Dallas Morning News*, September 5, 2007.

[29] For a more detailed (though dated) overview of CBN's establishment and later decline, see David Edwin Harrell Jr., *Pat Robertson: A Personal, Religious, and Political Portrait* (San Francisco: Harper & Row, 1987), 50–84.

tense criticism of Oral Roberts for his claims that God would take his life unless his viewers donated $8 million to his ministry caused public backlash against televised religious broadcasts in general.[30]

Beyond this general scrutiny of any televised religious broadcasting, Robertson himself would become a more divisive figure in the 1980s. Toward the end of the 1970s, CBN had begun adding news segments to its broadcasting schedule. These segments would take on more editorial tones through the 1980s as the Moral Majority began to take shape. This would culminate in Robertson's 1988 bid for nomination as the Republican Party presidential candidate. Despite an initially promising showing, several scandals and embarrassments came to light in this period, including Robertson's use of military connections to avoid serving in the Korean War and some (comparatively mild) financial improprieties at CBN. Robertson performed poorly in the primaries, and Christian Broadcasting Network's reputation was again tarnished. Decreased viewership and donation revenue led the network to sell off all of its broadcasting facilities in the 1990s, though always with the stipulation that the purchasing company continue to air *The 700 Club* on a weekly basis.[31]

Conclusion

In many ways, Baptist use of technology in the twentieth century reinforces the motifs discussed in the beginning of this chapter. New forms of technology inevitably became new means of evangelism, and Baptist adaptation to technological advancements proceeded closely behind the advancement's inception. Evangelical Baptist fervor for taking advantage of new communications technologies grew with every new development through roughly the 1980s, when rising production costs, public embarrassments, and general distrust of public religious personalities caused a sudden readjustment of

[30] For a recent and helpful overview of the rise to prominence and cultural backlash against televangelism in the 1980s and 1990s, see John Wigger, *PTL: The Rise and Fall of Jim and Tammy Faye Bakker's Evangelical Empire* (New York: Oxford UP, 2017). For a cultural and sociological analysis of the interplay between Christian theology and televangelism, see Quentin J. Schultze, *Televangelism and American Culture: The Business of American Religion* (Grand Rapids: Baker Book House, 1991).

[31] Randall Balmer, "Christian Broadcasting Network," in *Encyclopedia of Evangelicalism* (Waco, TX: Baylor University Press, 2004). Additional information on *The 700 Club*'s syndication agreements can be found in Tara Isabella Burton, "Understanding the Christian Broadcasting Network, the Force behind the Latest Pro-Trump TV Newscast," *Vox.com*, August 5, 2017.

broadcasting standards. Beginning in the 1990s and extending to the present day, Christian media in general turned from evangelistic efforts appealing to a broad audience to self-help and inspirational content designed specifically for the self-edification of religious communities.[32] Beyond the observation of this historical narrative, several key themes in evangelical Baptist adaptation of technology arise from this study.

First and most clearly, Baptist media in the twentieth century reflected the character of the Baptist movement. Baptist adaptation of these new forms of technology began with individual churches and preachers, and Baptist engagement with new media relied upon a few key denominational figures. It should be of little surprise that a denomination without formal centralized leadership adapted by looking to particularly popular individual leaders. While denominational bodies, especially the Southern Baptist Convention, played important roles in organizing and funding larger broadcasting products, popular personalities were key in the proliferation of Baptist mass media.

Second, the new media in the twentieth century were sources of strong contention between denominational conservatives and progressives, a point largely overlooked in contemporary scholarship. Mainline Baptists, typically more concerned with cultural acceptance than evangelicals, found new media to be a source of denominational embarrassment due to the often-amateurish productions. Mainline appropriation of new media was smaller in scope and typically focused on advocacy for social issues, with Harry Emerson Fosdick's use of radio and Martin Luther King Jr.'s use of television serving as the most important examples. For conservative and evangelical Baptists, the new mass media outlets provided an opportunity to broadcast the gospel to every American, churchgoing or not. For mainline Baptists, the new media were means by which culturally illiterate and evangelically aggressive fundamentalists tarnished the Christian reputation at a social level not previously possible.

Finally, the pragmatic bent of Baptist evangelism did not preclude moral reflection on new forms of technology. As historian David Morgan has cogently argued in his book *Protestants and Pictures*, the twentieth century was a time of dramatic expansion of the use of images in general

---

[32] Todd Brenneman, *Homespun Gospel: The Triumph of Senitmentality in Contemporary American Evangelicalism* (New York: Oxford University Press, 2014).

Protestant worship.[33] This tradition-wide debate on the relationship between images and faith is evident in the history presented in this chapter: Baptist radio broadcasts noticeably differed from other denominations in their tendency to prioritize the preached word over more aesthetically complicated musical productions. Similarly, depictions of Christ were commonplace in secular cinema from film's inception, but Baptists generally rejected direct portrayals of Christ in evangelistic films. To the best of my knowledge, the first film to contain a portrayal of Christ with any direct ties to any Baptist group was the film *Jesus* in 1979, which was produced by a parachurch ministry and not an actual denominational body. Pragmatism and theological and moral reflection were not opposed in the history of Baptist adaptation of new media; rather, new media frequently spurred on such conversations.

In short, Baptist use of technology in the twentieth century reflected both the unique character of the various Baptist denominational bodies of the United States and the character of the larger evangelical revival occurring throughout the twentieth century. Adaptation to rapidly changing mass media necessitated a combination of denominational organization and individual personalities to meet the increasingly high costs of entry into the sphere of mass public broadcasting. Enthusiasm to meet this challenge increased throughout the century but ultimately crashed as the denomination entered the twenty-first century. However, a societal return to low-cost, low-skill forms of communication as seen in the rise of the Internet and social media form an interesting parallel to radio in the start of the twentieth century. As such, the production and use of mass media by American Baptists merits further consideration and study.

---

[33] David Morgan, *Protestants and Pictures: Religion, Visual Culture, and the Age of American Mass Production* (New York: Oxford University Press, 1999).

Baptists in Europe

19

The "Monastic Way" of Russian Baptists and Eastern Orthodox Culture, 1960–1990

Constantine Prokhorov

Commonalities: Countercultural Worldviews of Russian Baptists and Russian Monastics

The isolation of the Union of Soviet Socialist Republics (USSR) from the West in the period of the Iron Curtain accentuated the preexistent distinctiveness of Russian culture, a culture that had a profound impact on the religious movements in the period of the Russian Empire and then in the Soviet era. Communists for a long time artificially separated the Soviet Protestants from their Western co-religionists and equally persecuted and discriminated against any religious communities in the USSR, unwittingly creating the conditions under which the Orthodox and Evangelical Christian Baptists (ECB)—the most important Christian trends within the country—paradoxically approached each other. In the present chapter I attempt to analyze the subject and, at the interconfessional level, in the context of church history in general, to demonstrate the legitimacy of the thesis of the "monastic way" of Russian Baptists, based in a certain measure on the Eastern Christian understanding of holiness.

The debated concept of "monasticism in the world," which became especially relevant following the Bolsheviks' rise to power in Russia, has been elaborated by a number of famous Orthodox authors.[1] Zealous Christians, living in a militantly atheistic state, raised, as it were, "a kind of monastery

---

[1] See, for instance, Archbishop Ioann (Shakhovskoi), "Beloe inochestvo" [White monasticism], in Archbishop Ioann (Shakhovskoi), *Izbrannoe* [Selected works] (Petrozavodsk: Sviatoi ostrov, 1992), 118–28; Archpriest Valentin (Sventsitskiy), *Monastyr' v miru* [Monastery in the world] (Moscow: Lestvitsa, 1999).

wall between one's soul and the world, which lay in evil."[2] For example, Archbishop Ioann (Shakhovskoi) wrote in the 1930s,

> Anyone can be a monk—in his heart....King David had several wives but was a monk....He became the most beloved teacher of the hermits, the great elder of all monks...."White monasticism" began to be restored....This is the first apostolic, martyr Christianity, the genuine discipleship of Christ....If you want to burn with love for the Lord, choose any way: the white or black monastic life....The Apostles were already the pure white monks, both Peter with his wife and Paul without wife....There are many covert monks and nuns in Russia now.[3]

It is interesting that Russian Baptists, for all their everyday critical attitude toward Orthodoxy, often spoke well of the monastic ("narrow") way, and compared themselves, whether intentionally or not, with those who have taken on the "angelic image." The intentional naming of the Russian Baptist Union *bratstvo* (the brotherhood), as well as the characteristic and indispensable reference of its members to each other as "brother" and "sister," suggest a parallel with a monastic brotherhood. One of the founders of the movement of the Council of Churches of ECB, Iu. K. Kriuchkov (brother of the leader G. K. Kriuchkov), for instance, writes, "We involuntarily adopted the mentality of the Russian Orthodox environment. In turn, that religious environment was based on the patterns of the 'Lives of the Saints,' various ascetics, monks and anchorites."[4]

An ECB church member from Gomel (Belarus), N. F. Mazhnaia, recollects with a positive Christian attitude that after her conversion in the 1950s, when she started to visit the Baptist church regularly, unbelieving neighbors called her a "Stundist" and a "nun" simultaneously.[5] B. M. Zdo-

---

[2] Deacon L. Kalinin, "Predislovie" [Preface], in Archpriest Valentin Sventsitskiy, *Dialogi* [Dialogues] (Moscow: Pravoslavniy Sviato-Tikhonovskiy Bogoslovskiy Institut, 1995), 10.

[3] Archbishop Ioann (Shakhovskoi), "Beloe inochestvo," 119–25.

[4] Iu. Kriuchkov, *Vnutritserkovnoe Dvizhenie EKh-B v Byvshem Sovetskom Soiuze* [Within the church movement of the ECB in the former Soviet Union] (Sacramento, CA: n.p., 2001), 57.

[5] Interview with N. F. Mazhnaia—Fresno, CA, 2006. Here and hereinafter, there are references to a number of interviews by the author with well-known Russian Baptist ministers and church members who emigrated from the Soviet Union to the United States during the years of perestroika. "Stundists" were Russian evangelical sects that emerged in the Ukraine about 1860.

rovets, who founded the "blue" (hectograph) press of the Council of Churches, very often uses monastic imagery and vocabulary in his recollections about the Russian Baptist brotherhood in the time of Khrushchev and Brezhnev. For example, he feels sorry for young sisters who sincerely turned to God and then after that realized that they had entered a "Baptist nunnery" (since the women in the congregations, as a rule, greatly outnumbered the men). Nevertheless, at baptism the young sisters were traditionally bound by making a promise in public, a kind of vow. To the question "If an unbeliever makes an offer of marriage to you?" the answer was, "No, I have fallen in love with Jesus!"[6] In this way, Russian Baptists actually preordained the mass female monastic way of life.

If we look at the matter from a different standpoint, one can say that monks themselves are a kind of sectarian community within Orthodoxy ("Orthodox fundamentalists"), whose mode of life often shocked the common laity of the Russian Church—and it shocked them no less than the Baptists' mode of life at that.[7] Therefore, it is no wonder that there was always a sympathy for monasticism within the ECB brotherhood (among the "true sectarians").

The main periodical of the ECB Union in the postwar period, *Bratsky vestnik* (Fraternal messenger), initiated some attempts to offer an interpretation of Russian Orthodox monasticism as a kind of forerunner of the evangelical movement in Russia: Orthodoxy gave rise to a great God-seeking among the Russian people....The infinite number of cloisters and hermitages,...churches and chapels testify to this....There was one thing that Orthodoxy did not bring to the Russian people,—knowledge of the Bible.[8] Russian monks...also wakened spiritual thirst.... [They] contributed to the strivings for spirituality in Russia.[9]

---

[6] Interview with B. M. Zdorovets—Spokane, WA, 2006).

[7] Nominal Russian Orthodox relatives of zealous Christians who have entered a monastery often mourn for them exactly as they would for people who have "gone into a sect." See, for instance: D. Iusupova, "Okhota na Ved'm" [A witch-hunt], *Ogonek* 40 (1998); N. Petrovskaia, "Ia ushel v monastyr', chtoby byt' shchastlivym chelovekom" [I entered a monastery to be a happy man], *Pravoslavnaia gazeta* (Ekaterinburg eparchy) 1 (1996); I. Podberezskiy, *Protestanty i drugie* [The Protestants and others] (St. Petersburg: Mirt, 2000), 89; and others.

[8] The words of A. Karev, cited in A. Bychkov, "100-letie Ob"edinitel'nykh S ezdov [The centenary of the uniting councils], *Bratsky vestnik* 6 (1984): 44–45.

[9] I. Gnida, "Dukhovno-patrioticheskoe sluzhenie" [Spiritual and patriotic ministry], *Bratsky vestnik* 6 (1984): 51. See also V. Popov, "Isikhazm kak chayanie dukhovnosti: Opyt

In spite of the stereotyped view of the lack of biblical knowledge in the Orthodox Church—paradoxically combined with gratitude to it, on behalf of the ECB, for the Synodal translation of Holy Scripture ("we appreciate the services of the Russian Orthodox Church, it provided...the Scripture: first in the Church Slavonic language, and then also...in Russian")[10]—the Baptists often cherished kindly feelings for the best manifestations of the monastic way of life.[11] A special ministry started in the monasteries—*starchestvo* (monastic elders' ministry), "which consisted in the spiritual care and guidance for souls seeking of salvation....Many people...followed the elders' admonitions."[12] "Faith without works is dead." Works of charity were an integral part of church life in Old Russia. The first hospitals and nursing homes originated in monasteries.[13]

> From the beginning of the Christianization of Russia, domestic monks did not lose contact with the life of common people. The suffering of one's neighbor and the needs of one's native land were cause for the concern of Christian ascetics. This is evident, for example, in the life of Sergius of Radonezh who had a humble monk's heart....Deep meditations on Divine truths and heavenly flights of the spirit did not isolate him from the surrounding world.[14]

People who think that such statements in the Baptist press before and during perestroika may be explained merely by the political correctness of Soviet censorship that "obliged" Protestants to be on friendly terms with the Orthodox Church are mistaken. The underground ("independent") publications of the Council of Churches of ECB were also entirely in accord with the opinion of the All Union Council of Evangelical Christians—Baptists (AUCECB) in respect of monasticism. If anything, the sympathies of the

---

istoricheskogo analiza" [Hesychasm as a spiritual aspiration: An attempt at historical analysis], *Bogomyslie* 2 (1991): 127–31.

[10] "Poslanie tserkvam ECB" [Epistle to the ECB churches], *Bratskyvestnik* 3 (1988): 71.

[11] See, for example, the many benevolent words about the Russian monasticism in I. Raimer, *Missionerskaia deiatel'nost' drevnerusskogo monashestva* [The missionary activity of the Old Russian monks] (Germany: Logos, 1996); Popov, "Isikhazm kak chaianie dukhovnosti," 115–34, etc.

[12] M. Chernopyatov and A. Vasiliev, *Pravoslavnaia Tserkov'* [The Orthodox Church], *Bratskyvestnik* 3 (1988): 50.

[13] These words of a Russian Orthodox priest are quoted with favor in V. Mazharova, "Byl bolen, i vy posetili menia" [I was sick, and you visited me], *Bratskyvestnik* 6 (1988): 69.

[14] Popov, "Isikhazm kak chaianie dukhovnosti," 125.

"unregistered" Soviet Baptists for monastic asceticism, contrary to the official dogma of the ECB (which was formally critical of monasticism), were even stronger. For instance, the service book (a kind of "Book of Needs" or "Ceremonial") by N. P. Khrapov contains such strict ascetic instructions that not many monasteries could require more.[15] A minister of the Kiev Baptist community of the Council of Churches (which later became "autonomous"), P. F. Kunda, testifies about the long and positive contact of their church members with a Russian Orthodox monk in the 1970s.[16] There are many examples of the close and friendly contacts between Orthodox people and Baptists before perestroika.[17]

The periodical of the Council of Churches, *Vestnik istiny* [Herald of truth], in an article related to Eastern Church history, stated in part,

> The monks read the Holy Scripture in their cells and worked to earn their daily bread. All of their property was held in common....They gathered for prayer and the singing of psalms at midnight....For four years John [Chrysostom—C.P.] dwelt as a hermit....In the desert [he] tempered his spirit, contemplated God in silence; at the same time, as a deacon, he served people....He gave his own silver to the poor.[18]

The Council of Churches notably published not only aphorisms of St. John Chrysostom (as was often done in the official *Bratskyvestnik*) but also entire homilies of this "great upholder of monasticism,"[19] for instance: *On*

---

[15] For example, the "closed" mode of Communion, preceded by strict fasting and confession of sins before the congregation; the continuous character of ministry, i.e., the absence of any "vacations" for the presbyter; the obligatory regular visiting of all church members by the presbyter; the gratuitousness of all kind of ministries in the community; fasting "for 10, 15, 30 days" with total abstinence from all food held up as a good example, etc. See *Dom Bozhy i sluzhenie v nem* [God's house and its service] (The Council of Churches of ECB), ed. N. P. Khrapov (1972–1974), http://www.blagovestnik.org/books/00280.htm#76.

[16] Interview with P. F. Kunda—Sacramento, CA, 2006.

[17] See, for instance, the memoirs of A. M. Bychkov: *Moy Zhiznenny Put'* [My life] (M.: Otrazhenie, 2009), 47–48. Also the interviews of Baptist ministers and church members: V. Ia. Bgatov—San Diego, CA, 2006; P. M. Abankin—Sacramento, CA, 2006; V. D. Bondarenko— Los Angeles, CA, 2006; L. E. Kovalenko—Sacramento, CA, 2006. See also the periodical *Bratskyvestnik* 2 (1976): 20; 5 (1985): 79–80; 5 (1988): 82, 88–90, etc.

[18] "Ioann Zlatoust" (editorial), *Vestnik istiny* 4 (1977): 30.

[19] The expression of A. Lopukhin. See A. Lopukhin, "Zhizn' i trudy Sv. Ioanna Zlatousta" [Life and writings of St. John Chrysostom], in *Polnoe Sobranie Tvoreny Sv. Ioanna Zlatousta* [The complete works of St. John Chrysostom], 12 vols. (Moscow: Pravoslavnaia Kniga, 1991), vol. 1, part 1, 20.

Prayer,[20] *Homily on Repentance*,[21] and so forth. *Vestnik istiny* also gives insight into the cause of the special sympathy of the Soviet Baptists for the saint: Chrysostom was baptized as an adult ("by faith"); he was strict and intolerant of any sin; he condemned the rich and the powers that be, as well as women—because of their fineries and adornments.[22] It probably also impressed radical Baptists that St. John was twice discharged from his hierarchic ministry "for the truth."[23]

The idea of "desert solitude" or "living in retreat" like monks was not alien to Russian Baptists either. For example, according to B. Zdorovets, the first leader of the Initiative Group, A. F. Prokofiev, shortly before the start of their famous movement, asked Zdorovets to find for him a "secluded room" in Kharkov (Ukraine) for fasting and prayer, and Prokofiev added, "I will not leave that place till I receive what I ask [from God] or die."[24]

All this could not just be a coincidence: from the beginning, Russian Baptists chose the most definitely ascetic, strictest mode of life that would be in the least measure possible for Protestants around the world.[25] And this yearning for the "strict faith" was truly Old Russian, monkish, natural only to the most sincere and unreserved religious feeling.

It is notable also how readily Soviet Baptists (both the "unregistered" and official groups) used certain words and special terms drawn from the monastery, for instance, *obitel'* (cloister, spiritual abode),[26] *kel'ia* (monastic cell), *podvizhnichestvo* (asceticism, selfless devotion), and so on.

He will raise the holy abode for us,

---

[20] See John Chrysostom, "O molitve" [On prayer], *Vestnik istiny* 2 (1987): 17–20.

[21] See John Chrysostom, "Slovo o pokaianii" [Homily on repentance], *Vestnik istiny* 1 (1990): 11–13.

[22] See "Ioann Zlatoust" (editorial), *Vestnik istiny* 4 (1977): 30–2.

[23] "Ioann Zlatoust," 32.

[24] Interview with B. M. Zdorovets—Spokane, WA, 2006.

[25] The "City of the Sun" (Evangel'sk), planned by I. S. Prokhanov, in the Siberian woods should be actually understood as a large "evangelical monastery": "The City of the Sun will be great: // The habit of drunkenness or the power of money // Will not reign there // But people will glorify God by their life" (*Khristianin* 1 [1928]: 15–16). Evidently, at a certain stage of its development, even the Protestant branch of Eastern Christianity automatically displays some monastic motifs.

[26] Both *Sbornik dukhovnykh pesen* (SDP) and *Pesn' vozrozhdeniia* (PV) have whole sections titled "Nebesnye obiteli" [Heavenly abodes]. See *Sbornik dukhovnykh pesen Evangel'skikh Khristian-Baptistov* [Songbook of the Evangelical Christians–Baptists] (Moscow: AUCECB, 1968), 344–72; *Pesn' vozrozhdeniia* [Song of revival] (GmbH: Christlicher Verlag, 1991), 325–52.

He will give us the golden crown....[27]

Time is passing; you and I are called
To another abode....[28]

Knocking, I stand at your door.
Admit Me to your cell![29]

In the innermost cell of the heart....[30]

Wherever you are: in the secluded cell or on the working place....[31]

We must reach the spiritual [mountain] peaks:...purity of heart, prayer, asceticism....[32]

We have to follow the example of spiritual leaders who gave their lives for the Lord...and continue [their] selfless devotion.[33]

Strive to do deeds for God's sake, to self-sacrificing devotion, to...asceticism on the narrow way.[34]

Some traditional mystical monastic motifs, for instance, of the "spiritual ladder"[35]—that is, the gradual, submissive climbing of the "ladder" to God in heaven—occupied the minds and struck a deep chord in the hearts of

---

[27] SDP, #106, 78. See also #130, 93; #285, 194; #464, 309; etc.

[28] PV, #296, 192. See also #92, 60; #200, 130; #312, 203; etc.

[29] SDP, #140, 99; PV, #332, 215.

[30] SDP, #122, 88; PV, #351, 226.

[31] "Nasha bran'" [Our battle] (editorial), *Vestnik istiny* 1 (1977): 9.

[32] "Semidesiatiletie Generalnogo Secretarya VSEKh-B A.V. Kareva" [The seventieth anniversary of the General Secretary of the AUCECB, A. V. Karev), *Bratskyvestnik* 1 (1965): 76.

[33] V. Zinchenko, "Prodolzhenie podviga" [Continuing the exploit], *Vestnik istiny* 2 (1986): 10.

[34] "Veroiu prines Bogu zhertvu luchshuiu" [He offered to God a better sacrifice] (editorial), *Vestnik istiny* 2 (2001): 36.

[35] See St. John Climacus, *Lestvitsa* [The ladder of divine ascent] (Sviato-Uspenskiy Pskovsko-Pecherskiy Monastyr', 1994); *Monasheskaia zhizn' (Vypusk 1)* [Monastic life, issue 1, 1885] (Sviato-Uspenskiy Pskovo-Pecherskiy monastyr', 1994).

Russian Baptists. In the preface of the monastic *The Ladder of Divine Ascent*, it is written,

> This book...presents to us a firmly based ladder leading us up from the earthly to the holy of holies, at the summit of which is the God of love. Jacob saw...this ladder also...when he slept on his ascetic couch. Let us ascend...with diligence and faith....The Holy Father, in arranging the ascent for us, wisely decided...to depict the ladder including thirty rungs of spiritual perfection.[36]

Respected Russian Baptist authors appealed many times to this favorite theme of the Orthodox monks as well:

> Like the ladder that Jacob saw in his dream, with the angels of God descending and ascending to heaven, we also have both descents and ascents in our spiritual life....The first rung...is forgiveness and justification....The second rung...is receiving the gift of the Holy Spirit.[37]
>
> The words of Scripture about the ladder that Jacob saw in his dream also light up the Cross of Christ on Calvary....Jacob's ladder joined earth with the heaven. The Cross of Calvary represents the reconciliation of heaven and earth....Millions of sinners have climbed this blessed ladder of Calvary...to heaven.[38]
>
> The Church is the ladder joining the earth with heaven ("because the Church is the threshold of heaven")—Genesis 28:12.[39]

In the words quoted above, we sense something far distant from the Protestant "instant sanctification" or—again—*instant* justification by "faith alone,"[40] while the Orthodox idea of the *long* daily spiritual transfiguration

---

[36] St. John Climacus, *Lestvitsa*, 5.

[37] Ia. Zhidkov, "Preobrazhenie Gospodne" [The transfiguration of the Lord], *Bratskyvestnik* 5–6 (1962): 40; See also I. Tatarchenko, "Dukhovnaia lestnitsa" [The spiritual ladder], *BV* 6 (1969): 47–48; S. Fadiukhin, "Bog Vsemogushchiy blagoslovil menia" [God almighty blessed me], *BV* 5 (1982): 18, etc.

[38] A. Karev, "Golgofa" [Calvary], *Bratsky vestnik* 3 (1964): 24. See also A. Karev, "Golgofa," *BV* 2 (1974): 25.

[39] N. Kolesnikov, *V pomoshch' propovedniku: Sbornik konspektov* [Assistance to the preacher: A collection of sermons] (Moscow: Zlatoust, 1995), vol. 2, 295.

[40] See, for instance, M. Erickson, *Christian Theology*, 2nd ed. (Grand Rapids: Baker Book House, 1998), 869; K. Bockmuehl, "Sanctification," in *New Dictionary of Theology*, ed. S. Ferguson (Downers Grove, IL: InterVarsity Press, 1988), 613–15.

and *theosis*, in our opinion, is clearly expressed.[41] The following is a pictorial description of the subject of the "spiritual ladder" by an anonymous Baptist author in *Bratskyvestnik*:

> Just one false step and we can…fall. This idea is well expressed by…a painting depicting people climbing a ladder to heaven. The angels of Satan are shown flying near the ladder. They hold steel hooks in their hands which they use to push people off the ladder. One man is already falling from the bottom rung of the ladder. There is even some stumbling among those who have climbed high….God holds out His hands…but a man is falling….This painting alerts all believers to the danger of a lapse at any time.[42]

What kind of striking painting the author of *Bratskyvestnik* had in mind is easy to understand if we acquaint ourselves with the description of the ancient Orthodox icon *The Ladder*.

> *The Ladder* from the cloister of St. Catherine on Mount Sinai is a unique icon created in the twelfth century….The ladder is going up to heaven where Jesus Christ meets those who have surmounted every hardship….Monks are climbing up the ladder, some of whom do not hold on and tumble down…into the paws of demons who are on the watch for their victims, using cords, pincers and shooting arrows from their bows….Before us is the way of ascetic righteousness, the way of the Christian ascent to eternal life.[43]

> There is a ladder from the earth to heaven. People in monastic dress are climbing it. The Lord holds out His hands to those ascending….This is an ancient Russian icon of the mid-sixteenth century. In the middle of the image there is a church representing the thresh-

---

[41] See, for instance, V. Losskiy, *In the Image and Likeness of God* (Crestwood, NY: St. Vladimir's Seminary Press, 1974), 97–110; N. Russell, *The Doctrine of Deification in the Greek Patristic Tradition* (New York: Oxford University Press, 2004); Archbishop Georgy, *Obozhenie kak smysl' chelovecheskoi zhizni* [Theosis as the meaning of human life] (Izdanie Vladimirskoi Eparkhii, 2000).

[42] [Anonymous], "Na rasput'e" [At the crossroads], *BV* 4 (1972): 66.

[43] O. Popova, "Vizantiyskie ikony VI–XV vekov" [Byzantine icons of the sixth to fifteenth centuries], in *Istoriia ikonopisi: Istoki, traditsii, sovremennost'. VI–XX veka* [History of icon painting: Origin, traditions, the present. Sixth to twentieth centuries] (Moscow: ART-BMB, 2002), 64–65. See also P. Rak, *Priblizheniia k Afonu* [Approaches to Mount Athos] (St. Petersburg: Satis, 1995), 10.

old of Paradise....Monks on their way above meet with temptations—demons with hooks and pincers pull them off the ladder of salvation into the pit of hell.[44]

Comparing these texts, which undoubtedly describe the same canonical iconic plot (the ladder to heaven, Christ above, the demons with "hooks" flying in the air, etc.),[45] we can draw the following conclusion. By replacing the word "icon" with the neutral word "painting," the editorial board of *Bratskyvestnik* once again characteristically identified Soviet Baptists with Russian Orthodox monks in their highly demanding divine ascent, as well as in their spiritual struggle against the powers of darkness. The spiritual ladder, starting on the earth with its top lying hidden high up in clouds, so delighted Soviet Baptists that they composed devotions about it,[46] wrote poetry on the subject,[47] dreamed about it,[48] and so on.

The monastic orientation of the brotherhood of ECB can also be seen in the traditional political indifference and pacifism of the Russian Baptists. Many of them refused to participate in Soviet public life: they did not take part in elections, refused to work in "Communist" organizations, nor even visited such,[49] and refused military service and medical assistance in times of illness. Some congregations rejected any "red" certificates (including regular

---

[44] E. Stepanova, "Za tri shaga do nimbi" [Three steps from the nimbus], *Neskuchniy sad* [Orthodox life periodical], 2 (2008), http://www.nsad.ru/index.php?issue=45§ion=10019&article=879.

[45] There are two main versions of the icon *The Ladder*, which in terms of narrative bear a strong likeness to one another: the Byzantine (twelfth century) and the Russian (sixteenth century). The images can be seen on the official Russian Orthodox website *Pravoslavie.Ru*, http://days.pravoslavie.ru/Images/ii9868&66.htm (accessed December 11, 2019)

[46] For example, the following words were spoken during a church service of the Petropavlovsk Baptist community (Kazakhstan) at the end of the 1980s (the author of this paper noted them in his diary): "Saving faith has three steps, like ladder rungs....The first two are able to save no one, but the third one will save. However, it is impossible to rise to the third rung, not having risen previously to the first two."

[47] See, for instance, the poem "Lestnitsa zhizni" [The ladder of life], http://www.blagovestnik.org/books/ 00430/db/ v6171177.html.

[48] See, for instance, the chapter "Ladder to Heaven" (interview with A. T. Kharchenko) in the book *Podvig very: Unikal'nye svidetel'stva o zhizni khristian v SSSR* [The battle of faith: Unique testimonies about the life of Christians in the USSR] (n.p.: Pacific Coast Slavic Baptist Association, 2009), 371–77.

[49] As the saying goes, "Believers should not go to *sobes*—since they do something there *together with demons*," etc. (*sobes* was the official abbreviation of the "social security department" of the USSR; *bes* in Russian means *demon*; in addition, the first part of the abbreviation [*so*-] in Russian means "together with").

passports)[50] and even some evangelical Christians, living by natural economy, tried to do without Soviet money (in villages).[51] All of this was very similar to the pattern of life of the "true Orthodox Christians" who lived as monks in the world.[52] There is information from a report of the Communist Central Committee of Kazakhstan concerning a true Orthodox Christians' village near Temirtau at the end of the 1950s: "They do not read any newspapers and books,…nor take part in elections; they refuse military service."[53] Some Russian Old Believers of the "priestless" persuasion also rejected passports, military service, and the use of money in their time.[54]

In 1967 a young Baptist woman was on trial in Novosibirsk for the illegal printing of literature of the Council of Churches of ECB. When the accused was asked who had managed the printing process at her home, she answered simply, "Christ," and judges were unable to get any more out of her.[55] N. Struve wrote about a similar incident with a member of the community of true Orthodox Christians in Tambov province. He burned his identity card and refused to serve in the army. Standing trial, he was asked his name and answered, "God knows it." When he was asked, "Who are you?" he replied, "God's servant." The judge tried to arouse his public spirit: "But are you also a citizen of the USSR?" The answer was, "No, I belong to

---

[50] See Biuleten' Soveta rodstvennikov uznikov Evangel'skikh Khristian-Baptistov v SSSR 21 (1975): 46; Iu. Kuksenko, "Nashi besedy" [Our conversations], Kazakhstan's Baptist Union Archives, 2002, 113; A. Vlasov, *Ot izbytka serdtsa* [From the heart's fullness] (Idar-Oberstein, Germany: Titel Verlag, 2000), 10.

[51] Interview with B. M. Zdorovets about the "evangel'skie khristiane sovershennye" [Perfect Evangelical Christians] (Spokane, WA, 2006).

[52] See, for instance, I. Brazhnik, *Sotsial'naia sushchnost' sektantskogo ekstremizma* [The social essence of sectarian extremism] (Moscow: Znanie, 1974), 21–23. A considerable number of the True Orthodox Christians were former monks. The Communists destroyed their last large secret cloister in the 1950s. See M. Shkarovskiy, *Russkaia Pravoslavnaia Tserkov' pri Staline i Khrushcheve* [The Russian Orthodox Church under Stalin and Khrushchev] (Moscow: Krutitskoe Patriarshee Podvor'e, 1999), 252–54.

[53] Cited in Shkarovskiy, *Russkaia Pravoslavnaia Tserkov' pri Staline i Khrushcheve*, 259. See also D. Pospielovsky, *Russkaia Pravoslavnaia Tserkov' v 20 veke* [The Russian Orthodox Church in the twentieth century] (Moscow: Respublika, 1995), 317–20.

[54] See, for instance, S. Zenkovskiy, *Russkoe staroobriadchestvo* [Russian Old Believers] (Minsk: Belorusskiy Ekzarkhat, 2007), 497–99.

[55] A. Pakina, *Raskol Evangelskikh Khristian-Baptistov 1961 g. i ego vliianie na obshchiny Novosibirskoi oblasti* [The 1961 split of the Evangelical Christians-Baptists and its influence on the congregations of Novosibirsk province], dissertation (Novosibirsk: Novosibirskiy gosuniversitet, 2000), 33. The author makes reference to records of the local religious affairs officer, which she found in the State Archives of Novosibirsk province.

God."[56] Undoubtedly, this is one and the same Russian religious type, no matter whether they call themselves Orthodox or Baptist.

Lives of Holiness

The Russian Orthodox interpretation of holiness evidently exerted influence on the ECB brotherhood. The absence of official church canonization is not by any means an obstacle to general public reverence for one saint or another. In the Russian Orthodox Church, alongside of universal canonization, there is also a local one, concerning a certain diocese or even a monastery or church closely associated with the life of a particular saint.[57] We see a similar state of things among the Russian Baptists.

For example, testimonies about the holy lives of brethren Iosif Andreevich Laptev and Ivan Vladimirovich Ivolin became widespread among the Baptist congregations of the Volga River region and South Russia. Some actual hagiographic features of their life stories follow.

In the 1950s and 1960s Iosif Andreevich Laptev lived in the small town of Shakhuniia (Gorky province) and served as a rural preacher. He was never married, giving his whole life to God. According to eyewitness accounts, Laptev was a good, humble shepherd who was constantly fasting and praying. He never accepted any presents, no matter much he was offered. He refused even meals in the villages where he served. When Laptev was invited to the table, he usually answered, "Thank you! There is nothing I want; I am fasting today." In the difficult postwar time, Iosif Andreevich earned his daily bread by weaving wicker baskets and gluing together galoshes out of old car tires. He loved to copy cautionary Christian books by hand, as well as texts of the Holy Scripture (which decorated the whole room where he lived). I. A. Laptev was on friendly terms with a local Orthodox priest; they used to sit together for hours, conversing with pleasure about spiritual things—both what unites all Christians and, delicately, about where Orthodox and Baptist ways have parted.[58]

In the 1960s Ivan Vladimirovich Ivolin served as the pastor of Piatigorsk Baptist Church (Stavropol region). According to testimonies, he was a

---

[56] N. Struve, *Christians in Contemporary Russia* (New York: Charles Scribner's Sons, 1967), 247–48.

[57] See, for instance, G. Fedotov, *Svyatye drevnei Rusi* [The saints of old Russia] (Moscow: Moskovskiy Rabochy, 1990), 34–35.

[58] Interviews with several ECB church members from Gorky province and Krasnodar region—for instance, M. A. Vasiliev and O. E. Avdeeva (Everett, WA, 2006).

humble servant of God, a preacher of the gospel who lived a holy life, almost in complete poverty. Brothers and sisters wanted to help him; they often left some food or clothes in his house without being noticed, but Ivolin immediately dealt out all gifts to the poor. When church members awarded a salary to the pastor, ninety rubles a month, he accepted only thirty. Ivolin visited every church member seven times a year, encouraging them, consoling and praying. The pastor was an outstanding preacher, a disciple of I. V. Kargel. Even visitors from Moscow said many times that they had rarely heard such simple and, at the same time, deep sermons that stayed in the mind.[59]

Such are some of the stories about the "holy paupers" of God (*sviatye bessrebreniki*), their pious lives and service to the Lord. The accounts do not seem to suppose any shortcomings in these people. Even stylistically the stories bear a strong resemblance to the Russian Orthodox *Lives of the Saints*.[60] The unmarried state of some holy Baptists also comes to the fore, which again mirrors the ancient monastic tradition. Having no space to retell here the many hagiographical narratives of the ECB brotherhood, we merely mention several typical plots.

The above-mentioned theme of holy self-neglect may be supplemented with testimonies about a Baptist congregation treasurer in Kazakhstan, A. L. Maniakin, who, in the 1960s, not having any money of his own, walked a long distance with the church's entire treasury in his hands without taking (either as remuneration or a loan) even a small sum for carfare. When the brethren asked the treasurer about this, he answered, "How could I have taken a penny from there? It is God's money!"[61] Another minister of a large Baptist church in Kazakhstan, through whom considerable donations for the

---

[59] For example, interviews with Baptist church members from Krasnodar, S. G. Odariuk and N. M. Odariuk (Everett, WA, 2006). Some sermons of I. V. Ivolin were published. See, for instance, I. Ivolin, "Ogon' Svyatogo Dukha" [The fire of the Holy Spirit], *Bratskyvestnik* 3 (1969): 45–46.

[60] See, for instance, the life stories of Russian paupers for God: Sts. Feodor and Vasiliy, Tikhon Lukhovskiy, St. Evstratiy Pecherskiy, etc.—*Zhitiya Svyatykh, na russkom iazyke izlozhennye po rukovodstvu Chet'ikh-Miney Sv. Dimitriya Rostovskogo* [Lives of the saints, in the Russian language, retold according to the cycle of readings by St. Dimitriy of Rostov], 12 vols. (Moscow: Sinodal'naia Tipografiia, 1903–1911), vol. 12 (August): 160-72; vol. 10 (June): 389; vol. 7 (March), 573–77.

[61] Interviews with Baptist church members I. M. Kaplenkov and A. M. Kaplenkov (Petropavlovsk, Kazakhstan, 1997).

poor were distributed, wore such threadbare clothes himself and was so modest in everyday life that he became a proverb among many people.[62]

Many times, the author heard numerous testimonies of aged ECB church members about showing Christian fortitude, both during Stalin's years and subsequently. In Soviet labor camps they were beaten and starved, and guard dogs were set on them. According to one reliable story, on one occasion the dogs miraculously did not touch a couple of Russian Baptists who were ready for a martyr's death.[63] It is interesting that the theme of the meekness of the most dangerous beasts toward God's people blends well with the Russian Orthodox *Lives of the Saints*. For example, it is reported that when St. Sergius of Radonezh lived in the forest, ravenous wolves and bears did not touch him.[64]

In ECB literature about the martyrdom of Nikolai Khmara (Altai territory, 1964), one also recognizes some hagiographical features, pious interpretations of his exploit: "Khmara witnessed for Christ until the end and therefore his captors tore out his tongue."[65] Similar firmness of faith has inspired Christians throughout the ages.[66]

Another testimony of the ECB brotherhood tells of a Soviet Baptist woman with four small adopted children who barely survived the terrible famine and then suffered many indignities and persecutions for her Christian faith in her village in the 1930s. At the beginning of the Great Patriotic War when their area was occupied by the Nazis, all of the village activists and Communists were arrested; the German authorities then compelled the peasants who had suffered as victims of the Soviet regime to give their accusatory evidence. Many people willingly put their signatures to the charges against the Communists, but a Baptist woman refused and said that she had

[62] The author is well acquainted with this remarkable minister. Since he is alive, his name is not mentioned here, knowing that he would not approve.

[63] For instance, see the interviews with Baptist ministers: V. N. Khot'ko (Petropavlovsk, Kazakhstan, 2000), Ia. A. Meleshkevich (Bishkul, Kazakhstan, 2003), etc.

[64] *Zhitie prepodobnogo Sergiia Radonezhskogo* [Life of Saint Sergius of Radonezh], ed. M. Pis'menny (Moscow: RIPOL KLASSIC, 2003), 32–33. See also Cloistress Taisiia, *Russkoe Pravoslavnoe zhenskoe monashestvo* [Russian Orthodox women's monasticism] (Minsk: Izd-vo Belorusskogo ekzarkhata, 2006), 15, 32, 245.

[65] Cited in W. Sawatsky, *Soviet Evangelicals since World War II* (Kitchener, Ontario: Herald Press, 1981), 143.

[66] See analogous pious stories: "Stradanie Sv. Muchenika Gordiia" [The sufferings of St. Gordius the Martyr], in *Zhitiia Svyatykh* 5 (January): 146–47; "Zhitie Prep. Maksima Ispovednika" [The life of St. Maximus the Confessor], in *Zhitiia Svyatykh* 5 (January): 715.

already forgiven her persecutors, as Christ taught. The Germans then threatened her and finally lashed her cruelly with a whip. However, she endured this suffering too, with all humility. This Christian did many simple, good works during her long life. When she died in the 1980s, many people in the area, both Baptists and Russian Orthodox (this woman's holiness was also recognized by Orthodox people who knew her well), gathered for the funeral. Above her, as she lay in her open coffin, according to eyewitness accounts, "heaven was weeping"—out of the cloudless midday heat, large, sparse raindrops suddenly started to fall.[67]

The general secretary of the AUCECB, A. M. Bychkov, also related that Orthodox people treated some pious Baptists with special respect:

> Recently, there was the funeral of an elderly Baptist presbyter in a small town in Central Russia. When the procession approached the local Orthodox church, the priest ordered that the bells should be rung as a sign of respect for the deceased servant of Christ.[68]

Analyzing the above-mentioned life stories, it should be noted that the Baptist hagiographies, as well as the Orthodox *Lives of the Saints*, often omit the essential details of the events described; it is not always clear where and when the events are taking place. The moral example and spiritual edification definitely come first, not the historical context. No doubt, this is a reflection of a well-known feature of the Slavic soul—the tendency toward the spiritual and mystical rather than the rational perception of the world. Here, for example, is a characteristic entry that many Soviet Baptists of the 1950s–1970s jotted down in their notebooks: "The Christian's address: Spiritual Homeland, Gospel Region, District of Zion, City of Heaven, Street of the Narrow Way, Thorny Lane, House of the Tabernacle. The Holy Spirit is the guide; inquire of the Watchman of conscience."[69]

---

[67] Testimony from the website of the Russian Baptist Union, http://old.baptist.org.ru/forums/archive/index.php/t-89-p-3.html. Several characteristic features of this report are typologically similar to the hagiographical story about the robbers' assault on St. Seraphim of Sarov: he did not resist them and was severely beaten, but when the robbers were caught, the saint announced his forgiveness to them and interceded for mercy, which caused finally their repentance. See "Zhitie prep. Serafima Sarovskogo" [The life of St. Seraphim of Sarov], in *Zhitiia Svyatykh* 5 (January): 77–79.

[68] A. Bychkov, "110-letie russko-ukrainskogo bratstva ECB" [The 110th anniversary of the Russian-Ukrainian brotherhood of ECB], *Bratskyvestnik* 5 (1977): 70.

[69] From the personal files of G. E. Kuchma, member of Omsk Central Baptist Church.

Such words are nonsense to an outsider. However, the essence of the allegorical text (copied down by both young and mature Soviet Baptists!) is slightly clearer if we compare it, for instance, with the following words of a Russian Orthodox hagiographical author: "But from what town or hamlet and from what family such a leading light was descended, we do not find in the writings; God knows this; for us it is enough to know that he was a citizen of the Heavenly Jerusalem, God was his Father and the Holy Church was his Mother, his relations were tearful, all-night prayers and unceasing groaning; his neighbors were the vigilant desert works."[70] The general, nonrationalistic approach, in which there is little about abstract spiritual and moral notions and very little about actual historical data, is to a considerable degree typical for both Russian Orthodox and Soviet Baptist hagiography.

God's Fools

In the Russian context, the unique spiritual phenomenon of foolishness for Christ's sake is closely related to the theme of holiness. In the Eastern Christian tradition, the Savior Himself, who rejected the values of this world and taught that His kingdom is "not of this world," was often interpreted as the first of "God's fools."[71] Although foolishness for Christ is, strictly speaking, an "anti-canonical" deed, many Russian Orthodox people consider God's fools the most honored saints.[72] Their "wretchedness" and "insanity," their unconventional lifestyle in society, demonstrate sincerity of religious feeling, childlike trust in God—an extreme form of Christian asceticism. Hundreds of fools for Christ's sake became famous in Russia, and dozens of them were canonized.[73]

In such an atmosphere, it is little wonder that the Russian Baptists had many fools for Christ as well. According to a curious legend, Ivan Grigorievich Riaboshapka, one of the pioneers of the evangelical movement

---

[70] Cited in V. Kliuchevskiy, "Istochniki russkoi istorii" [Sources of Russian history], in V. Kliuchevskiy, *Sochineniia* [Works], 9 vols. (Moscow: Mysl', 1989), 7:74–75.

[71] See, for instance, Iu. Riabinin, *Russkoe iurodstvo* [Russian foolishness for Christ] (Moscow: RIPOL klassik, 2007), 5.

[72] See, for instance, S. Ivanov, *Vizantiyskoe Iurodstvo* [Byzantine foolishness for Christ] (Moscow: Mezhdunarodnye otnosheniia, 1994), 4–5.

[73] See, for instance, S. Iurkov, *Pod znakom groteska: Antipovedenie v russkoy kul'ture, 11–Nachalo 20 vv.* [Under the sign of the grotesque: Anti-behavior in Russian culture, eleventh to early twentieth cent.] (St. Petersburg: Letnyi sad, 2003), 52–53; *Khristianstvo: Entsiklopedicheskiy slovar'* [Christianity: An encyclopedic dictionary], ed. S. Averintsev, 3 vols. (Moscow: Bolshaia rossiyskaia entsiklopediia, 1995), 3:286–87.

in South Russia, who lived during the second half of the nineteenth century, "played the fool" at the fairgrounds, where he liked to cry loudly, "He has stolen it! He has stolen it!" People gathered around him and asked what had been stolen. Riaboshapka answered, "Satan has stolen the people's salvation!" After a while he cried out again, "I have found it! I have found it!" The onlookers gathered again: "What you have found?" This time Riaboshapka said joyfully, "I have found my eternal salvation!" And then he began his unusual "popular preaching" to the large group of people who had gathered.[74]

In the period under review, dozens of fools for Christ became known among Soviet Baptists. The most famous of them was probably Vania Moiseev. He came from the Moldavian village of Volontirovka and was a member of a congregation of the Council of Churches. In 1972, during the second year of his military service in the Crimean city of Kerch, Vania suffered the death of a martyr for his Christian faith. He was distinguished among many other Baptist sufferers during Communist times by his "holy simplicity," amazing spiritual insight, and evident foolishness for Christ's sake. Even the official sources of the Council of Churches of ECB report many more extraordinary things about Vania Moiseev than are strictly allowed from the point of view of Baptist dogma. For example, they make no secret of the fact that he saw visions of the heavenly Jerusalem, Old Testament saints, and apostles of Christ, as well as communing with angels of God.[75] During his military service in the Soviet Army, Vania prayed many hours a day, as he had done before at home. He simple-heartedly told other soldiers and commanders (Communists) about Jesus Christ, enduring much mockery

---

[74] *Riaboshapka* (typescript), from the personal files of Russian Baptist historian S. N. Savinskiy (Salt Lake City, UT, 2006). See also V. Koval'kov and E. Sokolov, "I. G. Riaboshapka," *Bratskyvestnik* 6 (1981): 60. A peasant by birth, I. G. Riaboshapka used the language of the common people. For example, there is a testimony about the following expression from Riaboshapka's "baptismal formula": "You make a vow…to serve God faithfully to the coffin of your life." Cited in S. Savinskiy, *Istoriia evangel'skikh khristian-baptistov Ukraini, Rossii, Belorussii* [History of the Evangelical Christians–Baptists of Ukraine, Russia, and Belorussia, 1867–1917] (St. Petersburg: Bibliia dlia vsekh, 1999), 323. His appearance also often corresponded to that of a fool for Christ: for instance, there is a report about his visit to the capital city St. Petersburg. Riaboshapka arrived there for a meeting of the brethren dressed in a red shirt and wide trousers—one of the trouser legs was tucked into his shabby boot, and the other was "rolled high up." See *BV* 6 (1981): 57.

[75] See *Podrazhaite vere ikh: 40 let probuzhdennomu bratstvu* [Imitate their faith: The fortieth anniversary of the revival brotherhood] (Moscow: Sovet tserkvei ECB, 2001), 350, 355–56.

and beatings because of this. Once he publicly prophesied that an unbelieving sergeant would get a furlough ("I prayed with my spirit, and the Lord revealed it to me"). This sergeant was someone who, it seemed, had no chance to visit his home in the foreseeable future (but it happened!). Vania miraculously recovered after a severe injury without the help of any doctors; he could get along without food for several days; in the winter cold, he walked for the entire nights outside in just his summer uniform without detriment to his health; he took all punishments from his commanders without a grumble and even with joy (for example, he gladly scrubbed the floor of a big barracks with a brush and soap, which was always considered especially humiliating work for second-year soldiers). And with the same simplicity he became a martyr for Christ.[76]

Comparing the Christian exploits of Vania Moiseev with the *Lives* of well-known Russian fools for Christ's sake, we find many essential common features, such as meekness and love for the people around them, including their oppressors; "strange" public conduct; great zeal in prayer; visions of the spiritual, angelic realm; gifts of wonder-working and prophecy; and an ascetic mode of life. Thus St. Procopius of Ustiug suffered with humility many "vexations, reproaches, and beatings" for his foolishness for Christ;[77] St. Michael Klopskiy was known for his special asceticism, as well as for his indefatigable praying and miracles;[78] St. Simon of Iureivets walked in the winter in a flaxen shirt and without any footwear;[79] St. Vasiliy the Blessed was considered worthy of angelic visions and had a great prophetical gift,[80] the same as Procopius of Viatka, Nikolai of Pskov, and many other well-known fools for Christ's sake.[81]

---

[76] See *Inye zhe zamucheny byli* [Others were tortured] (CCECB booklet, 1970s), 1-32; *Podrazhaite vere ikh*, 340–61; interview with ECB church member from the Crimea, V. P. Litovchenko, who was personally acquainted with Vania Moiseev (Los Angeles, CA, 2006).

[77] See Fedotov, *Sviatye drevnei Rusi*, 202–3.

[78] Fedotov, *Sviatye drevnei Rusi*, 203–4.

[79] See A. Panchenko, "Smekh kak zrelishche" [Laughter as a spectacle], in D. Likhachev, A. Panchenko, and N. Ponyrko, *Smekh v drevnei Rusi* [Laughter in old Russia] (Leningrad: Nauka, 1984), 119.

[80]See A. Panchenko, "Iurodivye na Rusi" [Fools for Christ in Russia], in A. Panchenko, *Russkaia istoriia i kul'tura* [Russian history and culture] (St. Petersburg: Iuna, 1999), 397; *Khristianstvo: Entsiklopedicheskiy slovar'*, 1:338–39.

[81] See, for instance, Hieromonk Alexei (Kuznetsov), *Iurodstvo i stolpnichestvo* [Foolishness for Christ and pillar asceticism] ([1913]; Moscow: Izd-vo Moskovskogo Podvoria Sviato-Troitskoi Sergievoi Lavry, 2000), 202–4.

Boris Maximovich Zdorovets from Kharkov (Ukraine) is another famous Soviet Baptist fool for Christ. A well-read and highly gifted person, he often put on the "mask of foolishness"[82] during his life to condemn the vices of the powers that be, both the representatives of the state atheistic authority and some Baptist leaders. During his first arrest (in December 1961, because of many activities among Christian youth), Boris "played the fool" with KGB agents and militia for about three hours, not opening the door of his house in spite of all the latter's demands. The militiamen had the imprudence to come at 5 a.m., and Zdorovets lectured them with characteristic humor, saying that only bandits make a living at that hour so they should come at 8 o'clock. The militiamen froze outside for a while, and then began to break the door down, while Boris, who was, like many Soviet Baptists, an absolute pacifist, shouted at them menacingly through the door: "Hey, woman! Bring me the axe; some bandits are forcing their way into the hut!" That frightened everyone.[83]

When Zdorovets was imprisoned, he fasted for fifteen days and nights (drinking only water) every time he was put into the punishment cell. And Boris was there because of his "misbehavior" quite often. When the policy of the Council of Churches toward its own "dissidents" became especially tough, and excommunications even of reputable ministers were common practice, Zdorovets once interrupted the accustomed flow of a church service during the sermon of a well-known Baptist leader who was guilty of a great abuse of power. Suddenly Zdorovets publicly handed him a rope and bar of soap, saying, "That's enough of you tormenting God's people!"[84]

Boris Maximovich had many visions of God during his life; he prophesied ("to talk with the Lord through the Bible alone is the same as communicating with your father by letters; it is not enough"), used prayer beads he made himself out of thirty-three apricot stones[85] at a labor camp in the

[82] Concerning the foolishness for Christ of sane Orthodox people in Russian history, see, for instance, Panchenko, *Iurodivye na Rusi*, 392–93.

[83] Interview with B. M. Zdorovets (Spokane, WA, 2006).

[84] That was probably a hint at the dismal end of Judas Iscariot. See B. Zdorovets, *Kakim sudom sudite* [The way you judge], http://www.praize.com/denominations/group650/index.shtml.

[85] Incidentally, beads are one of the mandatory attributes of an Orthodox monk, and thirty-three beads symbolize the number of years of the earthly life of Jesus Christ. See, for instance, S. Trofimov, *Chetki* [Beads] (Moscow: AST, 2001), 16–25; *Pravoslavnaia entsiklopediya* [Orthodox encyclopedia], ed. O. Markicheva (Moscow: AST, 2007), 373.

1960s, and so on.[86] Some people, of course, denounced such unusual conduct for a Baptist, but others certainly found a display of God's grace, called "foolishness for Christ's sake," in Boris Zdorovets.[87]

In his life, yet another important facet of traditional Russian foolishness for Christ was illuminated, namely the courageous denunciation of the powers that be. What was unthinkable for common people, and even those from the nobility, was often permitted to fools for Christ, through whom, according to a pious belief, God Himself spoke.[88] For example, when St. John Big-Cap (*Bol'shoi kolpak*) met Boris Godunov, he openly (and in rhyme!) warned the tsar about the consequences of his unrighteous government: "Clever mind / Understand what God is doing; God waits long / And beats hard."[89] Another sainted Russian fool for Christ, Blessed Nikolai of Pskov, according to legend, once during Lent offered Tsar Ivan the Terrible a piece of raw (bloody) meat. "I am a Christian and do not eat meat during Lent!" the tsar turned pale. "But you drink Christian blood!" said the saint.[90] Against such a historical background, Boris Zdorovets of Kharkov, denouncing a "Baptist tsar" with rope and soap in his hands, no longer looks so strange.[91]

Another interesting case of "Christian foolishness" in the ECB brotherhood took place in Karaganda in 1986. A certain brother N.N., known to the Kazakhstan churches, had a supernatural revelation to visit a local high-ranking officer of the KGB. N.N. asked for an audience at the time revealed to him from above. Miraculously, without any previous appointment, a brief

---

[86] Interview with B. M. Zdorovets (Spokane, WA, 2006).

[87] For instance, a Kharkov newspaper *Sobytie* [The event] once published a lengthy article about Boris Zdorovets's life in which he, with evident sympathy and unequivocally, was called a fool for Christ (S. Rudenko, "Vashe vremia konchilos'" [Your time is up], *Sobytie,* August 29, 1992).

[88] See, for instance, *Sviatyni drevnei Moskvy* [Sacred places of ancient Moscow] (Moscow: Nikos, Kontakt, 1993), 7.

[89] See Hieromonk Alexei, *Iurodstvo i stolpnichestvo*, 187.

[90] See, for instance, Fedotov, *Sviatye drevnei Rusi*, 207–8.

[91] Perhaps one should also add two handkerchiefs to the symbolical presents of Baptist fools for Christ that were presented to the newly elected presbyter of the Chernovtsy community, K. S. Sedletskiy, in the late 1950s–early 1960s. It was correctly prophesied that the young presbyter would experience "many tears," and it was added that the big handkerchief was for crying privately before God, while the small one was for weeping in public (K.S. Sedletskiy, "Vospominaniia" [Memoirs], personal files of P. K. Sedletskiy [Omsk, Russia, 2007], 92).

meeting took place. During the meeting, there was the following remarkable dialogue.

> —...The Lord Himself has sent me to you to say that you should repent and believe in the Gospel.
>
> —...What is your business with me?
>
> —There is just one piece of business: the salvation of your soul....
>
> —If that is the business, I do not want to talk with you. . . .
>
> —"This is the only one."...I got up, moved to the door, stooped down and said, Shake off the dust from your feet (Luke 9:5)...."I do not know when [your soul] will pass into eternity—tomorrow or the day after tomorrow. I had an occasion to talk with Volodia in the coal mine. I have enough time—he said, but he did not have enough time, he departed into eternity early. . . ."
>
> —You know, there is a penal code article on intimidation. I can inform the right people, and you will be punished.
>
> —I stand ready for any punishment, so long as you are saved....I will continue to pray for you. God bless you....
>
> O Lord! ...I beg of you: help him not to perish.[92]

In this story, we see another version of the sacral plot about the meeting of a "holy fool" with a "tsar." It all begins with the revelation ("The Lord Himself has sent me to you"). "God's fool" feels without the slightest doubt that he is an instrument in the Lord's hands, the executor of His will, so the meeting, unexpected for the "tsar," for all his many engagements, cannot but take place at the strictly fixed (or "preordained") time. "God's fool" speaks about the noble's soul, just as if he was speaking to one of the common people. Meeting with a rebuff, "God's fool" immediately resorts to dramatic effects: defiantly "shaking off the dust from his feet," referring to known, literally interpreted words of Scripture, and also predicts the future, mystically hinting at the death of a certain man who also did not listen to him....Finally, "God's fool" concludes his speech with a prayer and a wish for his interlocutor's eternal salvation (apparently he has no doubts about his own salvation).

---

[92] V. Zhuravlev, *Velika vernost' tvoia, Gospodi: Svidetel'stva iz zhizni* [Great is thy faithfulness, Lord: Life testimonies] (Steinhagen, Germany: Samenkorn, 2006), 1:309–10.

A very similar picture of this kind of "playing the fool" can be seen, for instance, in the description by Protopop Avvakum (who was a leader of the Old Russian Orthodox Church in the second half of seventeenth century) of his famous meeting with the Greek Patriarchs, Paisiy and Makariy, during the Russian Orthodox Moscow Council in 1667.

As usual, "God's fool" speaks not his own, but the words of the Lord: "I was brought to the Eastern Patriarchs....God opened my sinful mouth, and Christ disgraced them by my mouth...."[93]

Avvakum, grieving over Greek Orthodoxy, exhorts the newly arrived patriarchs and frightens them with coming destruction: "I said much to the Patriarchs from the Scripture....Rome fell long ago and lies yet without rising, and the Poles perished with it...and your Orthodoxy has turned motley."[94]

When all words are unavailing, "God's fool," the better for people to remember his message, animatedly accompanies it with shocking acts. Protopop Avvakum continues his narrative: "I have a clear conscience, and I shake off the dust from my feet before you, as it is written....They started to push me and beat me, and the Patriarchs themselves ran at me....I retreated to the door and lay down on my side there and told them, 'You can sit, but I will lie here for a while.'"[95]

The encounter closes with words of admonishment, Avvakum doubtless enduring deep moral suffering because of the "ruinous way" of the Greek and Russian Orthodox mainstream: "They laughed, 'The Protopop is a fool. He does not even honor the patriarchs.' But I told them, 'We are fools for Christ's sake! You have honor, but we are despised! You are strong, but we are weak!'"[96]

In response to even seemingly the most insignificant events, Russian Baptists sometimes involuntarily reacted in a way that, on closer inspection, reveals its roots in the old Eastern Christian tradition. Here, for example, is one of the pious reflections known to the author of a Baptist minister during Soviet times. During a church service, a fly alighted on presbyter N.N. and bit him painfully. At first the presbyter drove the fly away, but when it settled on him again, he meekly decided to put up with it, thinking about how

[93] Avvakum, *Zhitie Avvakuma i drugie ego sochineniia* [Life of Avvakum and his other writings] (Moscow: Sovetskaia Rossiia, 1991), 60.

[94] Avvakum, *Zhitie Avvakuma i drugie ego sochineniia*

[95] Avvakum, *Zhitie Avvakuma i drugie ego sochineniia*, 60–61.

[96] Avvakum, *Zhitie Avvakuma i drugie ego sochineniia*, 61.

much greater were the sufferings Christ endured: "Just as I could drive the fly away at any moment, Christ might also have stopped His torments in a flash, too. But He decided…not to come down from the cross."[97]

This is also a kind of foolishness for Christ in miniature, bringing to mind the many holy men who worked for God in humility and patience, full of suffering. For example, St. Simeon Stylites, according his life story, fed worms on his open wounds and even put them back when they fell off, saying, "Eat what God has given you."[98] Nikita of Pereiaslavl voluntarily exposed his naked body to the bites of mosquitoes and midges that densely swarmed all over him.[99] And many other Russian saints did the same: Seraphim of Sarov, Theodosius of the Cave, Nicander of Pskov, Sabbas of Vishera….[100]

Russian Baptists, who have many times criticized all monastic extremes in words,[101] would probably prefer now to dissociate themselves in every possible way from this kind of Christian experience, all the more in the above-mentioned context; however, in practice the problem appears much more complex. The fact is that it would be scarcely possible to distinguish fundamentally between the behavior, as well as—what is more important—the *motivation* of holy Orthodox monk-ascetics on the one hand and, for instance, the same remarkable Baptist presbyter, N.N., on the other. Whether we like it or not, this is the same radical religious spirit that testifies: scratch a Russian Baptist and you will find a monk.

The deliberate "playing the fool" that took place during some Soviet-era trials of Baptists was also notable before perestroika. There are, for instance, some expressive passages from the full trial transcripts of "Baptists' trials" in Semipalatinsk in 1962 and in Fergana in 1971.

Judge: "Who is the leader of your illegal community?"

---

[97] V. Zhuravlev, *Sila v nemoshchi: Svidetel'stva iz zhizni* [Strength in weakness: Life testimonies] (Steinhagen, Germany: Samenkorn, 2008), 2:90.

[98] Zhitie prep. Simeona Stolpnika [The life of St. Simeon Stylites], in *Zhitiya Svyatykh* 1 (September): 26.

[99] Hieromonk Alexey (Kuznetsov), *Iurodstvo i stolpnichestvo*, 320.

[100] See *Zhitiya Svyatykh* 5 (January): 69; 9 (May): 133; 1 (September): 486; 2 (October): 26.

[101] See, for instance, A. Karev and K. Somov, *Istoriia khristianstva* [The history of Christianity] (Moscow: AUCECB, 1990), 88–92.

Accused Baptist: "I have already told you—Christ and the Holy Ghost."[102]

[The accused decline any assistance from state advocates and announce the wish to use the New Testament for their own defense. The latter was not allowed.]

Question: "One of your psalms has the following words, It is worth working, it is worth struggling....Tell us: to work—with whom, to struggle—against whom?"

Answer: "We wrestle not against flesh and blood, but against spiritual wickedness in high places."

Question: "You must have an official certificate confirming that you are a presbyter."

Answer: "A presbyter should work not by certificate, but by inspiration."

Question to a Baptist witness: "What do you know about the accused?"

Answer: "I know that their names are written in the Book of Life, that theirs is the kingdom of Heaven, and that their reward in heaven is great!"

Question: "Show us...this book, we need documents!"

Answer: "This book is in heaven."[103]

It is possible to imagine what an awkward situation the atheist judges found themselves in during such trials, sentencing believers to long imprisonment for their "religious fantasies" (as the Communists said) rather than for criminal offenses. Such sentences inevitably were a heavy blot on the judges' names. It is no coincidence that centuries-old Russian public opinion held that no one can offend God's fool without punishment.[104] It is significant that one of the distinguishing marks of the true church in the Eastern

---

[102] Zapis' sudebnogo protsessa nad Baptistami g. Semipalatinska, 1962 g. (Record of Baptists' trial in Semipalatinsk, 1962), *Istoriia evangel'skogo dvizheniia v Evrazii* [History of the evangelical movement in Eurasia] *4.0* (Odessa: EAAA, 2005) [Windows CD-ROM].

[103] *Sud nepravedny: Stenogramma sudebnogo protsessa* [Unfair trial: Full trial transcript], *Vestnik spaseniia* 1 (1973): 22–26.

[104] See, for instance,*Nebesnye pokroviteli Sankt-Peterburga* [The patron saints of St. Petersburg], ed. O. Nadporozhskaia (St. Petersburg: Izdatel'skiy Dom "Neva," 2003), 87.

Christian tradition is the unfailingly kind, patient, and caring treatment of "God's fools."[105] Communities that spurn them are thereby displaying a serious lack of charity within their own ranks.[106]

In general, in the widespread Russian Baptist interpretation of holiness before perestroika, which sometimes reached evident foolishness for Christ's sake, one cannot help but see significant Russian Orthodox influence.[107] It is notable that, in Soviet labor camps (where prisoners were not divided into groups on the basis of their religion), there were even some instances of joint "playing the fool" by the Orthodox and Baptists. Such well-known past leaders of the CCECB as Iosif Bondarenko and Boris Zdorovets testify to this in their memoirs.[108]

Many Soviet Baptists before perestroika were not ashamed to admit that they were "poor sinners"[109] who needed the purification of "weeping over their sins"[110] and "could not be pure."[111] Such a worldview was often in contrast with their genuine Christian, "ascetic," and even sometimes anguished lifestyle in an atheistic Communist state. It was probably close to holiness in the Eastern Christian sense of the word. From our point of view, the root of Russian Baptist specificity is to be sought first of all in its common history with Orthodoxy, in its life in the same country, in the unconscious following of the general Eastern Christian tradition (including monastic trends) that was especially noticeable in the postwar years, when the Western world and socialist countries were separated for a long time by the Iron Curtain. But already since the end of the 1980s, in the atmosphere of glasnost and perestroika, other theological trends—represented, for instance,

---

[105] See, for instance, Panchenko, *Smekh kak zrelishche*, 72–73.

[106] For instance, the senior presbyter of the Baptist Churches of Kazakhstan, F. G. Tissen, once remarkably developed this theme in the Soviet Baptist tradition (Saran, Kazakhstan, 1999).

[107] Not the church members who consider themselves holy (even referring to Scripture), but the Christians who, feeling their own imperfection, repent before God even for their smallest sins, have the true sense of holiness. See, for instance, the following materials in *Bratskyvestnik* 5 (1985): 12–13; 5 (1972): 26; 6 (1975): 29–35; 3 (1976): 28, etc.

[108] See I. Bondarenko, *Tri prigovora* [Three verdicts] (Odessa: n.p., 2006), 122–23; interview with B. M. Zdorovets (Spokane, WA, 2006). At the "churchy" camp in Mordovia where the latter was imprisoned in the 1960s, there was even a Russian Orthodox "stylite" who sat, telling the beads of his rosary, on the upper plank bed for several years, ignoring any work and roll calls. As spiritual kin, he and Zdorovets were on friendly terms.

[109] See SDP, #42, 35; PV, #68, 46.

[110] SDP, #62, 48. See also SDP, #36, 43, etc.

[111] PV, #77, 51. See also #7, 86, etc.

by numerous Western missionaries and preachers—appeared in Russia. As a result, the Occidental wing of the Russian Baptists (which undoubtedly always existed too) quickly grew in strength and began to put considerable pressure on their "Slavophil" brothers, which is the situation as we see it today.

20

Baptists in Georgia and Orthodox Culture, 1944–2008

Malkhaz Songulashvili

Baptists in Georgia have a rather unique story to tell. Frequently used terms in the life of the Evangelical Baptist Church of Georgia—such as "Baptist liturgy, "Eucharistic anaphora," "epiclesis," "bishops," "archbishop," "vestments," and "icons"—have been quite simply considered anomalous and self-contradictory among Baptists in Europe and elsewhere. Baptists of Georgia have challenged such a stereotype, offering a Baptist form of the church with distinctly Eastern Orthodox features: a threefold ministry of bishops, presbyters, and deacons, and a Baptist school of iconography that has been supplying a great variety of Christian churches around the world with icons. Some Georgian Baptist icons are displayed in cathedrals and churches of Great Britain, Germany, Switzerland, Norway, and the United States.

In this chapter I address how, when, and why Georgian Baptists developed their admiration and adaptation of the Eastern Orthodox cultural settings and heritage in the country of Georgia. I shall also try to identify some major factors at work that have shaped this particular expression of the global Baptist family.

The main chronological framework of this chapter covers the period between two wars: World War II and the Russo-Georgian War. I personally participated in the history of Georgian Baptists as the leader of the denomination for almost twenty years (1994–2013). I am not, however, drawing upon ethnographic methods,[1] but rather I aim to work as a historian and theologian in handling the available written and oral sources, some of which

[1] Ethnography is based on participant observation, a method used in ethnology. See H. Becker and B. Geer, "Participant Observation and Interviewing: A Comparison," *Human Organization* 16, no. 3 (1957): 28.

I have already used in my book.[2] This is a historical paper dealing with the history of theology and ecclesiastical practice of Georgian Baptists, but putting them in their social and intellectual setting.

Preconditions

Georgia is a land of ancient civilization. Archaeological finding of the first Europeans in Dmanisi, eighty-five kilometers (fifty-three miles) from Tbilisi, leads archaeologists to conclude that Georgia was located on the crossroad of migration routes that brought humans from Africa to Europe. In accordance with *Encyclopedia Britannica*, "Dmanisi is thus one of the most ancient human habitation sites anywhere in Eurasia."[3] In the course of history, Georgia has always been a place for cultural, religious, linguistic, and political convergences. It is not a great surprise that the convergence of Eastern Orthodoxy and European Radical Reformation has also taken place in this land.

Georgian culture owes more to the conversion of Georgia to Christianity than to any other single event in its centuries-long history. According to legend, Mary the God-birther and the apostles divided up countries of the world among themselves for preaching of the gospel.[4] Iberia, which was an East Georgian kingdom, fell to the lot of Mary the God-birther, who was designated as the missionary to this country. However, she was not able to accomplish her mission. This legend may bear a witness to the fact that the first encounters of Georgian culture with Christianity took place very early. The actual story of the national conversion to Christianity is associated with the name St. Nino, a woman who played a key role in this endeavor. The church history of Rufinus of Aquileia tells us that "Georgians who dwell in the region of Pontus accepted the word of God" through "a woman captive who lived among them."[5] Georgian documentary sources have more detailed narratives of the conversion where St. Nino plays a key role in the conversion of the East Georgian kingdom of Kartli as early as the early

[2] M. Songulashvili, *Evangelical Christian Baptists of Georgia: The History and Transformation of a Free Church Tradition* (Waco, TX: Baylor University Press, 2015).

[3] "Dmanisi Archeological Site," *Encyclopedia Britannica*, https://www.britannica.com/place/Dmanisi (accessed September 7, 2018).

[4] P. Ioseliani, *A History of the Georgian Church*, trans. and comments by S. C. Malan (London: Sanders, 1866), 1–2.

[5] Rufinus of Aquileia, *Church History*, bks. 10 and 11, trans. P. R. Amidon (New York: Oxford University Press, 1979), 20.

fourth century.[6] Since that time Christianity was established in this land in the form of Eastern Orthodoxy.

The Baptist movement reached Georgia in the nineteenth century, by which time the country had been incorporated into the Russian Empire. In the Russian Empire, the Baptist movement started in three different places almost at the same time. One was South Ukraine, where German settlers influenced the growth of Baptists. The ethnic Russians began to attend Bible study groups from about 1861. The second place was St. Petersburg, where Baptist life started in 1855. The third and perhaps most important place was Tiflis (as it was called in the nineteenth century, now known as Tbilisi). Martin Kalweit (1833–1918) to whom the establishment of the Tiflis Baptist Church is chiefly due, moved to Georgia in 1862. In August 20, 1867, Kalweit baptized a local convert from the Russian Molocan community in the river Mtkvari, which divides the city of Tbilisi into two parts. Thus, this date marks the beginning of the Baptist movement among Russians in the Russian Empire. In 2017 the Baptists of Georgia celebrated their 150th anniversary of the movement by public baptisms on the river of Mtkvari and by the consecrating of a new altar at the Peace Cathedral, which is the heir of the first Baptist congregation established in 1867. The ethnic Georgian Baptist Church was established much later in 1919, under the leadership of Ilia Kandelaki who was martyred by communists in 1927.

Restoring Religious Life at the End of World War II

By the time World War II broke out, religious life in the Soviet Union had been reduced to an absolute minimum. Most of the religious establishments had been closed down. There were no religious publications from 1931, and the Bible had not been printed in the country since 1927. Religious instruction was restricted to the context of the family. However, rampant antireligious campaigns had also slowed down. Some antireligious museums began to put up the shutters, and taxes on religious buildings were reduced.[7] Some scholars speculate that had Hitler not attacked the Soviet Union, all reli-

---

[6] *Life of St Nino*, trans. M. Wardrop and J. O. Wardrop, in *Studia Biblica et Ecclesiastica: Essays Chiefly in Biblical and Patristic Criticism by Members of the University of Oxford*, vol. 5 (Oxford: Clarendon, 1903); C. B. Lerner, ed., *The Wellspring of Georgian Historiography: The Early Medieval Historical Chronicle of the "Conversion of K'artli" and the "Life of St. Nino"* (London: Bennet & Bloom, 2004).

[7] J. S. Curtiss, *The Russian Church and the Soviet State: 1917–1950* (Boston: Little, Brown, 1953), 274–76.

gious organizations in the country would have been completely destroyed.[8] While such a view may be exaggerated, it is true that wartime religion showed that it was able to offer an indispensable service to the Soviet regime, for Soviet irreligion had a weakness when it comes to issues of death and disaster. The official propaganda machine would never report on mass deaths and disasters in the Soviet Union, for irreligion was not able to offer any comfort to the bereaved and mourning, while religion could.

The largest religious group in the Soviet Union was the Russian Orthodox Church, and therefore, when the crisis of war occurred the state sought to restore relations with this church and with other religious groups, both Christian and otherwise. For their part there was also a readiness within the leadership of the Russian Orthodox Church to cooperate with the state and secure some rights for the church. Accordingly, Hitler's attack on the Soviet Union on June 21, 1941, provided an opportunity for the Soviet state and the Russian Orthodox Church to resume relations that had been broken for some time. When Patriarch Tikhon died in April 1925, his nominee Metropolitan Peter of Krutitsky became patriarch locum tenens for eight months until he joined other metropolitans in prison in December 1925 (dying in exile in Siberia in 1946). With Peter's removal, Metropolitan Sergius of Nizhni-Novgorod took over with the curious title of "deputy to the locum tenens."[9]

Stalin, who was shocked by the unexpected invasion of the Soviet Union by Germany in June 1941, offered no personal comment on the war for ten days while Metropolitan Sergius immediately reacted to the German invasion and urged the people to support the government in the war immediately after it war broke out, on June 22, 1941. This is what the deputy locum tenens wrote: "Today the church will not forsake her people. She gives her heavenly blessing to this sacrifice which now is to be offered by the whole nation....May God grant us victory."[10]

Milovan Djilas, a Yugoslav communist politician, theorist, and author, was right in saying that the locum tenens appeals "were also attractive in form: against the monotony of Soviet propaganda they shone out with the freshness of their ancient and religious patriotism. The Soviet government quickly adapted itself, and it, too, began to look to the Church for support,

[8] W. Alexeev and T. G. Stavrou, *The Great Revival: The Russian Church under German Occupation* (Minneapolis: Burgess, 1976; repr., 1999), 63.

[9] T. Ware, *Orthodox Church* (London: Penguin, 1993), 151.

[10] *The Russian Orthodox Church and the Great Patriotic War* (Moscow, 1943).

despite the fact that they continued to regard it as reminder of the old order."[11]

Along with the Russian Orthodox Church, other churches and religious groups also offered full support to the Soviet state in the fight against Nazi Germany. On the other hand, the Soviet state also granted certain rights to religious groups. Metropolitan Sergius, who had been evacuated to Ulianovst, was brought to Moscow in the summer of 1943. On September 4, 1943, a most significant event took place: Stalin and Molotov, minister of foreign affairs and Stalin's confidant, received an ecclesiastic triumvirate—Metropolitans Sergius, Alexis, and Nikolai—in the Kremlin. This was the first meeting of the era between the leadership of the Orthodox Church and the head of the state. They were invited by Stalin to articulate the needs of the church. Sergius asked for the right to convene a synod of bishops to elect a new patriarch.[12] Sergius thought that a month would be needed to convene the synod, but Stalin was in a hurry. He offered airplanes to bring the hierarchs to Moscow. The synod was convened in four days after the meeting with Stalin, on September 8, 1943.

The metropolitans received more than they had expected; Stalin even offered the patriarchal office the premises that in the past belonged to the former German ambassador. However, at the same time Stalin instituted an organ to control their activity: the Council for the Affairs of the Russian Orthodox Church (CAROC), which would be headed by G. Karpov, a man with NKVD (People's Commissariat for Internal Affairs) background. It is interesting to note that Stalin's biographer, Dimitri Volkogonov, argues that Stalin reestablished the Moscow Patriarchate for two reasons: first to recognize the patriotic value of the church and, second, to secure military support from the West at the Tehran conference of the Big Three, which was to be held in December 1943. Stalin believed that the British Aid to Russia Fund—which was led by Dean Hewlitt Johnson (1874–1966), the so-called Red Dean of Canterbury—could play an important role. Volkogonov argues that "having received a number of messages from the Dean of Canterbury Cathedral, he [Stalin] decided it was time to make a public gesture to demonstrate his loyalty to the Church. He believed the West would acknowledge this signal and that it would evoke the desired response. His main motive, therefore, was not to gratify his vanity as failed seminarian.

---

[11] M. Djilas, *Conversations with Stalin* (London: Rupert Hart-Davis, 1962), 47.

[12] D. Pspielovsky, "The 'Best Years' of Stalin's Church Policy (1942–1948) in the Light of Archival Documents," *Religion, State & Society* 25, no. 2 (1997): 141.

Rather, his action was aimed purely pragmatically at relation with the allies.[13]

The creation of the CAROC on October 8, 1943, exclusively for dealing with the Orthodox Church, did not mean that Stalin's strategy concerned only the majority religion. He was going to deal with all religious groups step by step. The second-most-widely spread indigenous religion in the Soviet Union consisted of the Baptist and Evangelical Churches. After settling the issue of the Russian Orthodox Church, Stalin had a plan to sort out all faith communities, including these two groups. Five months after the establishment of the Council for the Orthodox Church on June 30, 1944, the Council for the Affairs of Religious Cults (CARC) was established, which provided a framework for dealing with other religious groups.

From October 26 to 29, 1944, the remaining leaders and faithful of the Baptist and Evangelical Christian Unions came together in Moscow to merge and form one single religious body, which was called the All Union Council of Evangelical Christians—Baptists (AUCECB). In the resolutions of the council, patriotic motives similar to those presented in the book published by the Moscow Patriarchate in 1942 are evident. Resolution 5 reads, "This resolution stresses the participation of large numbers of Evangelical Christians and Baptists in the war and the many awards won by them for gallantry; it stresses the hope that all Evangelical Christians and Baptists will follow the example and exhort them to fight against Fascism."[14]

The state's interest in the merger of these two unions was made clear by the publication of the note about the merger in the most influential Communist Party central newspaper, *Izvestia*, on November 10, 1944: "In the creation of the new ALL Union Council of Evangelical Christians and Baptists the most prominent and popular leaders of the Evangelical Christians and Baptists merged." This *Izvestia* news was proudly reprinted in the *Bratskiy Vestnik* (Fraternal herald) magazine, which came out with the permission of the Soviet authorities.[15]

The merger in Tbilisi took place in 1945, a few months after the merger in Moscow. In Tbilisi five groups—Russian Evangelical Christian and Baptists, Georgian Evangelical Christian and Baptists, and Armenian

[13] D. Volkoganov, *Stalin: Triumph and Tragedy*, trans. Harold Schukman (London: Weidenfield & Nicolson, 1991), 487.

[14] Materials of the All-Union Council of Evangelical Christians and Baptists held in Moscow, October 26–29, 1944.

[15] *Bratskiy Vestnik* 2 (1945): 20.

Evangelical Christians—were amalgamated into one church with three ethnolinguistic congregations. V. P. Krasinsky (1893-1983), a Baptist, was elected as a presbyter of the united Russian congregation; T. P. Kochoradze (1897–1967) was elected the presbyter of the Georgian congregation, and A. V. Arutinov was elected presbyter of the Armenian congregation. All three congregations were very small. The Russian congregation was the strongest of the three and therefore assumed the leading role.

After the merger, the AUCECB appointed Ter-Avanesov as presbyter of Baku Church in Azerbaijan. M. S. Dushenko (1888–1967) from the Tbilisi Russian congregation was made his deputy for Georgia. After the death of Ter-Avanesov, Dushenko became the senior presbyter for the three Caucasian republics of Georgia, Armenia, and Azerbaijan, and Tbilisi became the ecclesial center for these three republics. With its growing influence in the region, Dushenko's successors were recruited from the Tbilisi Georgian congregation. Dushenko was succeeded first by P. Janishvili (1903–1968), an ethnic Georgian who died under very suspicious circumstances, and Nodar Kvirikashvili (1925–1995), also Georgian by nationality, the last senior presbyter of the AUCECB in the Transcaucasia. After the breakup of the Soviet Union, Georgian Baptists were first to declare their independence from the AUCECB and establish their distinct ecclesiastical structures. The Evangelical Baptist Church of Georgia gradually transformed its life, ministry, liturgy, and ecclesiology in the light of Eastern Orthodox culture.

Factors at Work for Adaptation to the Eastern Orthodox Cultural Setting

Even though Georgian Baptists were a part of the AUCECB they never felt fully comfortable within this religious body. The longing for a distinct way of being church was always a part of the life of the Georgian Baptist community. Several factors were at work that paved the way to the transformation among the Georgian Baptists, but here I address only three main factors.

The Founding Father Factor

The missiological vision of the founding father and the martyr of the church, Ilia Kandelaki, was rather different from that of the Russian Baptist movement of his time. In his address to the twenty-sixth Assembly of the

Russian Baptists in 1926 he spells out his vision.[16] Kandelaki's faith in the gospel placed him in a closer relationship with his Georgian culture and spirituality. Explicitly proud of his Georgianness, he spoke enthuasistically about the glory and suffering of his people in the course of history. He also spoke affirmatively of Eastern Orthodox Christianity: "Georgians have long had their own church literature, and the main source of Georgian culture from ancient times has been the Georgian church."[17] Although he was sad to have to admit that in the heart of the Georgian people religious feeling had almost totally atrophied, he did not blame the Orthodox Church for such a situation. Rather, he blamed Russian imperial policy in regard to Georgian Orthodoxy:

> In order to avoid any kind of political threat from the Georgian side before the Revolution, the tsarist government invested a lot of effort and made vigorous attempts to weaken and russify the Georgian nation....The Georgian Church had been oppressed, and the Georgian priests who opposed the implementation of the tsarist policy had been exiled....The Georgian language was not taught to future Georgian priests in any teaching establishments. Subsequently even [ethnic] Georgian priests became agents of russification in many cases. This is how the Georgian Church was defiled. Georgians first lost respect for the Church, then all religous feelings cooled and died in them. Now we can openly say about them as in a song we sing: "Your temple, once so beautiful, has been desecrated, the altar of the Lord is piled up with a heap of ashes."[18]

He believed that there was a time when Georgian Christianity, which was Eastern Orthodox, was "once so beautiful" but now it was deprived of its former beauty and sanctity. However, Kandelaki did not think that it was "a hopeless case, because this religious feeling has not been quenched by evolution, but rather it was artificially suffocated from outside."[19] In Kandelaki's view the disciplship spelled out in the gospel was the way to

---

[16] I. Kandelaki, "Preaching of the Gospel among the Georgians," in *The 26th Congress of Baptists of the USSR: Protocols and Materials* (Moscow, 1927 [in Russian]). For an English translation, see M. Songulashvili, *Evangelical Christian Baptists of Georgia: The History and Transformation of a Free Church Tradition* (Waco, TX: Baylor University Press, 2015), 369–76.

[17] Kandelaki, "Preaching of the Gospel among the Georgians," 369.

[18] Kandelaki, "Preaching of the Gospel among the Georgians," 373.

[19] Kandelaki, "Preaching of the Gospel among the Georgians," 373.

spiritual regeneration of the Georgian people. In the search for spiritual revival, the Georgian cultural legacy—its literature and its musical traditions—could be utilized creatively. Perhaps this explains why Kandelaki admired Georgian literature and singled out three Georgian writers in his report to the Russian Baptist assembly: "Georgians who have a rich history, rich literature, who have produced such famous poets and writers as Shota Rustaveli (twelfth century), Ilia Chavchavadze and Akaki Tsereteli (ninteenth century), such famous public and political figures, statesmen, people who have a rich Christian past...these people do not have the Gospel in their contemporary, understandable language."[20]

Kandelaki was a great champion for translating the Bible into Modern Georgian, and in this endeavor he was keen to cooperate with Georgian Orthodox Church authorities. In his plea for the publication of the translation, he wrote, "When it is completed this translation will be sent over for inspection and confirmation by the Georgian clerical authorities."[21]

Sadly Kandelaki was never able to complete his dream project of translating the Bible into Modern Georgian. He was assassinated by Communist authorties in 1927 when he was returning from a mission trip in East Georgia. His martyrdom was graphically recorded in Russian by I. F. Arshin and translated into Georgian. In his report Areshin wrote, "Ilia Kandelaki died a martyr's death, having laid down his soul for Christ and for his neigbours, out of love for Georgia."[22] Kandelaki has became a role model for the Georgian Baptists. Later on, his icon was painted, and his remembrance day was entered into the liturgical calendar. Georgian Baptists inherited his admiration of Georgian culture and literature. In 2013, Georgian Baptists produced a new Eucharistic liturgy. The text of the Eucharistic anaphora is based on the work of Shota Rustaveli, the poet Kandelaki admired most.[23]

---

[20] Kandelaki, "Preaching of the Gospel among the Georgians," 373.

[21] "Ilia Kandelaki's Plea for the Translation of the Bible into the Modern Georgian Language," see Songulashvili, *Evangelical Christian Baptists of Georgia*, appendix 5, 368.

[22] I. F. Areshin, "The Death of Brother I. M. Kandelaki"—see Songulashvili, *Evangelical Christian Baptists of Georgia*, appendix 7, 376.

[23] For Georgian Eucharistic Liturgy, see Songulashvili, *Evangelical Christian Baptists of Georgia*, appendix 17, 425.

The Ecumenical Factor

The second factor that enabled Georgian Baptists to reform their religious practices and aesthetics was an ecumenical dialogue with the Georgian Orthodox Church. This dialogue was not approved by the Baptist ecclesial authorities of the AUCECB. In fact, they furiously opposed this dialogue and did their best to stop it.

In 1967 two pillars of the Georgian Baptist community, Thedo Kochoradze and Ekaterine Kutateladze, died. Kochoradze left behind his will, in which he urged the faithful to accept his successor, Giorgi Bolgashvili. This is what he wrote in his will:

> I, Thedo Kochoradze, the presbyter of the Georgian Evangelical Christian Baptist Church, leave to my beloved brothers and sisters a sufficiently prepared brother, Giorgi Bolgashvili, who loves the Church and serves her with all his energy—with all his heart. I know beloved brothers and sisters that you will not have bad memories of me: I served the whole church in general and each and every one of you with fear and trembling and if anyone can remember something unpleasant I ask your forgiveness....I taught what the Lord had taught me.[24]

Kochoradze's will was accepted by the Georgian Baptists unanimously. Giorgi Bolgashvili, "Brother Gogi" as everybody called him, was the right kind of leader. He served Georgia's Baptists from 1967 until his death in 1984. He filled the void left by the two prolific and deeply loved leaders of the church. Brother Gogi was very different from his predecessors. Perhaps this explains why Kochoradze is not more complimentary about his successor. He could have said of Bolgashvili more than just that he was "sufficiently prepared." He was not a calm, quiet, humble, and patient character. Quite the opposite: he was stormy, outspoken, energetic, and impatient. He often upset fellow clergy, ecclesial leaders, and Moscow-based ecclesial bureaucrats, but he was universally loved by the faithful and admired for his courage even by his foes, of whom he had many. He was a war veteran and a university graduate. Under his leadership the Georgian Church became the fastest-growing congregation not only in Tbilisi and Georgia but in the region of Transcaucasia. In 1982, a couple of years before his death, the Euro-

[24] Thedo Kochoradze, *Will*, translated from Georgian into Russian by N. Kvirikashvili, Archives of the Evangelical Baptist Church of Georgia, located at the Angus Library, Regent's Park College, Oxford, U.K.

pean Baptist Federation press service reported that there were forty-five hundred Baptists in Transcaucasia in twenty-five Russian-speaking churches, six Armenian, two Ossetian, and only one Georgian. But the Georgian congregation numbered fifteen hundred members and therefore was the largest church in the region.[25]

As early as in 1937, lamenting the activities of Baptists and other smaller groups whom they considered sectarian, the Communists noted that "fighting against sectarians is far more difficult than fighting against Orthodox Church and clergy."[26] During the ministry of Giorgi Bolgashvili, atheist watchdogs became more and more nervous about the Georgian Baptists. "In the course of the work against Baptists we should remember V. I. Lenin's comment that 'a Catholic priest who rapes virgins...is far less dangerous... than a frockless presbyter...who preaches....It is one thousand times more difficult to unmask them."[27] Gegeshidze suggested four reasons for the vitality of the Georgian Baptist community. First was the participation of the members in the mission of the church: "almost every member of the community is inspired by the idea that it is their duty to take care of religious propagation."[28] The second was the revival of the church's liturgical and musical life: "in recent times clerical circles pay more attention to the celebration of religious feasts." Third was the encouragement of the youth to participate in the liturgy: "young ministers and presbyters are entrusted to carry out religious practices and rituals."[29] Fourth was individual work: "the main attention is paid to the individual work with the people and the faithful."[30]

These atheist studies from a not friendly perspective give us a picture of Baptist strategy in the time of Giorgi Bolgashvili. Bolgashvili's main concern was the freedom to spread the gospel. He thought that the first and foremost obstacle for promoting knowledge of the gospel was the denominational seclusion of the church. He openly spoke about it, upsetting clergy and denominational leaders both in Moscow and Tbilisi. The senior presbyter of Transcaucasia, complaining about Bolgashvili, wrote, "Regretfully in

---

[25] J. M. Wilkes, "Many Languages, Spirit of Unity," *European Baptist Press Service*, November 23, 1982, 3.

[26] "Anti-Religious Education at School," *Fighting Atheist*, nos. 1–2 (1937): 51.

[27] D. Gegeshidze, *History of Religion Atheistic Propaganda in Georgia* (Tbilisi: Metsniereba, 1982), 53 [in Georgian].

[28] Gegeshidze, *History of Religion Atheistic Propaganda in Georgia*, 114.

[29] Gegeshidze, *History of Religion Atheistic Propaganda in Georgia*, 114.

[30] Gegeshidze, *History of Religion Atheistic Propaganda in Georgia*, 114.

some churches, mostly in the Georgian congregation in Tbilisi, the presbyter does not stick to the teaching of the Evangelical Christians and Baptists; he insists that 'the Baptist movement has secluded Christianity in bondage and prevents the spread of the gospel.' Because of this, some of the people became interested in Orthodoxy."[31]

Bolgashvili thought that for the spreading of the gospel, an understanding of Orthodoxy and a strong ecumenical partnership with the Orthodox Church was essential. In Bolgashvili's words, "secluded" Christianity needed to be liberated through the study and understanding of Orthodox Christianity and its legacy for Georgia. Both senior presbyter and other pro-Moscow clergy were not happy at all with such an approach. The opposition decided to strike. Kvirikashvili directly asked for help from the Council of Presbyters and the AUCECB representative to discipline the uncontrollable presbyter:

> Presbyter G. I. Bolgashvili and his consorts started consultations with Orthodox bishops in secret. Recently Presbyter G. I. Bolgashvili himself started forcefully preaching from the pulpit on icons, the souls of the departed, and on the intervening role of the Theotokos. Having noticed his deviation I warned him about the need to keep in line with the Evangelical teaching in the spirit and truth. But he did not accept my counsel, ignoring me as the arch-presbyter. Then I was to address two members of the Presbyters' Council, but he would not accept their counsel either, declaring that they do not represent any authority for him, implying they lacked understanding of Orthodox teaching....Today I am informing you about it, hoping that you will come to some conclusions about G. I. Bolgashvili or give me your advice as to what I shall do in order to eradicate this teaching which is still strange to our churches.[32]

Despair can easily be detected in the words of the senior presbyter, who was trying hard "to eradicate this teaching" that was strange to the church authorities. Bolgashvili's teaching was about renewal of Baptist life and ministry in light of the cultural legacy of Eastern Orthodoxy. He thought that the popular Georgian incomprehension of traditional Baptist ways was a hindrance for preaching the gospel, and Eastern Orthodox theology and

---

[31] *Report of the Senior Presbyter of the Transcaucasia at the Presbyters' Council*, August 6–7, 1982, archives of the Evangelical Baptist Church of Georgia.

[32] *Report of the Senior Presbyter of the Transcaucasia at the Presbyters' Council*, August 6–7, 1982.

practices could help people to accept the timeless teaching of Christ. For this reason he had entered theological dialogue with the Orthodox Patriarchate of Georgia. In 1977 on December 25, the day the new catholicos patriarch of Georgia was enthroned, the forty-five-year-old Ilia II became the new head of the church. At his enthronement, three ecumenical delegations were present from Georgia at the Svetitskhoveli cathedral in Mtskheta: the Latin Rite Roman Catholic delegation, the Armenian Apostolic delegation, and the Baptist delegation, which outnumbered the other two. In the delegation there were both Giorgi Bolgashvili and Nodar Kvirikashvili. That was the first time Ilia II and Giorgi Bolgashvili met. The next year the catholicos patriarch was elected as one of the presidents of the WCC, which was very helpful for the younger leader to strengthen the profile of the Orthodox Church both in relations with the state authorities and with the wider public. The new catholicos patriarch started his ministry as a reformer. He initiated the translations of the Bible into the modern Georgian language from the Hebrew and Greek originals. For the first time, the Orthodox Church recognized the need for a new translation of the Bible. The translation project was an ecumenical venture by its nature; the translating committee was composed of a couple of Orthodox, a Baptist, and a Jew. Bolgashvili introduced novelty in iconography and started building bridges with various layers of Georgian society—with scientists, poets, writers, and artists.

With the assistance of an Orthodox bishop, Kristephore Tsamalaidze, who had his conversion experience in the Baptist church and was formerly a Baptist lay preacher; Givi Gomelauri, a Baptist lay preacher; Ilia II; and Giorgi Bolgashvili had a series of encounters, at which it was decided to start a formal Baptist-Orthodox theological dialogue. Of course, Bolgashvili knew that this would upset his own clerical superiors, but he did not mind. In the dialogue, there were to be five Orthodox representatives and five representatives from the Baptists. The representatives were carefully selected; in each group there were two clergy officers and three laypersons. The Orthodox cochairship was assigned to Metropolitan Konstantine Melikidze. Orthodox members were: Archpriest Amiran Shengelia, Guram Shalamberidze, Micheil Tarkhnishvili, and Giorgi Tsintsadze. The Baptist cochairship was taken by Presbyter Giorgi Bolgashvili himself. The Baptist members of the dialogue were Presbyter Estate Gogebashvili, Givi Gomelauri, Malkhaz Dutchidze, and Avtandil Darbaidze.

The representatives of the dialogue worked hard and produced a document that recorded the results of their collaboration. The goal of the dialogue was clearly defined on the very first page of the document: "With the blessing of the preceptor of the Georgian Orthodox Church, the catholicos patriarch of Mtskheta-Tbilisi, the president of the World Council of Churches, Ilia II, on the one hand and the preceptor of the Georgian evangelical Christian-Baptists on the other hand, a foundation has been laid for a regular dialogue between believing Christians. The goal of the dialogue is to bring Christian believers into closer spiritual and fraternal relations, exchanging views about the faith and consequently implementing common liturgy by believing Christians in Georgia."[33] For the participants of the dialogue, the liturgy—that is, the Eucharistic worship service—was the crucial point for bringing "believing Christians" from both traditions into closer spiritual relations. The common liturgy was to be both a symbol of Christian unity and a starting point for further cooperation. They were naively convinced that every obstacle on this journey could be overcome. They even singled out three means for overcoming possible difficulties in the dialogue: "divine love," "patriotism," and "unbreakable faith."

The document reveals, however, the tension between two sides about locality and catholicity. The Baptists were insisting on the catholicity of the mission of the church while the Orthodox underlined the significance of locality and patriotism. In the concluding part of the document, it became clear that the question of patriotism and cosmopolitanism was discussed at length. They believed that, because of allegiance to Christ and in the affirmation of their Georgianness, Christian unity was mandatory. "Disunity and every kind of separation do not bring us closer to the head of the Church—Christ—but rather drives away from him. Consequently, to refuse Christian unity is to refuse Christ."[34] This led one to a jubilant statement about the religious unity of the Georgian people: "The participants in the dialogue deeply believe that an idea to build bridges of love between Christian denominations has already matured among believing Christians. Let Georgian believers sincerely celebrate in our homeland the establishment of a common Christian faith and its practical implementation."[35]

---

[33] "Dialogue between the Representatives of the Georgian Orthodox Church and the Georgian Evangelical Christian Baptists," Archives of the Evangelical Baptist Church of Georgia. See Songulashvili, *Evangelical Christian Baptists of Georgia*, appendix 8, 381.

[34] "Dialogue between the Representatives of the Georgian Orthodox Church and the Georgian Evangelical Christian Baptists," appendix 8, 393–94.

[35] "Dialogue between the Representatives of the Georgian Orthodox Church and the Georgian Evangelical Christian Baptists," appendix 8, 393–94.

The participants in the dialogue realized that there could be no common faith and common liturgy as its practical implementation, unless they learned more about the beliefs and practices of each group. Accordingly, they laid out a necessary program of mutual study. In order to secure implementation of a common Christian liturgy, the participants in the dialogue put their efforts into the study of crucial questions of teachings of the Christian religion; rituals and symbols; researching a common, holy, and worthy confession of faith; and coming to adequate conclusions and giving an adequate definition of them. Among the subjects they discussed there were questions of the sacraments (Baptism and Eucharist), the cross, Mary the Theotokos, the saints, icons, anointing with oil, foot washing, vestments, and candles. Due to fierce opposition from the pro-Moscow Baptist hierarchy and the Soviet authorities, this most radical ecumenical project of establishing an Orthodox-Baptist common liturgy was not implemented in practice. One of the participants in the dialogue, Malkhaz Dutchidze, a Baptist lecturer at Tbilisi State University, wrote years later, "The dialogue proved to be bilaterally beneficial. It was made extremely clear that the Orthodox and Baptists ought to love each other and confessional differences ought to be tolerated and understood. The death of the blessed Giorgi Bolgashvili put an end to the dialogue."[36]

Despite the failure of the plan to start an ecumenical Baptist-Orthodox Church, there were some impressive results that followed the dialogue. Estate Gogebashvili, one of the Baptist participants in the dialogue, wrote that in those days the new church was not launched, but the Orthodox "let Giorgi Bolgashvili preach in the Sioni Cathedral in Tbilisi. It lasted for almost one year. Brother Gogi was accompanied there by us, the preachers, and the choir....I am still so keen on restarting preaching in one of the [Orthodox] churches. I will put a frock on, will hang a pectoral cross on my neck and preach Christ crucified."[37] Even though the project of creating a Baptist-Orthodox liturgy failed, the dialogue made a significant impact on the development of the Georgian Baptist community. In 2005, about twenty-five years after the Baptist-Orthodox dialogue, the National Council of the Evangelical Baptist Church of Georgia adopted a document that confirms most of the decisions made during the Baptist-Orthodox dialogue. It seems

[36] M. Duchidze, "Shall We Trust the Archpriest?" unpublished manuscript, 1990, 7, Archives of the Evangelical Baptist Church of Georgia.

[37] E. Gogebshvili, "My Conversion to Christ," unpublished manuscript (Rustavi, 2001), 2, Archives of the Evangelical Baptist Church of Georgia.

we may not always see the results of our work. The document is called "The Liturgical Vision of the Evangelical Baptist Church of Georgia."[38] It covers the liturgical calendar, lectionary, the shape of Worship, Eucharist, Baptism, anointing with oil, the presentation of children, marriage, anointing of the sick, ordination of ministers, funerals, the service book, vestments, and the worship space (including icons).

The Political Factor

From February to March 1990, three countries, Lithuania, Estonia, and Georgia, declared independence from the USSR. Their example was followed by the rest of the Soviet republics. On December 8, 1991, the presidents of Russia, Belarus, and Ukraine sealed the fate of the Soviet Union by signing the agreement that established the Commonwealth of Independent States and declared the end of the USSR.

After independence Georgia had to go through a variety of political, social, and economic challenges. The downfall of the first president of Georgia in 1991 was followed by a series of conflicts and wars. Eduard Shevardnadze's return to Georgia and his election as president marked yet another stage in Georgia's national development. President Shevardnadze brought relative peace to the country, but he was not able to stop Georgian-Abkhaz and Georgian-Ossetian conflicts, nor was he able to run the government and rebuild the nation.

The last years of Shevardnadze's time in office were marked by the punitive action taken against religious extremist groups, including all non-Orthodox ethnically Georgian religious groups in the country. On March 14, 2003, Shevardnadze attended an ecumenical service at the Baptist cathedral in Tbilisi and made a public promise to stop religious violence in the country.[39] But it was the Rose Revolution of November 2003 that was destined to change the religious situation in the country. Many Georgian Baptists participated in the protest demonstrations that brought a new parliament into being. This period after the dissolution of the Soviet Union and establishment of independent nation of Georgia was marked by dramatic changes in the sociopolitical and cultural life of the country.

---

[38] "The Liturgical Vison of the Evangelical Baptist Church of Georgia," 2005, see Songulashvili, *Evangelical Christian Baptists of Georgia*, appendix 14, 411–17.

[39] President Shevardnadze's speech at the Baptist Cathedral, 2003, Archives of the Evangelical Baptist Church of Georgia.

This age of changes coincides with reforms in the life of the Baptist community as well. This was the age when new ecclesial structures were designed (threefold ministry of bishops, presbyters, and deacons); the Baptist School of Iconography was established; Orthodox-type liturgical features and religious practices were introduced; Orthodox aesthetics were affirmed; and the first female deacons, presbyters, and even a bishop were ordained and consecrated. The spirit of continuous political changes in the wider society stimulated and encouraged Georgian Baptists to introduce more changes into their lives. They embraced Eastern Orthodox features after adapting them to their Baptist legacy and spirituality.

Conclusion

Georgian Baptists have affirmed Orthodox culture from the very beginning of their faith journey. They have inherited from Kandelaki his admiration of Georgian Orthodox literature and music, they studied closely Orthodox religious practices and spirituality following the Baptist-Orthodox dialogue led by Giorgi Bolgashvili and Ilia II, and during the time of great political changes they absorbed the best of Orthodox culture: its iconography, liturgy, and liturgical aesthetics. But this does not mean that the Baptists have indiscriminately accepted everything that belongs to the dominant culture. They distanced themselves from religious nationalism, a characteristic feature of many Orthodox cultures. Georgian Baptists believe that the religious nationalism that is deeply entrenched in Georgia's culture is so inimical to the gospel that it has refused the idea of interpreting and reinterpreting the gospel. While Georgian Baptists encourage a patriotism that represents a love of people and culture, they reject a nationalism that alienates people from one another.

Robert Taft, a well-known expert on Orthodox liturgy, is right in suggesting that "cultural rejection as well as adaptation has always been integral to the process of inculturation. The church does not just borrow and adapt from local cultures: it also resolutely rejects aspects, even fundamental religious aspects, of those cultures."[40] Baptists affirm the Orthodox legacy. They embrace Orthodox aesthetics, liturgy, literature, and music but they also critique the nationalism and numerous phobias that are characteristic of Or-

---

[40] R. Taft, "Missionary Effort of the Eastern Churches as an Example of Inculturation," in *Le Chiese Orientali e la missione in Asia: Riflessioni in preparazione all'Assemblea del Sinodadei Vescovi* (Vatican City: Vatican Publishing House, 1998), 35.

thodox culture, whether Islamophobia, xenophobia, or homophobia. Baptists adopt the threefold ministry of deacons, presbyters, and bishops from the Orthodox culture, but they also open ways to these ministries for women. Cultures not only ought to be affirmed but should be critiqued as well. This is what Georgian Baptists did and still do in relation to Orthodox culture.

21

Against the Tide: Main Features of Latvian Baptist Interaction with Culture, 1900–1915

Valdis Tēraudkalns

This chapter analyzes the interaction of the Baptist movement in Latvia with local and transnational cultures at the beginning of the twentieth century. Baptist periodicals of that period are used as main sources for research; 1915 has been chosen as the final year of the researched period because in that year *Avots* and *Kristīgs Vēstnesis*, two major Latvian Baptist periodicals, ceased publication.[1]To many readers the first thought that comes to mind when they hear the words "religion and culture" is H. Richard Niebuhr's classic *Christ and Culture* (1951) and well-known categories proposed by him: Christ against culture, Christ of culture, Christ above culture, Christ and culture in paradox, and Christ the transformer of culture.[2] Niebuhr was not dogmatic about this classification because he understood well that these are more like Weberian ideal types than strict categories. However, many changes have taken place in cultural studies and theology since the 1950s when Niebuhr wrote this work; therefore, Niebuhr's approach has inevitably been criticized. American scholar Linell Cady stated, "There has been a change from interpreting cultures as bounded wholes, with large measure of integration and coherence, towards interpreting them as far more fragmented and contested."[3] More recent scholars have moved away from an essentialist understanding of culture and religion to an understanding that cultur-

---

[1] This article has been published as part of the project "Interaction between the Individual, the Society, and the State in Process of the History of Latvia: Conflicting Values and Formation of Shared Values during Historical Turning Points" (VPP-IZM-2018/1-0018).

[2] H. Richard Niebuhr, *Christ and Culture* (New York: Harper and Brothers, 1951).

[3] Linell E. Cady, "Loosening the Category that Binds," in *Converging on Culture: Theologians in Dialogue with Cultural Analysis and Criticism*, ed. Delwin Brown, Sheila Dawaney, and Kathryn Tanner (Oxford: Oxford University Press, 2001), 21.

al and religious identities are not stable and are constantly negotiated. There is no Christ apart from culture—whether it be the New Testament sociocultural environment or the numerous cultures that have influenced representations of Christ throughout the centuries. At the same time the image of Christ prompts us to apply hermeneutics of suspicion toward cultures we live in—be it the ecclesial culture or wider society.

Culture of Reading

The first printed texts in Latvian appeared in the sixteenth century. These were products of Protestant and Catholic strategies of persuasion as both divisions of Christianity competed for Latvian souls (mainly peasants then). Books were rare and expensive, and levels of literacy were low; therefore, these publications did not have much impact on wider Latvian society. Newspapers in the territory of Latvia were already published in the seventeenth century but these were in German and print runs were small. Even at the beginning of the nineteenth century in the Kurzeme and Vidzeme regions of Latvia there were only three journals and three newspapers, all still in German. Only occasionally, such as during the Russian-French War of 1812, did some of them reach a print run of several hundred copies. In the eighteenth century, attempts were made to start publishing periodicals in Latvian (*Latviešu Ārste*, 1768–1769; *Latviska Gada Grāmata*, 1797–1798), but these didn't last long, and their impact was probably not large due to the low level of literacy and the small print runs. Calendars were much more popular.[4] In the 1770s and 1780s, *Jauna un veca latviešu laika grāmata* published twenty-one hundred copies, and *Vidzemes kalendārs* published three thousand copies in the beginning of the nineteenth century.[5]

The situation slowly changed in the nineteenth century, and some Baltic-German Lutheran pastors like Karl Friedrich Watson, influenced by the Enlightenment, were instrumental. But they had a hard time convincing tsarist censorship that sometimes denied requests to start new publication, stating that there were already too many periodicals in the Russian Empire. This was the case with the project to publish the religious journal *Dieva Vārdu Mīļotājiem*.[6] In the 1850s with reforms undertaken by Tsar Alexander

[4] Calendars were yearbooks that published information on state and religious holidays, and often included very short articles giving practical advice and articles of general interest.

[5] Vita Zelče, *Latviešu avīžniecība: Laikraksti savā laikmetā un sabiedrībā 1826–1865* (Rīga: Zinātne, 2009), 66–70.

[6] Zelče, *Latviešu avīžniecība*, 110.

II, the spread of newspapers received new impetus. There were periodicals specializing in Christian "matters" with appendixes (church news or mission news) to secular newspapers. *Evaņģēlists*, the first Latvian Baptist periodical,[7] was published from 1881 to 1887; its editor was Baptist pastor and Union leader Jēkabs Rumbergs, who also published the first Baptist calendar in Latvian (1885). The first known Baptist book in Latvian was Johann Gerhard Oncken's *Confession of Faith*, translated by Mārtiņš Rīss (1875).[8] The next Baptist periodicals started only at the beginning of twentieth century: *Avots* (The spring [water]) (1905–1915); *Jaunība* (Youth) (1907–1909); *Jaunības Draugs* (Friend of youth) (1905–1915);[9] *Kristīgs Draugs* (Christian friend) (1903–1905), *Draugs* (Friend) (1906–1915, 1917), *Kristīgs Vēstnesis* (Christian messenger) (1906–1915); and so on.[10]

Instrumental in spreading Baptist literature in Latvia was Jānis Aleksandrs Freijs (sometimes in English texts his surname is transliterated as Frey), who was not only a Latvian Baptist pastor and Union leader but also the owner of a publishing house. He started to work as a colporteur at the age of seventeen in 1881; then some years later he established the publishing house. It was reorganized in 1906, but in 1914 it was taken over by the publishing house *Avots*.[11] Freijs and his publishing activities are examples of a selective attitude toward modernity. He was a wealthy person, which allowed him to travel more than many of his fellow believers. *The Land Where Jesus Walked* (1895), written in the tradition of popular travel books of his day, was reprinted several times and translated into several languages (Estonian, German, and others). If read from the postcolonial outlook of a contemporary reader, Freijs's reflections about his trip to Palestine reveal typical features characteristic of many people in the West of his time—referring to Muhammad as a false prophet, the description of Istanbul as a luxurious and superficial city,[12] and fascination with Egypt (an entire chapter of his book is

---

[7] By "Baptist periodicals," I mean publications edited or published by Baptists.

[8] Jānis Tervits, *Latvijas baptistu vēsture: faktu mozaīka* (Rīga: LBDS, 1999), 69, 415.

[9] The publication with that title was published from 1901 by Lutheran pastor Jānis Rozēns until Freijs bought from him a concession to publish it. From 1905 it was published as an appendix to *Avots* (Jānis Kronlīns, *Gaišā ceļā. Dr. theol. h.c. Jāņa Aleksandra Freija dzīve un darbi 1863–1950* [Amerikas Latviešu baptistu apvienības izdevums, 1964], 62).

[10] Publication years of periodicals are taken from Kārlis Egle, Velta Lūkina, Ārija Brempele, and Voldemārs Jauģiets, *Latviešu periodika*. 1. sēj. (Rīga: Fundamentālā bibliotēka, 1977).

[11] Jānis Tervits, *Latvijas baptistu vēsture: faktu mozaīka* (Rīga: LBDS, 1999), 81.

[12] Jānis A. Freijs, *Zeme, kur Jēzus staigāja* (Rīga: J. A. Freijs un biedri, 1910), 14–15.

about the ancient Egyptian religion).[13] As a Protestant, Freijs chose to worship on Sundays in the German Lutheran Church of Jerusalem that functioned as a familiar place, partly because, as he describes, the pastor speaks in "simple and sincere words."[14] In the same book, in lengthy detail, Freijs describes Eastern customs, warning readers to avoid some practices, such as tattoos.[15]

Freijs embraced the usage of modern printing technologies and book distribution methods, at the same time remaining within the framework of the evangelicalism of his day. The editorial in the first issue of the magazine *Jaunība* shows it well—its promise to provide readers with texts on science and issues of everyday life as well as the main political news—all to go hand in hand with setting its goal as "fighting against Satan and evils of the world."[16] Popular science was a regular subject in Baptist periodicals. *Kristīgs Vēstnesis* even called itself "a spiritual newspaper of popular science," in spite of the fact that this was not a main topic for this publication (later this was dropped from the front page of the newspaper and it advertised itself as "a newspaper of the spiritual awakening of Latvia").[17] This was an influence from the wider culture of reading that under the impact of the Enlightenment concentrated on issues of science, setting as their goal the enlightenment of readers in various fields of human knowledge. In the 1850s and 1860s a Latvian graduate of the University in Tērbata (now Tartu, Estonia), Andrejs Šūlmanis, published *Pasaule*, a series of small books in which the largest number of essays (twenty-two) were on zoology, followed by technology (eleven), natural phenomena (eight), architecture (five), geography of exotic lands (five), and others. Most of the pictures were borrowed from the English *The Penny Magazine* (used also in German [*Das Pfenning-Magazin*] and Estonian [*Ma-ilm*]).[18] Baptists followed a similar pattern; however, they also used science to defend some evangelical beliefs of that day. For example, one article in *Avots* refers to the theory of a German astronomer that explains the flood in the Bible.[19] Evangelicalism's interest in science can also

[13] Freijs, *Zeme*, 39-48.

[14] Freijs, *Zeme*, 205–6.

[15] Freijs, *Zeme*, 276.

[16] "Ievadam," *Jaunība*, June 1907, 1–2.

[17] "Vēstuļnieks," *Kristīgs Vēstnesis*, May 1914, 119.

[18] Aleksejs Apīnis, *Soļi senākās latviešu grāmatniecības un kultūras takās* (Rīga: Preses nams, 2000), 275–78.

[19] "Jauna teorija par grēku plūdiem," *Avots*, November 15, 1906, 545.

be observed in other countries. Congregationalist Leonard Woods Jr. wrote in 1822 that "the best method of Bible study is that which is pursued in the science of physics, [regulated by] the maxims of Bacon and Newton."[20] During the course of the nineteenth century, "scriptural geology" gained some support among evangelicals on both sides of the Atlantic. For example, a Bible-only approach to science was also advocated by Edward Irving, a leading figure of the Catholic Apostolic Church (an English Protestant group also with a presence in the territory of Latvia).[21]

In Latvian Baptist periodicals, as in other publications of that period, one can also notice the influence of romanticism, with its emphasis on nature and sentimentalism. The poetry by pastor Augusts Mēters is typical of the time:

> Again, I am in the wild nature,
> Too long I chucked in the dust of the city.
> I enjoy listening to the breeze,
> And watching how night is coming.[22]

Another author reporting about youth work writes, "With the awakening of nature, some Christian young men and women also woke up."[23] Romanticism was a characteristic of Keswick spirituality, a movement well known to Latvian Baptists. Keswick's speakers employed the use of poetry, appeals to nature, and expressions of personal feelings. The same can be said about the Russian evangelical leader Ivan Kargel, who visited Latvia and whose sermons and lectures were translated into Latvian. Keswick meetings took place in an area of England known for its beautiful natural surroundings. Kargel enjoyed holidays he spent in the seaside town of Haapsalu (Estonia) and on the Pashkov Estate Krekshino.[24]

The distribution of Christian literature was promoted in all possible ways and presented as a duty of believers. One of the authors writing for *Avots*, a periodical published by Freijs, reacted against what he considered

---

[20] Mark A. Noll and Christopher M. Rios, "Evangelicalism and Fundamentalism," in *Science and Religion: A Historical Introduction*, ed. Gary B. Ferngren (Baltimore: John Hopkins University Press, 2017), 272.

[21] Noll and Rios, "Evangelicalism and Fundamentalism," 278.

[22] Augusts Mēters, "Atkal es atrodos brīvā dabā," *Avots*, December 28, 1911, 618.

[23] J. Dubelzars, "No Kuldīgas," *Jaunība*, September 1907, 60.

[24] Gregory L. Nichols, *The Development of Russian Evangelical Spirituality: A Study of Ivan V. Kargel (1849–1937)* (Eugene, OR: Pickwick, 2011), 234–37.

immoral calendars and stated that "our sacred duty is to distribute among people good calendars of healthy contents."[25] Another author called for the mobilization of a Christian audience because "we have a great work in front of us. We should build God's kingdom through good, useful writings."[26] One Latvian Baptist wrote about his experience of traveling to other churches like the Gospel House in St. Petersburg, where books were sold in the church lobby. He suggests introducing this practice also to Latvian congregations and complains that most Baptist chapels are not built in a way that would allow selling books in the lobby.[27] Reports of colporteurs often were published. They traveled long distances around Latvia and sometimes worked also outside its territory. For example, Teodoras Gerikas, who was instrumental in spreading the Baptist faith in Lithuania, from 1908 assisted J. A. Freijs as a colporteur and also translated literature into Lithuanian.[28]

At the same time the culture of reading was a field of tension because opinions on what constituted a bad and good reading differed. One of the correspondents reported from the Latvian Baptist congregation in Philadelphia, "Young people love books, music and a lot of other things and they do not like that these things are always despised. They do not see them as a sin."[29] However, another article lamented that there are so many books, including bad novels ("stories of robbers") "that some young people do not fulfil their assignments in school, some go astray, crimes have been done. . . ."[30] In Baptist periodicals, more traditional views critical of new trends in literature and arts prevailed, with some exceptions. One such case is an article in *Jaunība* on Leo Tolstoy that provoked criticism. The author is positive about Tolstoy and states that "In the coming of God's kingdom the substance is not disputes between denominations, nor quarrelling about baptism

---

[25] Kārlis Ruševics, "Ienesīgs apsākums," *Avots*, October 25, 1906, 510.

[26] "Uzsaukums kristīgajiem," *Avots*, October 11, 1906, 490.

[27] R. Ozols, "Mūsu sapulču namu iekārtojums," *Avots*, May 15, 1912, 234. His proposal was criticized by other authors who said that many Russian Baptist churches are against this practice because they believe that selling books on Sunday is sinful. However, it is possible to distribute tracts at the end of the service ("Mūsu sapulču namu iekārtojums," *Avots*, June 6, 1912, 269).

[28] Lina Toth (Andronoviene), "Revival among Aliens: The Case of Lithuanian Baptists," in *Baptists and Revivals: Papers from the Seventh International Conference on Baptist Studies*, ed. William L. Pitts (Macon, GA: Mercer University Press, 2018), 313.

[29] Junagu Fricis, "No Filadelfijas draudzes," *Avots*, March 1, 1906, 104.

[30] J. Putnuērglis, "Ko tu lasi?," *Avots*, December 29, 1910, 615.

that can help, but rather the inconceivable love of Christ to people and all living creatures."[31]

The Baptist Movement as a Reaction against Dominant Mass Culture and Dominant Church Culture

Early Latvian Baptists often criticized the wider society and the Lutheran Church in particular for being worldly; "according to Baptist views the world and the church are separate things, not only in teaching but in everyday life."[32] However, we need to keep in mind that the Baptist movement in the territory of Latvia started among Pietist circles; therefore, some of the criticisms of the movement were shared with Lutheran Pietists. Later, Pietistic Lutherans and Baptists also sometimes cooperated when Baptists established themselves as independent and often as a rhetorically anti-Lutheran movement. A report from the village of Kaltene says, "Most honest of the Lutherans have prayer meetings together with Baptists on Sunday and Saturday nights in every house in turn."[33]

Some concerns expressed by most of the Lutherans (for example, about secularization) were identical to ones Baptists raised. But things like abstinence from alcohol and rejection of theatre and other leisure activities became symbolic signs of the borderline that separated Baptists from others. However, one can find a similar rejection outside Baptist churches. Even in the 1930s Lutheran Dean Kārlis Irbe divided dances into folk dances and "sexually stimulating dances."[34]

The nineteenth century and the beginning of the twentieth century were an age of establishing all kinds of nongovernmental organizations. There was a boom of social life. Baptists followed the same pattern, and their prayer houses became centers of activities that extended far beyond the main service on Sunday morning. Similarly, in England the chapel became "an organization offering a complete educational and leisure programme."[35] One of the articles on youth work starts with a motto by Atis Kronvalds, activist of the movement of New Latvians (a middle-class movement in-

---

[31] A. J-nf-ns, "Atdzimšana literatūrā un dzīvē," *Jaunība*, July 1909, 205.

[32] "Grēka tiesāšana mūsu draudzēs," *Draugs*, January 20, 1907, without pagination.

[33] 'No Kaltenes,' *Kristīgs Draugs*, March 30, 1905, 5.

[34] Kārlis Irbe, "Dzimstības mazināšanās kā tikumības pagrimšanas sekas," *Svētdienas Rīts*, April 24, 1938, 132.

[35] John H. Y. Briggs, *The English Baptists of the Nineteenth Century* (Didcot: Baptist Historical Society, 1994), 333.

strumental in the development of nationalist ideology): "Dear friends! Join together, join together because only joining together has a power!"[36] The pattern of democratic, self-governed congregations was often described as a modern type of organization as opposed to the Lutheran ecclesial system that still, in most parishes, kept patronage (with local nobility appointing clergy). The report on excursions following the conference of Sunday school teachers at the Riga Dome Church and looking to the church building that is below street level states, "If our whole life has adjusted to the needs of our age and has been raised up by some feet, how about the church of our land? It seems that it is still reluctant to accept the demands of our age."[37] Another author who reflects on Baptist contributions to the Latvian spiritual life mentions all the different activities and structures Baptists had created—choirs, societies of young men and women, and Sunday schools. According to this author, "strict morality" (he calls it a basic Baptist principle) is a common purpose of all these activities.[38]

Due to the influence of nationalism and a cultural memory that, in the eyes of many Latvians, turned Baltic-Germans into oppressors, the social life of Latvians and Baltic-Germans often took place in separate organizations. The same can be said also about Baptists who, after being a mission station of the church in Memel (now Klaipeda in Lithuania), became independent and often positioned themselves as a church started by Latvians and born out of Latvian aspirations for a new type of Christianity. There was a tension between Germans and Latvians that showed up in small details of various reports on local church life. For example, news came from the Liepāja Zion Church that there was also the German choir present but "we need to ask whether it is appropriate to sing German songs in the Latvian meeting."[39] Similarly, Estonian Baptists reacted against their German co-believers. Their leader, Karl Kaups, stated in 1934 that Roman Catholicism and Lutheranism came to Estonia from Germany and the Orthodox faith from Russia, but the Baptist movement "was born in Estonia and by Estoni-

---

[36] A. Liepiņš, "Mūsu jauniešu biedrību nozīme," *Avots*, January 21, 1909, 30.

[37] Vircavnieks, "Gājiens caur Rīgas pilsētas muzeju, Doma baznīcu, pilsētas bibliotēku un mākslas muzeju," *Avots*, January 21, 1909, 30.

[38] Alberts, "Baptistu nozīme latviešu tautas garīgās dzīves pacelšanā pēdējos 50 gados," *Avots*, May 9, 1912, 219.

[39] "Vēstis iz biedrībām," *Jaunība*, October 1908, 318.

ans themselves."[40] Today this view is considered a one-sided exaggeration, and Latvian historian Kristīne Ante has written, "Among Latvians there were groups of people who wanted to promote piety. However, it is arguable to what extent the members of these pious communities were informed about the basics of the Baptists and followed its postulates."[41]

Latvian Baptists were people of their time in relationship to the First World War, as many of them joined in the patriotic excitement of their fellow citizens. For example, the Baptist congregation in Smiltene organized a patriotic concert. The program includes anthems of the Russian Empire, Great Britain, France, and other countries of the Allies; Luther's hymn "A Mighty Fortress Is Our God"; and the song "God Bless Latvia" that later became the anthem of independent Latvia. J. A. Freijs read a poem written by Grand Duke Konstantin Konstantinovich, a grandson of Emperor Nicholai I.[42] *Avots* also praised the Allies and published in English and Latvian the British patriotic song "Rule, Britannia."[43]

Societies for young people supported not only devotional activities but also educational projects like libraries. When in 1870 the Riga Society of Baptist Young Men was founded, they also established the library, even though for some it looked like a "worldly" idea. At the beginning, only church members where admitted to the society, but later all who declared that they loved God were eligible.[44] Typical of associations of that time, Baptist youth organizations also had their flags. Likewise, literary evenings where young people presented their work was not something unique to that time. However, the topics of Baptist conversations were different because they debated works written by Moody, Torrey, and other evangelical authors.[45] This is a sign of how Baltic provinces were culturally interwoven in the web of transnational networks (including religious ones).

Baptists commented on activities of organizations connected to Lutheran churches. These reports show that their attitudes toward some expressions of secular culture were a dividing issue. For example, the report on

---

[40] Toivo Pilli, "Baptist Identities in Eastern Europe," in *Baptist Identities: International Studies from the Seventeenth to the Twentieth Centuries*, ed. Ian M. Randall, Toivo Pilli, and Anthony R. Cross (Milton Keyes: Paternoster, 2006), 96.

[41] Kristīne Ante, "The Religious and Socio-Political Context for Establishment of the First Baptist Parishes in Courland," *Latvijas Vēstures Institūta Žurnāls* 3 (2017): 59.

[42] "Smiltenes latviešu baptistu patriotisks koncerts," *Avots*, April 15, 1915, 120.

[43] "Rule Britannia" *Avots*, May 13, 1915, 147.

[44] Jānis Tervits, *Latvijas baptistu vēsture: faktu mozaīka* (Rīga: LBDS, 1999), 381–82.

[45] "Jaunekļu svētki Mateus draudzē," *Avots*, February 1, 1906, 57.

an evening organized by the Evangelical Society of Young Men in Liepāja (a German Lutheran organization) criticized it for showing a theatre play, declaring, "This is reversed, corrupted Christianity!"[46] There are parallels with English Victorian Nonconformist rejection of theatre plays; however, interestingly, most British evangelicals did not object to "sober" reading of plays.[47] Modesty in lifestyle and chastity was frequently promoted. Religious arguments for disciplining bodies of believers were sometimes coupled with techniques for a healthy lifestyle as promoted by health reformers. For example, young men were encouraged to fight "temptations of the flesh" by washing in cold water and exercising.[48] However, sport among Latvian Baptists remained a controversial topic for a long time. In illegal youth camps of the 1980s during the Soviet era, football was one of the main recreational activities that was more acceptable to Baptist leadership than going to the opera, theatre, or cinema. But before the First World War, *Avots* in reporting on sport games was quick to note, "It does not mean encouragement for our young men to participate in sport societies. These are worldly. Some believers by taking care of the flesh there have lost the blessing of their soul."[49] It also argued that sports take away Sunday rest. However, it invited readers to debate about the subject. There was an earlier article in *Avots* sympathetic to sports. Its author argued that an urban lifestyle requires exercising. He also referred to ancient Greeks and the deuterocanonical Ecclesiasticus to defend his argument.[50] The question about the role of sports should be placed in the wider context of the society of that time. In the nineteenth century it was considered a recreational activity of the German elite. Only at the end of the nineteenth century did Latvians and Russians start to be involved in sports in a more systematic way. The first Latvian sport organization—the Riga Second Society of Bicycle Riders—was established in the 1890s.[51] Unlike nineteenth-century England, churches in Latvia did not yet construct their version of "muscular Christianity."

---

[46] "Liepājas Evaņģēliskā Jaunekļu biedrība," *Jaunība*, November–December 1907, 135.

[47] Doreen M. Rosman, *Evangelicals and Culture* (Eugene, OR: Pickwick, 1984), 129.

[48] "Nopietns vārds jaunekļiem viņu mūža jaukākajā un bīstamākajā laikā," *Kristīgs Draugs*, August 10, 1905, 6.

[49] "Viskrievijas otrā olimpiāde notiek Rīgā," *Avots*, July 16, 1914, 224.

[50] "Kādēļ vajadzīga ģimnastika?," *Avots*, January 25, 1912, 43.

[51] *20. gadsimta Latvijas vēsture*, Vol. 1, ed. Valdis Bērziņš (Rīga: Latvijas Vēstures institūta apgāds, 2000), 330.

Baptist cultural separatism was criticized by both secular society and Lutherans. In 1909 *Kristīgs Vēstnesis* reacted against an article in the Lutheran *Evaņģēliuma Gaisma* where Baptists were depicted as narrow-minded sectarians who reject folk songs. This was a serious criticism if we take into account the fact that Latvian nationalism granted almost sacralized status to folk songs. An unnamed Baptist author, referring to Pietists, answered that Baptists are not the only ones who do not sing secular songs. He also wrote, "Baptists have kept the spirit of Latvian folk songs because they still are singing—they have large choirs and many songs. They only sing what expresses what their heart feels."[52] However, division between secular and religious singing remained strict. Baptist minister Miķelis Latons warned that through secular singing, young people were tempted to go to "places that corrupt the spirit."[53]

Latvian Baptists were very active in propagating abstinence from alcohol, but at least in the nineteenth century and at the beginning of the twentieth century, drinking among Latvian Baptists was more widespread than is later formally admitted in Baptist texts that emphasize the tradition of teetotalism. In 1912 it was reported in *Avots* that in some rural Baptist churches "this 'forefathers' custom' of brewing on farms is still supported to a large extent, and its practitioners argue that it should not be equated with 'ordinary drinking.'"[54]

At the beginnings of the Latvian Baptist movement, an argument was often made that Lutheran pastors are drinking and smoking and thus they do not motivate their church members to abstain. However, this can be said only about some of the Lutherans. Temperance and later abstinence societies at the beginning of the movement were closely related to the Lutheran Church. During the first half of the nineteenth century a number of Lutheran pastors, especially Otto Girgensohn from the town of Alūksne, promoted their work. During a two-month period, about seven thousand persons signed the promise to abstain from drinking vodka. Later this movement lost its popularity; however, at the end of the nineteenth century it was renewed in a secularized form. In 1891 in Riga, Auseklis, a temperance (later abstinence) society for workers, was started. It provided a wide range of cul-

[52] "Evaņģeliuma Gaisma," *Kristīgs Vēstnesis*, February 1909, 5–6.

[53] M. Latons, "Dziedāšana," *Kristīgs Vēstnesis*, August 1914, 110.

[54] O. Legdziņš, "Sakas,"*Avots*, September 19, 1912, 452.

tural activities with well-known writers and publicists involved.[55] Of course, involvement in the temperance movement is not exceptional to Latvian Baptists. The movement was strong also in England, and under its influence by the beginning of the twentieth century, 2,077 out of some 2,900 Baptist congregations abandoned fermented wine in their Communion services.[56]

Because of its dualistic attitude toward the wider society, the Latvian Baptist attitude toward education was complex. In the Baptist Congress of 1876, various views about education for ministers were expressed; however, already in 1876 the first Bible course took place in the city of Liepāja.[57] In 1910 at the Latvian Baptist Congress in Riga, in his paper on the future of Latvian Baptist ministry, Pastor Pēteris Lauberts gives his vision: since most of secular education is "ungodly," Baptists should use all efforts possible to establish their own schools, including German style gymnasiums. They should also open institutions to offer training courses for ministers and use opportunities to send their young people to study at Baptist institutions abroad.[58] Reasons for supporting theological education were not only to provide potential ministers with the knowledge of the Bible but also to teach them "fine speech [because] this age demands that Christ's unmeasurable riches should be preached in decent and attractive language."[59] The text just quoted (in an appeal of Latvian Baptist leaders to take a collection for the seminary in Hamburg) mentions, among other skills, learning languages and studying the "everyday life of people."[60]

In the nineteenth century and the beginning of the twentieth century, liberal theology was not something that influenced Latvian Baptists. (This experience came later, after the First World War.) It was viewed as a problem of mainline churches. In the report on the First European Baptist Congress held in Berlin in 1908 an unnamed author wrote with satisfaction that he had listened to numerous lecturers and "none of them had doubts about the Bible as the Word of God and Jesus as Son of God and our Reconciler

---

[55] "Atturība," *Konversācijas vārdnīca*, vol. 2 (Rīga: RLB Derīgu grāmatu nodaļa, 1910), 223–24.

[56] Briggs, *English Baptists of the Nineteenth Century*, 332.

[57] Jānis Tervits, *Latvijas baptistu vēsture: faktu mozaīka* (Rīga: LBDS, 1999), 266.

[58] Pēteris Lauberts, "Pamata līnijas latviešu baptistu turpmākam garīgam darbam," *Avots*, January 9, 1911, 65–66.

[59] J. Iņķis, J. A. Freijs, and J. Kurcīts, "Kolekte priekš sludinātāju semināra Hamburgā," *Avots*, September 12, 1912, 434.

[60] Iņķis, Freijs, andKurcīts, "Kolekte priekš sludinātāju semināra Hamburgā."

through his blood."[61] Baptists reacted against tendencies of liberalism among Lutherans—for example, against the content of "Faith of Modern Man," a series of lectures in Riga by pastor, writer, and later controversial politician Andrievs Niedra. *Kristīgs Vēstnesis* positively responded to the fact that he was rebuked by the Lutheran Consistory and expressed the hope that further disciplinary measures would follow: "Let's wait whether he will stay in his position of pastor. He has no right to remain."[62] However, not all Baptist publications were equally polemical about theological liberalism. *Avots* was more general in its reflections on this issue, for example, saying that "there are 'reformers' appearing who are trying to destroy this fundamental faith in the Bible and to God."[63] Pastor Pēteris Lauberts encountered liberalism during his studies in Hamburg, where in the library he found the commentary on Genesis by Hermann Gunkel, one of the leading scholars in the history of religions school.[64] After returning, he wrote books titled *Bible in the Fire of Criticism* and *The World without a Living God*,[65] where he argued against theological liberalism.

Baptists also went against the tide in their liturgical life. They differed from Lutherans with a simpler and more flexible liturgy, thus continuing Moravian worship traditions practiced in Latvia since the eighteenth century. Baptists often reacted against written liturgies that were considered too formal and stilted. According to one of the first descriptions of Latvian Baptist life and worship, published by Lutheran pastor Ferdinand Seeberg in 1861 (second edition in 1866), Baptists considered fixed prayers a "pagan habit."[66] A negative attitude toward written prayers included many but not all Baptists also in other countries. Charles Spurgeon refused to include prayers in produced daily Bible readings with brief comments and hymns.

[61] "Pirmais Eiropas baptistu kongress," *Kristīgs Vēstnesis*, September 1908, 3.

[62] "Apskats," *Kristīgs Vēstnesis*, March 1910, 4–5.

[63] A. Liepiņš, "Mūsu jauniešu biedrību nozīme," *Avots*, January 21, 1909, 30.

[64] Pēteris Lauberts, *Dieva roka manā dzīvē* (Liepāja: P. Lauberts, 1928), without pagination.

[65] Pēteris Lauberts, *Bībele kritikas ugunīs* (Priekule: P. Lauberts, 1908); Lauberts, *Pasaule bez dzīvā Dieva* (Priekule: P. Lauberts, 1906).

[66] F. Seeberg, *Kas tie tādi ir, baptisti? Pamācīšana par to jaunu ticību, kas vietām saceļas Kurzemē* (Jelgava: J. F. Stefenhāgens un dēls, 1866), 24.

He said that "it would be the height of hypocrisy for me to compose prayers for the use of others."[67]

However, exactly what the "Baptist liturgical style" was is not so clear, and it was also a cultural issue—what sort of music, style of language, and gestures were considered appropriate. Opinions were divided between supporters of more structured worship services and ones enjoying experiential, emotional types of services. Seeberg's account provides a description of a Baptist worship service. It is very much a pastor-centered liturgy: the hymn is followed by the prayer said by minister, then comes his sermon and another hymn. At the beginning, after the sermon and at the end of the service, people hug and kiss each other (women and men separately).[68]

Later Latvian Baptists learned about different worship styles from their Russian, German, British, American, and Estonian connections. After visiting Estonian churches, pastor Jānis Iņķis praised their worship style. There are several preachers as well as several people who pray in one service; before the service starts, the minister of the congregation meets with elders to find out who would like to preach. The meeting also does not have a strict beginning and end because people are singing before the minister comes to the church. Iņkis acknowledges that there could be problems with this liturgical approach but he thinks that the congregation can handle these problems and that he as a minister cannot take the place of the Spirit.[69] In 1907 one reporter described an evening service in Jelgava where the usual worship order (hymn, prayer, sermon, hymn) was changed and a revivalist type of meeting was introduced with testimonies, then more singing by both choir and by all, an invitation to come forward, and so forth. It was led by Latvian pastor William Fetlers, a graduate of Spurgeon's College (UK).[70] The reporter suggests that "in leading meetings we should try also new ways."[71]

---

[67] Quoted from Ian M. Randall, "'Take My Life': Evangelical Spirituality and Evangelical Identity," *British Evangelical Indentities Past and Present*, vol. 1, ed. Mark Smith (Milton Keyes: Paternoster, 2008), 217.

[68] Seeberg, *Kas tie tādi ir, baptisti,* 24. Here Seeberg distances himself from those who believe that the ritual of sharing the peace is evidence that Baptists are immoral.

[69] Jānis Iņķis, "Igauņu baptisti," *Kristīgs Draugs*, October 5, 1905, 5–6.

[70] In English Fetler's surname is often transliteraed as Fetler, or he is called Basil Malof. For his biographies, see John Wood, *Born in the Fire: The Story of William Fetler alias Basil Malof (1883–1957): Church Planting Evangelist in Russia and Latvia* (Author's publication, 1998); James A. Stewart, *A Man in a Hurry: The Story of the Life and Work of Pastor Basil A. Malof* (Asheville: Russian Bible Society, 1968).

[71] 'Evaņģelizācija Jelgavā,' *Kristīgs Vēstnesis*, August 1907.

Traveling preachers and Latvian Baptists' own inter-European contacts introduced churches to revivalism, Holiness, and later, Pentecostal movements. Sometimes the new movement was a cause of fragmentation. At the beginning of the twentieth century a group of German Baptists separated from their church in Riga. They were influenced by Holiness ideas from Germany, called themselves Evangelical Christians, and used unleavened bread during Holy Communion. This group also found supporters among Latvians.[72] Pastor Juris Puķukalns in 1914 wrote that after learning about revivals in America and Wales, some Latvians started to organize prayer groups. He is sympathetic to the practice and encourages it to continue; however, he admits that there are tensions and admonishes "that in God's church speaking in tongues and healing is not the first priority."[73] Similar tension between revivalism and a more traditional, local church–centered approach was also evident in other countries. In the United Kingdom the Home Mission Society was born out of eighteenth-century revivalism; however, later it became more distanced from revivalist methodologies of conversion, but this did not prevent local churches from taking up revivalist agendas with open-air evangelism and mass meetings in secular halls.[74]

There was also a question of power among various Baptist organizations and opinion makers. F. B. Meyer, influential author known to Latvian Baptists, experienced the Welsh revival in 1905, and soon thereafter the Azusa Street Pentecostal revival in Los Angeles. Others, including William B. Riley of Minnesota, questioned the emotionalism of these meetings and the insistence on tongues as initial evidence of Spirit baptism. Fundamentalist Baptists employed dispensational exegesis to adopt secessionism.[75] In 1909 *Draugs* published the Latvian translation of the Berlin Declaration,[76] which was signed in September 1909 by a group of Holiness-Pietist leaders who opposed Pentecostalism. For decades it had a negative effect on Pentecostal-evangelical relationships in Germany.[77] In Latvia, W. Fetlers wrote several

[72] Ģ. Krauls, 'No Rīgas,' *Draugs*, June 12, 1910, 3.

[73] J. Puķukalns, "Par lūdzēju pulciņiem," *Kristīgs Vēstnesis*, August 1914, 178.

[74] Briggs, *English Baptists of the Nineteenth Century*, 299–301.

[75] C. Douglas Weaver, "Baptists and Early Pentecostal Revivalism," in *Baptists and Revivals: Papers from the Seventh International Conference on Baptist Studies*, ed. William L. Pitts (Macon, GA: Mercer University Press, 2018), 64–87.

[76] "Revivalu lietā," *Draugs*, November 7, 1909, 1–2.

[77] Cecil M. Robeck Jr., *The Azusa Street Mission and Revival* (Nashville: Nelson Reference & Electronic, 2006), 245.

articles full of excitement about the Azusa Street Revival.[78] He never became Pentecostal; however, as an independent-minded, energetic personality he was a supporter of all kinds of revivalist and Holiness movements. After the First World War, the conflict between Fetlers and other Baptists who disagreed led to the split and the formation of the Second Baptist Union (1926–1934). In 1934, Baptists again had one union, but within that union, contradicting theologies and practices remained.

Conclusion

During their more than 150-year-long history, Baptists in Latvia have changed significantly, becoming more flexible, more diverse, and more acceptable of various forms of culture. Baptist pastor Kaspars Šterns, in his speech to the Congress of the Union of Baptist Churches in Latvia in May 2018, where he was elected as a bishop, said that there is a need to establish local churches that are not isolated but interested in society.[79] What this means in practice is a question, because, as with other social groups, Latvian Baptists are selective in relating to the dominant cultural currents and patterns of everyday life. For example, drinking of alcohol, formally still condemned, has been practiced by some clergy as well as laity. Latvian Baptists are more visible in politics, but their agenda is not against what most Christian denominations would believe. They now focus on right-wing politics, defending what they and most other denominations believe to be "Christian values." The Baptist movement in Latvia is ethnically diverse (Latvian and Russian churches both belong to the union); however, many Baptists also embrace the ethnic divide between Latvian and Russian parties characteristic of society in general. When in 2018 former Baptist bishop Pēteris Sproģis unexpectedly announced that he had agreed to be a presidential candidate, most of the criticism among Baptists and others was not theological but political—that he had agreed to cooperate with the "wrong" political force for Latvians: the Harmony Centre, which is considered an alliance of Russian

78 See, for example,V. Fetlers, "Kristīgās draudzes pamošanās," *Avots*, February 21, 1907, 85–87; Fetlers, "Svētā Gara kristība," *Draugs*, February 17, without pagination.

79 "Baptistiem jauns bīskaps," https://www.lbds.lv/zinas/baptistiem-jauns-biskaps (accessed September 2, 2018).

political parties. Public pressure was so high that after some days he withdrew his candidacy.[80]

In the period analyzed in this chapter, the Latvian Baptist attitude toward culture was selective. In many ways—accepting new technologies and more participatory ecclesiology—it was in accord to its time. On the other hand, Baptists shared with some other Christian groups (Lutheran Pietists and other Nonconformist groups) a dualistic attitude toward prevailing culture. This account suggests that social groups use cultures as tool boxes to legitimatize and propagate certain ideas. The same cultural tools, like the Bible, are used by competing groups in different ways.[81] The theological question to be asked is what it means today to be countercultural and whether it is not something that is always contested by the time and space we live in, something that is not given but should be negotiated again and again anew.

---

[80] Ervīns Jākobsons, "Pētera Sproģa krustaceļš nedēļas garumā," http://www.laikmetazimes.lv/2018/07/09/petera-sproga-krustacels-nedelas-garuma/ (accessed September 3, 2018)

[81] Craig Martin, *A Critical Introduction to the Study of Religion* (London: Routledge, 2017), 106–7.

Baptists in the Majority World

22

"More Christian, More Chinese, and More Efficient:" Herman C. E. Liu and the University of Shanghai (1928–1938)

Marina Xiaojing Wang

> The Baptists of the world have lost one of their most stalwart young leaders, the Christian forces of China one of their foremost representatives, and the Chinese Nation a distinguished educator and patriot.[1]

The University of Shanghai (滬江大學) was founded in 1906 as a cooperative effort between the Southern Baptist Convention (SBC) and the American Baptist Missionary Union (ABMU). Herman C. E. Liu (劉湛恩) was appointed its first Chinese president in 1928 and had been highly esteemed in both Christian and Chinese educational circles. Although I focus in this chapter on the history of the University of Shanghai during the period from 1928 to 1938, I first give a brief account of the early history of the university, as well as the nationwide Anti-Christian Movement (1922–1927), which resulted in the transition of the university leadership from foreign to Chinese. Then I examine how the university, under Liu's leadership from 1928 to 1938, attempted to achieve the goal of "more Christian, more Chinese, and more efficient." My aim is to explore the complexity of the interaction between a Christian institute and Chinese society, particularly in the face of fierce nationalist tensions. The history of the University of Shanghai reflects the trend of the evolution of a Christian establishment from its denominational (Baptist) background to a more general and diverse character, and from Western to Chinese culture. I contend that this evolution was a natural step during the growth of the "selfhood" of Christianity in early twentieth-

---

[1] Yale University [YU], Day Missions Library [DML], UBCHINA Archives, College Files, "Resolution Adopted by the Executive Committee of the Baptist World Alliance," in *In Memoriam: Dr. Herman C. E. Liu, University of Shanghai*, April 7, 1939, 8.

century China; meanwhile, however, the trend also reveals an obliged response to a politically hostile environment. In addition, I argue that, while making itself more indigenous and relevant to Chinese society, the university was quite exceptional by keeping and emphasizing its Christian essence. This owed much to Herman Liu's own vision and practice in Christian education in China, which reflects a contextual understanding of the Christian message and its social application.

A Brief Early History of the University of Shanghai

The early history of the University of Shanghai reflects some general trends in the history of the modern missionary movement and the development of Christianity in the mission fields.

Cooperation between Two Baptist Missions

The history of the university can be traced back to the year 1900, when Baptist missionaries took refuge in Shanghai because of the Boxer Uprising. A good number of the Baptist missionaries had sensed the demand for establishing an educational institute to train efficient Chinese church leadership at the turn of the century, thus reflecting the Baptists' deficiency in developing Christian higher education in China. Northern Baptist missionary Francis Johnstone White recorded that, by 1900, "Not one Chinese teacher or layman in the whole Baptist constituency was a full graduate of a secondary school, much less a graduate of a college."[2]

In the early stage of Protestant expansion in China during the nineteenth century, the majority of the missionaries regarded Christian education as being secondary to direct evangelistic work.[3] For example, during the 1877 General Conference of the Protestant Missionaries of China, L. H. Gulick of the ABMU expressed his attitude that education should be employed only if it "directly subsidized" evangelistic work.[4] By the late nineteenth century, however, when mission work became stable and institution-

---

[2] Francis Johnstone White, "A Christian College in China: The Story of the University of Shanghai, From the Year 1906 to the Year 1934," Shanghai Municipal Archives [SMA], U106-0-63: 3.

[3] Ryan Dunch, "Science, Religion, and the Classics in Christian Higher Education to 1920," in *China's Christian Colleges: Cross-Cultural Connections, 1900–1950*, ed., Daniel H. Bays and Ellen Widmer (Stanford, CA: Stanford University Press, 2009), 60.

[4] *Records of the General Conference of the Protestant Missionaries of China, held at Shanghai, May 10–24, 1877* (Shanghai: American Presbyterian Mission Press, 1877), 198.

alized, the problem of the shortage of capable Chinese pastors, preachers, and other Christian workers was exposed. Considering the urgent need of training efficient Chinese workers for ministry, together with the rising tide of the Student Volunteer Movement for Foreign Missions, which "contributed to a changing emphasis in mission theory and methods" with more professional and culturally oriented young missionaries rushing into the mission fields,[5] the 1890s therefore saw a rapid expansion of Christian education in China, especially in higher forms. Baptist missions in China, however, fell far behind in this trend due to their evangelistic-oriented approach.

Cooperation in the mission fields to a large extent prompted similar trends of cooperation at the home base. The establishment of a Baptist educational institute required the cooperative effort of both the central China mission of the SBC and the East China mission of the ABMU. A proposal for the formation of a united college was then sent to both mission boards in the United States. Neither of the mission boards approved this educational union scheme at first.[6] Regardless of the initial refusal of home boards, both missions in China persisted in working out a union scheme and approved Articles of Union in 1904.[7] The year 1905 was significant in the history of education in modern China: the old system of civil service examination was abolished by the Qing government, and Western learning was spreading fast in Chinese society. Regarding the changes as a rare opportunity for the formation of a modern Christian educational institution, both missions strongly urged their home boards for immediate action. Owing to their cooperative efforts, a plan was eventually agreed to in 1905.[8] The early history of the University of Shanghai marks the evolution of Christian education in China. Additionally, it is part of the tide of world ecumenism.

---

[5] Jessie G. Lutz, *China and the Christian Colleges, 1850–1950* (Ithaca: Cornell University Press, 1971), 99. For instance, the two key founders of the University of Shanghai, John Thomas Proctor and Robert Thomas Bryan, both valued the importance of Christian education in missions. Proctor was deeply influenced by the SVM, while Bryan dedicated himself to the founding of a Baptist seminary.

[6] Having recognized the advantage of cooperating with the SBC in Christian education, the executive committee of the ABMU, however, did not believe the time for working on such a union scheme had come. The SBC simply preferred to establish a seminary of its own and disapproved the union plan. See John Burder Hipps, *History of the University of Shanghai* (Board of Founders of the University of Shanghai, 1964), 10–11.

[7] Hipps, *History of the University of Shanghai*, 11.

[8] White, "Christian College in China," 22.

Early Development

The University of Shanghai opened in 1906, with two separate institutions under the same board of trustees and on the same campus—a seminary (1906) and a college with an academy that provided secondary education (1908).[9] In 1912 the college and the seminary were united, with F. J. White serving as president. The university thus was composed of three parts: a college, an academy, and a seminary. In 1926, twenty years after its establishment, the staff number had reached eighty and students numbered nearly 700.[10] By 1926, of its 184 college graduates, 16 dedicated themselves to church ministry, 10 to the YMCA and other social and religious organizations, 77 had taught in Christian schools and fourteen other schools, 3 became doctors, 33 had been in business, and the remainder served in other careers or studied overseas.[11]

Shanghai University was the first institution in Chinese higher education to introduce and adopt coeducation in China, with four female students being enrolled in 1920.[12] The enrollment of female students had increased to sixty-six in 1926.[13] By the mid-1920s, according to White, the university was listed in "the front rank of Christian colleges" in China, and Baptist missions were thus regarded "second to none in higher education in China."[14]

The Anti-Christian Period and Nationalist Challenges during the 1920s and 1930s

While the university entered an era of high-speed development in the mid-1920s, the tide of nationalism in Chinese society also reached a peak, one of whose main targets was the Christian presence in China. The nationwide Anti-Christian Movement of 1922–1927 delivered Christian missions and Chinese churches a heavy blow. This modern Chinese nationalism had been

---

9 The seminary was opened first in 1906 under the name "Shanghai Baptist Theological Seminary" (上海浸會道學書院). In 1908 the college was opened with the name "Shanghai Baptist College" (上海浸會大學堂).

10 YU, DML, UBCHINA Archives, College Files, 240/3949, Shanghai, Administrative, President's Annual Reports, F. J. White, Annual Report of Shanghai College for the year 1925.

11 White, "Christian College in China," 60.

12 White, "Christian College in China," 46–52.

13 White, Annual Report 1925, YU, DML; White, "Christian College in China," 59.

14 Hipps, *History*, 63–64.

fermenting during the first two decades of the twentieth century, stimulated by a series of political and social events: the Revolution of 1911, which overthrew the Qing dynasty and established the Republic of China; the New Cultural Movement since 1915; and the October Revolution and the birth of Soviet Russia in 1917–1918 with the spread of Bolshevism in China. The May Fourth Movement of 1919—triggered by China's diplomatic failure in claiming territory back from a former German treaty and territory in Shandong from Japan during the Paris Peace Conference, further stirred the outrage of the Chinese nation and sparked protests in urban China, marking the upsurge of a new ideological direction of Chinese nationalism. Under the influences of Soviet Russian Bolshevism, this new type of nationalism embraced a number of new concepts, for example, imperialism, cultural imperialism, warlordism, colonialism, and semicolonialism. Based on the discourse of anti-imperialism and anti-warlordism, both the Guomindang (GMD, the Nationalist Party) and the Chinese Communist Party (CCP) developed their Bolshevik revolutionary strategies.[15] Owing to its entanglement with Western powers, the Christian presence in China—whether missions, churches, schools, or other institutions, and regardless of denominations or confessions—was condemned by the nationalists as an agent of Western imperialist invasion and oppression to the Chinese nation, a representative of cultural imperialism.[16]

Meanwhile, the goal of "national salvation" centered in this newly emerged nationalist discourse. The sovereignty and self-determination of a nation were highly valued as keys in the process of building a strong nation-state. Education, for instance, came to be seen as a vital dimension of national sovereignty. Under the vision of "saving the nation through education," which became prominent in the early twentieth century, the main function of education was deemed to "serve the state" in enhancing national identity and disseminating patriotism among the Chinese people, particularly among younger generations.[17] By contrast, Christian education was suspected by a good number of Chinese educators, intellectuals, nationalists,

---

[15] Dong Wang, *China's Unequal Treaties: Narrating National History* (Lanham, MD: Roman and Littlefield, 2005), 72.

[16] Daniel H. Bays, "Foreign Missions and Indigenous Protestant Leaders in China, 1920–1955: Identity and Loyalty in an Age of Powerful Nationalism," in Brian Stanley and Alaine Low, eds., *Missions, Nationalism, and the End of Empire* (Grand Rapids: Eerdmans, 2003), 146.

[17] Lutz, *China and Christian Colleges*, 232.

and patriots of cultural invasion, aiming at "denationalizing" the country by eliminating the national consciousness and identity among students.[18] Control over the educational rights in Christian schools was thus brought onto the agendas of the nationalist campaigns. Under such circumstances, one of the major claims of the Anti-Christian Movement since 1924 tended to focus on taking educational rights away from the Christian schools and placing control in the hands of the state. It became intensified after the May Thirtieth Incident in 1925, when thirteen Chinese students were shot dead by British police in Shanghai, which pushed anti-imperialist sentiments to its climax.

Agitated by nationalist hatred, a large number of urban Chinese Christians, including Christian school students, actively participated in patriotic campaigns and protests.[19] According to F. J. White's reports, it was difficult for the University of Shanghai to maintain a normal atmosphere, and "all schoolwork throughout China was suspended" for the last few weeks of the spring school term. During the next four to five years, even though the total number of students continued to increase every year, "the spiritual tone was at a low ebb."[20] In the meantime, the government urged all Christian schools to register with the Ministry of Education, which was viewed as a vital step in the restoration of educational rights. The regulations for registration issued by the government required:

1. That all religious instruction be placed upon a voluntary basis.
2. That the majority of the board of managers be Chinese.
3. That the president be Chinese.[21]

The university began to prepare for registration in 1926–1927, regardless of the opposition from many missionaries and some Chinese Christian leaders. The first step was taken on March 26, 1926, when F. J. White submitted his resignation, which resulted in Herman C. E. Liu's election as president. In the spring of 1927 an additional eight Chinese members joined the board of managers to make the board meet the standard of a majority of

---

[18] 陳啟天 [Chen Qitian], 新國家主義與中國前途 [New nationalism and China's future], 少年中國 [Young China] 4, no. 9 (1924): 8–9.

[19] Jessie G. Lutz, *Chinese Politics and Christian Missions: The Anti-Christian Movements of 1920–28* (Notre Dame, IN: Cross Cultural Publications, 1988), 160–65, 170–73.

[20] White, "Christian College in China," 56–57.

[21] White, "Christian College in China," 70.

Chinese members.[22] When it opened in 1906, university affairs had been directed by a board of trustees, which consisted of five missionary members from each mission (SBC and ABMU). Also, a Chinese advisory board of ten members, five Chinese Baptists representing each mission, was constituted in the same year.[23] Meanwhile, the matter of Chinese Christians serving on boards of control of the educational and other missionary institutions had been brought to the agenda. Baptists generally valued autonomous local congregations, and its missions encouraged both native leadership and self-support of individual churches. White's resignation can be seen as a move in full compliance with the government's regulations. However, when it came to the issue of Chinese participation in university management, attitudes of the Baptist missions varied in different regions of China.[24] Not until 1927, when the university faced frequent nationalist challenges, was the majority of the board of managers Chinese.

In the meantime, the university started to conduct all religious courses and activities under voluntary principles of instruction in accordance with the government's requirements. This had been the key obstacle causing a good number of Christian schools to be hesitant to register with the national government. Some missionary educators regarded it as a "violation of the principle of religious liberty which the constitution of the Republic guaranteed," and they were concerned about losing the religious life and functions of Christian schools.[25] Many schools therefore refused to register and had been closed down, with the huge cost of their graduates being denied entrance to higher education or not being recognized with a government-stamped diploma. To the board of managers, it seemed to have "no choice" but register as long as the university was "not required to deny" its faith.[26]

---

[22] White, "Christian College in China," 65.

[23] White, "Christian College in China," 65.

[24] There was in general a negative attitude toward this matter among missionary schools outside of East China: some suggested that the acceptance of a Chinese Christian on the boards of control should depend on the financial contribution of Chinese Christians. One mission strongly disagreed with passing the control of missionary funds to the Chinese. Baptist institutions in East China, by contrast, generally held a more positive attitude and acknowledged the tendency of applying the principle of Chinese representation in boards of control to missionary institutions "without any financial conditions." There were eventually two Chinese representatives appointed into the board of trustees of the university in late 1912 (see Hipps, *History*, 26–27).

[25] White, "Christian College in China," 69.

[26] White, "Christian College in China," 69.

After the government's requirements were fulfilled, the university applied for registration in the autumn of 1927, and it was eventually granted after Herman Liu was elected as the president.

Herman C. E. Liu's Vision for the University of Shanghai

Another important event in the history of Shanghai College, Yangtsepoo, took place on Saturday afternoon when Professor Herman Chen-En Liu, M.A., Ph.D., was inaugurated as President, the first Chinese to hold that position. The installation ceremony was presided over by Dr. C. S. Miao, Secretary of the China Christian Educational Association, who was chairman of the College Board of Directors, and there were present, among others, Dr. Tsai Yuan-pei, President of the Nationalist Board of Education; Dr. H. H. Kung, Minister of Industry and Commerce; Dr. F. L. Hawks Pott, President of St. John's University; Dr. H. T. Hodgkin, Secretary of the National Christian Council; Gen. Chang Ting-fan, Mayor of Greater Shanghai....[27]

Liu's inauguration took place on February 25, 1928; it was a sensational event in Chinese educational circles. Liu's address, "The Mission of a University [Daxue zhi Shiming, 大學之使命]," identified three major tasks: to train qualified people in both knowledge and character, to conduct and enhance academic research, and to transform society.[28] Liu took the opportunity to speak of his vision of making the university a better educational institute along Christian lines, with the goal of being "more Christian, more Chinese, and more efficient."[29]

Herman C. E. Liu was born in 1895 in Yangxin, Hubei. He was a third-generation Chinese Baptist who had a poor childhood due to his father's early death. Nonetheless, Liu's educational profile was outstanding. After being educated in William Nast College (Methodist) in Jiujiang, he studied science in Soochow University, one of thirteen Christian universities in the republican era. He then furthered his study at Rush Medical College in Chicago after graduation in 1918, but later transferred to the University of Chicago to study toward a master's degree in education. In 1922 he re-

[27] 教會新聞：滬江新校長劉湛恩就職記 [Church news: Inauguration of Herman Liu, New president of the Shanghai Baptist College"], 通問 [Tongwen] 1287 (1928): 8.

[28] Church news: Inauguration of Herman Liu, 8.

[29] *Bulletin of the University of Shanghai*, July 1933, 8.

ceived his doctoral degree from Columbia University. Before taking up the position as president of the university, Liu served as a key leader in several national Christian organizations, including national educational secretary for the YMCA from 1922 to 1928, research director of the National Vocational Education Association, secretary of the educational commission of the national government, chief Chinese delegate to the world YMCA conference in Helsinki in 1926, and one of the founders of both the China Institute of International Relations and the Anti–Civil War League of China (1933). He also held other positions as professor in education in Great China (大夏) and Kwanghua (光華) Universities.[30] His Christian background, his academic training in China and overseas, his working experience in the educational field, as well as his international fame and broad professional network qualified him to become the college president. Liu's presidency from 1928 to 1938 was a vital period for the university to engage actively and deeply in Chinese society on the one hand, while maintaining its Christian character on the other. This was also a period of turbulence and turmoil due to the outbreak in 1931 of the Second Sino-Japanese War.

Liu's vision in making the university "more Christian, more Chinese, and more efficient," in fact, corresponded to the advice of the Committee of Reference and Counsel of the Foreign Missions Conference of North America, based on their survey of Christian education in China in 1922, in which the committee urged each Christian school in China to be "thoroughly *Christian* in its character and thoroughly *Chinese* in its atmosphere, raised to a high level of *efficiency*, it can render a service which a school lacking any of these characteristics cannot at all perform."[31] Liu reaffirmed this goal in 1933 at the annual meeting of the board of directors of the university when he formulated and launched a five-year program by further explaining his aims in detail:

> • More Christian. We reaffirm that we should continue to preserve the Christian purpose of the university and make the institution more Christian than ever before. This is a sacred trust. It is absolutely vital to the development of our institution.

---

[30] YU, DML, *In Memoriam: Dr. Herman C. E. Liu.*

[31] Committee of Reference and Counsel of the Foreign Missions Conference of North America, *Christian Education in China: A Study Made by an Educational Commission Representing the Mission Boards and Societies Conducting Work in China* (New York, 1922), 14. Emphasis added.

> • More Chinese. By "more Chinese" we mean that we want to make our institution meet the needs of China more adequately than ever before. We should not try to achieve some American or European standard but to reach a standard that is fitting for China. In our method of instruction and teaching material we should take the best from all foreign countries but keep the best that is Chinese and adapt the whole to the peculiar needs of China.
>
> • More Efficient. We are known to be one of the most efficient and economical institutions of higher learning in China. We should uphold that reputation and continue with the minimum of expense and get the maximum result.[32]

"More Chinese"

One of the first matters Liu was facing after his inauguration to presidency was to secure registration with the government. Registration, to a large extent, was significant in changing the public attitude toward the university so that they would accept it as a Chinese educational institute. This was similar to Liu's appeal for "more Chinese" and conformed to his attitude about the future of Christian education in China. Right after the outbreak of the May Thirtieth Incident in 1925, Liu commented on the incident's influence on Christian schools in China and brought forward suggestions to help Christian schools reform:

> 1. To appoint Chinese to be school principals and to make Chinese the majority of faculty members and board of directors;
>
> 2. To enhance more studies on Chinese culture and to use Chinese instead of the English language as the medium of teaching;
>
> 3. To adopt a voluntary principle on religious education and to focus more on fostering students with Christ-like characters;
>
> 4. To register with the national government.[33]

Prior to the issue of the government regulations for registration, Liu had already held a similar view, especially toward the voluntary policy on reli-

---

[32] Hipps, *History*, 92.

[33] 劉湛恩 [Liu Zhan'en], 五卅慘案與教會學校 [The May Thirtieth incident and Christian schools], 教育季刊 [Education Quarterly] 1, no. 3 (1925): 15–17.

gious education. His sympathy lay with the national government on this matter.

One of the major obstacles during the university's registration process was the opposition from the central China mission of the SBC. The mission strongly opposed registration at the cost of making religious education voluntary and decided to withdraw in 1927.[34] Liu, after his inauguration as president, visited all the stations of the central China mission, explaining in detail the registration process and its advantages, and eventually received approval from the mission.[35] One year after Liu becoming president, the university was finally registered on March 18, 1929, and became the first registered Christian university in Shanghai.[36] In 1931 the English name, Shanghai Baptist College, was changed to the name "University of Shanghai" to match the Chinese name Hujiang Daxue (Hu Kiang Ta Hsioh, 滬江大學), which was adopted as early as 1915. Although the process toward registration began before Liu's inauguration as president, the symbolic meaning of Liu's leadership in the university—together with his supportive attitude toward school registration, his actual ability in administration and negotiation, as well as his fame and personal contact in Chinese educational circles—played a great part in the registration process and in making the university "Chinese" and thus gain wide recognition among the Chinese.[37]

After registration, the Christian school curriculum conformed to the standard of the Ministry of Education. The national government determined to reinforce patriotic education in schools by enforcing military training and the study of the Three Principles of the People. The Three Principles of the People, also known as *Sanmin Zhuyi* (三民主義), which were developed by Sun Yat-sen to express his revolutionary ideas and served as the fundamental doctrine of the GMD, refer to the principles of *Minzu* (na-

---

[34] Southern Baptist Convention [SBC], Central China, Minutes: Executive Committee, Mission, Reference Book and Minutes, 1927, 9–14.

[35] SBC, Central China, Minutes: Executive Committee, Mission, Reference Book and Minutes, 1927, 32–33; Hipps, *History*, 81–82.

[36] YU, DML, UBCHINA Archives, College Files, 滬江大學同人 [The University of Shanghai], 劉校長與滬江大學 [President Liu and the University of Shanghai], in 劉公湛恩逝世週年紀念 [*One Year Anniversary of the Death of Dr. Herman C. E. Liu*], April 7, 1939, 8.

[37] Liu's methods to make the university "more Chinese" included strengthening the Chinese members of the faculty and staff and self-fundraising to realize financial independence. In 1928 the ratio number of foreign and Chinese professors in the university was 11:8, while in 1937 it changed to 11:14 (see Hipps, *History*, 85).

tionalism, 民族), *Minquan* (popular sovereignty / democracy, 民權), and *Minsheng* (people's livelihood, 民生). From many of his articles on the topics of citizenship, education, and social engagement, one may find Herman Liu a fervent patriot. In fact, Liu participated in Sun Yat-Sen's revolutionary campaigns in his early years.[38] Additionally, citizenship education and vocational education were Liu's lifetime focuses.[39] To him, one of the main tasks of education was to train "good citizens" for the nation. When he served as national educational secretary for the YMCA from 1922 to 1928, a campaign for citizenship education was launched throughout China by the YMCA to strengthen the national identity and patriotism of the Chinese people. A good number of Liu's writings during that period focused on this topic.[40] He welcomed the teaching of the Three Principles of the People in schools and combined it with his own vision of citizenship education to forge students' personality and patriotic loyalty and to train them to dedicate themselves to serve the society.[41] It should be noted, however, that Liu, as a Christian educator, emphasized learning autonomy, free discussion, and field investigation during the study process, instead of propagating lectures favored by the party.[42]

Furthermore, the university engaged itself in the New Life Movement in 1934–1935, which was launched by the national government to strengthen Chinese people's national identity, loyalty, and collective solidarity, and to embark on social and moral reform in Chinese society.[43] Xing Jun points out that the New Life Movement and the YMCA "held so much common

---

[38] YU, DML, UBCHINA Archives, College Files, 劉王立明 [Liu Wang Liming], 劉公湛恩之生平 [The life of Dr. Herman C. E. Liu], in *One-Year Anniversary of the Death of Dr. Herman C. E. Liu*, 1.

[39] 劉湛恩 [Liu Zhan'en], 中國教育之將來 [The future of Chinese education], 上海青年 [Shanghai Youth] 34 (1930).

[40] 劉湛恩 [Liu Zhan'en], 公民教育運動計劃 [Scheme for Citizenship Education Campaign] (Qingnian Xiehui Shuju, 1925); idem, 公民與民治 [Citizenship and people's rule] (Qingnian Xiehui Shuju, 1926); idem, 五年來之公民教育運動 [Five years of the Citizenship Education Campaign"], 青年進步 [Youth progress] 100 (1927): 244–49; idem, 民族復興與公民教育 [Nation's revival and citizenship education], 湖北教育月刊 [Hubei Education Monthly] 2, no. 5 (1935): 43–46.

[41] 劉湛恩 [Liu Zhan'en], 高級中學研究三民主義的方法 [Methods of studying the Three Principles of the People in high schools], *Jiaoyu Jikan* 4, no. 1 (1928).

[42] Methods of studying the Three Principles of the People in high schools.

[43] Mayling Soong Chiang, "'New Life' in China's Resistance," *China Christian Year Book*, 1938–39, 78.

ground in terms of their ideological objectives and personnel."[44] Liu's own vision and patriotism, as well as his close association with the YMCA and the National Christian Council (NCC), could have been important factors behind the university's active social engagement, determining to share the fate of the nation. On the other hand, this reveals a deep permeation of the nationalist ideology into all corners of society, a tendency of the nationalization of education. Liu and the university seemed not to be alert to implications of participating in the movement, which was "significantly suggestive of Italian Fascism."[45]

"More Christian"

From the outset, the university endeavored to create a Christian atmosphere by ensuring the Christian identity of all faculty members and the majority of the students. All subjects were taught from a Christian point of view, and all courses in Bible study, Christianity, and Christian ethics, as well as all religious activities, were made compulsory.[46] After becoming president, Liu continuously emphasized and enhanced the Christian character of the university, by seeking well-trained Christian teachers and making every effort to increase the number of Christian students.[47] He also launched a bureau of extension work to connect the university with churches and their "Baptist constituency" in China.[48]

J. B. Hipps regarded Liu himself as a "leading Chinese Baptist."[49] His fame and influence were not limited to the university but spread to a larger circle. For example, in 1930, the Baptist Alliance in China was organized at his suggestion.[50] He was one of the key figures in pushing a "forward movement" launched by the Baptist Alliance in 1936 and in organizing in the same year the Jiangsu Baptist Convention, which he served as president until 1938.[51] Liu's educational ideas were closely related to his Christian con-

---

[44] Xing Jun, *Baptized in the Fire of Revolution: The American Social Gospel and the YMCA in China, 1919–1937* (Bethlehem, PA: Lehigh University Press, 1996), 280–81.

[45] Jun, *Baptized in the Fire of Revolution*, 282.

[46] Hipps, *History*, 65. This was permitted since his stated goal was character formation.

[47] Hipps, *History*, 104–5.

[48] Hipps, *History*, 88–89.

[49] J. B. Hipps, "In Remembrance—Herman C. E. Liu: An Appreciation," *Chinese Recorder* 69, no. 4 (1938): 193.

[50] Hipps, "In Remembrance,"193.

[51] YU, DML, *In Memoriam: Dr. Herman C. E. Liu*, 5.

victions. He claimed that Christian education in China, "with Christ-like spirit of sacrifice," could "make a contribution" to Chinese society and "mark a new era in the history of education in China."[52]

Given the government's control of education, instead of conducting "religious education," Liu stressed "personality education," through which the university aimed at forging students with Christ-like characters. This was a general trend for Christian schools in order to maintain their Christian features after registration. To Liu, to make Christian schools "more Christian" required the four following steps:

> 1. Christian teachers and students "must live real Christian lives. It is up to them to create a Christian atmosphere and make it so contagious that all who come in contact with it cannot but be benefited by it."
>
> 2. "The teaching in Christian institutions should adhere to Christian principles" and Bible instruction and modern scientific thought should be "harmonized in the classroom."
>
> 3. The teaching staff should "vitalize their religious instruction as to make it attractive to the students and effective in leading them to Christ."
>
> 4. Christian schools "must have a Christian constituency to support and serve them" to be able to remain Christian.[53]

Based on such perspectives, Liu stressed the university as "a big family" (滬江大家庭) and encouraged organization of Christian fellowships, especially fellowships between teachers and students, and to strengthen the Christian atmosphere on campus.[54] It was reported that, in 1931, 95 percent of the faculty and 43 percent of students were Christians.[55] There were altogether twenty-eight Christian fellowships on campus with three hundred

---

[52] 劉湛恩 [Liu Zhan'en], 近今美國之教育運動及其民眾對於國外宣教事業的態度 [The recent educational movement in America and people's attitude towards foreign missions], *Jiaoyu Jikan* 10, no. 3 (1934).

[53] H. C. E. Liu, "Christian Education in China," *Chinese Recorder* 59, no. 12 (1928): 763–66.

[54] 滬江大學三十週年紀念 [Thirty years anniversary of the University of Shanghai], 7.

[55] *Bulletin of the University of Shanghai*, July 1931, 4.

members, two hundred of whom were Christians and one hundred non-Christians.[56]

The university's emphasis on personality education had to work alongside the government-enforced nationalist education on the Three Principles of the People. As mentioned previously, for Liu these two types of education did not conflict with each other. However, his understanding of the Three Principles of the People took an ethical approach in shaping citizenship in China, which bore the color of social gospel teaching and liberal and progressive ideas. This fundamentally differed from the intention of the "party transformation education,"[57] which aimed at incorporating Christian education into the national educational system to serve the party's political purposes. The two would severely conflict with each other when the government's control over Christian education tightened.

"More Efficient"

The goal of "more efficient" reveals a strong influence of early-twentieth-century American educational theories, especially John Dewey's "social efficiency" as an educational aim, which links education with social application and contribution.[58] As some scholars have pointed out, the development of the University of Shanghai manifests how reforms in American educational philosophies and practice during the late nineteenth and early twentieth centuries made an impact on modern Chinese education.[59] For instance, the curriculum and organization of the university had gradually become more vocationally oriented.[60]

---

[56] "Report of the Christian Universities" Group to the Conference on Religious Education, *Educational Review* (1931).

[57] Susan Rigdon, "National Salvation: Teaching Civic Duty in China's Christian Colleges," in *China's Christian Colleges*, 202–6.

[58] John Dewey, "My Pedagogic Creed," *School Journal* 54 (1897): 77–80.

[59] For example, 王立誠 [Wang Licheng], 美國文化滲透與近代中國教育—滬江大學的歷史 [American cultural penetration and the modern education of China: A history of the University of Shanghai] (Shanghai: Fudan University Press, 2001); 朱嫿玥 [Zhu Huayue], 美國南北浸會在華教會大學的地方化實踐—以滬江大學職業化教育為例 [The localization of the Christian University of ABMU and SBC: A case study of the vocational education of the University of Shanghai"] (MA diss., Shanghai Academy of Social Sciences, 2016).

[60] It had developed from a replica of the pattern of American arts colleges since 1908, to a "group system" (language and education, social sciences, natural sciences, and religion) in 1916, and to a college system after registration (College of Arts, College of

As noted previously, education was expected to serve the GMD's political need for reinforcing a centralized government and spreading nationalist ideology. The university attempted to accommodate its own vision and practice with the government's policy by emphasizing its educational function in improving *Minsheng* (people's livelihood).[61] This enabled the university to take advantage of its vocational education and social service, which the university had stressed since establishment. These were also Herman Liu's lifelong concerns, which not only were largely related to his early life experience and his pragmatic character, but also bore the mark of the educational philosophy of his mentor in Columbia University, Paul Monroe.[62] The most prominent case of making the university more efficient was the development of the College of Commerce, which became one of the university's most advanced subjects. Largely owing to Liu's initiative, a Downtown School of Commerce was established in 1932 to provide evening classes for young men and women to prepare for business positions, which were in high demand in the Shanghai area.[63] Additionally, the Yangtsepoo Social Centre started to serve industrial communities in northeast Shanghai as early as the era of the university's founding.[64] The university encouraged social application of knowledge, with the aim of rendering "real service" to the communities and the nation.[65] Through social application, the university formed and expanded its social network. By 1936 the total number of alumni reached 905,[66] a great number of whom played active roles in all walks of life and contributed to building a "new China."

The university's vocational focus and social engagement reflect the belief that the ideas of pragmatism and progressivism, which developed in early twentieth-century America, met the needs of a transforming and professionalized Chinese society. The vocational focus and social engagement

---

Science, and College of Commerce). See White, "Christian College in China," 72; YU, DML, University of Shanghai, "Liu and University," 8.

[61] Wang, *American Cultural Penetration*, 246–50.

[62] Wang, *American Cultural Penetration*, 202–3.

[63] Liu corresponded several times with Hu Shi (胡適), one of the best-known Chinese educators in the republican era, regarding the planning of the downtown school of commerce. 劉湛恩致胡適函 [Herman Liu's letters to Hu Shih], in 劉湛恩文集 [Collections of Herman Liu] (Shanghai: Jiao Tong University Press, 2011), 197.

[64] YU, DML, UBCHINA Archives, College Files, University of Shanghai, "Liu and University," 10.

[65] White, "Christian College in China," 74.

[66] Hipps, *History*, 95.

were also attempts to negotiate the government's policy, based on its own Christian convictions on social service, colored by liberal-humanist theology and social gospel teachings. However, this more liberal approach caused the Baptist missions much concern.[67] To some extent, this demonstrates a tendency toward secularization of Christian education with high social goals in both China and America.

Herman Liu himself was trained as an educator, and his perspective on the development of the university was one of the key factors in making the university outstanding among various government or private colleges and universities. By 1936, the school's thirtieth anniversary, the university had incorporated a college, a secondary school, a primary school, a downtown school of commerce, a well-established social center, and a village and community center. The total enrolment was 2,834, including 627 in college, 399 in middle school, and 140 in elementary school. The faculty had increased from six in 1906 to sixty-six, of whom forty were Chinese and twenty-two American.[68] Herman Liu's presidency ended in 1938, not because of the completion of his service but due to a tragic assassination, which was believed to be premeditated by the Japanese authorities, for Liu was well known for his patriotism and loyalty to the Chinese government:

> Assassins fatally shot Dr. Herman C. E. Liu, president of the University of Shanghai, at 8:30 o'clock this morning as he stood at the corner of Bubbling Well and Majestic Roads with his young son and a sister-in-law, waiting for an eastbound bus which was just drawing to the curb.... He was pronounced dead at Pauline Hospital fifteen minutes later.[69]

The Baptist world expressed its grief at the funeral service on April 9, 1938, at which it was reported that over four thousand ordinary Chinese people attended: "A Chinese patriot, an educational leader, a true Christian, a man of vision and statesmanship, his cruel murder causes grief around the world."[70]

---

[67] SMA, Q242-66, G. Poteat to H. C. E. Liu, July 29, 1935; Y. C. Tu to G. Poteat, August 3, 1935.

[68] Hipps, *History*, 95.

[69] *Evening Post and Mercury*, April 8, 1938.

[70] YU, DML, UBCHINA Archives, College Files, "Resolution Adopted by the Foreign Mission Board of the Southern Baptist Convention," in *In Memoriam: Dr. Herman C. E. Liu, University of Shanghai*, April 7, 1939, 10.

Conclusion

"More Christian, more Chinese, and more efficient"—the goal of the University of Shanghai brought forward by President Herman Liu—to a large extent describes the nature of the forty-six-year history of the evolution of the University of Shanghai, as well as the interaction between the Baptists, the gospel, and Chinese society and culture.[71]

First, the history of the University of Shanghai reflects the trend of the evolution of an educational institution, from a Baptist background to a more general and diverse character, and from Western to Chinese. The four decades witnessed the growth of Chinese leadership over the university, particularly significant in the aftermath of the Anti-Christian Movement. The history is a story of the university getting closely involved in Chinese society and rooting itself deeply in the Chinese soil, which can be seen as a natural step given the growth of the "selfhood" of Christianity in early-twentieth-century China. On the other hand, the university's registration process in the face of nationalist challenges reveals that the sociopolitical context did not provide churches and Christian schools with much space to make their own choices. The Sinicization of the university, in this regard, was also an obliged response to a politically hostile environment.

Second, "more Chinese" and "more Christian" describe the dual character of the university. While making itself more indigenous and relevant to Chinese society, the university also kept and emphasized its Christian essence. The national government determined to de-Christianize mission schools through enforcing party transformation education as a replacement for religious teachings.[72] The University of Shanghai, however, was quite exceptional during this process by reinforcing and further enhancing its Christian character. The university also kept close connection with churches and its Baptist constituency. This may have had much to do with President Liu's own vision, and the university being the sole denominational university.

Third, the case of Herman Liu, as manifested through his vision and practice in Christian education in China, reflects a contextual understanding of the Christian message and its social application, which many Chinese Christian intellectuals and metropolitan elites adopted. Influenced by social

[71] Christian education came to an end in 1952 when the Communist Party expelled all foreign missionaries.

[72] Rigdon, "National Salvation," 202–6.

gospel teachings and a metropolitan intellectual elitist culture,[73] the emphasis on social transformation through the application of an ethical Christianity became a common vision and mind-set of the YMCA activists in early-twentieth-century China. Interestingly, many of the leaders were educated at the University of Chicago or Columbia University, where Liu studied.[74] By engaging Christian teachings and ethics in the theme of "national salvation," Christian leaders intended to seek common ground between Christianity and China's reality, to demonstrate the positive role that Christianity could possibly play in China's quest for national salvation and reconstruction, and to solve Chinese Christians' identity crisis between being a citizen of China and a citizen of the kingdom of God. When the crisis became more acute, however, national identity took priority over Christian identity. Liu's convictions played a significant part in keeping the university both more Chinese and more Christian. Nonetheless, Liu's effort in bridging Christianity and the fate of China did not convince most non-Christian intellectuals and the nationalists, as fully demonstrated in the communist reorganization of Christian higher education. Christian education eventually came to an end in communist China in 1952, when all foreign missions were expelled from the mainland.[75]

In sum, Christian education in China created great opportunities for the missions, including the Baptist mission, to be involved in and to influence Chinese society in wider and deeper ways. Christian education in fact played a significant part in China's process toward modernization during the late nineteenth and early twentieth centuries, but was then excluded by the nationalists. Christian education provided a platform for the interaction between missions, the gospel, and Chinese society and culture, and it could also turn into a battlefield when missions and the gospel conflicted with Chinese society and culture.

---

[73] Bob Whyte, *Unfinished Encounter: China and Christianity* (Glasgow: W. Collins Sons, 1988), 156–57.

[74] The leaders included such men as Tu Yuqing (涂羽卿), professor at the University of Shanghai, president of St. John's University, and general secretary of YMCA in China; Tao Xingzhi (陶行知), Chinese educator and reformer; Wu Yaozong (Y. T. Wu, 吴耀宗), YMCA secretary and advocate for the social gospel and the Three-Self Patriotic Movement in China [TSPM]; and Ting Guangxun (K.H. Ting, 丁光训), YCMA activist and chair of the TSPM.

[75] Lutz, *China and Christian Colleges*, 473–84.

23

Baptist Warriors Who Changed the World: Latin America, the Moral Majority, and Reagan's Foreign Policy

Ivan Dias da Silva

In the third installment of the six-hour 2007 miniseries *God's Warriors*,[1] called "God's Christian Warriors: Evangelicals,"[2] British Iranian journalist and television host Christiane Amanpour, CNN's chief international correspondent, featured the powerful political influence of the evangelical Christian leaders in the United States who seek to reorder the culture and the seats of power in America to include God and religion into everyday social routines and the government.

A similar bellicose term had been used by sociologist Nancy Tatom Ammerman in her book *Baptist Battles: Social Change and Religious Conflict in the Southern Baptist Convention* (1990), winner of the 1992 Society for the Scientific Study of Religion Distinguished Book Award. In this book, Ammerman "provides a historical and sociological context to unfold the historical events and issues that have dramatically changed the shape of Southern Baptists" in the 1980s.[3] During the same decade, Jerry Falwell, the independent (and, later, Southern) Baptist pastor from Lynchburg, Virginia, used to say that "a fundamentalist is an evangelical who is angry about

---

[1] *CNN Presents: God's Warriors* is a three-part August 2007 "CNN Presents" documentary produced by Christiane Amanpour in which she examines the rise of religious fundamentalism as a political force in the world. The documentary was filmed in the United States, Europe, and the Middle East. It focuses on the three major monotheistic religions of the world: Judaism, Christianity, and Islam.

[2] "Amanpour: Christian warriors," https://edition.cnn.com/videos/international/2012/08/23/amanpour-christian-warriors-a.cnn (accessed July 1, 2018).

[3] Nancy Tatom Ammerman, *Baptist Battles: Social Change and Religious Conflict in the Southern Baptist Convention* (New Brunswick, NJ: Rutgers University Press, 1990).

something."[4] In accordance with this assertion, but in a more accurate statement, Marsden declares,

> An American fundamentalist is an evangelical who is militant in opposition to liberal theology in the churches or to changes in cultural values or mores, such as those associated with "secular humanism." In either the long or short definitions, fundamentalists are a subtype of evangelicals and militancy is crucial to their outlook. Fundamentalists are not just religious conservatives; they are conservatives who are willing to take a stand and to fight.[5]

Barry Hankins observed,

> The traditionalists and conservatives become known as "fundamentalists" in 1920, when a Baptist preacher and magazine editor coined the term. Curtis Lee Laws of the *Watchman Examiner* said that a fundamentalist was one who was ready to do "*battle royal*" for the fundamentals of the faith.[6]

Fundamentalism brought division to Baptists. In a book Walter Shurden called this division "the struggle for the soul of the SBC."[7] This chapter addresses the influence of evangelical activism on Baptists in Brazil. It is divided in three parts: Brazilian Baptists learning how to battle for the faith, how to battle for the culture, and how to understand U.S. president Ronald Reagan's foreign policy.

Brazilian Baptists Learn How to Battle for the Faith

The first Baptist missionary couple sent by the Southern Baptist Convention's (SBC) Missionary Agency to Brazil was Jefferson Thomas Bowen (1814–1875), who had previously worked in Nigeria (1850–1856), and his wife, Laurenna Henrietta Davis Bowen (1832–1907). During his time on the African continent, Bowen had learned the Yoruba dialect and had even written an English-*yorubá* dictionary. Following his return to the United States, Bowen determined in 1860 to go as a pioneer missionary to Brazil,

---

[4] George Marsden, *Understanding Fundamentalism and Evangelicalism* (Grand Rapids: Eerdmans, 1991), 1.

[5] This description is found on the cover of Marsden's book (emphasis added).

[6] Barry Hankins, ed., *Evangelicalism and Fundamentalism: A Documentary* (New York: New York University Press, 2008), 5 (emphasis added).

[7] Walter Shurden, *The Struggle for the Soul of the SBC: Moderate Responses to the Fundamentalist Movement* (Macon, GA: Mercer University Press, 1994).

the largest South American country. Since he was fluent in the *yorubá* dialect, the American missionary opened a specific Sunday school with the purpose of sharing the gospel with the African slaves in Brazil and prepare black preachers to share the good news. Slave owners called this to the attention of the Brazilian authorities, who limited Bowen's work in the country.[8] Due to restrictions imposed by the Brazilian government, the opposition of the Roman Catholic Church, divergences with the Richmond Board regarding methods of missionary work, and his poor personal health, Bowen returned to the United States in 1861, where he disseminated the idea that Brazil was not a good country to invest in foreign missions.

Bowen's return to the United States coincided with the beginning of the Civil War (1861–1865). After the war between the Union and the Confederate states, with its accompanying economic recession, many Confederates left their nation and immigrated to other countries; many came to Brazil, where they found fertile soil to plant familiar crops such as cotton, corn, and watermelon. They settled at first in the cities of Santa Bárbara d'Oeste and Americana (both in São Paulo state). Among the group of Americans in Santa Bárbara d'Oeste were a number of Baptists who established the first Baptist church on Brazilian soil in September 10, 1871, with twenty-three members, including Richard Ratcliff (1831–1912), their pastor. But this was an English-speaking church for the settlers.

General Alexander Travis Hawthorne visited Brazil, saw the religious opportunities, and encouraged the opening of a Southern Baptist mission for Brazilians. In late 1880, in a worship service at the First Baptist Church of Waco, Texas, William Buck Bagby and Anne Luther Bagby[9] were commissioned as the first Southern Baptist missionaries to Brazil. They arrived

---

[8] The Brazilian authorities and the slave owners accused Bowen of trying to convert the "poor black slaves" and establish in Brazil an alternative sect. The first Baptist American missionary stayed in Brazil for just eight months and nineteen days, from May 21, 1860, to February 9, 1861. See Betty Antunes de Oliveira, *Centelha em restolho secco: uma contribuição para a história des primórdios de trabalho Batista no Brasil* (São Paulo: Vida Nova, 2005), 105-31, here 108, and Zaqueu Moreira de Oliveira, *Um Povo chamado Batista: história e princípios.* 2ª edição revista e corrigida (Recife: Kairós Editora, 2011), 103–4; also see José dos Reis Pereira, *Breve história dos Batistas.* 3ª edição (Rio de Janeiro: Juerp, 1987). 88.

[9] William Buck Bagby (1855–1936) and Anne Luther Bagby (1859–1942) married in Texas on October 21, 1880. They had nine children, of whom five survived and were also missionaries (Ermine, Taylor Crawford, Alice Anne, Helen Edna, and Albert Ian). The Bagby couple dedicated their lives full-time to the missions work in Brazil. In addition to being missionaries they were also educators and denominational leaders (Oliveira, *Centelha em restolho secco*, 306–11).

in the country on March 8, 1881. After six weeks on board the ship, when William Bagby saw the shape of the Brazilian mountains, near Rio de Janeiro, he said to his wife, "Anne, Brazil for me is a giant. Gigantic in territory, in minerals, in the production of coffee and sugar, but it is a giant that sleeps spiritually, and God has sent us here to awaken it from its sleep."[10] William Bagby became the pastor of the First Baptist Church in Santa Bárbara d'Oeste and began to learn the Portuguese language with Antonio Teixeira de Albuquerque, an ex–Roman Catholic priest, who was the first Brazilian to adopt the Baptist faith and the first Brazilian Baptist pastor.[11]

With the cooperation of another couple of American missionaries who arrived in Brazil in 1882, Zachary Clay Taylor (1851–1919) and Katherine Crawford Taylor (1862–1894), the Bagbys organized the first Portuguese-speaking church in the country with the assistance of Albuquerque. This church was established in Salvador city, Bahia, on October 15, 1882. Describing the progress of the Baptist work in Brazil, Pereira wrote,

> In four years, there were already four Baptist churches in Brazil. In these eighty years [since the founding of the Brazilian Baptist Convention in 1907][12] all of them [the four churches] have had an enormous importance in the progress of the Baptist work in Brazil.... Over the years the Brazilian Baptist Convention is getting stronger continuously. Its meetings have become a model of inspiration and encouragement. New service agencies were created to improve the implementation of the work. In addition, the State Conventions, to coordinate the cooperative efforts of the existing churches in each State have been also created on similar basis of the national Convention [Brazilian Baptist Convention]. Therefore, large and expensive undertakings, as for example, the sending of missionaries to the Brazilian hinterland and to foreign countries, the founding of seminaries and orphanages, the intense evangelization, became possible because the churches have joined their efforts in favor of the general work.

---

[10] Helena Bagby Harrison, *O gigante que dorme: biografia de William Buck Bagby. Série missionária heróis cristãos* (Rio de Janeiro: UFMBB, 2001), 5.

[11] Oliveira, *Um Povo chamado Batista*, 108.

[12] José dos Reis Pereira, *Breve Historía dos Batistas*, 3rd ed. (Rio de Janeiro: JUERP, 1987), 92,96. The four churches he mentions are FBC Salvador (October 15, 1882), FBC Rio de Janeiro (August 24, 1884), FBC Maceió (May 17, 1885), and FBC Recife (April 4, 1886).

At the same time that the mission work experienced advance, persecution was also present and growing.[13] As Pereira states, "In that time of [Brazilian] Empire, the Catholic Church was linked to the State and many times the authorities, attending the requests of the priests and friars, intervened in the activities of the preachers of the gospel."[14] The first incident happened when William Bagby and Zachary Taylor were preparing to baptize two converted ladies on the beach. A crowd of people circled the missionaries and began to threaten and intimidate them. One of the persecutors held Bagby by the collar and punched his face. The next day Bagby and Taylor went back to the beach to conduct another worship service and once again the crowd stood around them and threw wet sand and little rocks at them. When the police officer arrived at the place, he defended the aggressors instead of the missionaries. In a similar situation, Bagby was preaching in a home and was hit by a rock that left him unconscious. Taylor, who was absent that time, visited his partner and said to him, "Bagby, that injury is more horrible than I've ever seen. How I would like to have been there too. I'd rather have acquired an injury the same way that you did than to receive the crown of any king of Europe."[15]

In a letter sent from Rio de Janeiro to the SBC's Foreign Mission Board, dated March 15, 1860, Ashbel Green Simonton, a missionary of the Presbyterian Mission Board, had already explained that the influence of the Catholic clergy would be an obstacle to the Protestant evangelization in Brazil.[16] Baptist missionary to Brazil Elias Hoton Quillin[17] wrote to the Foreign Mission Board,

> The [Brazilian] government though constitutionally liberal and tolerant, it is, in its administration, strictly Catholic, and even though the persecution is forbidden by law, there are many places that could be highlighted by the fire of the Inquisition. The Imperial Constitution

---

[13] Bill J. Leonard, *Baptist Ways: A History* (Valley Forge, PA: Judson Press, 2003), 256. Leonard notes that "when the Portuguese empire fell to the Brazilian republic in 1889, there were four churches claiming a membership of some three hundred converts."

[14] Pereira, *O Jornal Batista*, 83.

[15] Harrison, *O gigante que dorme: biografia de William Buck Bagby*, 10-12.

[16] Oliveira, *Centelha em restolho secco*, 424–25.

[17] Among the Baptist immigrants who settled in Santa Bárbara d'Oeste (SP), four of them were pastors—in addition to Quillin (founder of Second Baptist Church in Brazil) were Richard Ratcliff (founder of First Baptist Church in Brazil), Robert Porter Thomas (who was an interim minister of the two mentioned churches), and Samuel M. Pyles (who eventually preached in both churches). See Oliveira, *Centelha em restolho secco,* 469.

> permits the exercise of all religions, but it guarantees and protects Catholicism. All the staff, from the Emperor to the less categorized ones, are admittedly Catholics, and swear to protect the established religion. And there are many of this group that use the religion as a political force.[18]

Catholics persecuted Masons as well as Protestants "because its ideals were practically identical," that it is to say, Masons held "Republican ideals such as religious freedom, progress, and education."[19] Beyond the common ideals, Vieira highlights that other motives helped create the rapprochement between Protestants and Masons. For example, both held an appreciation for the Holy Bible,[20] which for Lyra is the source of the largest part of the Masonic philosophy.[21] As Oliveira notes, a considerable number of the American immigrants who went to Brazil to begin a colony were Masons, where "in 1874, excited and hopeful, they founded [in Santa Bárbara d'Oeste] the 'George Washington' Masonic Lodge, under the leadership of Hutchinson Norris, who was elected the Venerable."[22]

According to Crabtree, despite not having a religious creed, Masonry always protected religious freedom, worked for a liberal government, and stood beside the evangelical movements in Brazil.[23] For this reason it joined forces to battle the Catholic power that persecuted the Protestants. A converted Jew, Salomon Ginsburg (1867–1927),[24] a Mason who became a mis-

---

[18] Oliveira, *Centelha em restolho secco*, 469. The defense of religious freedom would be official in Brazil from November 11, 1889, with the Proclamation of the Republic that established the republican-presidential system of government.

[19] José Pereira Sobreiro, *A contribuição da maçonaria para a consolidação do protestantismo no Brasil* (Ciberteologia—Revista de Teologia & Cultura—Ano XI, n. 52, 2015). 99, 92.

[20] Davi Gueiros Vieira, *O protestantismo, a maçonaria, e a questão religiosa no Brasil* (Brasília: Editora Universidade de Brasília, 1980), 47.

[21] Buarque Jorge Lyra, *A maçonaria e o cristianismo,* 5ª ed. (Niterói: Gráf. Ed. Aurora, 1970), 121, 228.

[22] Oliveira, *Centelha em restolho secco,* 72.

[23] A. R. Crabtree, *A história dos batistas do Brasil até 1906* (Rio de Janeiro: Casa Publicadora Batista, 1962), 47.

[24] Salomon Louis Ginsburg was a Jew who was born in Poland and raised in Germany and England; he was completely rejected by his family when he became a Christian. Feeling that he was called to preach, Salomon studied and presented himself to a missionary society, being sent to Portugal, where he began to learn the Portuguese language. From there he was sent to Brazil as a Congregational Church missionary, where he met American Baptist missionary Zachary Taylor and was convinced to adopt the Baptist faith. Ginsburg became a Baptist preacher and was appointed as a missionary of the Foreign Mission Board of the

sionary of the Richmond Board, describes in his autobiography how often the Masons saved him from oppositions and difficulties.[25] Lyra reports that on many occasions the Masons acted on behalf of the Protestants, delivering them from death, supplying their needs, and ensuring the freedom of belief and conscience in the country.[26] In the beginning of the Baptists' work in Brazil, various denominational meetings, such as for the issue of letters to the Foreign Mission Board and the ordination to the pastoral ministry of Antonio Teixeira de Albuquerque, took place in a Masonic lodge.[27] Sobreiro judges that, through Masonic assistance, God was assuring "that the mission could succeed in Brazilian soil."[28] Ribeiro declares, "For the Protestants all support that they received from Masonry was welcomed, because it enabled the success of the mission in Brazilian land and it was understood as an effort in favor of the gospel."[29] In the new Brazilian setting, Protestants and Masons shared cultural values in opposition to the majority Roman Catholic culture.

In 1884 the Bagbys left the Taylors and Albuquerque in Salvador, and headed to Rio de Janeiro, the capital of Brazil at that time. One month later an Irish lady named Mary O'Rorke and a British woman named Elizabeth Williams (who offered her home as a place to meet) established on August 24, 1884, the First Baptist Church of Rio de Janeiro, the second Portuguese-speaking church in the country.

After six years as the pastor of the church in Rio, Bagby was succeeded by Francisco Fulgêncio Soren, the first Baptist Brazilian pastor with formal training, who led the church from 1900 to 1933.[30] When he left the ministry

---

Southern Baptist Convention. He preached in many places across the country during almost forty years. Ginsburg was also a singer and writer. The missionary translated more than a hundred hymns and composed others that are part of the Brazilian Baptist Hymnal. (Pereira, *Breve Historía dos Batistas*, 92-93.

[25] Salomão Ginsburg, *Um judeu errante no Brasil* (Rio de Janeiro: Casa Publicadora Batista, 1970), 82.

[26] Lyra, *A maçonaria e o cristianismo*, 251.

[27] Oliveira, *Centelha em restolho secco*, 182, 703; also Oliveira, *Um Povo chamado Batista*, 107.

[28] Sobreiro, *A contribuição da maçonaria para a consolidação do protestantismo no Brasil*, 100.

[29] Boanerges Ribeiro, *Protestantismo e cultura brasileira* (São Paulo: Casa Editora Presbiteriana, 1981), 303.

[30] Francisco Fulgêncio Soren (1869–1933), born in São Gonçalo (Rio de Janeiro), was the son of Pierre Soren, a French goldsmith, and a Portuguese mother, Candida Pires Soren. F. F. Soren was converted to Protestantism in 1890 during the pastoral ministry of William

at First Baptist Church of Rio, William and his wife, Anne, went to the United States for a one-year furlough. Following that, they returned to Brazil to open a new mission work in São Paulo state. There the Bagbys opened a Baptist school to evangelize children and established churches in many cities of the state. The Brazilian Baptist School in São Paulo (SP) was bought by Anne Bagby in 1902 from a Presbyterian lady, Mary Ellis McIntyre, with thirty-two students, and was called at that time the Brazilian Progress School. This academic institution was a success, and Anne Bagby served as its director until 1919.[31] The school has been operating for 117 years and is still open.[32]

When William Bagby was seventy-two years old, he and his wife moved to Porto Alegre in the south of Brazil to help their daughter Alice and her husband, Harley Smith, open a Baptist school there in 1926, working with them for almost twelve years.[33] After fifty-eight years of ministry in Brazil, William Bagby died in Porto Alegre city on August 5, 1939, at age eighty-three, having arrived at age twenty-five. After the death of her husband, Anne Bagby moved to the northern area of the country, Recife, Permanbuco (PE), to live with her daughter Helen. There Anne died on December 24, 1942, at age eighty-four. She had arrived in Brazil at age twenty-three.

Buck Bagby at FBC Rio de Janeiro and soon developed abilities for preaching. He came to the United States, where he studied for eight years at William Jewell College and Southern Baptist Theological Seminary (see Lewis Malen Bratcher, *Francisco Fulgêncio Soren: intérprete de Cristo em muitas terras*, trans. Israel Belo de Azevedo [Rio de Janeiro: JUERP, 1985], 15, 39–40). Returning to Brazil, Soren became the pastor of the church where he was converted (which during his ministry became the largest Baptist church in Latin America), from where he exercised a denominational leadership that lasted more than thirty years. F. F. Soren soon became a prominent leader on the Baptist Brazilian scene. He was the first president of the Baptist Brazilian Convention, established in 1907, and reappointed in 1908, 1909, and 1916. Dr. F. F. Soren married American Jane Filson, and after his death at age sixty-four, he was succeeded by one of his sons, João Filson Soren, pastor of the First Baptist Church of Rio for fifty-one years (1933–1985) (see Pereira, *Breve Historía dos Batistas,* 95, 97; see also Othon Ávila Amaral and Celso Aloísio Santos Barbosa, *O livro de ouro da CBB: epopéia de fé, lutas e vitórias* [Rio de Janeiro: JUERP, 2007], 40–41).

[31] Oliveira, *Centelha em restolho secco,* 370, 311.

[32] "Institucional," https://batistabrasileiro.com.br/conteudo.php?p=institucional (accessed January 23, 2019).

[33] The Baptist School of Porto Alegre (RS) was established in February 1926 and continues to operate with success ninety-three years after its founding

("O Colégio," http://colegiobatista.org.br/ocolegio/historia/ (accessed January 23, 2019).

This year (2019) will be the 137th anniversary of the founding of the First Baptist Church of Salvador, Bahia (BA), but it is no longer a member of the Brazilian Baptist Convention (BBC). The church passed through two doctrinal divisions over Pentecostalism. First it became a Pentecostal Baptist church, and more recently the Pentecostal community divided and a new neo-Pentecostal group assumed control of the church; its leaders are a couple of "apostles," Milton Ebenézer and Niara Souza. This is significant because the first Baptist church established in Brazil is no longer a traditional Baptist church, but a neo-Pentecostal one; consequently, the Brazilian Baptist Convention no longer recognizes this church as part of the Convention. Clearly, Pentecostalism has changed Protestant culture in Brazil and significantly influenced Baptists.

According to the official Brazilian Census 2010, the country had 3,723,853 Baptists, divided into many different subgroups.[34] Leonard says, "At the end of the twentieth century, there were at least fourteen distinct Brazilian Baptist groups, some located in a single congregation."[35]

The oldest and largest Baptist Convention is the Brazilian Baptist Convention, established in 1907.[36] In 2018 it had 8,753 churches, 4,944 missions and 1,706,003 members (representing about 0.8 percent of Brazil's 208.5 million population[37]). The other major Conventions are the National Baptist Convention (NBC, Pentecostal orientation), established in 1967 (the fruit of a division inside the BBC), in 2015 having 2,271 churches, about 2,000 missions, and 412,750 members, and the Convention of the

[34] In 2010 the population of Brazil was 190.7 million ("Censo 2010: Número de católicos cai e aumenta evangélicos, espíritas e sem religião," https://censo2010.ibge.gov.br/noticias-censo.html?busca=1&id=3&idnoticia=2170&t=censo-2010-numero-catolicos-cai-aumenta-evangelicos-espiritas-sem-religiao&view=noticia [accessed September 1, 2019]).

[35] Leonard, *Baptist Ways*, 257.

[36] Between Census 2000 and 2010, Brazilian Baptists grew 17.74 percent between the groups referred as "evangelicals of mission" ("Entre os pentecostais, os batistas e adventistas cresceram no Brasil," April 27, 2013, https://institutoparacleto.org/2013/04/27/entre-os-pentecostais-os-batistas-e-adventistas-cresceram-no-brasil).

[37] "Quem Somos," July 17, 2018, http://www.convencaobatista.com.br/siteNovo/ pagina.php?MEN_ID=19; "Estatísticas dos Batistas da CBB—2016," http://igrejamultiplicadora.org.br/new/estatisticas-dos-batistas-da-cbb-2016/ (accessed September 1, 2018); "População brasileira ultrapassa 208 milhões de pessoas, revela IBGE, http://www.brasil.gov.br/noticias/cidadania-e-inclusao/2018/08/populacao-brasileira-ultrapassa-208-milhoes-de-pessoas-revela-ibge (accessed January 24, 2019).

Independent Baptist Churches, established in 1952, which had 800 churches and 68,000 members in 2013.[38]

The BBC faced two great challenges in its first 135 years. The first significant conflict happened in the 1920s, rooted in the prior decade, beginning at the North of Brazil Baptist Theological Seminary in Recife, when some Brazilian pastors questioned sharply the American missionaries' form of leadership. This movement was called "Radical" or the "North movement." It reflected some of the world's typical tendencies of upheavals against American imperialism (the military, cultural, and economic influence of the United States on other countries). But it was also a perception that the Baptist work in Brazil was already mature enough to have more national leadership, without being dependent on other foreign missions. Anderson writes,

> An objective, missiological evaluation of this period reveals that the FMBSBC [Foreign Mission Board of the Southern Baptist Convention], as its highly dedicated, capable core of missionaries, unconsciously and with good intention, sparked many of the conflicts of the period due to its insensibility to the growing spirit of nationalism in Brazil. It insisted on unilateral control of personnel and funds, plus overall hegemony in the development of national work.[39]

Those who supported the cause against the American missionaries became known as "radicals," and all who advocated the missionaries' position were "constructives." The movement became broader and reached all the northeast of Brazil, and other areas of the country. The radicals began a new Baptist school and seminary in Recife, and also founded the Brazilian Baptist Association, which operated until 1938 when it was dissolved, "bearing in mind that the New Basis of Cooperation [between the nationals and Americans], that had been approved by the BBC in 1936 met with the missionary expectations of the dissidents' group." Then the churches that had turned away from the BBC returned to it.[40] According to Anderson,

---

[38] "Nossa história," http://www.cibi.org.br/nossa-historia/ (accessed January 23, 2019.

[39] Justice Anderson, *An Evangelical Saga: Baptists and Their Precursors in Latin America* (Maitland, FL: Xulon Press, 2005), 158.

[40] Oliviera, *Um Povo chamado Batista: história e princípios*, 146.

> W. C. Taylor[41] became the champion of the devolution of leadership to the nationals. He had several violent clashes with his missionary colleagues, but he seemed to be one of the first missionaries to catch and promote a unified, integrated Baptist work under national direction and leadership.[42]

With W. C. Taylor's help the national leadership of the BBC was confirmed. Anderson affirms that "although this period was characterized by internal controversies, fomented by a mixture of missionary paternalism and national sectionalism, there was a steady numerical growth and increased evangelistic fervor among Baptist churches."[43]

The second great challenge for Baptists in Brazil was Spiritual Renovation. This was a Pentecostal movement among the Baptists in the 1960s that caused the largest division in the history of the BBC. The so-called Renovation movement emphasized charismatic worship, glossolalia, and the baptism of the Holy Spirit as a second blessing (after conversion). Leonard affirms that "these practices created a schism and the foundation of a new denomination, the National Baptist Convention, with connections to the Baptist World Alliance and the ABC-USA."[44]

Many people believe that the forerunner of this movement was American missionary Rosalee Mills Appleby (1895–1991), who spoke and wrote about the need of a spiritual revival in Brazil. Appleby began a radio program called *Spiritual Renovation* in Belo Horizonte city, that was heard in 1960 by Pr. José Rego do Nascimento of Lagoinha Baptist Church in Belo Horizonte, who is known as the founder of the Renovation movement. In 1962 the BBC elected a commission with theologians on both sides of the controversy within the BBC: "renovationists" and "traditionalists." This group became known as "Commission of the 13," and in the very first year of the commission's work, Nascimento and Enéas Tognini, the key leaders

---

[41] William Carey Taylor (1883–1971) was a Southern Baptist missionary in Brazil. He published the *Doctrinal Courier* (*Correio Doutrinal*) for the constructive orientation of the churches that continued to cooperate with the BBC and was an author of a grammar of the Greek New Testament and a Greek Dictionary, both in Portuguese (A. R. Crabtree, *Baptistas in Brazil* [Rio de Janeiro: Baptist Publishing House of Brazil 1953], 174, 230; Oliveira, *Um Povo chamado Batista: história e princípios*, 143).

[42] Anderson, *Evangelical Saga*, 158.

[43] Anderson, *Evangelical Saga*, 158.

[44] Leonard, *Baptist Ways*, 256, 257.

of the Renovation, left the commission.[45] The final report of this commission was given in the BBC's Meeting of 1964,[46] and after much discussion, it was decided that the BBC would "cut off from its cooperative roll all churches that were excluded from the State Conventions for its practical-doctrinal identification with the Pentecostal-renovationist movement." These excluded churches gathered to found the National Baptist Convention in 1967.[47]

The most recent survey of the BBC reveals that the largest number of Baptists in Brazil is in Rio de Janeiro state (497,415 members in 2,882 churches and missions) and that São Paulo state is in second place (283,000 members in 1,676 churches and missions); both are located in the southeast of the country. The Brazilian state with the smallest number of Baptists is Amapá, in the north of the country, with 3,000 members in 55 churches and missions.[48] For a century, Baptists engaged varieties of cultural forms—Roman Catholics, Masons, Pentecostals—and American missionary practices. In the 1980s, still influenced by American precedents, they engaged in what became known as "culture wars."

Brazilian Baptists Engage in Cultural Warfare

The political lobbying organization called the Moral Majority was established and led by the fundamentalist evangelical pastor Jerry Falwell. This organization, which was the most prominent expression of the New Religious Right, flourished in the U.S. political landscape between 1979 and 1989 in an attempt to implement a theological agenda in the political arena, based on its religious and moral values. The Moral Majority's action prohibited outcomes that significantly modified the political dynamics of the United States. The Moral Majority considered that American society was under

---

[45] Enéas Tognini (1914–2015) was the first president of the National Baptist Convention. Author of more than forty books, Tognini established and was professor of the Theological Baptist College of São Paulo and of the National Baptist Theological Seminary of São Paulo State. He also established and led the People's Baptist Church. In 2009 Tognini was elected Honorary President of the Biblical Society of Brazil ("Morre aos 101 anos o pastor Enéas Tognini," https://www.ultimato.com.br/conteudo/morre-aos-101-anos-o-pastor-eneas-tognini [accessed January 27, 2019]).

[46] Oliveira, *Um Povo chamado Batista,* 147–49.

[47] Pereira, *Breve Historía,* 257.

[48] This information was published by the Convention in the book of its recent Annual Meeting (April 2018), which occurred in Poços de Caldas, Minas Gerais state (Livro da 98a. Assembleia da Convenção Batista Brasileira [Rio De Janeiro: CBB, 2018]).

the threat of "great evils" and acted to mobilize the conservative religious people who shared their perspectives. Whereas conservatives had generally kept religion and politics separate, they were now mobilized to engage in political action. This change created a new kind of sociopolitical cleavage and culture wars between different moral and religious understanding systems. Although dissolved at the end of the 1980s, the Moral Majority contributed significantly to polarization of American public life and culture, expressed nationally in the two major political parties.[49]

The Moral Majority was not just a Protestant coalition. There were Catholics and Jews on its staff. Among their ranks were people of all creeds, and even members of no religious circles. However, their common viewpoint was the conviction that "the majority of the people live their lives based on a moral code handed down from the founders of this country, a code which corresponds to the Ten Commandments," who also believed that the government was "listening and responding to the wishes of a vocal minority."[50] Describing the diversified composition of the Moral Majority, Flippen highlights that Falwell had

> now acknowledged the advantages of reaching across denominational lines. Just weeks before, he had met with Catholic cardinal John O'Connor, and the two had agreed that homosexuality and abortion were sins to battle. Nevertheless, Falwell still harbored reservations about Washington for Jesus. Even as [Pat] Robertson pressed for his involvement, Falwell replied that he feared the rally would fizzle, discrediting its architects. In fact, Falwell had other reasons, which he confessed in later years. "The rally appeared too heavily charismatic," he admitted, referring to the flamboyance of many charismatic pastors. "I was afraid of a loose cannon in an uncontrolled environment saying something that would hurt us." It was, in short, an admittance that, even as Washington for Jesus loomed, he still had problems overcoming the historic animosities that had divided the Christian

---

[49] Ivan Dias da Silva, *Jerry Fawell e a Maioria Moral: um estudo sobre a relação entre religião e política no espaço público americano entre 1979 e 1989.* Tese de Doutorado em Ciência da Religião (Universidade Federal de Juiz de Fora: Juiz de Fora, 2016), 139–42.

[50] Patricia Pingry, *Jerry Falwell, Man of Vision* (Milwaukee: Ideas Publishing Corporation, 1980), 6.

community. After the rally concluded, however, he never experienced any reluctance again. Falwell had, it appeared, learned his lesson.[51]

Jerry Falwell had lived all his religious experience as a separatist Christian, who did not worry about getting along with other kinds of Baptists, let alone with Methodists, Presbyterians or Catholics. "To be yoked together with unbelievers" for any reason was something even more unthinkable. However, the Moral Majority reversed this position in order to gain political power. According to the televangelist, such aggregation was possible because the Moral Majority was not structured as an evangelistic enterprise, nor even as a religious movement, but as a political organization that was linked to a moral agenda.

What, if any, was the influence of this American experience in Brazil? Camurça writes that the religious-political phenomenon of the Moral Majority in the United States

> bears much relationship with the Brazilian situation of the last years, which points to a growing and unstoppable expansion of the evangelicals and Pentecostals in Brazil's political and public space.…It must be acknowledged in the American example…thirty or forty years before, the current situation in Brazil of the conservative evangelical presence in national politics.[52]

In Brazil the evangelical groups that first took part in movements that aligned religion and politics during the 1990s were the Pentecostals, represented mainly by the Universal Church of the Kingdom of God, Assemblies of God, International Church of God's Grace, and Methodist and Baptist Pentecostals.[53] The Brazilian churches more closely related to historical Protestantism inherited the traditional theological perspective of the separation of church and politics, but the tradition within the Baptist group seems to be changing, expressing a reorientation of Baptist tradition.

---

[51] J. Brooks Flippen, *Jimmy Carter, the Politics of Family, and the Rise of the Religious Right* (Athens: University of Georgia Press, 2011), 5.

[52] Ivan Dias da Silva and Wilmar do Valle Barbosa, *Religião e Política nos Estados Unidos: Jerry Falwell e a presença do fundamentalismo evangélico no espaço público americano.* (Curitiba: Editora Prismas/Editora Appris, 2019), 7–8.

[53] Maria das Dores Campos Machado, "Aborto e ativismo religioso nas eleições de 2010," *Revista Brasileira de Ciência Política,* no. 7 (Brasília) (January–April 2012), http://www.scielo.br/scielo.php?pid=S0103-33522012000100003&script=sci_arttext(accessed February 4, 2014).

In the article "Iniquity or Neo-Fundamentalist Élan? Remarks about Religion and Politics in Brazil," Barbosa and Souza consider that a group of "evangelical Brazilian Baptists show a tendency to assume approaches of the American evangelical discourse, using a religion-politics agenda and similar strategies of action in the public space, organizing politically, bringing the politic to the pulpit and carrying the religious discourse to the public and political space."[54] The authors are referring to a position assumed by one of the most prominent Brazilian Baptist leaders in a video produced (available online and nationally distributed to evangelical churches on a CD) during the 2010 campaign for the presidency of Brazil.[55] In this video, Paschoal Piragine Júnior, pastor of the First Baptist Church of Curitiba (one of the largest of the country) and president of the BBC[56] at the time, takes a stand against what he calls "institutional iniquity"[57] and calls on the Brazilian Baptists not to vote for the Workers Party, which had held the nation's presidency for nine years. Barbosa and Souza write that, according to Piragine, "iniquity" means

> evil's dissemination and trivialization, since sin condemns one to an inclination to the practice of evil, namely, individuals, become used to the existence of the evil in the world and in their lives, because of the peaceful coexistence with frequent and repeated examples of evil, lose the capacity to perceive its presence in the society as the degradations deriving from it.[58]

---

[54] Wilmar do Valle Barbosa and Andréa Silveira de Souza, "Iniquidade ou elã neo-fundamentalista? considerações sobre religião e política no Brasil," *Numen: revista de estudos e pesquisa da religião* (Juiz de Fora) 19 no. 2 (2016): 115.

[55] This video was posted on the network in September 3, 2010, and had 98,552 views through January 3, 2019 ("Posicionamento do Pr. Paulo Piragine Júnior sobre as eleições 2010" (http://www.youtube.com/watch?v=aUcc4e-aLcA; accessed January 30, 2019). The video also appears at two other addresses, with different names: "Não votem no PT—Pr. Paulo Piragine Júnior—2010" (http://www.youtube.com/watch?v=NaGBrs7J6O8; accessed January 30, 2019, with 68,548 views, and "Pastor Paschoal Piragine fala do perigo de votar no PT" (http://www.youtube.com/watch?v=lxRof2j9XdU), with 55,737 views, all of them posted between September 3 and 15, 2010. This video time is eleven minutes, twenty-two seconds recorded during an evening worship of the First Baptist Church of Curitiba (PR—Brazil).

[56] Piragine was in his second term as the president of the BBC.

[57] "Posicionamento do Pr. Paulo Piragine Júnior sobre as eleições 2010," http://www.youtube.com/watch?v=aUcc4e-aLcA (accessed January 30, 2019; see 0 minutes, 07 seconds–0 minutes, 59 seconds)

[58] Barbosa and Souza, "Iniquidade ou elã neo-fundamentalista?," 125.

The 2010 Piragine discourse echoes ideas that can be found in American evangelical fundamentalism, beginning in the 1970s, especially in neo-fundamentalism.[59] The presence of "evil" described by the pastor of FBC Curitiba is very similar to the discourse of the Moral Majority and Jerry Falwell, who declared that his country was under the menace of "great evils" that were supposedly threatening his nation, colliding with Judeo-Christian ethics and contributing to the degradation of the original morality of the United States.[60]

The Baptist Brazilian pastor's speech is similar in content to what Falwell said in the 1970s and 1980s. In his book *Listen America*, a kind of manual for the Moral Majority, Falwell writes about his concern with his country and the great ills threatening America, saying that the 1980s would be a

> decade of destiny. During the crucial years of the 1980s it will be determined whether we continue to exist as a free people. It is now past time for the moral people of America to fight against those forces that would destroy our nation....It is time that we faced reality. We are in trouble as a nation. We are very quickly moving toward an amoral society where nothing is either absolutely right or absolutely wrong. Our absolutes are disappearing, and with this disappearance we must face the sad fact that our society is crumbling. I cannot keep silent about the sins that are destroying the moral fiber of our nation. As a minister of the Gospel, I have seen the grim statistics on divorce, broken homes, abortion, juvenile delinquency, promiscuity, and drug addiction. I have witnessed firsthand the human wreckage and the shattered lives that statistics never can in their totality.[61]

Before showing a PowerPoint presentation with many impactful images (domestic violence, infanticide) and short videos (with scenes of a gay pride parade and an abortion ultrasonography), Piragine states,

> I need to tell you something that during thirty years in my [pastoral] ministry I never did. I completed thirty years of ministry on August

[59] While fundamentalism has as one of its outstanding characteristics the tendency to separate from secular society, as well as from the other religious groups that do not align with its interpretation of the Bible narrative, the neo-fundamentalism that Falwell launched is a movement of the cobelligerence suggested by Francis Schaeffer, stimulating an "ecumenical coalition" of those who believe that the United States is under the menace of "great evils" caused by the secular modernity.

[60] Silva and Barbosa, *Religião e Política nos Estados Unidos*, 182.

[61] Jerry Falwell, *Listen America!* (New York: Doubleday, 1980), 117.

> 08 [2010], and in these thirty years I never did what I did today during the morning [worship] and will do now at evening [worship]. I want to tell you that we need to take much care with the next election.[62]

While defending the creation of the Moral Majority, Jerry Falwell said that he had set aside pietism and the principle of separation between church and state, which had been one of the marks of his pastoral ministry, and began to defend the participation of leaders and laypeople of various evangelical religious affiliations in the political/party scenario.[63] In the Baptist Brazilian case, Piragine also justified his position of involvement with politics, declaring,

> *As a pastor I never did that.* I'm not telling you to vote in A or B, I'll tell you in whom you must not vote: in people that are working in favor of the iniquity in our land. Because if not, dear [brothers], God will judge our earth. And if God judge our land, this will happen in your life, in my life, because we are part of this land. Because God doesn't tolerate iniquity. Amen?[64] [This declaration is followed by effusive applause from the people present in the worship service.]

According to Flippen, the leaders of the New Religious Right believed that the sins of America could be named, such as

> Homosexuality, abortion, feminism, and what some termed 'secular humanism.' A repugnant cultural liberalism in all of its manifestations had for almost two decades rapidly consumed the traditions that had made America special in God's eyes. Indeed, the very core of America—the nuclear family—was in danger.[65]

Considering the perceived menace of these great evils in Brazilian society, through the political "institutionalization of the iniquity" in the country, Piragine assumes a political discourse, in a frontal abandonment of the sepa-

[62] "Posicionamento do Pr. Paulo Piragine Júnior sobre as eleições 2010," http://www.youtube.com/watch?v=aUcc4e-aLcA (accessed January 30, 2019), at 1 minute 00 seconds–1 minute, 25 seconds.

[63] Patrick Allitt, *Religion in America since 1945: A History* (New York: Columbia University Press, 2003), 152.

[64] "Posicionamento do Pr. Paulo Piragine Júnior sobre as eleições 2010," http://www.youtube.com/watch?v=aUcc4e-aLcA (accessed January 30, 2019), at 10 minutes, 34 seconds to 11 minutes, 8 seconds (emphasis added).

[65] Flippen, *Jimmy Carter*, 1–2.

ration between church and state, and an alignment with the tendency assumed by the conservative Southern Baptists during the 1980s, expressing a fundamentalist élan. Continuing his statement before his congregation, Piragine advises the audience that they should be careful about the 2010 elections

> because there are a series of laws that are being discussed, that will depend on the federal representative's vote, that will depend on the senator's vote, which will be incorporated by the action of the State machine, through the Republic Presidency, and we will vote on those people.…That is, in the next month, it will strengthen also inside the State chambers, in the actions performed through the State. And we need Christian values working in these contexts.[66]

The Brazilian Baptist pastor presents a clear perception of the need for an organized Christian political stance against alternative legislative agendas based on a moral vision that would strengthen the mentioned iniquity in the country. Continuing, the pastor says that because of this evident conflict between the secular and religious agendas, a conservative coalition is being organized, and

> I'm now a part of it, thank God,…of Christian leaders, from various denominations, evangelicals and Catholics, that are working [together] in a way that we may prevent that the iniquity become institutionalized as a law. Because of this some pastors took a firm stand on the radio and TV with their churches, and also the CNBB, the National Conference of Bishops from Brazil. This last week [they] wrote a document, published it and put it in the hands of all the press taking a stand about these issues.[67]

Similar to what happened with America's neo-fundamentalism in the 1980s, Piragine mentions that to face the Brazilian moral conflict, an organized and interdenominational religious movement would be needed "to obstruct the implementation of certain legal or political public agendas, and

[66] "Posicionamento do Pr. Paulo Piragine Júnior sobre as eleições 2010," http://www.youtube.com/watch?v=aUcc4e-aLcA (accessed January 30, 2019), at 1 minute, 26 seconds–2 minutes, 3 seconds.

[67] "Posicionamento do Pr. Paulo Piragine Júnior sobre as eleições 2010," http://www.youtube.com/watch?v=aUcc4e-aLcA (accessed January 30, 2019), at 2 minutes, 3 seconds–2 minutes, 48 seconds.

benefit other ones."[68] The media and mass movements would be needed. Since the end of the 1980s, Brazilian evangelicals aggressively began using the mass media, especially radio and TV, to spread their moral perspective. More recenty the Internet has become an essential way to propagate these values. Piragine's discourse in the video clearly illustrates the importance of the media in cultural conflict.

When Piragine completed his statement in this 2010 video, he rallied his audience to assume the "commitment of fighting in the National Congress, of fighting in the state machine against the legalization of the iniquity."[69] With this action the Baptist Brazilian pastor shows a clear alignment with the discourse of the American Baptists with a fundamentalist tendency, articulating a political confrontation in the public space around moral propositions and against antagonistic visions. So, we may conclude that the Brazilian Baptists learned with the American Baptists how to battle for the culture.[70] But they learned more still.

Brazilian Baptists Adopt American Anticommunism

The Moral Majority's heyday (and of the New Religious Right as a whole) occurred during Ronald Reagan's presidency.[71] In *Listen America!* Falwell talks about the purpose of influencing the government by

> (a) mobilizing the grassroots of moral Americans in one clear and effective voice; (b) informing the moral majority what is going on be-

---

[68] Barbosa and Souza, "Iniquidade ou elã neo-fundamentalista?," 132.

[69] "Posicionamento do Pr. Paulo Piragine Júnior sobre as eleições 2010," http://www.youtube.com/watch?v=aUcc4e-aLcA (accessed January 30, 2019), at 8 minutes, 19 seconds–8 minutes, 27 seconds.

[70] In 2018, Josué Valandro Jr., pastor of the Atitude Baptist Church (Rio de Janeiro), prayed on the altar of his megachurch for the Federal representative Jair Bolsanaro, then candidate for president of Brazil. Bolsonaro's wife, Michele, was a member of this church, but Bolsonara, a Catholic, was not. After praying for the candidate, asking God to "put his hand upon the head of his servant" and to bless him to be elected in October as the new president of Brazil, Valandro gave him the opportunity of speaking to the church gathered for worship. Bolsanoro introduced himself as a Christian and as someone prepared to battle against communism, to value the family, and to protect the children at school. Bolsonaro was elected president of Brazil in October and took office on January 1, 2019, with the support of Brazilian evangelicals, including the Baptists, because of his conservative agenda ("Pastor Josué Valandro Jr. ora por Jair Bolsonaro—Notícias Gospel +," https://www.youtube.com/watch?v=VxaMa2oamI0 [accessed February 13, 2019]).

[71] Jerry Falwell, *Falwell: An Autobiography* (Lynchburg, VA: Liberty House, 1997), 388–89.

> hind their backs in Washington and in state legislatures across the country; (c) lobbying intensely in Congress to defeat left-wing, social-welfare bills that will further erode our precious freedom; (d) pushing for positive legislation such as that to establish the Family Protection Agency, which will ensure a strong, enduring America; and (e) helping the moral majority in local communities to fight pornography, homosexuality, the advocacy of immorality in school textbooks, and other issues facing each and every one of us.[72]

Matthew Avery Sutton says,

> Reagan spoke the language of evangelicalism fluently and believed in many of the issues that conservative Christians cared about. He was a strident anticommunist, he denounced the decline of the family, he praised the "old-time religion," and he criticized the permissiveness of the sixties generation. He questioned the validity of evolutionary theory and supported the teaching of creationism in the public schools.[73]

The official White House site affirms that at the end of his two terms (1981–1989), President Ronald Reagan

> viewed with satisfaction the achievements of his innovative program known as the Reagan Revolution, which aimed to reinvigorate the American people and reduce their reliance upon Government. He felt he had fulfilled his campaign pledge of 1980 to restore "the great, confident roar of American progress and growth and optimism."[74]

Through all this, Balmer declared that Reagan left the White House with "the status of an icon among many American evangelicals, despite the fact that he failed in fulfilling his central promises" made to the fundamentalists.[75] Reagan visited Brazil one time, from November 30 to December 2, 1982, during the presidency of General João Batista Figueiredo, when Brazil

---

[72] Falwell, *Listen America!*, 258.

[73] Matthew Avery Sutton, *Jerry Falwell and the Rise of the Religious Right: A Brief History with Documents* (New York: Bedford / St. Martin's, 2013) 22.

[74] "Ronald Reagan," http/www.whitehouse.gov/1600/presidents/ronaldreagan (accessed February 9, 2015).

[75] Randall Balmer, *God in the White House: Ahistory History—How Faith Shaped the Presidency from John F. Kennedy to George W. Bush* (New York: Harper One, 2008), 124.

was under a military dictatorship.[76] Reagan committed two mistakes: (1) During the dinner he saluted the "people of Bolivia." Then he tried to fix it, stating that Bolivia would be his next destination, but it was not. He went next to Colombia, Honduras, and Costa Rica. (2) He used the phrase "Onward, Brazil," from the hardline time of the Brazilian military dictatorship, in a moment when President Figueiredo was thinking about again democratizing the country.[77] With these statements, Reagan was showing support for the Brazilian military dictatorship.

In reality, the Brazilian Baptists had shown alignment with Reagan's foreign policy against communism even before the American president disembarked in their country. In January 1980, the sixty-second Assembly of the BBC approved a manifesto to be sent to the military president, General Figueiredo. This document, containing a brief presentation about the Baptist denomination, was handed to the Brazilian president during an official audience. The document ended with the statement, "Our disposition to pray for Your Excellence and the Government, at the same time that we offer you all moral and spiritual support."[78] This support was given even in a moment when the military regime was weakened.[79]

Hankins affirmed that

> From the 1930s a smattering of individual fundamentalists was deeply involved in politics and are often referred to as the Old Religious Right. Of course, this name did not surface until there was a New Religious Right against which to compare the old. The Old Religious Right consisted primarily of fundamentalists who rejected liberal po-

---

[76] João Baptista de Oliveira Figueiredo (1918–1999), a Brazilian geographer, politician, and military leader, was the thirtieth president of Brazil, from 1979 to 1985, and the last president of the Brazilian military dictatorship. The Brazilian military dictatorship (April 1, 1964–March 15, 1985) ruled the South American country as an authoritarian military regime, implemented by a coup d'etat by the armed forces upon the president João Goulart's administration. The military government ended on March 15, 1985, when José Sarney took office as president, replacing General João Batista Figueiredo ("The Military Republic, 1964–1985, http://countrystudies.us/brazil/18.htm (accessed January 16, 2019). See Rex A. Hudson, ed., *Brazil: A Country Study* (Washington: GPO for the Library of Congress, 1997).

[77] "Em tempos de Donald Trump, gafe de Ronald Reagan no Brasil," https://osdivergentes.com.br/orlando-brito/em-tempos-de-donald-trump-gafe-de-ronald-reagan-no-brasil/ (accessed July 17, 2018).

[78] Anais da 63ª Assembléia da Convenção Batista Brasileira, 1981: 6.

[79] S. R. Dusilek, C. F. da Silva, and A. C. Castro, *A igreja de farda: os batistas e a ditadura civil-militar. Estudos Teológicos. Faculdades EST,* 58, no. 1 (São Leopoldo, EST, 2017): 196.

> litical theory and the spiritualization of the church in order to engage in selected political causes, chiefly anticommunism during the Cold War era....The Old Religious leaders were given to conspiracy theories about Communist infiltration and clandestine plots to destabilize America.[80]

This anticommunist agenda of the Old Religious Right continued with the New Religious Right. Donald Anderson describes a Falwell discourse about the Liberty Federation,[81] an organization that was formed in 1986 to substitute for the Moral Majority. According to it, the new organization aimed to show

> a special interest in foreign affairs; not in assisting the needy and urging greater assistance to the poor and deprived overseas, but in spearheading an anti-communist campaign. The priority is not the famished Horn of Africa but embattled Central America. Its influence is seen in the appointment of Ambassadors and in US policy towards family planning programmes.[82]

The New Religious Right and Reagan shared support for this anticommunist agenda and intended to spread it to other countries as well. The Brazilian Baptists had already supported this position since the 1960s. In an editorial of the *Baptist Newspaper*, the BBC's newspaper, editor José dos Reis Pereira states, regarding the Brazilian military regime, "We like the anticommunist aspect of the triumphant revolution, as we have already said in a previous editorial."[83] Examining the relation between the Baptists in Brazil and the national dictatorial regime, Dusilek, Silva, and Castro conclude,

---

[80] Barry Hankins, *American Evangelicals: A Contemporary History of a Mainstream Religious Movement* (Lanham, MD: Rowman & Littlefield, 2009), 193.

[81] The Liberty Federation was founded in 1986 by Jerry Falwell to be the new political arm of the New Religious Right, and the Moral Majority was absorbed in it, temporarily remaining as a separate entity, but under the wider jurisdiction of this new organization, until being finally dissolved about two years later (Herbert N. Foerstel, *Banned in the Media: A Reference Guide to Censorship in the Press, Motion Pictures, Broadcasting, and Internet* [Westport, CT: Greenwood Press, 1998], 233).

[82] Donald Anderson, "Neither Majority nor Moral (The View from Westminster)," in Tim Dean, *Third Way* (Knaphill: Elm House Christian Communications Ltda., February 1986), 27.

[83] *O Jornal Batista* [da] Convenção Batista Brasileira (Rio de Janeiro), editorial, April 26, 1964, 3.

> As a channel of the denominational leadership thinking of that time [1960s], José dos Reis Pereira[84] pointed the way to the Baptists of that time: a) face the changing as a divine intervention in the history, that avoided the greater evil of the communism; b) strengthen the pilgrim condition of the Baptist believers, by which they were to set their sights on their heavenly citizenship and not become entangled in Brazilian politics, given that particular circumstance; c) urge the believers to pray for the country and the governing authorities. Given that the editor was aligned with the dictatorship, it was to be expected that the otherness of "The Baptist Newspaper" would cease.[85]

Therefore, when Reagan visited Brazil, Brazilian Baptists had already been supporting the military government for decades, with a clear influence of the U.S. way of dealing with communism and with American support of the Brazilian military coup d'état.

In the article "The Church in Military Uniform," Dusilek and his coauthors suggest that the Brazilian Baptists supported the military government from the beginning; also, the role of United States in these events

> was complex and at times contradictory. An anti-[João] Goulart press campaign was conducted throughout 1963, and in 1964 the [Lyndon] Johnson administration gave moral support to the campaign. Ambassador Lincoln Gordon later admitted that the embassy had given money to anti-Goulart candidates in the 1962 municipal elections and had encouraged the plotters; that many extra United States military and intelligence personnel were operating in Brazil; and that four United States Navy oil tankers and the carrier *Forrestal*, in an operation code-named Brother Sam, had stood off the coast in case of need during the 1964 coup. Washington immediately recognized the new government in 1964 and joined the chorus chanting that the coup d'état of the "democratic forces" had staved off the hand of international communism.[86]

---

[84] José dos Reis Pereira was elected the new editor of the Baptist newspaper at the end of 1963; was inaugurated on March 1, 1964; and his first column was published in the April 5 edition, right after the military coup d'etat in Brazil (April 1, 1964). His support of the dictatorship could be clearly perceived in the next edition of the newspaper, April 12, 1964 (*O Jornal Batista*, March 14, 1964).

[85] Dusilek, da Silva, and Castro, *A igreja de farda*, 193.

[86] "The Military Republic 1964-1985," http://countrystudies.us/brazil/18.htm (accessed January 16, 2019). See Hudson, *Brazil*. Lyndon Baines Johnson served as the thirty-

Sutton remarks that, during his term (1945–1953), U.S. president "Harry S. Truman believed that the United States had a divine calling to oppose the Soviet Union," and communism's explicit atheism. This perspective, adopted by other American leaders and policymakers, made the conflict about more than competing economic systems. According to Sutton, these leaders

> drew on religion as a source of inspiration and saturated their speeches with biblical rhetoric. Truman's successor, President Eisenhower, masterfully linked the cold war issues to religion. In 1954 he famously declared, "Our government makes no sense unless it is founded on a deeply felt religious faith—and I don't care what it is." Such claims tapped into a deep American tradition of civil religion that dated back to the Puritans. Many Americans believed that the United States—like ancient Israel—had been divinely chosen by God to play a major part in his plan for the ongoing redemption of the world. They believed that the United States was destined to bring God's message (economic, political, and religious) to the rest of the world. Such ideology melded perfectly with the cold war. Congress's addition of the phrase "under God" to the Pledge of Allegiance in 1954 (to distinguish it from so-called atheist pledges of communist countries) and its 1956 elevation of "In God we trust" to the national motto further demonstrated the hold of civil religion on the American consciousness in this period.[87]

The same anticommunist stance was shown in Brazil. Dusilek, Silva, and Castro also mention that concerning "the Annual meetings of the BBC the prevailing stillness is impressive in the minutes about the two great events headed by the generals: the military coup d'état of 1964 and the IA-5 in 1965."[88] The authors ponder that "the historical reality invited the Bap-

---

sixth president of the United States, from 1963 to 1969. João Belchior Marques Goulart was the twenty-fourth Brazilian president, serving from 1961 to 1964, when the military dictatorship occurred. Abraham Lincoln Gordon was U.S. ambassador in Brazil from 1961 to 1966.

[87] Sutton, *Jerry Falwell and the Rise of the Religious Right*, 8, 10.

[88] Dusilek, da Silva, and Castro, *A igreja de farda*, 199. "IA-5: On the night of December 13, 1968, the Institutional Act number five (IA-5) was issued and Congress was closed indefinitely. The government of the new President, Artur da Costa e Silva was under tight watch after a speech in which Marcio M. Alves called citizens to boycott the September 7 [celebration of Brazil's] Independence Day festivities. Characteristics of the AI 5: (1) granted power to the President to intervene, as he desired in state and national laws without any regard to the Constitution, (2) further granted the President the right to suspend citizens' rights for a period of up to ten years, (3) banned any type of political manifestation against

tists to face the moment of tension that the country was undergoing at that time," but that the reality was being neglected at least in the formal historical notes.[89] The article affirms,

> The Brazilian Baptists echoed the stance of their American patrons. It is in this way that the American missionary in Brazil John Landers, writing about the Baptist Principles, criticizes the abandonment of Walter Rauschenbusch's social gospel by the majority of this segment.[90]

In Brazil in March 1964 José dos Reis Pereira took office as the new editor of the *Baptist Newspaper*. In his second editorial Pereira defined the military coup as a democratic act for freedom:

> The victory of democracy, the restoring of respect to the Constitution, the vote of confidence given to the National Congress, all of this means for us, believers, opportunity. It is not now that censorship and limitation of freedom will be established in Brazil. But that such time may never come. Pray the believers, veil the believers, work the believers.[91]

Pereira continued, saying that the Brazilian people "by their very nature, by their background, reject the totalitarian systems, and particularly the communist regime."[92] In a previous editorial of the *Baptist Journal*, Pereira had said that "to be quite clear, if someone decides to send us an apology for Communism...[it] will not see the material published by us."[93]

---

the government. Most importantly, it suspended the right to *habeas corpus*, (4) and this act imposed heavy censorship in all aspects of society including, but not limited to newspapers, magazines, plays and music. Censorship, tortures, and murders of opposition leaders were confirmed by IA-5. In practical terms this was an amendment to the Constitution of 1967, which was based on the National Security Doctrine, which instituted a police state. As a result, Brazil became highly indebted because of the various groups that helped finance the 1964 coup" ("The AIs," https://www.mtholyoke.edu/~athay20m/classweb/ censorshipbrazil/page3.html [accessed January 16, 2019]).

[89] Dusilek, da Silva, and Castro, *A igreja de farda*, 199; Atas Da Convenção Batista Brasileira, Anos 1964-1974. Arquivos do Conselho de Coordenação e Planejamento, Convenção Batista Brasileira.

[90] Dusilek, da Silva, and Castro, *A igreja de farda*, 199.

[91] *O Jornal Batista*, April 12, 1964, 3.

[92] *O Jornal Batista*, April 12, 1964, 3.

[93] *O Jornal Batista*, April 5, 1964, 3.

In the United States during the 1980s, the anticommunist feeling was still high. Jerry Falwell considered the Soviet Union an enemy nation, whose communist system of government was seen as a threat to freedom and to democracy, a form of a sociopolitical and economic organization to be fought at any cost, since

> Americans have been fooled by the Communists long enough. It is time that key figures in our government begin to awaken to the fact that communism is a vicious attack upon what was once a free world. Communists have dedicated themselves to world conquest....When communism takes over a nation, the first thing that happens is that the churches are shut down, preachers are killed or imprisoned, and Bibles are taken away from the people. Communists are expert deceivers. In Moscow today we see little churches that are merely there as window dressing to fool people as to communist intentions. There is in the Soviet Union today no religious freedom, no freedom of speech, no freedom of the press.[94]

In the 1980s the Brazilian Baptists' leadership adherence to the military regime seemed to be more explicit during João Batista Figueiredo's term as the nation's president (1979–1985), the last leader of the military dictatorship. Approval of this convergence between the Baptist leadership and the military president was already articulated in January 1980, during the sixty-second BBC Annual Meeting, when a manifesto was prepared by a commission nominated by the Convention and then sent to President Figueiredo. Dusilek, Silva, and Castro highlight that

> the most visible part of this engagement was the president Figueiredo and his delegation's celebrated attendance in two worship services specially promoted by the Baptist leadership. The first one, whose preparation occupied a considerable part of the meetings of the Brazilian Baptist Convention's Executive Board during the first semester of 1980....The *Baptist Journal* reported [it] with emphasis, as if marking the Baptist leadership prestige because of a Federal President's presence in one of his meetings.[95]

---

[94] Falwell, *Listen America!*, 85–87.

[95] Dusilek, da Silva, and Castro, *A igreja de farda*, 207–8. See *O Jornal Batista*, July 6, 1980, 1, 6.

During the 1980s the BBC demonstrated proudly a clear alignment with the discourse of the Southern Baptist Convention, articulating and spreading a message of anticommunism.

Conclusion

The Baptists in Brazil began with the work of American missionaries in the 1880s, who learned how to battle for the faith at several stages in their early history. But such battles are not restricted to the past. Most recently Brazilian Baptists also learned with the Americans how to battle for the culture, especially under the influence of the example of Jerry Falwell's Moral Majority and other American Baptists who adhered to the New Religious Right's neo-fundamentalist perspective. Finally, at the international level, Brazilian Baptists agreed with Reagan's anticommunist foreign policy. This meshed well with the Brazilian military dictatorship regime. Brazilian Baptists clearly borrowed from American political, social, and religious culture in shaping their own Brazilian Baptist Christianity, morality, and political commitments.

Index